Ho

Also available from Pluto Press

Postmodernism and the Other
New Imperialism of Western Culture
Ziauddin Sardar

Aliens R Us
The Other in Science Fiction Cinema
Edited by Ziauddin Sardar and Sean Cubitt

Islam, Postmodernism and Other Futures
A Ziauddin Sardar Reader
Edited by Sohail Inayatullah and Gail Boxwell

How Do You Know?

Reading Ziauddin Sardar on Islam, Science and Cultural Relations

ZIAUDDIN SARDAR

Introduced and edited by
EHSAN MASOOD

Pluto Press

LONDON • ANN ARBOR, MI

First published 2006 by Pluto Press
345 Archway Road, London N6 5AA
and 839 Greene Street, Ann Arbor, MI 48106

www.plutobooks.com

British Library Cataloguing in Publication Data
A catalogue record for this book is available from the British Library

ISBN   0 7453 2515 7 hardback
ISBN   0 7453 2514 9 paperback

Library of Congress Cataloging in Publication Data applied for

10   9   8   7   6   5   4   3   2   1

Designed and produced for Pluto Press by
Chase Publishing Services Ltd, Fortescue, Sidmouth, EX10 9QG, England
Typeset from disk by Stanford DTP Services, Northampton, England
Printed and bound in the European Union by
Antony Rowe Ltd, Chippenham and Eastbourne, England

Contents

Introduction:
The Ambiguous Intellectual

Ehsan Masood

Writer, thinker, scholar, theorist, broadcaster, critic, journalist and futurist; Muslim, British, Pakistani, South Asian. Ziauddin Sardar has many occupations and more than one identity. Indeed, many of his critics complain that he deliberately cultivates 'a carefully calculated ambiguity' projecting several things at once, yet none of them on their own. He wants to be seen simultaneously as both traditionalist and modernist – while at the same time being a severe critic of both.

Sardar's evolution into a polymath began with a much more defined intellectual range: the modernisation of traditional societies, particularly those with predominantly Muslim populations. It is his extensive writings on this theme that form the core of *How Do You Know: Reading Ziauddin Sardar on Islam, Science and Cultural Relations*. The book is intended as a companion volume to *Islam, Postmodernism and Other Futures: a Ziauddin Sardar Reader*, which is concerned largely with Sardar's writings on postmodernism and futures studies.

Some of the essays in this new volume are drawn from Sardar's earliest books, written in the late 1970s and the 1980s, such as *Explorations in Islamic Science* and *Islamic Futures: The Shape of Ideas to Come*. This was also the formative period of his own ideas and position. During the 1970s and 1980s he travelled and wrote prodigiously about science, technology, international development, Islam and the environment. Part of the aim of *How Do You Know* is to introduce Sardar's ideas that were formed in that period to a generation of English-speaking readers who have come to know him largely from his columns in the *New Statesman*, his contributions to newspapers like the *Independent* and the *Observer*, popular science writing, and television and radio appearances.

The question that Sardar has always asked is: how do you know? For Sardar, the answers we get from using particular methods – such as the scientific method – provide at best partial answers. He says that a great deal depends on who 'you' are: how you look at the world, how you shape your inquiry, the period and culture that shapes your

1

outlook and the values that frame how you think. In Islam, Sardar insists, knowing is always accompanied by shaping: to know the world is to interact with it, to shape it and understand it according to the principles, values and worldview of Islam. Much of his work on Islam seeks to combine theory with practice. Indeed, Sardar and his network of intellectuals, the Ijmalis, pioneered concepts – such as definitions of knowledge (*ilm* in Arabic) and public interest (*istislah*) – as analytical tools that can be used to develop practical policies from theoretical work.

KNOWING ISLAM AND THE WEST

For Sardar, Islam is not merely a religion, culture or civilisation. It is, above all else, a worldview. It is a way of looking at the world and shaping it. It is a way of knowing, being and doing; a way of being human. Like conventional theorists, Sardar does not 'locate' Islam anywhere; he has consistently argued that Islam is located everywhere, not least in the west, which has its own Islamic history and inheritance, and now a major Muslim presence in Europe and America. Similarly, the west is now everywhere: 'there is now as much "west" in Bombay and Kuala Lumpur as in Europe', Sardar believes. The difference between Islam and the west is a difference of perception. In Sardar's eyes, Islam, or being Islamic, is a different way of perceiving the world than that to being western, or of the west. By contrast, Sardar sees 'the west' not so much as a culture, or a place, but as a concept and epistemology: as a specific way of knowing. In much of the west, he has argued, rationalism is considered the only way (or the best way) to Truth. The knowledge categories emerging from the west – such as natural science, social sciences and humanities – are both a product and an embodiment of this way of wanting to know; or wanting to ask questions.

Today it is the west that provides the dominant way of thinking and asking questions. People all over the world think, plan, work, play, study, consume, or waste increasingly as is done by people who live in western countries. Islam, for Sardar, provides as an alternative mode of inquiry to that of the west. For him it is a way of knowing that will generate different answers to questions about equality and justice, rights and duties, accountability and responsibility – or what it means to be human in a non-western sense.

Most of his writings on Islam are an exploration. Each of the five chapters in the part on 'Islam', for example, explores the idea of knowledge and historiography within the Muslim faith. In the chapter 'Faith and the Written Word', for example, Sardar explores the relationship between Muslim civilisation and the written word. In 'Re-reading the Life of Muhammad', he calls for opening up the biography of Prophet Muhammad to critical analysis – something that Muslim scholars are still largely reluctant to do. In the chapter 'What Do We Mean by Islamic Futures?', Sardar returns to a favourite theme: creating a distinct discipline geared to shaping viable futures for Muslim societies.

Social and physical reality can never be defined by a single knowledge system and for Sardar the idea that reality can be compartmentalised into 'physics', 'sociology', 'religion' and 'politics', 'law' and 'ethics' is not based on some universal axiom. Rather, it is a product of asking questions in a certain way. These questions, in turn, are based on the needs and requirements of a certain set of people in a given time in our history. One of those 'requirements' was the colonial project of European countries.

Much of Sardar's intellectual energy has been devoted to arguing that many western knowledge categories are inherently Eurocentric because they supported the growth and material prosperity of the west at the expense of non-western peoples. Many of these disciplines have evolved and changed with time. But for Sardar, if anything, they have become more and not less Eurocentric. Just as ideas of modernity represent a more sophisticated form of Eurocentrism than colonialism, so the evolution of knowledge categories has made them more and not less Eurocentric. In colonial times, Eurocentrism was overt and obvious. In their modern incarnation, Eurocentrism, for Sardar, is deeper, though not so easily discerned.

When he worked for the magazines *Inquiry*, *Nature* and *New Scientist*, Sardar took off on several grand tours of Muslim countries in the 1970s and 80s. These resulted in a series of essays and later a clutch of books that explored the relationship between science, technology, development, environment, ethics and values, both in Muslim countries as well as in the broader developing world. Sardar's articles frequently tackled the wider questions relating to science, such as its history, sociology, implications, and its relationship to colonialism. Colonialism has been a recurring theme in Sardar's work – the earliest work being no exception. Sardar discovered that throughout the southern hemisphere, centuries-old traditions of learning and scholarship had been erased, replaced by a set of ill-fitting western-style institutions. Moreover, these institutions had little grounding in the history or culture of the countries they were in, with the result that they were often unable to function once the overseas sponsor had left for home. Throughout his travels, Sardar saw, in addition, how colonialism had given way to technological colonialism in the form of technology transfer, led by consultants, many of whom had little time (or inclination) to transfer anything more than 'black box' technologies, which had been developed with little consideration for their users, nor taken into account any knowledge that users might have been able to contribute.

Indigenous knowledge systems is a second thread in Sardar's early writing. A third is the poor state of Muslim intellectual life. Sardar discovered the depth of the malaise experienced by Muslim writers and thinkers while working on his first book: *Science, Technology and Development in the Muslim World*. Many writers and researchers, Sardar found, struggled with being able to think and write critically and were very much prisoners of their own history. This closing of so many minds was partly down to the belief (still widespread in the Muslim world) that the faith of Islam discourages independent inquiry and that certain topics are off-limits to freethinking. This is also very much a function of a university system where pedagogy and rote-learning are the rule.

In his essay 'What Makes a University Islamic?' Sardar directly challenged those in power to allow universities in Muslim countries to probe the boundaries of knowledge. His particular target was a then newly-established network of 'Islamic universities' in Muslim states that were being established in the 1980s under the enthusiastic patronage of Pakistan's military ruler General Zia ul Haq. The idea behind these universities was to develop a generation of scholars who would be able to synchronise modern knowledge with the teachings of the Qur'an. However, these were not intended to be open-ended centres for knowledge – for example, they would not be allowed to conduct open-ended research into the Qur'an itself; nor would there be any engagement with Muslim historiography. This was partly out of a fear that opening the fundamentals of Muslim history to new inquiry could open the doors to new and different interpretations of sacred texts, and indeed new interpretations on the history of Islam, which is mostly taught and studied (in Muslim countries) in hagiographic terms.

MUSLIMS AND THE ENVIRONMENT

Sardar's explorations of science in developing countries were taking place at a time in which the relationship of science to people and the environment had already come under intense scrutiny in western countries. Conventional (western) science had (for the previous two decades) been subjected to the microscope of philosophers and sociologists of science such as Jerome Ravetz, author of *Scientific Knowledge and Its Social Problems* (Oxford University Press, 1971); and before that by environmentalists such as Rachel Carson, author of what would later become a seminal work on chemicals and the environment, *Silent Spring* (Houghton Mifflin, 1962). Carson, Ravetz and many others were arguing that human-induced environmental degradation (such as pollution from chemicals) was in part a result of the reluctance of scientists to consult or to submit their work to wider peer-review (beyond their own expert community). Another reason was the hasty desire among policymakers and industry for countries to industrialise without asking questions about social and environmental costs of industrialisation.

Not surprisingly, Sardar was strongly influenced by these writers (Ravetz soon became a close friend and long-term collaborator). This was partly because Sardar could see a connection between sociology of science, environmentalism and Muslim ethics and values – such as the idea that scientists should pay more attention to the implications of a course of action before taking that course. But Sardar also had an additional motive: he wanted to show a predominantly Muslim audience that ideas such as environmental ethics were inherently Islamic. In 'Towards an Islamic Theory of the Environment', for example, Sardar was the first Muslim writer to show how the practice of Islam is naturally at home with environmentally sustainable development.

Sardar also suggested that Muslim states should aim to develop technologies appropriate to local needs and conditions – instead of spending large amounts of money on advanced technologies developed out of western laboratories. This was one of the messages in the essay 'Islamic Science: The Way Ahead'. A parallel aim was to lay bare the contradiction at the heart of science policymaking in some countries with predominantly Muslim populations, such as Iran, Pakistan and Saudi Arabia. These are countries where Islam is enshrined in the constitution and where Islamic law has a place in the legal system, yet where, at the time Sardar was writing, concepts such as appropriate technology and sustainable development were being dismissed as western fads.

DESPERATELY SEEKING ISLAMIC SCIENCE

Sardar's numerous journeys throughout the Muslim world led him to the conclusion that there was a need for a distinct practice of science, which he called 'Islamic science'. Pakistan was among a number of Muslim states that Sardar toured in the 1970s and 1980s talking to researchers, politicians, scholars of religion, clerics, professional development practitioners, and recipients of formal 'aid' programmes from international agencies. He discovered that some things were common to most of the countries he visited. He found, for example, that large-scale international assistance was having little impact on the daily grind of poverty. He also found that research and teaching at universities had almost no relevance to the problems of poverty and underdevelopment; that open-ended inquiry, a plurality of views and freethinking was either absent or strongly discouraged; and that scientists in Muslim countries seemed to make few connections between the science they were doing and their personal ethics or values.

Today, the links between knowledge, poverty and development are fairly well-established. Even the large development agencies inside the UN system and the World Bank recognise that development works best when you listen carefully to the needs of those you want to help. It is vital that donors pay close attention to the history of indigenous attempts to find solutions through local traditions; and that they encourage free inquiry, innovation and creativity. But in the 1970s and early 1980s, Sardar's combined scholarly and journalistic assault led the way; but his ideas and interventions to this effect were not seen as welcome. International donors were very much of the view that they understood development better than most; and their 'clients' in developing countries were in no position to argue, nor did most possess the capacity to suggest alternatives.

Sardar argued that science in Muslim societies should not only be based on certain values, but that these values need to be up front. He used Arabic words for these concepts, which included *khilafa* (trusteeship), *istislah* (public interest) and *adl* (social justice). These are discussed in more detail in his essay 'Arguments for an Islamic Science'.

Sardar saw 'Islamic science' as *science*: a puzzle-solving activity based on rigorous research and experimentation, subject to a peer-review process, whose results were universally applicable across all cultures. His argument was that the *content* of science will change if it reflects the values and ethics, needs and questions of different cultures – including the culture and worldview of Islam. Science, if funded by and organised by pious Muslims in China, for example, will inevitably ask different questions, reflect different priorities and operate to a different set of ethics from, say, the science of more materialistic people in Russia. Because so much of western science was developed by men of power and influence, often during times of war and with little thought to its long-term implications, Sardar argued, it was inevitable that much of the results of this science and technology would end up benefiting the west and being destructive. In other words, science had a political economy as well as a cultural dimension.

ARGUMENTS AND MISUNDERSTANDINGS

Sardar's attempts to help shape an Islamic science were often misunderstood, even by some of his closest associates. Some commentators understood Sardar's Islamic science to mean a type of science and technology that only Muslims could do – even though the framework that he helped to develop was not at all a science for religious people. In the end, out of all of his ideas, it is those on science that have had the least impact on a Muslim audience.

Why couldn't Sardar's Islamic science in itself become more mainstream? There are several reasons, but an important one is that Sardar and his colleagues became distracted by a public clash of ideas with three of the existing (and more dominant) schools of thought on science and the Muslim world. The clash became increasingly personal, and it undoubtedly turned off many of Sardar's Muslim readers from engaging with his work any further.

In the debate about science in Islam, an important strand is represented by Seyyed Hossein Nasr, a historian at George Washington University. Unlike Sardar, Nasr comes from Islam's Traditionalist (or Sufi) wing. Nasr regards Islam as a perennial tradition in which the place of science is as a way of appreciating the complexity of creation.

Muslims of Traditionalist schools do not see science as a set of tools to solve problems, but as a way of appreciating the greatness of God, which they do by extolling the wonder of living things, the symphony of heavenly objects and the harmony of the natural environment. The solutions to life's myriad problems for Traditionalists are more likely to be found in the pages of the Qur'an and in the practice of the Prophet Muhammad as well as the lives of the earliest Muslims. Traditionalists are wary of new knowledge, of open-ended thinking or inquiry (or interpretations of the Qur'an that have not been authorised by their own recognised teachers). They argue that it is the freedom to think beyond the bounds of what they see as divine limits that has led to death, destruction, extremism and holocausts in the modern world. Their objection to Sardar is that, despite his call for respect and understanding of indigenous traditions, he makes little room for the spiritual, or non-rational dimension to knowledge and research; and they wonder why he is so strongly opposed to using science as a way of appreciating the wonders of nature.

A second strand of thinking in Islam and science is represented by conventional scientists trained in the west, who seek to replicate western styles of scientific organisation in developing countries. Among the better known exponents of this method of thinking was the late Pakistan-born Nobel laureate, Abdus Salam, who established an international centre for theoretical physics in Italy, which was aimed at helping scientists from developing countries to attain the standards of their developed-country counterparts. Even though Sardar and Salam were good friends, Salam rejected a link between science and values as well as science as culture. He saw science as a neutral and objective 'international culture', and argued that the scientific method is a universal way of knowing that applies to all people and all times.

The third strand is represented by a French-born surgeon, Maurice Bucaille. Bucaille wrote a series of books that tried to analyse religious texts in the light of modern knowledge. The biggest-selling title was his first, *The Bible, The Qur'an and Science* (Seghers, 1976). He placed the Qur'an next to the Bible and the Torah and discovered that descriptions of natural phenomena in the Qur'an were closest to the results of modern scientific discoveries. As a result, Bucaille's books remain bestsellers in Muslim countries, despite the contradiction in Muslims needing to have a non-Muslim scientific expert validate a book that they otherwise regard as the word of God. Sardar dubbed this feeling of inferiority 'Bucaillism'.

Sardar's early books heavily criticised both Nasr and Bucaille. In *Arguments for Islamic Science*, Sardar devotes a whole chapter to dissecting Nasr's oeuvre; and labelled him 'Nowhere Man'. But the extent of disagreement between the schools came to a head at a high-level international conference in Islamabad in April 1995 that had been organised by the Organization of the Islamic Conference (OIC), the 57-member intergovernmental body of Muslim states. The event had been convened to help chart a new strategy for science in Muslim states with the help of Sardar and Nasr. The organisers had hoped to bring about peace between Islam's top two Diaspora intellectuals. But instead, Sardar mounted a strong attack on both Nasr as well as the Bucaillists (who were once particularly influential in Pakistan).

In retrospect, Sardar probably lost more than he gained by taking on the Traditionalists and the Bucaillists with the vehemence with which he did. He alienated many readers with the nature of his attacks and if his aim was to influence the course of thinking among Muslims, this largely did not happen. Traditionalism and Bucaillism remain, for the most part, the dominant frameworks of thinking about science and Islam among believing Muslims.

FROM POSTMODERN TO TRANSMODERN

Part III of this book highlights key essays from Sardar on the theory and practice of cultural relations. It includes his thoughts on relations between India and Pakistan, where he was born; as well as his ideas on how postcolonial Britain now needs to view the rest of the world.

Of all the countries that Sardar has travelled to, analysed, advised, or written about, Pakistan, the land of his birth, is clearly the one that troubles him the most. For Sardar, it is almost as if the Radcliffe Line, drawn by Viscount Cyril Radcliffe as the border between India and Pakistan, had fallen on the wrong side. He is clearly more at home in New Delhi than in Islamabad, a city he describes in the first volume of his memoirs *Desperately Seeking Paradise* (Granta, 2004) as a 'confined autocratic eyesore'. Pakistan remains a state that is unable to shake off the 'troubled' label. It is among a dwindling group of (often Muslim) countries where representative government has yet to take root. The army is deeply embedded in politics and society, and religious extremism appears to be on the rise. But these are not the only reasons why Pakistan and Sardar have failed to gel.

Sardar sees Pakistan as a 'state of borrowed ideas'. As an 'Islamic state', Pakistan for Sardar has not only demonstrably failed, but it is one that is based on what he sees as imagined fantasies that have no bearing in Islamic history. 'The founding fathers', Sardar says, 'envisaged the Muslims of India as a "separate nation". In the early period of Pakistani history, this "nation" was said to embrace the "ideology of Islam". Later, the "ideology of Islam" became synonymous with the "ideology of Pakistan".' In either case, this ideology was not seen as a system of ideas and concepts, but as a catalogue of do's and don'ts whose only binding force was emotion and compulsion.

Sardar sees the concept of Pakistani nationalism as an artificial identity, in part because it was created by the force of colonial politics as much as a desire among ordinary people for an independent Muslim state. For Pakistan's leaders, a sense of national identity is now a necessity (given that Pakistan is a physical reality). However, for Sardar, there is something missing in what he regards as official monochromic nationalism, through, for example the suppression of the distinctive identities of Pakistan's many minority communities.

In contrast to his thoughts on Pakistan, Sardar sees in India a complex civilisation, with its different cultures, faiths, and identities. In his essay, 'Coming Home: Sex, Lies and All the "I"s in India', Sardar argues that India belongs not just to 'Indians' but also to Pakistanis – and by extension to Bangladeshis and Sri Lankans, for each of these nationalities is an essential component of the civilisation that is India. Sardar is arguably better known and read in India than in Pakistan. He has had a long and fruitful collaboration with the Indian intellectual Ashis Nandy and his essay introducing Nandy's thought – 'The A, B, C, D (and E) of Ashis Nandy' – was written as a tribute to someone Sardar regards as both equal and mentor.

Sardar's ideas on diversity, and his concern for shaping alternative ways of 'knowing, being and doing', are evident in the last two chapters in this volume. In 'Managing Diversity: Identity and Rights in Multicultural Europe', he argues for a history of European societies that sees Islam as an integral part of Europe's past, present and future. In 'Beyond Difference: Cultural Relations in a New Century', his British Council 70th anniversary keynote lecture, he develops his latest idea: what he calls 'transmodernity' and 'mutually assured diversity'. Transmodernity, Sardar argues, takes us 'beyond and above modernity'; it sees tradition as amenable and capable of changing and eager to change and it takes us beyond the geographical and intellectual matrix of the Enlightenment. Mutually assured diversity is what he calls 'a non-competitive conversation', which recognises that identities are not fixed in time and will change, so long as people recognise that identity includes the ability to know others and learn other things.

BACK TO THE FUTURE

Throughout his life Sardar has regarded himself more as a public intellectual, than an academic one. Indeed, his relationship with universities and the world of higher education is a mixed one. He has written extensively about the past, present and future of centres of learning. He has tried to help reform the intergovernmental system of Islamic universities of Muslim states, advised numerous ministers of education, and has probably spent more time inside the corridors, classrooms and offices of universities than many tenured academics. Yet he refuses to take on a full-time academic position; and has resisted offers to embed himself in a single institution – except one: the East West University in Chicago in the US, where he is an adviser and at one time headed its Center for Policy and Future Studies.

Sardar's influence is expanding and his audience growing – not least because of his bestselling book, *Why Do People Hate America?*, co-authored with Merryl Davies, and his work in film and television, including a 90-minute film for the BBC, *Battle for Islam*. Yet Sardar's challenging ideas on change within Islam will not have an easy ride into the future. To become more mainstream, they will need to shift the centre of Muslim opinion. Arguing the case for greater engagement with modernity, for the strengths of pluralism and the right to dissent, and advocating alternative visions for Muslim futures will be one of the biggest challenges in the coming years, both for Muslims and non-Muslims alike. The times we live in are likely to make the efforts of Sardar, as well as other pluralist voices within Islam such as Tariq Ramadan and AbdolKarim Soroush, both more difficult, but also more urgently needed.

On a personal note, I would like to thank all those who made this book happen, in particular Ziauddin Sardar, the staff of Pluto Press, Chase Publishing Services and The Gateway Trust. Special thanks also to Seema Khan for research assistance and careful fact-checking.

Part I

Islam

1
Jihad for Peace

The word Islam has the dual meaning of 'peace' and 'submission'. Islam seeks peace not just for its own sake, it is an essential precondition for, and consequence of submission to, the 'will of God', the creation of the circumstances in which the life of faith can be implemented in all aspects of human existence. So, why does Islam today appear to be synonymous with violence? And why are those who claim to be following the 'will of God' so bent on the path of war? As Anwar Ibrahim, the former Deputy Prime Minister of Malaysia, asked in an article written from prison, how 'in the 21st century, could the Muslim world have produced a bin Laden'? Or, as many supporters of Anwar, whose only crime is standing up against the corruption and despotism of Mahathir Muhammad, Malaysia's Prime Minister for two decades, are asking: why is the Muslim world so crammed with despots, theocrats, autocrats and dictators?[1] Or, to put it another way: why have Muslim societies failed so spectacularly to come to terms with modernity?

These are not new questions. I have raised them many times.[2] Other writers and scholars have asked the same questions; most notably, Kanan Makiya in his *Cruelty and Silence* (Penguin, London, 1994). But after September 11, these questions have acquired a new poignancy and a much broader currency. However, such debate and earnest discourse has some notable features. The debate is conducted, for the most part, by Muslim intellectuals and writers living and working in the west, though they enjoy a readership and close links within the Muslim world. The reason is not hard to find. Living in the west requires a direct response to the circumstances and human dilemmas of modernity; it also permits more ready access to sources of Muslim scholarship than in most Muslim countries; within the Muslim world dissent, wide ranging intellectual inquiry and argument has little if any public scope. So the central debate on the contemporary meaning of Islam is, in its most challenging form, doubly marginal. It occurs outside Muslim nations, where any attempt to apply its ideas is blocked by existing power structures and

This chapter was originally published in Anna Kiernan (ed.), *Voices for Peace*, Scribner, London, 2001, pp. 185–94.

entrenched vested interests. In the west it is hardly known, being the concern of a minority within a minority it is almost inaudible and invisible. Furthermore from a western perspective it is not consistent with popular perceptions of Islam, nor the *realpolitik* of relations with the Muslim world.

Defining the predicament of modern Muslim nations and Islam in the modern world is not difficult. Ascribing reasons is an equally effortless procedure. Muslims have tended to look to outsiders for answers to these questions. It is apparent, despite all the posturing of governments that the fate of the Muslim world is affected and determined by decisions taken elsewhere, there is a widespread sense of dispossession and powerlessness. Therefore, much energy goes into providing a critique of the actions and consequences of the centres of power, the nexus of western governments, economy, industry and popular culture where modernity is manufactured and exported to its recipients in the Muslim world.

For example, Muslims are quick to point out the double standards of America, both in its domestic rhetoric and foreign policy. The American support for despotic regimes, its partiality towards the Israelis, and a long series of covert operations that have undermined democratic movements in the Muslim world. There is truth in these assertions. But such truths cannot explain nor provide all the answers. Indeed, the most significant answers lie deep within the history, social practice, intellectual and political inertia of Muslims themselves. Holding a mirror to our own faults is the place Muslims are just too reluctant to look. And unless the Muslims re-examine their own assumptions, their own perceptions of what it means to be a Muslim in the twenty-first century, peace – in any meaningful sense – will continue to elude us.

The question of peace, then, is tied up with a re-examination of the meaning and nature of Islam in contemporary times. Muslims believe that their identity is shaped by the best religion with the finest arrangements and precepts for all aspects of human existence and the most glorious of all human histories. Muslim rhetoric is shaped by the ideals of Islam where all is sacred, nothing secular and justice the paramount duty. The problem, as acknowledged by all concerned, is that many Muslims, as individuals and nations, are neither expressly Islamic nor all that just. The problem of flawed humanity is answered, in the deepest core of Muslim being, by the unquestionable need to be more Islamic. So, we are constantly retreating to a more and more romanticised notion of 'Islam'. Time after time, we have watched as the definition of what is 'Islamic' in contemporary times and circumstances is shrunk and reduced to pathological levels. Our most sacred concepts have been monopolised and hijacked by under-educated clerics, by obscurantist sheikhs and '*ulema*' (religious leaders), fanatics and madmen.

This process of reduction itself is also not new. But now it has reached such an absurd state that the very ideas that are supposed to take Muslims towards peace and prosperity are now guaranteed to take them in the opposite direction. From the subtle beauty of a perennial challenge to construct justice through mercy and compassion, we get mechanistic formulae fixated with the extremes repeated by people convinced they have no duty to think for themselves because all questions have been answered for them by the *ulema* in previous times, men far better than themselves, but long dead. And because everything carries the brand name of Islam, to question it, or argue against it is tantamount to voting for sin.

Peace will elude the Muslim world as long as we Muslims continue to perform violence on our own ideas and concepts. Let me illustrate the nature of this violence by looking at two very common Muslim concepts: the notions of jihad (struggle) and *ijma* (consensus) that shape much of Muslim identity and outlook.

DOING VIOLENCE TO JIHAD

Jihad (in both Muslim and non-Muslim contexts) has now been reduced to the single meaning of 'Holy War'. This translation is perverse not only because the concept's spiritual, intellectual and social components have been stripped away, but it has been reduced to war by any means, including terrorism. So anyone can now declare jihad on anyone, without ethical or moral rhyme or reason. Nothing could be more perverted, or pathologically more distant from the initial meaning of jihad.

The primary meaning of jihad is peace, not war. Peace and justice are the core values of the message of Islam. War cannot, nor has it ever been, an instrument of Islam. Muslim polities, like all other societies, are no strangers to war. But conversion to Islam is unequivocally declared by the Qur'an and understood by the community to be a matter of private, personal conscience between each individual and God. The entire history of human experience testifies that war instigates, perpetuates and compounds all the conditions that negate justice and are not peace. War demeans the dignity of the human person, which Islam explicitly seeks to nurture and promote. Even if jihad is reduced to the sole meaning of war, it cannot be war by any or all means. The rules of engagement established by Prophet Muhammad are well known to all Muslims and explain why even the Taliban's clerics had to condemn the terrorist attacks in America and declare them unethical. The most central notion of Islam is *tawheed*, usually translated as unity of God. But this unity extends to, indeed demands, moral and ethical unity: Islam insists that there cannot be a distinction between ends and means, and just causes must be pursued by just means.

Given the violence done to the meaning of jihad, it is hardly surprising that in modern times no call for jihad has translated into securing justice for anyone, least of all those on whose behalf and in whose interests it has been proclaimed. A central principle of our faith has become an instrument of militant expediency and moral bankruptcy. Those who call Muslims to jihad are deaf to compassion and mercy, the most essential values by which justice and peace must and should be sought.

IJMA: CONSENSUS OF THE PUBLIC

Similarly, the idea of *ijma*, the central principle that guides communal life in Islam, has been reduced to meaning making decisions based on the consensus of a select few. *Ijma* literally means consensus of the people. The concept dates back to the practice of Prophet Muhammad himself as leader of the original polity of Muslims. When the Prophet Muhammad wanted to reach a decision, he would call the whole Muslim community – then, admittedly not very large – to the mosque. A discussion would ensue; arguments for and against would be presented. Finally, the entire gathering would reach a consensus. Thus, a democratic spirit was central to communal and political life in early Islam. But over time clerics and religious scholars have removed people from the definition – and reduced *ijma* to 'the consensus of the religious scholars'. Not surprisingly, authoritarianism, theocracy and despotism reigns supreme in the Muslim world. The political domain finds its model in what has become the accepted practice and métier of the authoritatively 'religious' adepts, those who claim the monopoly of exposition of Islam. Obscurantist mullahs dominate Muslim societies and circumscribe them with fanaticism and absurdly reductive logic.

The way to peace requires Muslims to move in the opposite direction: from reduction to synthesis. Ordinary Muslims around the world who have concerns, questions and considerable moral dilemmas about this current state of affairs must reclaim the basic concepts of Islam and reframe them in a broader context. *Ijma* must mean participatory consensus leading to participatory and accountable governance. In the same way, jihad must be understood in its complete spiritual meaning as the struggle for peace and justice as a lived reality for all people everywhere.

More specifically, we need to declare jihad for peace. In its original multi-dimensional meaning, jihad must involve Muslims in a concerted, cooperative endeavour to combat poverty, disease, the indignity of unemployment, the lack of educational opportunity and provision, the underachievement of economic institutions, all aspects of corruption, denials of basic rights to freedom, the oppression of women – all those things that afflict Muslim societies everywhere. And this jihad has to be conducted by intellectual and moral means. When the deformed political institutions of our nations impede the process of peace and justice, we have a duty to peacefully work together to bring meaningful change based on programmes of remedial action. Jihad for peace also involves intellectual efforts for peace, including the construction of a discourse for peace. When the inequities of the global system impede our efforts to bring improvement to the needy, it becomes a matter of jihad for every Muslim to engage in dialogue and not be satisfied with self-righteous denunciation. In such a jihad, it becomes a supreme duty of the *ummah*, the international Muslim community, to be part of the world community of faiths, nations and peoples. The essence of the Qur'anic vision is the duty of believers to take the lead in forming new coalitions across all dividing lines to promote what is right, and prevent what is wrong.

Muslims have no monopoly on right, on what is good, on justice, nor on the intellectual and moral reflexes that promote these necessities. The Qur'an calls on Muslims to set aside all sectarianism and work with people of good conscience whoever they may be, wherever they are, to serve the needs of the neediest. This, for me, is the true jihad; the jihad that is crying out for the attention of Muslims everywhere.

THE BETRAYAL OF REASONING

Jihad shares a root with another central Islamic concept, namely: *ijtihad*. *Ijtihad* means 'reasoned struggle for understanding', struggle to comprehend the contemporary meaning of Islamic precepts and principles. It is a cognate of jihad, and expands the meaning of the term. Interpretation of the meaning of Islam is an act of culpable negligence by educated Muslims the world over. We have left the exposition of our faith in the hands of under-educated elites, religious scholars whose lack of comprehension of the contemporary world is usually matched only by their disdain and contempt for all its ideas and cultural products. Islam has been permitted to languish as the professional domain of people more familiar with the world of the eleventh century than the twenty-first century we now inhabit. And this class has buried *ijtihad* – a conventional source of Islamic law and wisdom as well as the basic conceptual instrument for adjusting to change – into frozen and distant history.

The betrayal of *ijtihad* has enabled obscurantism to dominate the life of Muslim communities. It has led to the pernicious irreligion of the Taliban who deny women the right to education and work in direct violation of the responsibilities laid upon women by the Qur'an. They are akin to all those religious adepts who complain that democracy and human rights are 'infidel inventions' because their terminology and institutional form is not shaped in the conceptual framework of Islam. This is the unreason that has become the prime obstacle to the reasoned struggle of one fifth of humanity to live in dignity, freedom, justice and peace.

The events of 11 September 2001 make it clear that ordinary Muslims cannot be complacent about the interpretations of their faith. We have to find a way to unleash the best intentions, the essential values of Islam, from the rhetoric of war, hatred and insularity that is as much the stock in trade of mullahs as it is of unenlightened policy advisers in the United States. That means all educated and concerned Muslims must take responsibility for authoring twenty-first-century interpretations of the basic concepts of Islam.

We need to publicly and volubly reject jihad as Holy War and do more to promote the holistic view of jihad for peace. From a reductive interpretation that limits *ijma* to meaning the consensus of an authoritarian elite, we must develop contemporary, effective and workable models for democratic and participatory notions of consensus. Finally, we must revive *ijtihad* as the dynamic principle of seeking a more humane understanding of our faith. In short, we have to go forward to the intrinsic meaning of Islam: peace.

2
Re-reading the Life of Muhammad

Muslim societies are being relentlessly pulled in opposite directions. On the one hand, the onslaught of culturally-destructive 'modern' trends, for example in high technology and urban planning, threaten to decimate Muslim cultures *en masse*. On the other hand, the inertia of ossified traditionalism threatens to suffocate Muslim societies. The tension generated by these inimical lifestyles is now affecting the very being of Muslim personality. Indeed, the strain has now reached such a pitch that it has become a matter of urgent priority for Muslim intellectuals to take steps to preserve the Muslim personality and save the immediate future. In particular, there are four tasks which urgently need the attention of Muslim scholars:

- The *Seerah*, the life of the Beloved Prophet Muhammad, has to be made more meaningful and significant to Muslim individuals and societies.
- Muslim societies have to be liberated from 'development' and other similar mind-enslaving concepts so they can be intellectually free to explore alternatives within the purview of Islam.
- The environment of the Hajj – which includes the holy cities of Makkah and Medina as well as Muna, Arafat and Muzdalifah – has to be saved from total destruction and preserved in an enlightened way, to accommodate the needs of a growing number of pilgrims. The Hajj is the microcosm and heart of the Muslim world; when the environment of the Hajj suffers degradation and abuse, the whole of the Muslim world is affected.
- Islamic studies have to be delivered from the narrow confines of 'religious studies' and Islam has to be taught as a universal worldview, complete with the apparatus to build a dynamic civilisation, so that the future generations of Muslim intellectuals

First published as 'Rewriting the Seerah: Future Significance of the Life of Muhammad', in *Islamic Futures: The Shape of Ideas to Come*, Mansell, London, 1985, chapter 11.

and scholars can cope with the diversity and interconnected-ness so inherent in Islam and so much needed to survive the future.

Here, I would like to discuss the important issues of making the *Seerah* relevant to contemporary needs and future possibilities.

LEARNING FROM THE LIFE OF THE PROPHET

The *Seerah* literature is a unique institution of Islam. *Seerah*, the life of the Prophet Muhammad, is both history and biography. But more than that: it is a source of guidance as well as of law. It is in the *Seerah* that Muslims seek inspiration for their behaviour and understanding of the Qur'an. As such, the *Seerah* is an integral part of the Shari'ah of Islamic law. Thus the *Seerah* is biography, history, law and guidance all integrated together. It therefore transcends time and has eternal value as a model of ideal Muslim behaviour and a practical demonstration of the eternal principles and injunctions of the Qur'an.

The *Seerah* has mostly been written in a standard way. Literary biography was a particular strength of Arab literature and it was natural for writers who lived a few years after the death of the Prophet Muhammad to throw themselves wholeheartedly into writing his *Seerah*. Indeed, a massive attempt was made not just at writing the biography of the Prophet, but also of his companions as well as the narrators who related various traditions of the Prophet and formed a key link in the transmission of knowledge going back to the Prophet himself.

Classical studies on the *Seerah* approached the subject chrono-logically. This is hardly surprising, as in that period biography was valued largely as chronological history. Thus the celebrated work of Ibn Ishaq,[1] published in the middle of the eighth century, starts with a description of life in Arabia before the birth of the Prophet (described by early Muslim writers as the 'period of ignorance'), and continues by describing:

- His birth, childhood and first marriage
- How the Qur'an was first revealed
- Migration from Makkah to Medina
- Battles against the ruling elite
- Expeditions
- The peace treaty of Hudaibiyah

- The conquest of Makkah
- The last Hajj
- The Prophet's death
- Electing his confidant Abu Bakr, the first Caliph of Islam.

As many of the battles of the Prophet marked a turning point in the story, Ibn Ishaq gives a great deal of emphasis to them. But the emphasis on the battles was also due to the influence of a literary form very popular in Arabia during that period, known as the *maghazi*, or the literature of the military expedition. Thus biography written as chronological history and the *maghazi* literature became the main models for writing the *Seerah*.

THE *SEERAH* AS SELF-HELP MANUAL

For the Prophet's earliest biographers like Ibn Ishaq, Ibn Hisham, Ibn Sa'ad, al-Waqidi and a multitude of other scholars, this was the simplest and the most accurate way of furnishing the Muslim community with the basic details of the life of the Prophet. The accent was on what the Prophet did, and the overall emphasis was on providing detailed information on how he lived his life so that individual Muslims could follow his example. And this is precisely what many did with an attention to detail and care that is unique. The classical biographers were indeed very successful in achieving their objectives. They not only provided a reliable body of basic data but because the cultural and technological milieu in which they were writing was not much different from the time of the Prophet Muhammad, they made his life relevant to the community. Thus for the Muslim communities of early Islam, the Prophet was not just a fact of immediate history, but a living presence whose every action shaped their own behaviour.

However, the classical *Seerah* literature, cast as it is in an idiom that is over 1,200 years old, does not have the same impact on the modern mind as it had on the early Muslims. Facts of biography, as indeed of history, make sense when an individual can relate to them and when avenues for assimilating these facts into the individual's life are clear. One would expect more contemporary writers of *Seerah* to cast the life of Muhammad in an idiom that is instantly recognisable and relates to modern living. Unfortunately, modern authors, for some strange but compelling reason, have stuck to the classical method of writing the *Seerah*. The result is that the life of Muhammad makes no real sense to the vast majority of today's Muslims.

Thus most modern studies of the *Seerah* relate the life of Prophet Muhammad as a chronological story adding no new facts and emphasising exactly the same points once emphasised by classical authors for a community whose priorities and mode of production were radically different from those of contemporary Muslim societies. The widely read *Muhammad: The Holy Prophet*,[2] for example, presents a collection of facts from what the author calls 'The Age of Ignorance' to 'The Eleventh Year of Hegira'. Apart from the fact that much of the book is quite unreadable, written as it is in an over-the-top subcontinent version of Victorian English, the author makes no attempt to explain any of his facts, or to put the Prophet's actions in some sort of context, or indeed draw any lessons from the narrative. Quite often he is simply content to list things; as if knowing the 14 chiefs of the Quraish tribe who conspired to kill the Prophet in Makkah is an end in itself!

DEFENDERS OF THE PROPHET

Modern biographers of the Prophet are also plagued by another serious shortcoming: what I would call 'reaction syndrome'. Many contemporary studies of the *Seerah* amount to little more than benign apologia written in answer to various orientalist accusations. There are many orientalist studies of the *Seerah* from Andrae to Boswell, Carlie, Goldziher, Margoliouth, Muir, Noldeke, Sprenger, Watt and Weil. Much in the way of orientalist writings about the Prophet Muhammad, as Tibawi and Edward Said have pointed out so forcefully, were designed to show, both that Muslims are an inferior people; and that the imperial and political conquest of Muslim nations was in effect a conquest by people of a superior faith and intellect.[3] Christian missionaries, in their crude way, and the orientalists in a more subtle way, singled out the personality of the Prophet Muhammad for ridicule. Muslim scholars responded by presenting the *Seerah* in an apologetic mould. Whether they were denying the accusations of the missionaries and the orientalists or simply justifying them, they were, at best, wasting scholarly energy which could be better utilised in analysing the biographical narrative.

Two of the most respected studies of the *Seerah*, Shibli Numani's massive six-volume study in Urdu, *Seerat un Nabi*,[4] and Muhammad H. Haykal's *Hayat Muhammad* in Arabic,[5] are somewhat marred by both authors' obsessions with orientalist accusations.

Shibli Numani's *Seerat un Nabi*, is undoubtedly the best contemporary study of the *Seerah* in any language. Shibli wanted nothing less than to take on every orientalist who had written on the Prophet since the days of Hal de Bert in the twelfth century. He planned to devote an entire volume to the work of orientalists but was unable to finish his task. That, to some extent, is unfortunate, for Numani is a powerful writer who does not mince his words in dissecting the studies of the orientalists. For example, of Margoliouth's work he writes:

In all the written record of the world, his biography of the Prophet stands unsurpassed for lies, calumnies, misinterpretations, and biased expressions. His sole excellence lies in the art of giving, by dint of his genius, the ugliest colour to the plainest and cleanest incident in which it is not possible to discover the tiniest black spot.[6]

Despite clearly devoting much time, space and energy to attacking orientalists, Numani still managed to produce a monumental, balanced and guidance-orientated study of the *Seerah*. He was able to do this largely because he relied exclusively on classical Muslim authors. The second-half of the first volume presents a chronological account of the Prophet's life and the second volume – concerned with the battles the Prophet was involved in – are both almost entirely based on classical sources. But, while Numani relies on the traditional sources, he is not afraid to break with tradition in that he devotes separate volumes to discussing broader questions such as the organisation of state and society, forms of worship and the methods used to invite people to Islam. In this respect, Shibli Numani's *Seerat un Nabi* is almost unique. When one considers its authenticity and the wealth of detail it provides, his study stands out as a true giant among contemporary works on the *Seerah*.

However, Haykal is all too willing to concede authority to orientalist scholars and consequently is always forced to justify his arguments in their terms. The net result is an overly apologetic biography of the Prophet. He writes that he is concerned with writing what he calls 'a scientific study, developed on the western modern method' and considers his approach to the *Seerah* almost at par with that of the 'researcher in the natural sciences'.

The main motivating force behind Haykal's *Seerah* is his anger at what he calls the 'slanders', 'false charges' and the 'hostility' of the orientalists. This often leads him to judge particular events during the *Seerah* by the stand that an orientalist may have taken on them.

One of his repeated targets is the nineteenth-century British civil servant in India, William Muir.[7]

Haykal and Numani's anger with orientalism can be partly explained by the period (and the countries) they lived in. Numani's India and Haykal's Egypt were both under British occupation during the lives of the authors: they were writing from a defensive position in an era when western intellectual domination went unchallenged. Yet despite these circumstances, their studies of *Seerah* (as well as that of Syed Ameer Ali's *The Spirit of Islam*)[8] had a major impact on Muslim minds. Although their writings are undoubtedly apologetic, they were brave endeavours of their time – and, despite the passage of time, their works have mostly not been surpassed in scholarship, clarity or force of argument.

A BIOGRAPHY OF FACTOIDS

Indeed, it is fair to say that more recent biographers of the Prophet have achieved comparatively less. Biographies by Abul Hasan Ali Nadwi from India, founder of the Muslim educational system that bears his name, Muhammad Hamidullah and the British Muslim Martin Lings have each used traditional sources, but once more, they are afraid to tread beyond chronology.

All three authors quote generously from the Qur'an and Hadith, but differ in their secondary sources. Nadwi, for example, relies heavily in his biography *Muhammad Rasulullah* on the works of early Muslim scholars and commentators Ibn Hisham, Ibn Kathir and Ibn Qayyim.[9] In *Muhammad: His Life Based on the Earliest Sources*, Lings, in contrast draws more on the writings of Ibn Ishaq, Ibn Hisham, Ibn Sa'ad and al-Waqidi.[10] In terms of actual content, however, there is little difference between Nadwi and Lings. Both present the *Seerah* as chronological history, with the same stories making an appearance in both texts. Having said that, the two biographies are still very different. Nadwi, for example, makes no real attempt to explain the events of his narrative; Lings on the other hand uses the literary device of weaving relevant and explanatory quotations from the Qur'an and the Hadith into the narrative, thus increasing its informational content. Lings is a master story-teller whose prose and style is well suited to both the grandeur of the subject and the sublime personality which is the focus of the narrative. Nadwi is awkward (which is probably the fault of the translation), repetitious (probably because he dictated most of the book) and somewhat pedestrian in prose and style. The difference between Nadwi and Lings is not of scholarship or approach or the fact that either of them have come up with something new. The difference is in the style and the power one of them gives to his narrative. Lings' study has been described as the *Seerah* 'par excellence' and a 'work of art . . . a modern English classic'.

If the art of the story-telling is the criteria by which *Seerah* literature is judged, Lings certainly has produced a masterpiece. But if insight, analysis and contemporary relevance are the indicators to judge by, then it is Hamidullah's *Muhammad Rasulullah* (the same title used as in the Seerah by Nadwi), which is by far a superior work.[11] Hamidullah, like Lings, also bases his study on some of the earliest sources; however, he has tremendous problems with style. The style is stilted, often clumsy and difficult to read. But unlike Lings and Nadwi, Hamidullah tells his readers upfront that he is not there to tell a story. Instead, he sees it as his job to emphasise that which 'the classical biographers have not cared to lay much emphasis'.

In his *Seerah*, Hamidullah has essentially reorganised the material that traditional scholars mostly focus on. This incluces: politics, state administration, social institutions, economics, methods of creating inter-racial concord, blending of the spiritual and the material. The end result is that the guidance elements of the *Seerah* that emerge are not restricted to personal piety and tales of heroism in warfare. Indeed, *Muhammad Rasulullah* contains only the minimum amount of information on the battles that the Prophet fought. And in doing so, Hamidullah chooses to concentrate on the relationship between the Prophet and his enemies. *Muhammad Rasulullah* does not pursue arguments to the required depth but is nonetheless a valiant attempt at historiography and an indication of the direction that contemporary *Seerah* literature could take.

SEERAH AND THE FUTURE

The conventional method of writing the *Seerah* has provided us with a vast body of fact and information, what Hamidullah calls 'raw material', about the life of the Prophet Muhammad. However, while this approach to the study of *Seerah* has been invaluable in the past, it has shortcomings, which need to be supplemented by new and more innovative methods of studying the paradigm of Muslim behaviour.

Even from the viewpoint of modern writers, it should be obvious that the story-telling approach to writing biography or history is not going to break any new ground. Besides, if all one needs to do is to relate the story of the Prophet, then why is it necessary for new authors to relate the story over and over again? Whatever their individual merits and shortcomings, there is no recognisable difference, narratively speaking, between the studies of Hafiz Ghulam Sarwar, Muhammad H. Haykal, Abdul Hamid Siddiqui, Abul Hasan Ali Nadwi and Martin Lings. Moreover, the story-telling approach has the tendency of inducing intellectual and stylistic laziness in the writer. Thus many facts of the Prophet's life are narrated with hardly any variation of style and words. Sometimes, expressions that were used by as far back as Ibn Ishaq are reproduced verbatim by contemporary writers. This does not apply to Lings' *Seerah* because he has his own distinctive style.

There are other reasons why the conventional approach to writing the *Seerah* is now inadequate. While the conventional *Seerah*s furnish Muslim individuals and societies with facts, these facts by themselves are not enough to motivate individuals or solve problems in society. Knowing that during the Battle of Badr, 317 ill-equipped Muslims fought and defeated a well-equipped army of 1,000 Quraish warriors, tells us that the Muslims were brave in battle. But is bravery the only lesson to be drawn from the Battle of Badr? Or can the battle also tell us something about the conduct of war; the treatment of enemies; guidelines for intelligence and espionage; who can and cannot be killed during war; what can and cannot be destroyed; what action can one take from harming that which should not be harmed; and the conduct of foreign policy during hostilities? If the Battle of Badr is to have some meaning for us today and in the future, its lessons must be shown to be relevant to contemporary situations. The facts of the *Seerah* cannot just be stated; they have to be integrated, synthesised and analysed, turned into principles and models, so that they can be absorbed into contemporary and future life.

After the Qur'an and the Hadith, key sources for biographies of the Prophet were the written accounts of these battles known as *maghazi*. This partly explains why so many biographers focus on conflict and battles. Written mainly to record the events relating to expeditions and battles, the *maghazi* contain a wealth of detail; but it is detail that spans a relatively short period in the Prophet's life. In Islam's first 23 years (the period during which Prophet Muhammad lived), the Battles of Badr and Uhad did not last more than a day each. The longest battle, the Battle of Trenches lasted a month, but contained no fighting because the enemy could not cross a protective trench that the Muslims had built to shield them. The Prophet's biggest military triumph, the conquest of the city of Makkah, was also a bloodless affair. Indeed, in six decades of life, Prophet Muhammad spent less than a year in battle or physical conflict. Lings is not alone among the biographers to devote more than half of his book to warfare.

This over-reliance on early military history sources (such as the *maghazi*) means that social and economic life in Makkah and Medina, has been overlooked. There are authentic sources for such material and they include al Azraqi's *Akhbar-i-Makkah* and Umar Ibn Shaiba's *Akbar-e-Medina*, as well as others that could provide new insights into the cultural and technological milieu within which the Prophet moved. Even the *shamail* literature, which focused on the morals, character and habits of the Prophet, has been largely ignored.

Static description is the major instrument of conventional *Seerah* literature. As such, it is interested in answering one basic question: what did the Prophet do? As Hamidullah points out, classical biographers were not interested in cause and effect. But if today's Muslim scholars are to make the *Seerah* relevant to the present and the future, they have no choice but to tackle additional questions. These include: *how* did the Prophet do it? And *why* did he do it?

These two questions demand that the *Seerah* is subjected to searching analysis to discover the explanations behind the facts. And that requires going beyond the handful of traditional sources that have dominated the *Seerah* so far. The life of Prophet Muhammad has to be written as living history, not as distant, historical biography. As analytical history, *Seerah* is to understand the life of Muhammad as it shapes and motivates the behaviour of contemporary Muslim individuals and societies. Analytical *Seerah* aims at discovering and synthesising general principles from historical situations – principles with strong contemporary relevance, which would enable modern Muslim societies to make moral value-judgements in the face of complex reality.

In trying to answer the questions of how and why, analytical *Seerah* has to focus on the Prophet's ideas and concepts – in addition to his actions. The guidance aspects of the *Seerah* can best be brought to the fore by examining how the Prophet operationalised key Islamic concepts in his life. In trying to establish how the Prophet put certain ideas and concepts into action, the logic of detailed questioning often yields more productive results than simply examining anecdotal evidence. For example, in a short essay on how the Prophet

Muhammad implemented the idea of consultation in Islam (known in Arabic as *shura*), Tayeb Abedein provided more answers than many more fully-fledged biographies of the Prophet.[12] Starting from the premise that it is obligatory on Muslims to consult before making decisions, the writer suggests that we need to know: who is to be consulted – the wider public or a small section of society; on what issues does consultation become essential; and is the outcome of a consultation exercise binding on a leader?

Studying the *Seerah* in relation to the idea of consultation helps us with the answers to all three questions. Throughout his life, the Prophet consulted widely before making major (and often minor) decisions. Abedein explains who the Prophet consulted with. Shortly after the Battle of Taif, the defeated tribe accepted Islam. The Prophet was uneasy about taking their booty now that tribe members were brothers in faith. He asked his soldiers whether they would give back what they had taken. The soldiers agreed. But the Prophet needed further convincing, and told them: 'We do not know which one of you has agreed and which one has not, go back till your heads bring us your answers.'

On another occasion the Prophet decided to take action against members of his own Quraish tribe. Two of his companions agreed with him. But the Prophet sought out other representatives of the community and specifically asked for their opinion. On yet another occasion the Prophet wanted to sign a truce with a tribe living near Medina – so as to encourage them not to fight with other tribes. He thus called for the opinions of the heads of two dominant tribes in Medina.

From these incidents, Abedein tries to draw out a definition of *shura* from the perspective of Muslims. He writes: 'the ruler should obtain the approvals of individuals when the issues concern their right to property'. In matters of special experience and knowledge, a Muslim leader has to consult those who possess it irrespective of their representative power.

But what issues are to be put to consultation? Abedein argues that the whole of the *Seerah* is full of illustrations showing that the Prophet consulted the community on many, many problems that affected them. However, he cannot find any examples where the Prophet consulted his followers when appointing leaders of armies, district governors or judges. From this he concludes: 'perhaps such consultation would develop ill-feelings in the Muslim community, or possibly it should be a prerogative of the ruler to choose his subordinates'.

And finally: is the outcome of the consultation binding on the leader? Abedein notes that there is only one case when the Prophet consulted his people and did not accept the opinions to which they agreed. However, there are at least three recorded incidents where the Prophet submitted to the people's opinions, even though they differed from this own. One conclusion that can be drawn from this is that consultation is binding on a leader whatever his own opinion on the matter.

Even a simple interrogation of the *Seerah*, as Tayeb Abedein's analysis shows, can yield rich rewards. The answers to each of his three questions are based on evidence and can be translated into, for example, public policy legislation which makes public consultation mandatory on important issues, or for placing constitutional limitations on a government.

What is important about the *Seerah* of the Prophet Muhammad are the causes and principles for which the Prophet lived and the operational form he gave to concepts and ideas from Islam. Muslims should not be obliged to follow the Prophet's actions precisely to the letter. But they are required to promote the norms of behaviour and the principles for life that can be drawn as lessons from the *Seerah*. Only studies of the *Seerah* from the perspective of ideas and concepts, seeking to answer the questions of why and how, can turn the life of Muhammad into a living reality. And only by turning the *Seerah* from a historical narrative into a contemporary map of guidance can Muslims fully appreciate the future significance of the life of Muhammad.

3
Faith and the Written Word

The worldview of Islam furnishes us with a number of concepts which, when realised in all their sophistication at various levels of society and civilisation, yield an integrated infrastructure for distribution of knowledge.

At least five Islamic concepts have a direct bearing on the distribution of information. They are: justice (*adl*); knowledge (*ilm*); worship in its broadest sense (*ibadahh*); human trusteeship of the Earth's resources (*khilafa*); and philanthropic or charitable endowments (*waqf*). An examination of the early history of Islam reveals how these five concepts were given practical shape and generated a highly sophisticated infrastructure for the distribution of information and knowledge. The all-embracing concept of *ilm* shaped the outlook of the Muslim people, from the very beginning of Islam. Indeed, Islam made the pursuit of knowledge a religious obligation: by definition, to be a Muslim is to be entrenched in the generation, production, processing and dissemination of knowledge. Moreover, the concept of *ilm* is not a limiting nor an elitist notion. *Ilm* is distributive knowledge: it is not a monopoly of individuals, class, group or sex; it is not an obligation only on a few, absolving the majority of society; it is not limited to a particular field of inquiry or discipline but covers all dimensions of human awareness and the entire spectrum of natural phenomena. Indeed, Islam places *ilm* at par with *adl*: the pursuit of knowledge is as important as the pursuit of justice. Just as *adl* is essentially distributive justice, so *ilm* is distributive knowledge. One is an instrument for achieving the other. The ideal goal of the worldview of Islam, the establishment of a just and equitable society, cannot be achieved without the instrument of distributive knowledge. Only when knowledge is widely and easily available to all segments of society can justice be established in its Islamic manifestations. Early Muslim communities were well aware of this interconnection between *adl* and *ilm*. To begin with, they faced the question of distributing the Qur'an and the traditions of

First published as: 'Past and Present – Going Forward to the Islamic Heritage', in *Information and the Muslim World*, Mansell, London, 1988, chapter 2.

the beloved Prophet among the believers. The new Muslims needed access to copies of the Qur'an and authentic records of the Prophet's life (*hadith*). The first steps in this direction were taken by Uthman, the third Caliph of Islam, who was aware that the total memorisation of the Qur'an, and its preservation in the hearts and minds of the believers, was one manifestation of the distributive notion of *ilm*. Because the Qur'an could be easily memorised, its contents could be just as easily distributed. Nevertheless, in view of the variations of dialects, he felt it necessary to preserve it in a written form. As such he took the necessary steps for the preservation of the written text. The next step was taken by the compilers of *hadith* who evolved a sophisticated process of authenticating the traditions and made them widely available to all segments of society. During the first century of Islam, oral traditions predominated and were the chief vehicle for the dissemination of information. But it soon became clear that memory cannot be relied upon completely, and written notes began to circulate among seekers of knowledge. Thus, we hear from Saad Ibn Jubair (d. 714): 'In the lectures of Ibn Abbas [one of the Prophet's close companions], I used to write on my page; when it was filled, I wrote on the upper leather of my shoes, and then on my hand.' He is also reported to have said: 'My father used to say to me, "Learn by heart, but attend, above all to writing. When you come home from lectures, write, and if you fall into need or your memory fails you, you have your books."' But what did Ibn Jubair actually write his notes on? His 'page' was most likely papyrus made from the stem of a plant of the same name or a parchment prepared from the skins of goats. Notes gathered like that were freely exchanged among students and scholars. Indeed, quite often such notes were combined to form books. Evidence from earlier scholars and commentators such as Ibn Ishaq, al-Waqidi, Ibn Sa'ad, Tabari and Bukhari suggests that Urwa Ibn al-Zubair (d. 712–13) was the first to collect such loose-leaf books. And his student, al-Zuhri (d. 742) collected so many of these books that his house had space for few other things. His preoccupation with collecting these books and studying them occupied so much of his time that his wife was led to complain: 'By Allah! These books annoy me more than three other wives would (if you had them).'

Ruth Stellhorn Mackensen, who during the early 1940s carried out a pioneering study of the emergence of Muslim libraries, considers al-Zuhri's collection as the first Muslim library.[1] She notes:

Whether the early books were merely a collection of students' notes and little treatises in the form of letters or more formal books, of which there were at least a few, the collecting of them, the recognition that such materials were worth keeping, can legitimately be considered the beginning of Muslim libraries.

But even during this period, the book, as a coherent record of thoughts, had made its debut. Indeed, noted men of learning were commissioned to write books and persuaded by students who would take notes of their lectures and transform them into coherent books. Al-Amash Abu Muhammad Sulaiman Ibn Mihran (680–765), a fiercely independent and witty scholar of tradition was frequently approached to write books. Not all the commissions he received were worthy of his attention. The Caliph Hisham Ibn Abd Allah once approached him to write a book on the virtues of the third Caliph, Uthman and the crimes of his successor, Caliph Ali. Al-Amash read the note and then thrust it into the mouth of a sheep that must have been nearby. While doing so, he is believed to have said: 'Tell him I answer it thus.' When a few students arrived at his house early one day and insisted that he teach them some traditions (of the Prophet), he eventually came out, greeted them and said: 'Were there not in the house a person [his wife] whom I detest more than I do you, I would not have come out to you.' By the time al-Amash died, the book had become a common and widely distributed vehicle for the dissemination of knowledge and information, due largely to the emergence of paper, thanks to China. When Muslims came into contact with the Chinese in the latter part of the seventh century, they quickly realised that paper could play a key role in the distribution of knowledge. The first Muslim town to set up a paper industry was Samarkand in Central Asia, which came into Muslim possession in 704. It is understood that the paper industry of Samarkand was established by Chinese prisoners-of-war. From Samarkand the paper industry soon spread to the central provinces and major cities of the Muslim empire. In a matter of decades, paper replaced papyrus and parchment, becoming the main medium for the dissemination of written information, and by the end of the century had even replaced parchment in government documents. Along with paper-making, other industries connected with book production also developed rapidly. The preparation of ink in various colours and the technology of writing and illustrating instruments advanced considerably during this period. Bookbinding, too, acquired a degree of sophistication. The earliest books were stiff and hard because of the use of rough leather dressed in lime. However, a discovery in Kufa led to a more effective way of dressing leather, which used dates to produce softer leather.[2] At the same time, new skills for the ornamentation of bindings and techniques for the illumination of books were developed. The overall result was books which were breathtakingly beautiful, works of art in themselves. Even the oldest existing Arab bindings have tasteful cover designs of simple elegance and beauty all their own. Books of a later date are more elaborate, containing decorations and illuminations with a kaleidoscope of colour.[3] Just over one hundred years after the advent of Islam, the book industry had advanced to such an extent that Muslims became the 'people of the book' in the truest sense of that expression. Reading for its own sake (and not only reading the Qur'an) had become one of the major occupations and pastimes. The connection between reading and the Qur'an, however, is important: it enforces the notion that the pursuit of knowledge is a form of worship, that knowledge and worship are two faces of the same coin.

It was hardly surprising then that in the next two centuries the book industry spread to every corner of the Muslim world. Libraries sprung up of all types – royal, public-funded, specialised and privately endowed; as did bookshops of every colour including small bookstalls, adjacent to mosques and in bazaars, as well as large city-centre establishments. This period also saw the rise of what can only be described as 'bookmen' – authors, translators, copiers, illuminators, librarians, booksellers and book collectors. It is no exaggeration to say that the entire Muslim civilisation revolved round the book.

Listen to Ibn Jammah, writing in 1273 in *Books as the Tools of the Scholars*:

'Books are needed in all useful scholarly pursuits. A student, therefore, must in every possible manner, try to get hold of them. He must try to buy, or hire, or borrow them. However, the acquisition, collection and possession of books in great numbers should not become the student's only claim to scholarship.' He adds: 'Do not bother with copying books that you can buy. It is more important to spend your time studying books than copying them. And do not be content with borrowing books that you can buy or hire.' And he says: 'The lending of books to others is recommendable if no harm to either borrower or lender is involved. Some people disapprove of borrowing books, but the other attitude is more correct and a preferable one, since lending something to someone else is in itself a meritorious action and, in the case of books, in addition serves to promote knowledge.'[4]

Lending books came in vogue throughout the Muslim world. Libraries were therefore built in almost every major town. The first were the magnificent royal libraries of the Caliphs. Almost every dynasty, from the Ummayad and Abbasid Caliphs, to the Fatimids of Egypt, the Hamdanids of Aleppo, the Buwayhids of Persia, the Samanids of Bokhara, the Ghaznavid rulers and the Mughals of India all established major libraries in their respective seats of government.

HOW MUSLIMS BUILT AND MANAGED LIBRARIES

According to George Makdisi, several terms were used to designate libraries.[5] Three of these referred to a library as a space and included: house (*bait* or *dar*); space for a large collection (*khazana*). Other words referred to libraries in terms of their content. These words included: wisdom (*hikma*); knowledge (*ilm*) and books (*kutub*). Libraries were named using many combinations of these words, such as House of Knowledge, or House of Wisdom. Undoubtedly, the most famous of the Muslim libraries was the House of Wisdom (*Bait al-Hikma*), which was founded by the Abbasid Caliph Harun al-Rashid in Baghdad in 830. It was more than a library and included a research institute and translation bureau. The library included translations from non-Arabic languages, such as Greek and Sanskrit. Harun al-Rashid's son, the Caliph Mamun al-Rashid is reported to have employed scholars of the stature of al-Kindi, the first Muslim philosopher, to translate Aristotle's works into Arabic. Al-Kindi himself wrote nearly 300 books on subjects ranging from medicine and philosophy to music, copies of which which were stored in the library. Mamun generously rewarded the translators and as an incentive sealed and signed every translation. He also sent collectors abroad – to countries such as India, Syria and Egypt – to collect rare and unique volumes.

Bait al-Hikma had a number of well-known Muslim and non-Muslim scholars on its staff. They included: Qusta Ibn Luqa, Yahya Ibn Adi, and the Indian physician Duban. Musa al-Khwarizmi, the Muslim mathematician and founder of algebra, also worked at Bait al-Hikma, where he wrote his celebrated book: *Kitab Al Jabr Wal Muqabilah*. Bait al-Hikma, however, was soon to be surpassed by another library in Baghdad.

This second library, which boasted a collection equal to that of Bait al-Hikma, included the collections of the Nizamiyyah Madrassah, founded in 1065 by Nizam al-Mulk, prime minister in the government of Malik Shah. The collection at the Nizamiyyah library was gathered largely through donations: for example, Caliph al-Nasir donated thousands of books from his royal collection to the Nizamiyyah library. The library had many famous visitors including Nizam al-Mulk al-Tusi (d. 1092), author of a classic work on international law *Siyar al-Muluk*. Al-Tusi, during his visits to Baghdad, spent a lot of time at the Nizamiyyah.

The Nizamiyyah employed regular librarians on its staff who received attractive salaries. Among the better-known librarians were Abu Zakariyyah al-Tibrizi and Yaqub Ibn Sulaiman al-Askari. In 1116, the library survived a huge fire, and a new building was erected under instructions from Caliph al-Nasir. Still in Baghdad, Caliph Mustansir Billah established an exceptional library at the madrassah he founded in 1227. Madrassah Mustansiriyah, whose ruins are still visible on the banks of the Tigris, had a hospital attached to it, and the library served both the madrassah and the hospital. Thanks to the journals of globe-trotter Ibn Battuta, we have a vivid description of Mustansiriyah and its library of 80,000 books.

Baghdad, however, was not unique in magnificent libraries. Almost every major city in the Muslim world had a library equal to the other. Cairo, for example, housed the Khazain al-Qusu, the splendid library founded by the Fatimid ruler al-Aziz Ibn al-Muizz. In some 40 rooms, over 1.6 million books were stored using a sophisticated system of classification. Cairo also boasted its own House of Wisdom (*Bait al-Hikma*), which was established by al-Hakim, the sixth Fatimid Caliph, during 1005. It had a large collection, including the personal collection of the Caliph. The library was also open to the general public and free writing materials were provided to visitors; those who wished to spend time for study also received lodgings, meals and a stipend.

The Caliphs were not the only patrons of libraries. Lesser monarchs, too, were equally busy setting up libraries. For example, the library of Nuh Ibn Mansur, the Sultan of the central Asian city of Bokhara, is described by the philosopher and medical scholar Ibn Sina in the following words:

Having requested and obtained permission from Nuh Ibn Mansur to visit the library, I went there and found a great number of rooms filled with books packed up in trunks. One room contained philological and poetical works; another jurisprudence, and so on, the books on each particular science being kept in a room by themselves. I then read the catalogue of the ancient authors and found therein all I required. I saw many books the very titles of which were unknown to most persons, and others which I never met with before or since.

When Nuh Ibn Mansur offered the premiership of Samarkand to the scholar Sahib Ibn Abbad, the latter declined on the grounds that it would need 400 camels to transport his books to Samarkand. The Sultan understood the difficulty and accepted his apology. Like Nuh Ibn Mansur, most regional rulers of that period were also bibliophiles. The library of Abu al-Dawlah, one of the Buwayhid rulers, for example, was administered by a large staff and impressed Al-Maqdisi, the geographer, who has left a detailed description of it. As they were considered a trust from God, the central libraries were completely at the disposal of the public; as such they were truly public libraries, open to individuals from all backgrounds and classes who were invited to use them, to read and freely copy any manuscript they liked. Moreover, these libraries were not just storehouses of books, but working libraries in every sense. Apart from intensive research programmes, they were also the focus for discussions, lectures, debates and other public activities. Indeed, many of the manuscripts in the book of the tenth-century bibliophile al-Nadim were copied from the House of Wisdom, a point that has confused some Orientalists who have suggested that Nadim's *Fihrist*, which cites over 60,000 books, may possibly be the catalogue from the House of Wisdom.[6] Considerable thought was given to the design, layout and architecture of libraries to ensure that the public had easy access to books and appropriate facilities to study and copy manuscripts. Most of these libraries, such as those of Shiraz, Cairo and Cordova, were housed in specially designed buildings of their own. They had numerous rooms for specific purposes: galleries with shelves in which books were kept, reading rooms where visitors could comfortably sit to read books, rooms for public lectures and debates, and in some cases, rooms for musical entertainment. All the rooms were comfortably fitted out and the floors were covered with carpets and mats. Heavy curtains covered the windows and the rooms were maintained at an appropriate temperature. The description provided by the historian Yaqut of the library of Adud al-Dawlah in Shiraz gives a good general impression of the layout of these institutions:

The library consists of one large vaulted room, annexed to which are storerooms. The prince had made along the large room the store chambers, scaffoldings about the height of a man, three yards wide, of decorated wood which have shelves from top to bottom; the books are arranged on the shelves and for every branch of learning there are separate scaffolds. There are also catalogues in which all the titles of the books are entered.[7]

Larger libraries, such as Baghdad's House of Wisdom had separate rooms for copiers, binders and librarians. In his extensive survey of libraries, S. M. Imamuddin demonstrates that ancient Muslim libraries were designed in 'such a way that the whole library was visible from one central point'.[8]

As befits such institutions, the librarians were of exceptionally high calibre. The *Fihrist* mentions three librarians, all of whom were noted authors and translated works from Greek and Persian, who served at one time or another as librarians of the House of Wisdom. The library at Subur was headed by al-Murtada, a man of learning and considerable influence in scholarly circles. The Dar al-Ilm (House of Knowledge) in Cairo was headed by a judge, Abd al-Aziz. The profession of librarian commanded respect and a good salary. Throughout the *Fihrist* Nadim suggests that he might have been envious of the librarians in the House of Wisdom because of their high standing in society and their scholarship. Apart from central libraries, the Muslim world also housed numerous public libraries. In a city like Merv, the renowned traveller and geographer Yaqut found twelve libraries. During his three years of residence in the city, he gathered the greater part of the material for his geographical dictionary. He was able to borrow as many as 200 volumes at a time.

Baghdad, Damascus, Cairo, Cordova, Fez, Isfahan, Lahore, Delhi and Samarkand, major as well as minor cities, boasted a host of public libraries. Most of these libraries received government subsidies; some were endowments set up by individuals who wished to promote knowledge. The geographer al-Maqdisi tells us that during the tenth century, the visitors to the central libraries of Basra and Ramhurmuz received financial assistance to do their work. In addition, the Basra library also had a full-time professor under whom one could study Mutazilite thought and ideas. In addition to public libraries, special libraries for the cultivation of various departments of literature and sciences were also founded. Hence, we find collections of medical books in hospitals; works on mathematics, astronomy and astrology in observatories; religious and legal writings in mosques and colleges; and rich and more diverse collections in several great academies. Indeed, almost every social, cultural and scientific institution supported a rich library. Apart from the central, public and special libraries, there were also thousands of private collections. During the Abbasid period, Yahya Ibn Khalid al-Barmaki's private library in Baghdad was known to be among the richest. Each volume in the collection had three copies and most of the rare works from the House of Wisdom were also included. During the eleventh century the library of Mahmud al-Dawlah Ibn Fatik, a great collector and scribe, became famous because Ibn Fatik spent all his time in his library, reading and writing. His family felt so neglected that when he died they attempted to throw his books away in anger. The library of the noted ninth-century scholar al-Waqidi filled 600 chests and required 120 camels to transport it from Baghdad to beyond the Tigris. Book collectors took pride in establishing libraries and inviting scholars to use them; indeed, it was the main fashion of the time.

A frequently quoted anecdote in the literature of Muslim librarianship illustrates the extent to which private collectors, even those unable to read or write, went on to establish libraries. The historian Makari relates a story about al-Haddhrami, who is reported to have said:

'I resided once in Cordova for some time, where I used to attend the book-market every day, in the hope of meeting with a certain work which I was anxious to procure. This I had done for a considerable time, when on a certain day, I happened to find the object of my search, a beautiful copy, elegantly written and illustrated with a very fine commentary. I immediately bid for it, and went on increasing my bid, but to my great disappointment, I was always outbid by the crier, although the price was far superior than the value of the book. Surprised at this I went to the crier, and asked him to show me the individual who had thus outbid me for the book to a sum far beyond its real value, when he pointed out to me a man of high rank, to whom, on approaching, I said, "May God exalt you O doctor, if you desire this book I will relinquish it, for through our mutual bidding its price has risen far above its real value." He replied, "I am neither learned nor do I know what the contents of the book are, but I have just established a library, and cost what it may, I shall make it one of the most notable things in my town. There is an empty space there, which this book will just fill. As it is beautifully written and tastefully bound I am pleased with it, and I don't care what it costs, for God has given me an immense income."'[9]

Many private collectors helped visiting scholars financially and many libraries were turned into private endowments by their owners for the use of students and other knowledge seekers. For example, Ali Ibn Yahya al-Munajjim personally received visitors who came to study the books in his library, Khazanat al-Hikma (The Collection of Wisdom), and he also provided them with food and lodgings. It was such devotion to books and libraries that permitted the Muslims, in the words of Ruth Stellhorn Mackensen, to develop 'the library as an institution to unprecedented lengths. Not until recent times have libraries been so numerous, well stocked, and widely patronized as they were in Muslim lands.'[10]

FROM LIBRARIES TO BOOKSTORES

It is hardly surprising that such intense interest in books generated a thriving book trade. The state encouraged such trade and books were exempt from tax throughout the length and breadth of the Muslim world. Consequently, traffic in books between states was exceeded only by essential goods. Buyers representing rulers, private collectors, booksellers and scholars travelled to different countries, including non-Muslim lands, in search of valuable manuscripts. Adjacent to almost every mosque was a booth of a small bookseller, but it would be incorrect to say, as Khuda Bukhsh seems to suggest, that all bookshops in the golden period of Islam were small. On the contrary, al-Nadim's bookshop, which contained the books described in catalogue, the *Fihrist*, itself must have been several times larger than Foyles in London which describes itself as the biggest bookshop in the world. The historian Yaqubi tells us that there were more than 100 bookshops in Baghdad alone during his time, from small booths to larger bookstores. Almost all Muslim cities of the classical period had segments of the central bazaar reserved for book traders. In addition to bookshops, another institution of this period – the *ijarah* – seems to have been overlooked by Muslim historians. As a legal term, *ijarah* signifies permission granted for a compensation to use something owned by another person. In the specific context of bookshops, it refers to a book that has been loaned not just for study but also for the purpose of copying, and for the right to copy it. Up till the the end of the sixteenth century, *ijarah* institutions were common in Muslim urban centres. They were not merely commercial lending libraries, but also served as centres for the dissemination of books. For example, when he was young and poor, Ishaq Ibn Nusayr al-Abbadi went every evening to a certain bookseller in Baghdad and borrowed one book after another for the purpose of copying. Whenever the bookseller asked him to pay the hire fee that was due to him, Ishaq would tell him to be patient until he had a lucrative position. We do not know whether Ishaq ever paid the owner of the *ijarah*, but within a few years he had an impressive library of his own. This summary of the history of Muslim librarianship and book trade shows how the infrastructure for dissemination of information evolved naturally during the classical Muslim period. In one respect it is quite astonishing that in fewer than 100 years after the migration of the Prophet (*hijra*) from Makkah to Medina, the book had established itself as an easily accessible and basic tool for the dissemination of knowledge and information.

However, when viewed from the perspectives of knowledge (*ilm*), worship (*ibadahh*) and *waqf* (endowment), which the early Muslims put into operation at the level of the individual, society and civilisation, the phenomenal spread of books and bookmen in early Islam does not look all that astonishing. Indeed, when realised at all levels of society, the conceptual matrix of Islam would work to produce an infrastructure for the dissemination of information in any society, even if it had serious flaws. The eternal concepts of Islam are for the real world; they do not operate in or have much significance for an idealised society. During the early days of Islam, the dictates of distributive *ilm* and *waqf* were institutionalised in a society that had many serious problems, including sectarianism (numerous sects were constantly at war with each other and, indeed, many libraries were established to promote sectarian views), disunity and political divisions. In spite of this strife, the conceptual matrix produced an information infrastructure that took the Muslim civilisation to its zenith.

The contemporary Muslim *ummah* appears to be facing problems even more formidable than those of early Muslims, including dependency, parochialism, fatalism and economic and environmental disaster. In these circumstances the operation of the eternal concepts of Islam becomes even more significant. It was the internalisation of Islamic concepts that saved Muslims of the classical period from their follies and quarrels. Because they have eternal and universal validity, it is the actuality of these very concepts that can save the contemporary *ummah* from the obvious disasters that loom ahead. Only by rooting their information policy firmly in the matrix of Islamic concepts can Muslim countries generate the type of intellectual energy and productivity needed to meet the problems of the contemporary *ummah*.

4
Rescuing Islam's Universities

A clear manifestation of the rise in the intellectual consciousness of Muslims is the emergence of a number of new Islamic universities throughout the Muslim world. Outside the Islamic Republic of Iran, most of these institutions, such as the International Islamic University of Pakistan, the International Islamic University of Malaysia and the planned Islamic University in Niger, are backed by the Organization of the Islamic Conference (OIC), the intergovernmental agency for Muslim states. But independent efforts to establish Islamic institutions of higher learning are also being made, the most noteworthy being the Islamic Institute of Advanced Studies in Washington, D.C.

How do these institutions, both those functioning and those in the advanced stages of planning, differ from such classical Islamic seats of learning as al-Azhar University in Cairo, and the centres of learning in Qom (Iran) and Najaf (Iraq)? And how do they differ from the more recently established traditional models, such as the Darul Uloom (House of Knowledge) in Deoband, India, and the Islamic University of Medina, Saudi Arabia? Are these institutions going to perform the age-old function of producing religious scholars or will they have broader objectives? How will they differ from the western model of a university? Will they focus on traditional learning; will they concentrate on modern scholarship or develop a synthesis of both? Answers to these and similar questions have emerged over the last decade in two forms: theoretical discussions on the concept of the Islamic university, and the setting up of working models for such institutions. Thus theory and practice have developed almost simultaneously. However, enormous hurdles have to be overcome before both theory as well as operational models come up to acceptable levels. In the new universities it appears that more thought has been given to bureaucratic and administrative procedures than to academic content. For example, a single page out of a 43-page document, the International Islamic University Ordinance of 1985 (OIC, Islamabad), discusses academic matters. The rest of

First published as 'What Makes a University Islamic?' in *How We Know: Ilm and the Revival of Knowledge*, Grey Seal, London, 1991, chapter 6.

the document is concerned with the appointment of directors and sub-directors. In terms of the curriculum, a good deal of emphasis is placed on traditional Islamic disciplines (Qur'anic commentary; the life of the Prophet; jurisprudence etc.), as well as on producing scholars in Shari'ah and qualified people who can spread the message of Islam. There is also some awareness of contemporary knowledge and needs. As such, the new universities are not exclusively religious institutions in the traditional sense: they also produce graduates in social and natural sciences. The theoretical basis for the institutional structure of the new universities was hammered out in the late 1970s and early 1980s. Much of the theoretical understanding gained at the First World Conference on Muslim Education held in Makkah (31 March–8 April 1977) and the subsequent follow-up meeting, is summarised by Hamed Hasan Bilgrami and Syed Ali Ashraf.[1] They write that the Islamic university differs from the dominant western model 'in its wide concept of knowledge', which emphasises the spiritual basis of education. This concept of knowledge is based on the unity of God (*tawheed*), which 'reflects itself in all facets of Muslim life' and integrates the sacred with the profane. They identify three characteristics in the evolution of Muslim civilisation which they insist should become the basic building blocks of the Islamic university: the first is a willing submission to Islam (*tameel*); the second is a deep regard and realisation of the greatness of Islam (*tazeem*); and the third is reverence and respect for Islamic values (*adab*).

The Islamic university, the authors state, should start with 'the lowest rung of the ladder', that is: respect for Islamic values (*adab*). Such reverence is the 'very door of all knowledge', the authors say. They add:

The universities of the West in the past few decades have undergone tremendous changes; their technical, nuclear, industrial and other scientific researches have added much to the stock of human learning. If it is being misused, it is not the fault of the universities but of those who are wielding the power. The pity is that all over the world, even today, people are ignoring the real basis of education, which is spiritual in nature and not materialistic. The spirit has to be recaptured by the establishment of truly Islamic universities, not only in the interest of the Muslim countries but also for the benefit of the entire humanity.

Despite the Islamic trappings, the model that Bilgrami and Ashraf are offering differs little from western universities. In the structural framework of a western university, they seek a disciplinary topography, which is divided into perennial and the acquired. Examples of perennial knowledge include the Qur'an, *sunnah*, the Prophet's life, Arabic, jurisprudence, and so on. Examples of acquired knowledge include arts, social sciences, humanities, natural sciences and engineering. Within this overall division students are to pursue their religious and material studies in parallel. There is no real discussion of how genuine integration is to be achieved; nor is there much discussion on how a synthesis of traditional and modern is to be developed in the students. Bilgrami and Ashraf present an excellent example of widespread school of thought, which can be paraphrased as saying: 'let us show a complete and uncritical love of and devotion to Islam and everything else will fall into place'. Those in Sufi mould add the 'inner' ingredient of 'purifying the heart and enlightening the soul'. But on the whole, no one moves, not even marginally, from the well trodden but superannuated path laid down centuries ago by classical scholars.

WHAT MAKES AN ISLAMIC UNIVERSITY 'ISLAMIC'?

In particular, our understanding of key Islamic concepts has not progressed from the classical period. Most Muslim intellectuals rightly consider that it is the Islamic concept of knowledge (*ilm*), which must form the basis of the theoretical and institutionalised structure of an Islamic university. In other words, what makes an Islamic university 'Islamic' is the fact that it is based on the truly Islamic notion of knowledge. The concept of *ilm*, as has been argued by numerous Muslim scholars, integrates the pursuit of knowledge with values; combines factual insight with metaphysical concerns and promotes an outlook of balance and genuine synthesis. This is the ultimate difference between the Islamic idea of *ilm* and the western notion of knowledge. In the western notion of knowledge, 'knowledge' and 'values' are contained in two separate, vacuum-sealed compartments. Yet, when the Islamic concept of knowledge is given practical shape by Muslim intellectuals, it almost yields a dichotomous picture of the world. For example, Muhammad Naguib al-Attas in an essay which essentially reaches the same conclusions as Bilgrami and Ashraf (but is much more erudite and powerfully argued), rightly criticises the western notion of knowledge as being confined to the rational, intellectual and philosophical sciences and for the concept of dualism which encompasses their vision of reality and truth. He categorises western knowledge as containing:[2]

- Dualism of mind and body
- Focus on rationalism and empiricism
- Doctrine of humanism
- Secular ideology.
- Tragedy – mainly in literature.

Yet when it comes to expanding on what he means by knowledge in Islam, al-Attas falls back on established definitions developed by Muslim scholars of the classical period such as al-Kindi, al-Farabi and al-Ghazali. Under this definition, knowledge is divided into the religious sciences (the Qur'an, *sunnah* and so on) and 'the rational, intellectual and philosophical sciences' (human, natural, applied and technological sciences). This division of knowledge, while significant and of value in the classical period, introduces the same type of dichotomy which Muslim scholars find so objectionable in western thought and ideas. It makes 'religious science' appear as though it were less rational and intellectual; while at the same time presenting human, natural, applied and technological sciences as though they had little to do with religious concerns. This definition presents two parallel worlds, which, like parallel lines, only meet at infinity. The idea of a university based on a (theoretical) division of knowledge can never really achieve true integration between, for example, physics and metaphysics, which exist in different university faculties; nor can it synthesise knowledge and values to the level of sophistication needed to solve contemporary problems.

One result of such a theoretical division of knowledge can be found in the courses offered by the Islamic Institute of Advanced Studies in Washington, D.C.[3] The postgraduate programme has a core module on the Qur'an, *hadith* (traditions of the Prophet), Shari'ah, jurisprudence, Islamic history and social institutions. It also offers advanced seminars on Islamic literature, art, philosophy of history, ethics and mysticism. The world outside interferes with this course of study in the form of 28 what are called 'specialisation seminars'. These are on: Islam and philosophy of science, Islam and economics, Islam and public finance, Islam and management, Islam and political theory, Islam and international relations and so on. Courses that offer 'Islam and X' clearly view Islam as a kind of detergent which when used on economics and psychology or architecture; mass communications, logic or whatever, cleanses the latter of impurities and somehow yields a purified and Islamic discipline. Moreover, from a disciplinary perspective, the enforced dividing line between

'Islam and X' effectively makes Islam a subset of discipline X. For example, a course on 'Islam and political theory' makes the Islamic approach to political theory a subset of political theory. Similarly, courses in 'Islam and architecture', 'Islam and economics' and 'Islam and science' make Islamic architecture, Islamic economics and Islamic science subspecies of the disciplines architecture, economics and science, respectively.

This unintentional description of what appear to be Islamic alternatives to western disciplines has two consequences. First, by making Islamic alternatives a subspecies of western disciplines it makes the western discipline and its methodology the arbitrator of what is worthy and of value. Second, it denies the independent validity of such Islamic disciplines as Islamic economics, Islamic architecture, Islamic political theory and Islamic science. Of course, in reality all Islamic disciplines are subspecies of the genus Islam and derive their validity, value orientation and methodology from the worldview of Islam and not from the counter western disciplines.

THE ISLAMIC UNIVERSITY SYSTEM OF THE OIC

The Islamic universities established as part of the OIC have attempted a degree of integration and synthesis between 'religious' and 'rational' disciplines, but with varying degrees of success. For example, the International Islamic University of Malaysia has two main faculties: law and economics. It also houses what it calls a 'Centre for Fundamental Knowledge' where a more traditional Islamic curriculum is taught. The faculties of law and economics teach Islamic law and Islamic economics along with western law and western economics. However, at the larger and more complex International Islamic University of Islamabad, religious and rational sciences are taught and researched separately. The university contains separate faculties for Shari'ah and law; Usul al-Din (rules for faith), as well as a Shari'ah Academy, an institute of Islamic economics and institutes for applied sciences, social sciences, education, linguistics and languages, medicine and health, and engineering and technology. The fact that all disciplines are taught on a single campus could lead to the exchange of thought and ideas and may eventually produce some kind of integration, but that would be more a matter of coincidence than considered planning. While the institutional structure of the new Islamic universities appears adequate if not altogether original, in the long run it is unlikely that they will fulfil the main objectives for which they have been set up. According to the prospectus of the International Islamic University of Malaysia, for example, the main objectives of these centres of learning are to:

- Revitalise the Islamic concept of learning which considers the seeking of knowledge an act of worship.
- Re-establish the primacy of Islam in all fields of knowledge.
- Revive the ancient Islamic traditions of learning where knowledge was propagated and sought after in the spirit of submission to God.
- Widen the scope and options in higher education of the Muslim *ummah*.

The pursuit of a great part of knowledge in our times has become so perverse, so commercialised and industrialised that to consider it as a form of worship is to show an acute lack of appreciation of the ethics of Islam. The primacy of Islam can only be established if it can re-emerge as a complete civilisation, which can stand up to the dominant civilisation of the west and meet the challenges of the future. Institutions established on artificial divisions of knowledge, where knowledge generated, manufactured and packaged in an alien culture is given an Islamic gloss, where emphasis is given more to a traditional knowledge-base, which concentrates on esoteric subjects, authoritarian methodologies, learning by rote and ancient scholasticisms is hardly likely to transfer the power structures of the globe. We must not, however, be too demanding of the new universities. As Sher Muhammad Zaman, director-general of the Islamic Research Institute (now part of the International Islamic University, Islamabad) says, these are experimental models to 'be understood, in a context of a formative phase'.[4] Zaman, who is one of the few Muslim scholars to have contemporary insight into the notion of an Islamic university, also makes an important point that once these early models have been perfected they must be adopted by all institutions of higher learning: 'without this all-important understanding of the comprehensive goal, we shall be heading towards marshy ground and mortally aggravating the existing dichotomy between the traditional Islamic school (madrassa) and the modern secular or quasi-secular school, instead of eliminating (not bridging) the gulf by achieving a truly Islamic synthesis'.

In other words, the model must be perfected so that eventually it fulfils the needs covered by traditional and secular institutions in Muslim countries and can be universally adopted as the model institution of higher learning for all disciplines. Now, if this is the ultimate goal of an Islamic university, and it seems to me to be the only sensible justification for developing these institutions, then we are really talking about something radically different. Zaman argues that the real task of such institutions is the 'constant cultivation of knowledge in all spheres and disciplines, old and modern, occidental or oriental, with the application of an Islamic approach to the content of each of them'.What is 'Islamic' about an Islamic university then is that it is an uncompromisingly universalist institution where all branches of knowledge are pursued within an ethical and methodological framework that is unquestionably Islamic. It is clear that the existing institutional structures, both those which are indigenous to Muslim countries and those which are imported from the west, do not meet these criteria. Moreover, the new institutions cannot emerge by simply modernising the traditional sector which, as Zaman points out, amounts to little more than secularising them or adding 'Islamic' bits to modern universities, or combining two types of institution in any form whatsoever. We need to start with a clean slate.

CAN THERE BE AN ISLAMIC UNIVERSITY TEMPLATE?

The main objective of Islamic universities should be to build a comprehensive foundation for the reconstruction of Muslim civilisation. As such they are service institutions providing the knowledge base that carries Muslim civilisation forward. Classical Muslim scholars were well aware of the role of knowledge in sustaining a civilisation, which is why they paid attention to the concept of *ilm* and its exposition. When they sought to classify various branches of knowledge, they did it in the spirit of evaluating its needs for Muslim civilisation. They sought to identify important branches of knowledge which could not be ignored and to develop the methods by which these branches could be studied. Various classifications of knowledge produced by scholars such as al-Kindi, al-Farabi and al-Ghazali are not based on epistemological divisions as such modern Muslim scholars as al-Attas, Bilgrami and Ashraf project them to be. There is no such thing as religious knowledge and secular knowledge: all knowledge that promotes the goals of Islam – the ideas of *tawheed* and *khilafa*, justice and equality, understanding and brotherhood – is Islamic. When the Prophet said the ink of the scholar is holier than the blood of the martyr, he did not qualify the scholar or the discipline. Or when he gave a higher rank to learning over prayer, he did not put the adjective 'religious' before the word 'learning'. To spend more time in learning is better than spending more time in praying – the support of the religion is abstinence; it is better to impart knowledge one hour in the night than to pray the whole night. As such, a religious scholar is no more righteous than a scientist; under Islam both are equally religious and equally important. The new Islamic universities, therefore, cannot be based on a false dichotomy of religious and secular, rational and non-rational: by the very fact that they provide a knowledge base for Muslim civilisation, all knowledge they cultivate, whether based on reason or revelation, must be Islamic. This, however, should not be confused with the Aristotelian fallacy that the pursuit of all knowledge is virtuous: there are certain segments of modern science and technology (research on lethal weapons, sociobiology, bioengineering) and social sciences (Freudian psychology, aversion therapy) which cannot be described as virtuous by any ethical criteria. Moreover, because the Islamic universities aim to infuse the spirit into every human endeavour, every discipline, they must minimise the artificial disciplinary divisions that are dominant today.

Neither nature nor reality comes divided into neat subjects labelled physics or economics; design or political science. Disciplines, as I have written before, are born with a matrix of a particular worldview: they do not have an autonomous existence of their own but develop within a particular historical and cultural milieu and only have meaning within the worldview of their own origin and evolution.[5] The division of knowledge into various disciplines as we find them today is a particular manifestation of how western civilisation perceives reality in its own problems. As such, to impose the existing disciplinary division of knowledge on Islamic universities is to make them subservient to the western civilisation and its worldview. Apart from developing a new disciplinary structure which reflects the needs and requirements of Muslim civilisation and derives its value structure from the worldview of Islam, Islamic universities have to be shaped as future-orientated institutions. To function as institutions, which serve the knowledge base of Muslim civilisation, they must be capable of assessing the changing contemporary and future needs of Muslim people. Assessing and meeting the needs of the Muslim civilisation, generating the knowledge from within the worldview, and working towards the primacy of Islam and complete reconstruction of the Muslim civilisation are all normative activities; and an Islamic university, therefore, is a normative institution. Let me elaborate. If we say that an Islamic university is a normative institution, we are not saying that it is in any way a biased or prejudiced academy. A normative, goal-seeking institution is not a 'politicised' institution that takes sides with this or that political stance. It does not 'tilt' as universities in post-Reformation Europe were expected to tilt towards Protestantism or Catholicism; nor should they be expected to take a position (against an enemy) during times of war. Nor should they, as universities in the Muslim world and in the west do nowadays, adopt a conservative garb under a conservative board of trustees or when a conservative government is in power; and exchange this for a shirt of collectivisation when a Marxist Central Committee takes power. A normative institution is free from such scruffy sell-outs. A normative academy owes its loyalty only to norms and values that shape its outlook and goals. It is the objective and universal values of Islam – those enshrined in the concepts and injunctions of the Qur'an, which have the ultimate loyalty of an Islamic university. Within the normative framework of these values, there is complete freedom of inquiry and academic work. Some would argue that research is independent of values; that fundamental knowledge recognises no normative criteria. I would disagree. Just as disciplines have real significance within the cultural milieu of their origin and development, so too are facts recognised as such within a particular framework and worldview. There is no such thing as a neutral fact or an unaligned truth. Whether an action is determined by theology or biology; logic or axiology; physics or sociology; history or statistics; it is values that guide and shape an action. As Abraham Edel points out, whether a fact becomes a value, or value changes into fact, is determined by the office that the item is serving.[6]

Unlike the western university, which despite being guided in all its endeavours by hidden values (swept under the carpet so they may not be noticed), an Islamic university boldly states the values and norms which shape its goals and academic work. This is not only more honest, it is also less dangerous. Consider the stance of those who insist on value-neutrality of facts. Edel wrote:

Think of Kant badgering a mother who loves her child to find out whether she does it from a sense of duty or from natural affection. Or the free man in Russell's early essay, 'A Free Man's Worship', brandishing his fist at matter rolling on its endless way. Or of the scientist insisting that when he says that atomic warfare is evil he is saying so purely as an individual and not as a scientist. In all these, we get a sense of an extricated self that waits until the situation is completely mapped out and then reacts, wills, feels, commands – all of his own sweet arbitrary impulse or his own indeterminate fashion.

In contrast, if the values underlying the facts are appreciated, then the situation is not all that helpless: one moves in a determined direction, acts, wills, feels, commands as the situation unfolds itself. In other words, one can react and take precautions against those facts that prove destructive not just of certain cherished values but of life and of terrestrial environment itself. Thus, a normative institution, the Islamic university is not only a goal-seeking enterprise, but is in the healthy position of being able to guard, to a certain extent, against the type of fact-finding and problem-solving exercise which could lead to disastrous consequences for people, society and the planet. So how do we go about setting up such normative institutions, considering that contemporary disciplinary boundaries are artificial and reflect the worldview of western civilisation? Being the knowledge base of the Muslim civilisation, an Islamic university should reflect its essential conceptual nature and characteristics in its institutional and organisational structure. It should be a microcosm of Muslim civilisation as well as an instrument of meeting its intellectual and research needs. As such, at the core of each Islamic university must be an outreach research and development (R&D) programme geared to the study and contemporisation of the essential concepts of the worldview of Islam. Traditionally, the worldview of Islam, or rather 'Islamic ideology' has been studied in terms of Shari'ah, the rules of faith and so on. This approach has restricted the traditional content of Islamic thought and traditionalism and, some would say, suffocated the development of innovative thought. Thus, to make traditional thought relevant to contemporary and future times, the outreach programme should be structured on a conceptual matrix: as such, the programme should have departments devoted to the study and contemporary understanding of such key Islamic concepts as unity of God (*tawheed*); the Prophets (*risala*); human trusteeship of the Earth's resources (*khilafa*); worship in its widest sense (*ibadahh*); justice (*adl*), and Shari'ah.

In these departments all the traditional grounds should be amply covered, as, for example, that which is covered in the faculties of Shari'ah, rules of faith (*Usul al-Din*) and promoting Islam (*Dawa*) at the International Islamic University, Islamabad. But the emphasis would be on contemporisation: the Department of Prophethood (*risala*), for example, would seek not to produce scholars who have memorised 5,000 actions of the Prophet Muhammad – one would expect them to have these not so much in their heads but on a CD – but to seek to understand their relevance in meeting the needs of modern life in all its complexities. By organising the core programme in this fashion, the emphasis is shifted from a rigid traditional mould to dynamic conceptual analysis and synthesis, which will take Islamic thought forward. Apart from this core outreach programme, an Islamic university would cover all areas of knowledge while conforming to the needs and requirements of Muslim civilisation. To give this institution a structure that can be appreciated in modern terms, we can analyse the contemporary and future needs of the Muslim civilisation into certain familiar categories such as ideational, scientific, technological, informational, organisational, social and cultural. These categories should not be understood as conceptual, for they are purely functional. We can build an academic structure around these categories. Thus, for example, an Islamic university could have faculties, schools, institutes and centres around each of these categories with appropriate departments in each. What, for example, would the School of Ideational Science contain? It could have departments of contemporary ideologies and worldviews; history of ideas; history of religion; natural philosophy, and philosophy of science. Similarly, the School of Technical Science could have departments of food technology, health technology, defence technology, environmental technology, materials technology and so on. Departments within each school will vary from country to country, reflecting local strengths and needs. We must now address the critic who argues that this is the same old wine in somewhat different but not altogether new bottles. After rejecting the false disciplinary divisions of knowledge, we also rejected the western type university structure. But now, it appears, that by suggesting an academic structure based on faculties and departments, we have brought back the same disciplinary divisions. This is definitely not so. The disciplinary divisions in western epistemology are divisions of worldviews: western epistemology does not have a single worldview. Moreover, within each discipline certain theoretical as well as factual developments generate their own specific worldviews, which are sometimes imposed on the entire discipline.

For example, the theories of organic evolution and sociobiology have created their own specific worldviews that are extrapolated and imposed on the entire discipline. For example, if one wishes to study parasitology or bacteriology, one has to study it from the evolutionary perspective; other avenues of exploration are not open. Moreover, the worldview of a particular discipline is often exposed on the entire human existence. To continue our example of biology, the biologist now tells us what evolutionary purpose, if any, religion serves for us. Furthermore, the worldview of a particular discipline may often completely contradict the worldview of another: the worldview of elementary particle physics is not complementary to the worldview of evolutionary biology. As such, disciplines are forced to be mutually exclusive: to enforce this division, the practitioners of each discipline develop a highly mythical language that prevents any form of interaction. Our functional division of areas of knowledge into faculties and departments does not support disciplinary worldviews. There is only one worldview at operation here, and this worldview and its norms and values shape inquiry and academic work in each discipline. If disciplines are deeply entrenched into their own worldview, any notion of interdisciplinary research almost becomes meaningless. But where the operational divisions are part of a unified worldview, real interdisciplinary research has no boundaries. When results of research based on narrow, disciplinary, parochial worldviews are applied generally, they lead to serious social, economic, class, sexual and cultural dislocations. In contrast, the fruits of research derived from disciplines based on unified and universal worldviews are more likely to have universal applications. While on the surface the institutional structure of an Islamic university presented here may appear to retain some of the old forms, a little probing reveals a radically different institution. Finally, what kind of product would this normative, interdisciplinary institution based on a unified worldview produce? The answer is a creative individual who not only understands but is also capable of synthesising Islam to his or her personal and societal needs. This will be an individual who is not only socially responsible but also technically virtuous. It will be an individual who not only appreciates the dictates and complexities of contemporary life but can also adapt to a changing future. What useful function, after all, can an Islamic university serve if it cannot produce individuals of this nature?

5
What Do We Mean By Islamic Futures?

At the dawn of the twenty-first century, the Muslim world finds itself in a state of helplessness and uncertainty, marginalised, suppressed, angry and frustrated. While a great deal has changed in the last 100 years, little has changed in terms of power politics. At the beginning of the twentieth century, when the Muslim reformer Jamaluddin Afghani was calling for the revival of *ijtihad* (independent reasoning) and a global pan-Islamic alliance, most of the Muslim world was under colonial rule, but a fledgling Caliphate was still in existence. The condition of the Muslim people – the *ummah* – its subjugation by the west, poverty and dependence, engendered a mood of despondency. Within two decades the Caliphate had ended. A decade later a renewed struggle for independence began as calls for *ijtihad* and jihad reverberated throughout the Muslim world. Halfway through this century, most Muslim countries had gained their independence only to discover, after a couple of decades of development and westernisation, that economically and politically they were still the subjects of the west. In the 1970s and 1980s, there was a brief period of euphoria about 'Islamic resurgence' before, in the beginning of the 1990s, the rediscovery of their utter helplessness in a rapidly changing world brought the Muslims back to the cycle that began the century: as the French proverb has it, *plus ça change, plus c'est la même chose* – the more things change the more they stay the same.

During the twentieth century the Muslims stumbled from one crisis to another. Even the hard-won successes, like the creation of Pakistan as 'the first Islamic state', the liberation of Algeria after a bitter and savage struggle against the French and the strenuously gained independence of so many Muslim countries, have not improved the overall conditions of the Muslim people. In many parts of the Muslim world, particularly in Africa and in states like Bangladesh and Iran, the daily lives of ordinary folks are harsher and more poverty-stricken then during the colonial period. Large-scale

First published in the *Blackwell Companion to Contemporary Islamic Thought*, edited by Ibrahim Abu Rabi, Blackwell, Oxford, 2006.

famine is a constant presence in sub-Saharan Muslim Africa. Seven out of ten of all refugees from war, oppression and famine in the world today are Muslims. The total impotence of the Muslim states was revealed, in the glaring presence of global television networks, by their inability to prevent 'ethnic cleansing' and the genocide of Muslims in Bosnia. The 'war against terror' as well as internal feuds and strife has turned Afghanistan and Iraq into wastelands.

As things stand, this state of affairs is set to continue. In a world where the rate of change is itself rapidly changing, the structures that oppress and suppress Muslims will become even more entrenched. Under globalisation, change is characterised not just by its global nature but also by instant, rapid feedback, complexity, chaos and irreversibility. What this means is that the globe is constantly being transformed by swift scientific, technological, cultural and political developments. The power of those who are managing and enhancing these changes – North America, Western Europe and multinational corporations – is increasing in equal proportions. In the Muslim world, rapid and perpetual change will bring newer and deeper crises to the fore; will generate further confusion and bewilderment, and make Muslim societies even more volatile and unstable and thus more amenable to manipulation, subjugation and domination.

ACCELERATED RATE OF CHANGE

Consider how rapidly the Muslim world has itself been transformed in the last three decades. The early 1970s saw unbound enthusiasm and hope in the Muslim world. Muslim countries and communities were said to be going through a cultural revival. Everywhere there was talk of 'Islamic resurgence' and the dawn of a new glorious age. Islam, it was said, was fast becoming a force in international politics. The Organization of the Petroleum Exporting Countries (OPEC) had come of age and was beginning to flex its muscles; there was an infinite pool of financial resources for development and modernisation. The Sudan was going to be transformed into the 'bread basket' of the Middle East. A new kind of Muslim unity, hitherto unimagined, was in the air as the Organization of the Islamic Conference (OIC) held one 'Islamic Summit' after another. There were 'Islamic conferences' on every conceivable subject, held in almost every major location in the Muslim world. Apparently, Islamic thought was being dragged from the Middle Ages to contemporary times. The 'Islamic revolution' in Iran added extra fuel to this euphoria. Islam, it was announced, finally had a modern success story. And 'Islamic revolution' had produced the first 'Islamic state' in history; and where Iran led, other Muslim states were bound to follow. Suddenly, revolutions were supposed to break out everywhere in the Muslim world. Muslims everywhere demanded the implementation of the Shari'ah and Islamic movements in Pakistan, the Sudan and Egypt began their struggle to transform their respective countries into Islamic states. Pakistan and the Sudan even succeeded in implementing some form of the Shari'ah and declared themselves to be 'Islamic states'. In the 1980s, 'Islamisation' became the norm throughout the Muslim world. Meanwhile the mujahideen in Afghanistan took on the might of a superpower. With over $5 billion in aid from Saudi Arabia alone, and American weapons, they began to push the Russian bear out of Afghanistan and eventually, after a decade of bloody struggle, succeeded in driving the Soviet armies from their lands.

But then things began to go sour; or, perhaps, the real world intervened to bring the Muslim *ummah* down to earth. The political, administrative and organisational incompetence of various governments in Afghanistan, including the Taliban, produced a fractured and fragmented state. The mujahideen may have brought the disintegration of the Soviet Union, as Ali Mazrui has argued,[1] but replacing the government of President Muhammad Najibullah was another story. It proved beyond their capabilities to transform themselves from a band of undisciplined but fearless mountain warriers into disciplined, united party politicians capable of forming and leading a government.

Similarly, the revolution in Iran, despite its Islamic credentials, turned out to be no different from any other revolution in history. The petrodollars on which so much hope was pinned have been swallowed up by American and European banks and the bottomless purses of arms merchants. The 'Arab money' which found its way as aid to various Muslim countries has produced little or no dividends in terms of development or modernisation. On the contrary, absolute poverty increased manifold as certain Muslim countries, most notably the Sudan, Pakistan and Bangladesh, went into a downward spiral of poverty and degradation. The experiment with Islamisation and implementation of the Shari'ah turned out to be a superannuated farce, which succeeded only in subverting social justice and increasing communal strife. The Islamic movements, which only two decades ago were so buoyant and full of promise, revealed themselves not just to be totally out of touch with reality but intellectually bankrupt and dangerously incompetent.

WHAT WENT WRONG?

So, what went wrong? Why did the promises and hopes of the 1970s turn so quickly into nightmares and bitter haplessness in the 1990s? Why has terrorism suddenly become the dominant theme in Muslim societies during the last decade?

Where did the 'Islamic resurgence' take a wrong turn? Whatever happened to the Muslim reassertion of cultural identity? The failures of the previous two decades, indeed the shortcomings of the past century, have been the inability of Muslims to appreciate their own strengths, comprehend the reality of the contemporary world, and adjust to rapid change. Muslims have been forced to react to one challenge after another, moving from one *cul de sac* to another: reacting, reacting, reacting. The way forward, and it seems to me to be the only rational way ahead, is for Muslims to become proactive: shape the future with foresight and a genuine appreciation of their present predicament, truthful assessment of historical shortcomings and a deep understanding of contemporary, global reality.

The purpose of Islamic futures is to chart out a path from the present impasse, develop insights into managing and anticipating change and map out desirable alternative futures for Muslims. The enterprise of Islamic futures demands a sharp break from conventional Muslim thought – based as it is on ossified traditionalism and a one-dimensional understanding of the modern and postmodern world, and a bold and imaginative grasp of the challenges that confront the Muslim people. It requires a fresh, deeper, futuristic understanding of Islam and a conscious, collective, will to overcome the present impasse. And it needs intellectual boldness and imagination: to imagine what has hitherto been impossible to imagine, to develop ideas that have existed only on the margins, and envision what may appear to be unrealisable dreams. Let us then move to the future.

WHERE IS THE FUTURE?

It is not easy to think about the future; the very idea of working out what things might look like 20, 50, even 100 years from today is daunting. The difficulty is compounded by the fact that the future does not really exist: it is always a time that has yet to be reached.

Moreover, the future will not exist even in the future for the future exists only when it becomes the present at which point it ceases to be the future. As the future does not actually exist, it has to be invented; to put it another way, ideas about the future must be generated and studied. Ideas about the future are important because our thoughts and actions are influenced not just by our notions of what happened in the past but also by our images of what may yet happen in the future. Thus, while the future is elusive and uncertain, it is also a domain over which we can exercise some power. We cannot change the past; we can only interpret and reinterpret history; but we can't actually change it. We cannot change the present either: that requires instantaneous change, which is impossible. But our inability to have definite knowledge about the future is balanced by our ability to mould it. It is within the capabilities of individuals and societies to shape their own future.

How can we shape the future? Imagine a devout Muslim whose only desire is to visit the holy city of Makkah in Saudi Arabia and perform the pilgrimage, or Hajj. He knows how the Hajj is performed but he has never been to Makkah and he is not in Makkah now. There is no room for this image in the past or the present; but there is room for this cherished image to perform the Hajj in the future. Future time is the only domain where he is able to receive as 'possible' an image, which is 'false' in the present. And the future in which he now places his cherished image reaches out to him to make the image a reality. To transform this future image into reality, the devout Muslim begins to save up for his journey; and saves for a number of years before he has enough financial resources to undertake the journey to Makkah. But his plans are concerned not just with financial resources. He also plans to make arrangements for his family and business to be looked after while he is away, perhaps as long as two months. And he also plans for certain contingencies. What if, for example, due to unforeseen circumstances, he cannot perform the Hajj on the actual year he had planned? What if he is taken ill in Makkah; or, given his age, he dies. Thus, the realisation of a simple future image requires careful and detailed planning, which includes asking a number of 'what if?' questions.

What is true of individuals is also largely true of societies. To shape a viable future, a society needs an image, a vision, of its future. It then has to map out a path towards the realisation of that future: how is it going to move from 'here' to 'there'? Incorporated in that map must be a host of 'what if?' questions: the variables that could go wrong, the hurdles that could appear almost as though from nowhere, the different paths that are available, and the different alternatives and options that will generate different choices that will have to be made. What we are then presented with is not just one future but a whole array of alternative *futures*.

In futures studies we always think of 'the future' in terms of the plural: *futures*. The objective is not so much to predict the future (a highly hazardous exercise) but to anticipate possible futures and work towards shaping the most desirable ones. Consciously and rationally thinking and acting towards desirable futures implies developing a sense of direction: behaving in anticipation. A society with a sense of direction moves towards a planned future of desired goals and realisable visions and anticipates all the possible alternatives, including undesirable futures that it may encounter in its journey. In contrast, an aimless society drifts from one undesirable future to another. A society that is continuously reacting to one change after another will move from crisis to crisis until it reaches one from which there can be no escape.

An aimless society considers the future as a mighty river. The great force of history flows inexorably along, carrying everyone with it. Attempts to change its course amount to little more than throwing pebbles in the river: they cause a few ripples but have no real effect on the mighty river. The river's course can change but only by natural disasters such as earthquakes and landslides: by the will of God. This is fatalism in action. On the other hand, a society with a sense of direction sees the future as a great ocean. There are many possible destinations and many alternative paths to these destinations. A good navigator takes advantage of the main current of change and adjusts his course accordingly, keeping a sharp outlook for possible typhoons or changes in weather conditions, and moving carefully through fog or through uncharted waters thus getting safely to the intended destinations.

THINKING ABOUT ALTERNATIVE FUTURES

When thinking of alternative futures, we tend to think in terms of five basic time horizons.

1. The *immediate* future: the one-year time horizon. As a planning horizon it presents a rather limited choice for it is largely dictated by the past. Present decisions or actions have little or no effect over

this time horizon frame; only major events cause perturbations in this range.

2. *Near* future: from one to five years. This is the time frame chosen for conventional development plans of most Third World countries. Decisions and policy choices made now can cause certain shifts in this time frame; however, it is not really possible to bring about revolutionary change in this time horizon. The near future works well for evolutionary advances; development plans have succeeded only when success has been accumulated from one plan to the next. However the history of development planning teaches us that, in most developing countries, each five-year plan has marked a departure from the previous and the next five-year plan. The end result has been a sort of drunkard's random walk. After successive development plans many Third World countries have ended up exactly where they started.

3. *One-generation* future: 20 years from now. This is the time required for one generation to grow and mature. The decisions taken today will not change the world we will experience in the next five years, but they could dramatically change the world we experience 20 years from now; the next generation would be maturing with those experiences. Almost anything can be done in this time frame. This sounds astonishing but consider the fact that it took the Prophet Muhammad just 23 years to totally change the tribal society of Arabia and evolve a civilisation virtually from nothing; in more recent times, once the decisions had been made, it took just four years to build the atom bomb and just eight years to put a man on the moon! One generation is basically all it takes to realise any realistic vision of the future.

4. *Multi-generational* or *long-range* future: from one to several generations, extending up to 50 or 60 years. Although this is a largely uncontrollable, open-ended future, it is possible to see/ trigger the opportunities/crisis ahead.

5. The *far* future: from 50 years and beyond. The domain of science fiction: it is possible only to speculate in this time frame. However, this time frame is not as far out as one may think. Consider: yourself, your parents, your grandparents – that's at least 100 years of your personal history. Consider: yourself, your children, your grandchildren: that is another 100 years of your personal future. An individual walks around wrapped in 200 years of the extended present: the family chain.[2]

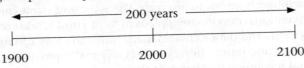

The extended present – a family chain:
grandparents – parents – self – children – grandchildren

← ———————— 200 years ———————— →

1900   2000   2100

Which time horizon is most suited for futures studies? Well, the faster the car, the further headlights need to be able to see if we are to avoid dangers and pitfalls. The faster the pace of change, the further into the future we must look. Given the extremely rapid rate of change, and its interrelated nature, we need to work with at least one-generation, if not multi-generational, time frames. Most futures planning and visionary work is thus carried out between 20 to 50 year horizons.

The future is, of course, a product of both the past and present. And both, our history, as well as our present circumstances, have to be taken into account in futuristic planning. That is to say futures thinking requires *prospective*: the inclusion of knowledge from the past and the present. History is the domain of identity; and a future without one's identity is no future at all. But not all history plays a part in the future; if it did then we would simply be living in history. All societies have living histories, often described as tradition, which mould their historical identity. It is tradition, in its living, life-enhancing form, and not its ossified, suffocating form that we must take into account when thinking about shaping viable futures. When considering contemporary reality, we have to ensure that we do not start from an impossible or untenable position. The modern world has to be appreciated in all its complexities and contradictions.

There are certain central features of contemporary reality that have to be taken into account in all futures-orientated work. In the globalised world, everything is connected to everything else. *Inter-connection* and *interdependence* are the dominant global norms. That means problems do not exist in isolation; neither can they be resolved in isolation. A 'simple' health problem, for example, does not only have a medical bearing but also scientific, educational, lifestyle, environmental, social and economic components. A viable solution would therefore require inputs from all these areas. Thus even apparently 'simple' problems turn out to be complex: *complexity* is the essence of contemporary problems, most of which seem to be interlinked to each other forming a web of problems – or *problématique*.[3]

The situation is made worse by the rapid pace of change. To appreciate the pace of change consider the fact that the evolution of the modern ship took over a thousand years but the airplane evolved in less then 60 years; the evolution of the personal computer has followed a path similar to that of the printed book, but in 40 years instead of 600; most high-technology becomes obsolete and is replaced in less then five years; the processing capacity of the microchip doubles every two years! The complexity of modern problems is thus being continuously enhanced by the changes ushered in by scientific and technological development. The truly mindboggling intricacy of our problems often generates a paralysis of decision-making processes characterised by perpetual postponement and avoidance of decisions – the so-called 'disappearing decision' syndrome.[4]

The interconnection and interdependence of the world also means that isolation is now untenable. Developments in communication and information technology, global television networks, and the evolution of the Internet, the network of all networks of computers around the world, means that the globe is shrinking rapidly. All cultures, big or small, are obliged to interact with each other, generating synthesis and counter-synthesis. Notions of cultural purity and monolithic institutions of all types are doomed. What has always been true in agriculture (a single crop, if repeatedly planted on the same field, exhausts the land and gives rapidly diminishing yields) is also true of human cultures: large structures dominated by single modes of thought or straightjacketed by a single, all-embracing ideology cannot sustain themselves. The rapid collapse of the Soviet Union was as much due to the vacuous nature of Soviet communism as the monolithic nature of the Soviet State. *Plurality* and *diversity* are not only the essence of sustainability in nature but also the bedrock of stable societies and dynamic cultures. Monocultures have no place in the future.

Given the nature of contemporary reality, it is not possible for futures studies to be a unified, single-subject discipline. By the very nature of what it sets out to tackle, futures studies is a *transdisciplinary* and *multidimensional* activity. It tackles both the *complexity* as well as the *contradictions* inherent in the world; it considers both the *global* as well as the *local* dimensions of planning; emphasises both *interdependence* as well as *interconnections*; and incorporates *plurality* as well as *participation* across all levels of societies and cultures. In as far as futures studies involves systematic and disciplined, empirical and rational exploration of future possibilities, futures studies is a science. But experimentation is not a possibility in futures studies; so, in that sense, futures studies is not a science. In as far as future studies involves foresight, prospective analysis, creation of visions and images, future studies is an art. It is the art of anticipation based on the science of exploration.

ISLAMIC FUTURES 40 YEARS FROM NOW

So how do we shape a desirable future, say, 20, or 40 years from now?

First, we need certain basic tools. We need pictures of what the future could look like. Essentially, we need two varieties of pictures. The first variety tells us what the future would look like if things continue as they are. We can get an idea of how the future is shaping up, given the present trends, by *projections* or *trend extrapolations*. Projections are linear analysis of current trends, which go from the past to the present and into the future. Demographic developments are often predicted on the basis of this kind of projection. Trends extrapolations can be simple, involving one variable, or highly complex and sophisticated involving a whole array of variables as well as the probabilities of their interdependence and occurrence – in the latter case it is normally referred to as *morphological analysis*. We can also get an idea of what the future will be like by asking a selection of experts: if this is done in a systematic manner, the experts are polled a number of times, allowed to challenge each others' opinion and rethink their opinions, a consensus emerges giving us a general idea of what the future has in store. This is known as the *Delphi method*. When the Delphi method is used to identify future trends and then linked with possible future events, as well as the impact of trends on events and is analysed in a systematic manner, a more sophisticated picture of the future emerges – this is known as the cross-impact matrix method.

A yet more sophisticated method is to develop a simulation model of a system – say the world, or a city, or an economy – and then use this to study what happens when various variables are changed. The first major study of the future in recent times, *The Limits to Growth*, sponsored by the Club of Rome, was based on computer simulation models.[5] These, and other methods, of studying the future generate *predictions* and *forecasts*. A prediction is a reasonably confident statement about a future state of affairs. A forecast is a more guarded statement of possible future outcomes based on a 'what if?' type of analysis: if a certain trend continues, and certain conditions are fulfilled, then we can expect a certain outcome with a certain level of confidence. Pictures of the future generated by these methods can be turned into *scenarios*. A scenario is defined as 'the description of future situations together with the progression of events leading from the base situation to the future situation'.[6]

Pictures of the futures generated in this way warn us of the potential threats and dangers ahead. They provide us with early warning signals so that we may change course, develop contingency plans, prepare ourselves to confront the emerging challenge. But this variety of futures images has a serious limitation: it contains only three types of basic information: (1) there will be continued growth and business as usual; (2) things will retard and there will be a backwards slide; or (3) there will be total collapse or catastrophe. Since change is inevitable, and we cannot stand still, there can only be three options: things go up or down or break apart. This type of futures analysis is too dependent on historical momentum and present complexities. Such images of the future do not have transformational potential.

A VISION FOR KARACHI IN 2040

The second archetypal variety of images of the future is concerned with what we would like the future to be. It is our individual or collective picture of the future. Here, we could be imaginative and bold. Instead of predicting the future, we try to invent it, to envision it. Our images of the future, both at the level of the individual and society, play an important role in actually determining the future. An enumerated image of the future, with most of the contours and details worked out, is a *vision*; and visions have transformational power. It is through well-articulated visions that societies break out of their cocoons, surpass their limitations, and transform, like a butterfly, into higher levels of existence.

How do visions help us shape the future? To transform visions into realisable futures we start with a vision and then plan backwards to present time. Consider, for example, a vision of a city like Karachi some two generations (40 years) from today. What is my vision of Karachi in 2040? Karachi today is a mega-city of more than 10 million people and suffers from the problems common to most Third World mega-cities. I envision Karachi free from ethnic and communal strife; free from pollution and traffic congestion; most of its inhabitants are in gainful employment and have adequate housing with clean water and electricity and a good network of public transport; business is booming thanks to the port which has become a focus for shipping in South Asia; there is law and order and a responsible and accountable local government. Now, while this is a pretty realistic vision of Karachi it is far removed from the Karachi of today.

To make this vision into a workable proposition we ask a series of questions working backwards from the year 2040: what conditions must be fulfilled in 2038 for my vision of Karachi to be in place by 2040? Well, for most of the inhabitants to be in gainful employment some sort of employment policy must be in full swing, the basic infrastructure of the city, including the public transport system, should be in position, an adequate number of low cost housing units directed towards the urban poor must have been built, and so on. For these things to have occurred by 2038, what should have happened by 2036? And 2034, 2032, 2030...and so on to the present time.

We also have to explore negative possibilities: what can happen to undermine successful implementation of certain targets? What could possibly go wrong? At the completion of the exercise, we have two products: a vision of Karachi in 2040 and a detailed plan, worked out backwards from 2040, with yearly goals and target, of how that particular vision could be realised. This kind of planning is known as *backcasting* (as opposed to forecasting) and is a highly empowering tool. It brings what appears to be unachievable, distant goals, into the realms of realisable alternatives. The more detailed and realistic the vision, the more thorough the backcasting, the more amenable the future. Of course, my individual vision and backcasting exercise is neither adequate nor, by itself, able to shape a viable future for Karachi. To be meaningful, both envisioning and backcasting must be a collective, social endeavour: shaping the future is a participatory endeavour.

Visions provide a society with a sense of direction, a future destination. Backcasting furnishes it with paths, ways and means to get 'there' from 'here and now'. This kind of futures studies is thus a highly empowering as well as an action-orientated process. It invites participation in both the formulation of, as well as developing routes towards, desirable futures. The purpose of generating images of the future, both by conventional methodologies of futures studies, by vision analysis and using backcasting, is to improve our decision-making processes. Futures studies is a highly practical and pragmatic undertaking. When the visions and images, ideas and empirical work about alternative futures are distilled, we are left with choices and options that have to be made now:

The fact is that problems of today did not appear suddenly out of thin air; they have been building up, often for many years, and might have been dealt with fairly easily if they had been tackled earlier. The crisis that we face today is generally the minor problem we neglected yesterday .... The whole point of studying future possibilities ... is to improve the quality of decisions that are *being made* right now. Today's decisions are shaping tomorrow's world, yet only too often we make decisions with little concern about their impact on the longer-term future.[7]

So, how does futures studies relate to Islam?

ISLAM AND FUTURE AWARENESS

Islam is intrinsically a future-orientated worldview. The Qur'an specifically asks the believers to be conscious of their history as well as their future: 'Beware of what lies before and behind you, so that you may be given mercy' (36:45). The idea of the future and the notion of accountability in Islam are tied up in two fundamental concepts: *akhira* (life after death, or hereafter) and *khilafa* (trusteeship of humans over God's creation). The concept of *akhira* is related to the Islamic notion of time. In rationalist and materialistic philosophies time is a linear progression: it ends with an individual's life. Beyond his/her life there is no time, at least as far as his/her own individual identity is concerned. In contrast, Islam sees time as a tapestry in which earthly time and eternal heavenly time are woven together. This life is life in earthly time, while *akhira* is the life in eternity, where we are able to pass beyond the limits of space, time and causality. One's life, thus, does not end with one's death and one's deeds on Earth continue to have an impact on one's life in the life to come. Future time, that is time both in this world and the Hereafter, is the time of accountability: a believer will produce results for his/her deeds both in this world and *akhira*, the Hereafter.

The concept of *khilafa* adds another dimension to the synthesis of accountability and future. As trustees of God's creation, believers are required to manage the trust (*amana*) in an ethically- and socially-responsible way. This means that the planet and the well-being of its people must be delivered to future generations in at least as good, if not better, condition than they found it. Certain Islamic social institutions inherently display the future orientation contained in the fundamental concepts of *akhira* and *khilafa*. For example, throughout history, Muslims have been keen to establish what is called *waqf* (an endowment or philanthropic foundation; plural, *awqaf*) for the needy. A *waqf* by definition looks after the welfare of future generations. For the donor, a *waqf* is also an investment in the life to come, as Muslims believe that a *waqf* will generate blessings in perpetuity for the individuals who established them, enriching their afterlife.

The same future-orientated logic is evident in the establishment of what are called *haram*, or inviolate zones in which development is prohibited by law; and what are called *hima* reserves, similar to conservation zones or national parks for the conservation of wildlife and forests. Concern for the future is thus intrinsic to Islam.

We can see a demonstration of future awareness in the life of the Prophet Muhammad (peace be upon him). The Prophet constantly anticipated future possibilities before taking action. For example, when he took the decision to relocate the fledgling community of Muslims from Makkah to Medina, he did so on the anticipation that the community had a more viable future in Medina. In his birthplace of Makkah the Prophet was facing hostility from the ruling authorities (the Quraish tribe). The migration was carefully planned, and the path for the migration was systematically cleared over several months. The Prophet anticipated that there would be a Quraish uprising against him. He prepared for this in advance and met the advancing Quraish army outside Medina, at a point he knew would give the small Muslim army a strategic advantage: this was the well at a place called Badr.

Later on in his life, the Prophet knew that the future viability of the Muslim community depended on a comprehensive, negotiated peace settlement with the Quraish; as well as a constitution for the pluralistic community of Medina where Muslims, Christians and Jews lived together. Despite complaints from his companions that he was giving too much away, the Prophet concluded an agreement (the treaty of Hudaibiyah), which he used as a basis to establish one of the first constitutions in the world.

Another example from the life of the Prophet comes in the months leading up to what is called the 'battle of the trenches'. Here, the Prophet anticipated further conflict with the Quraish (who wanted to wipe out the new Muslim community) and he prepared to defend Medina by digging a trench around the city. Once more, he demonstrated how, thanks to anticipation and planning, he was able, within a single generation, to the lay the foundations for a future global civilisation.

And after the Prophet's death, his successors (the Caliphs) continued the tradition of future-orientated thinking and actions. Abu Bakr, his close friend and the first Caliph, foresaw the expansion of Muslim lands and realised that future needs could not be fulfilled with the existing system of administration. He therefore developed a new, and more flexible, system of administration and management, which could adjust to future needs. Umar, the second Caliph, realised that the future survival of the Muslim community was dependent on available resources. This meant that all resources could not be consumed within a single generation. Against the explicit wishes of his companions and even at the risk of a conflict, he refused to distribute the conquered lands of Syria, Iraq, Iran and Egypt among the Muslims. Declaring that they were for 'succeeding generations', he set them aside as future resources for the rapidly expanding Muslim community.

Islam does not only emphasise that Muslims be aware of their future, it insists that believers should actively shape their future. By the very nature of their faith, Muslims are required both to engage with the world and change it. The Qur'an repeatedly asks the Muslims both to change themselves and to constantly strive to change the world so that it could become a more just, equitable and peaceful abode for humanity:

Man will only have what he has worked towards, that his labour will be seen and in the end he will be paid in full for it. (53: 39–41)

This is why at the core of Shari'ah, or Islamic law, we find the principle of *ijtihad* (sustained and reasoned struggle), which is concerned primarily with change and with shaping and reshaping the future.

HOW MUSLIMS FROZE THE FUTURE

Muslim societies have abandoned *ijtihad*, whose 'gates' were supposed to have been 'closed' some centuries ago. They have also ignored the future-orientated message of their faith – the very source of the dynamism inherent in Muslim civilisation. As a result, Muslim understanding of the worldview of Islam has been frozen in history. During its long decline and eventual colonisation, Muslims have lost the capability for developing fresh insights, appreciations and interpretations of the fundamental sources of Islam: the Qur'an and examples from the life of the Prophet Muhammad (known as *sunnah*). Colonisation produced further ossification where obscurantist traditionalism came to be seen as the sole protection from the encroachment of the west. Finally, development and accompanied westernisation has systematically stripped the holistic ethical layers from Muslim society leaving them with the fragmented shell of what the late Fazlur Rahman called 'minimal Islam' – rituals, pieties and a list of do's and don'ts. In the contemporary world, Islam manifests itself in a number of fractured, fragmented and reductive ways. Contemporary Muslim societies prefer to look back, wallow in nostalgia for their 'golden past' rather than plan and work towards a vibrant future.

The process of shaping desirable futures for the Muslim world must begin with an awareness of contemporary reality. From the perspective of futures studies, we know that there are no simple, one-dimensional answers to contemporary problems, let alone the increasingly complex web of problems that will confront us in the future. This means there is little room for the classical atomistic, jurisprudence-orientated methodology in which classical jurists try and solve problems by looking for guidance, arguments and positions of their predecessors and by quoting stand-alone verses of the Qur'an, or traditions of the Prophet Muhammad. Such simplistic legal rulings cannot engage the increasingly complex and rapidly changing world where problems are interconnected and interdependent. To transform the world proactively, the driving forces of contemporary world, science, technology, modernity and postmodernism, must be engaged at fundamental levels: at the level of axioms, values and ethical concerns. Thus, Islam must be seen not just as a faith and religion, but an integrated, holistic *worldview*.

Islam interacts with contemporary reality through an integrated matrix of concepts and values. These include: the unity of God, humanity and nature; humanity's trusteeship of God's creation; accountability; the life to come; as well as knowledge, justice, worship and public interest. Contemporary problems and challenges are analysed from the perspective of this matrix to generate a range of possible choices from which each Muslim society chooses those which are most appropriate to its needs. When contemporary problems are examined and analysed with ethical and value concepts, the Shari'ah is transformed, from a body of rules and injunctions from history into a multidimensional problem-solving methodology. This is the first principle of Islamic futures: *Islam engages with the contemporary world as a worldview whose conceptual matrix serves as a methodology for tackling problems and generating future choices and possibilities for Muslim societies.*

The fragmentation of the Muslim world means that Muslims appear to be little more than a collection of nation-states each with limited resources and a myriad of insoluble problems. In a globalised world, the nation-state is coming under pressure from two opposing forces. It is leaking power downwards to dissenting, and often suppressed and marginalised, ethnic groups and minorities. And it is diffusing power upwards by being forced into regional economic and political alliances. Global politics is now too complex either to be divided into three portions (first, second and third world) or analysed by pre-Cold War logic. The emerging political divisions are increasingly being based on what Samuel Huntington has called the 'civilizational paradigm'.[8] Global politics will thus increasingly become civilisational politics. Thus, it is imperative for Muslims to see themselves not in terms of nation-states and national interests, but as a civilisation and in terms of civilisational interests.

As a global civilisation, Muslims possess vast resources and enormous potentials, which would enable them to solve most of their problems.

This is the second principle of Islamic futures: *Only when moulded into a civilisation, which involves pooling of resources and sharing of potentials of Muslim countries to tackle common problems and goals, would Muslims be able to move beyond parochial concerns of fragmenting nation-state and acute global marginalisation towards shaping a vibrant and dynamic future for themselves.*

One of the main strengths of Islam is its diversity: a diversity that exhibits itself in numerous ways: a diversity that is enveloped by a unity: a unity that manifests itself as a matrix of concepts and values that all Muslims accept without qualification. Those who see Islam simply as a private faith; those who are committed to various traditions within the religion – such as the trend of literal interpretation of the Qur'an and the *sunnah* – those who subscribe to the established trend of mystical interpretations, the Sufis; those who emphasise juristic traditions; those who are committed to the political differences arising from various interpretations, the Shias: each group contributes to the richness and diversity of Islam and each group has an important contribution to make in shaping the future civilisation of Islam in a collective, cooperative framework. When this religious diversity is combined with an ethnic plurality, the bewildering number of ethnicities within the world of Islam, the true multicultural nature of Islam comes to the fore. Here then we have the third principle of Islamic futures: *The plurality and diversity of Islam are the cornerstones for shaping a dynamic, thriving Muslim civilisation of the future.*

This principle has profound consequences for certain exclusivists and isolationists, more commonly known as the fundamentalists. The Qur'anic directive to 'change things', to work towards shaping a future, writes Anwar Ibrahim, former Deputy Prime Minister of Malaysia, is to

Emphasize collectivity and cooperation, self-development and self-adjustment. From the Islamic perspective, it is not man but God who created values. For Islam, values are a *priori*, given. Moreover, values do not change; they are eternal. There are no new values out there waiting to be discovered. There is complete consensus of the ummah on this issue; in fact, the definition of a Muslim is one who accepts the values and norms laid down in the Qur'an and the Sunnah of the Prophet Muhammad. The ummah (international Muslim community) tries to 'change things' with a consensus of values; consensus rather than conflict and competition become the operating parameter. Moreover, as things are being changed with a cooperative endeavour, there is no place for domination and control in this framework.[9]

Shaping Islamic futures is thus a participatory exercise based on exploration of alternatives and possibilities and making choices. A puritan and dominating interpretation of Islam cannot engage in such an exercise for in its framework there are no alternatives, no choices to be made: there can be only one future, the inevitable extension of the perpetual and brutal struggle of the present.

Islam is pre-eminently a doctrine of truth. But believing in Islam is not tantamount to *possessing* the truth. Those who claim that only their version of Islam is the absolute truth, not only deny the manifest diversity and plurality of Islam, but also arrogate divine powers to themselves. What distinguishes fundamentalism from traditional Islam, as Parvez Manzoor, Professor of Linguistics at the University of Stockholm, has argued so convincingly, is that 'the cognitive theory of the "state" is "fundamental" to its vision of Islam and represents a paramount fact of its consciousness'. Thus, from a 'totalistic theocentric worldview, a God-centered way of life and thought, of knowledge and action', Islam is transformed into a 'totalitarian theocratic world order that submits every human situation to the arbitration of the state'.[10]

When society and state become one, politics disappears, cultural and social spaces are homogenised, and the end product mirrors fascism. When Islam is transformed into an exclusivist ideology, the sacred is politicised and politics becomes sacred and everything is bulldozed into uniformity. The fundamentalist interpretation of Islam not only does violence to its tradition, history and pluralistic outlook, but has no appreciation of either the complexity and interdependence of contemporary reality nor of the ecological laws of nature. Fundamentalism is 'all cause and no programme' and thus superfluous and irrelevant to contemporary times. As an homogenised, mentally monocultural, monolithic outlook on state and society, it is an unnatural phenomenon: it cannot survive; therefore it has no future; and, as such, it has no place in the purview of Islamic futures.

Pluralism and diversity lead by necessity to participation and hence to the fourth principle of Islamic futures: *Shaping viable and desirable futures for a Muslim civilisation involves the active participation of communities and conscious effort at consultation (shura) at all levels of society with the aim of achieving a broad consensus (ijma).*

Both *ijma* and *shura* are the basic and essential values of governance in any Muslim community. The process of consultation and consensual politics not only strengthens civic institutions within Muslim societies but also legitimises pluralistic identities and interests within a Muslim community. While a liberal polity allows the loudest, most powerful voices to win out, participatory structures of governance based on *ijma* and *shura* ensure equality and justice by making consultation mandatory with all segments of society – thus giving voice and power to all minorities. The direct articulation of interests, needs and preferences peculiar to different groups in society enables more appropriate and just policies to be formulated. New agents of social and economic change are produced moving society towards healthier and positive directions. Conflict is reduced if not eliminated and a cohesive society generated.

In contrast, the fundamentalist agenda, as Anwar Ibrahim notes, 'sets a false agenda of peripheral issues as the only topics that get serious and sustained attention' and thus violates the necessary moral meaning of the concept of ummah because it 'causes division and engenders unnecessary conflict' and 'enables some expressions to become Muslim imperialism writ large or writ small'. Classical Muslim discourse, on the other hand, emphasised ideals of *ijma* and *shura* as well as the notion of a pluralistic community bounded by faith, the *ummah*. Ibrahim sees the *ummah*, which is 'not a cultural entity patterned upon the norms of any one dominant group' but 'exists within and is expressed through diverse cultural groups', as the basis for a viable future for the Muslim civilisation. The Muslim identity, he argues, is not only rooted in Islamic history and tradition, it is also intrinsically connected to the notion of the *ummah*. The idea of the *ummah* is not simply that Muslims are a community, but:

How Muslims should *become* a community in relation to each other, other communities and the natural world. It is manifesting in thought, action and openness a distinctive moral vision that is the raison d'être of the ummah. It is enduring commitment to the dynamism of a constant set of moral concepts and precepts that creates the contours and ultimate configuration of the ummah.[11]

Pluralistic participation and consultative and consensual politics, at the level of society, nation and civilisation, provide the circumference within which Muslims become a community in relation to each other.

The interconnected and interdependent nature of the modern world makes isolation a thing of the past. Even when it is desired, it is not possible for a society or a state to exist in splendid cultural, economic or political isolation. Moreover, the complexity and contradictory nature of modern times means that is not possible to consider, or label, a single institution, idea or group of people as all bad or all good, all black or all white. The world consists not of dichotomies, and bipolar choices but of complexities that have reduced everything to shades of grey. This is why the ethical concepts of Islam are of such paramount importance in analytical and methodological explorations. *To shape desirable alternative futures Muslims must engage constructively with the contemporary world in all its dimensions*. This is the fifth – and last – principle of Islamic futures. There is, for example, no escaping the west: there is nowhere on this globe that one can hide to get away from the western civilisation! However, constructive engagement with the west could not only produce dividends for Muslim societies but also has the potential of actually transforming the west to the benefit of the entire planet! This principle also contrasts sharply with the clannish approach to Islam, evident in even the names of certain groups, such as Egypt's Muslim Brotherhood; Pakistan's Jamat Islami (Islam's Party); Lebanon's 'Hizbullah' (God's Party); and even in Britain's Hizb ut Tahrir (Liberation Party); which encircle a minority to the exclusion of the majority. The very nature of these insular movements, based as they are on the idea that an imagined 'pristine' beginning needs to be retrieved, leads them to engage with the world in terms of dichotomies, such as: fundamentalism versus modernism; normativism versus acculturationism; revivalism versus re-entrenchment; Islam versus the west. Thus everything must be rejected; and the rejection begins by cutting off ties with the west and all its ills and ends with intolerance of all interpretations of Islam, which differ from those of the clan.

Similar ideas lead to a total rejection of democracy. But democracy, or indeed any notion, western or non-western, clashes with Islam only when it conceives itself as a doctrine of truth or violates one of the fundamental notions of Islam. Only when democracy becomes wedded to atheistic humanism and lays claims to being a dogma of truth, or when secularism interprets itself as an epistemology, does it clash with the faith of Islam. As a mechanism for representative government, devoid of its ideological pretentions and trappings, democracy hardly clashes with Islam. Similarly, a total rejection of modernity is insane. In a world dominated by technological development, one cannot create a non-technological society. What is needed is a detailed analysis of modernity and rejection of its core values such as instrumental rationality, alienating modes of production, artificial and conflict-ridden nation-states etc. But, in the end, Muslims will have to engage with modernity by producing their own ways of being (traditionally?) modern. Rejectionist ideologies produce one-dimensional answers far removed from contemporary reality. Once Islam is isolated from the real world and framed into a cardboard ideology, it ceases to be an actor shaping individuals and societies but becomes a simple point of reference. Islam therefore becomes an instrument in attempts to create a totalitarian state based on intolerance and martyrology. This type of reductionism is the product of intellectual capriciousness and exaggeration, wavering and anaemia, and pretension and intolerance, none of which were dominant in pre-modern Islamic history.

Constructive engagement involves reducing conflict both within Muslim societies and between Muslims and western systems of thought. Conflicts within Muslim societies can be tackled by successfully managing competing interests and loyalties on the basis of *shura* and consensual politics. Imparting humility to the west involves a great deal more. Muslim understanding of western civilisation, tempered by centuries of conflict and the experience of colonialism, is extremely skewed. On the whole, Muslims have developed stereotyped images of the west as pernicious and immoral ('the Great Satan') just as the west has developed orientalist images of Islam and Muslims. The myopic understanding of the west means that Muslims are unable to see the contradictions within western societies nor are they able to martial their natural allies within the west who are often alienated by extreme and one-dimensional rhetoric.

There are essentially two points of conflict between Islam and the west. The first point is that economically and technologically, the world is structured as though the developing countries were the colonies of the industrialised states of the west. The vast majority of the world's most productive scientists are from developed countries and technology is one of their main exports. Banks and insurance companies, airlines and shipping companies, and multinational corporations of the west all tie the world together. Multilateral institutions such as the World Bank, the International Monetary Fund (IMF) and the World Trade Organization (WTO), ensure that the oppressive and the unjust nature of the system is maintained. Muslims have to change the global system by managing the conflict through alliances with other civilisations – China, India, Latin America – and taking advantage of the contradictions and fractures within the western alliance. To some extent this process has already begun with the industrialisation of South-East Asia and the re-emergence of China as an economic and military superpower.

The second point relates to the west's insistence on demonising Islam and Muslims and flaming the fires of conflict. That a bloodthirsty Muslim civilisation is ready to pounce on the west is one of the main assertions of Huntington's 'Clash of Civilization' thesis; and it is an intrinsic assumption of such notions as 'axis of evil' and the 'war on terror'. Demonisation of Islam in western thought has a history going back even before the Crusades.[12] It is, in fact, very much part of the western psyche and consciousness. At this juncture of history, we should not be too surprised by it. Far from being hurt by this type of stereotyping, Muslims must engage with the west and demonstrate the false nature of these earlier images. Instead of being alarmed by western sabre-rattling, Muslims have to manage this variety of perceived conflicts by creative tension where resolution is achieved by the qualitative transformation of the opponent.

It is quite evident that the principles of Islamic futures are as much about the future as they are a critique of the existing Muslim thought. When the concerns of the future are brought to bear on contemporary situations a critique is always generated and the critique *per se* becomes a programme of action. The function of the principles of Islamic futures is to enable Muslim societies to creatively manage the four global features of our time: change, complexity, contradictions and conflicts. The process of managing the four C's – improving upon the present – is related to operationalising the principles that will shape desirable and possible futures for Muslims. The future is a function of the present. And the present demands a set of pragmatic first steps. A fresh, contemporary understanding of Islam, that transforms Islam from a mere faith, to which it has been reduced, into an integrative worldview with an analytical ethical and conceptual matrix, has to be developed. Muslim states have to reconstruct and transform themselves, almost brick by brick, into a dynamic, contemporary, global civilisation. Isolationist, puritanical and monolithic tendencies have to be checked. Plurality and participation, on the basis of consultation and consensual politics have to be instituted. And Muslims have to avoid being cast as a new demon or become entangled, like the Ottoman Caliphate at the beginning of the twentieth century, with the rivalries of old adversaries. Formidable though these challenges are, they are, nevertheless, not as daunting as they first appear. Already, there are considerable intellectual and scholarly resources to draw upon; and the momentum of history is on the side of the Muslims.

FUTURE PATHS ALREADY TAKEN

The euphoria and upheaval, the swings of the pendulum, over the last two decades has generated an important side-effect: Muslims everywhere have realised the acute need for Islamic reform, a realisation that has acquired urgency after the tragic events of 9/11 and its aftermath. Numerous calls for internal reforms in Islam and to shape a new, 'progressive' Islam have been made. The American group 'Progressive Muslims' has presented an agenda for change, including ideas on justice, gender relations, sexual orientation and pluralism.[13] While wishing to engage seriously with Islamic thought, tradition and practice, Progressive Muslims want to 'translate' the social ideals of the Qur'an into contemporary idiom, seek full 'human and religious rights' for Muslim women, and aim at restoring 'compassionate humaneness' into contemporary Islam.

In contrast, Malaysia's Prime Minister, Abdullah Badawi, has proposed another model of progressive Islam he calls 'Islam Hadhari'.[14] The term *hadhari* is taken from the first recognised Muslim sociologist Ibn Khaldun and signifies urban civilisation. Islam Hadhari places considerable emphasis on economic development, civic life and cultural progress. It gives equal emphasis to the present and the future, encourages moderation and pragmatism, emphasises the central role of knowledge in Islam, preaches hard work and honesty and appeals to Muslims to be 'inclusive', tolerant and outward-looking towards other faiths and ideologies. Both the work of the Progressive Muslims and Islam Hadhari are contemporary efforts at a new *ijtihad*.

Elsewhere, the emphasis has been on what I have called the three 'metaphysical catastrophes'[15] that have undermined our ability to undertake *ijtihad*: the elevation of the Shari'ah to the level of the Divine, the equation of Islam with the state, and the removal of agency from believers. Muslims throughout the world now realise that much of Islamic law and jurisprudence is socially constructed and has little relevance for contemporary society. We need to reconstruct Islam, law and ethics from first principles – from the matrix of concepts and values embedded in the Qur'an that define the spirit of Islam. Moreover, the spectacular failure of contemporary 'Islamic states' – in Iran, the Sudan, Saudi Arabia, Afghanistan, Pakistan and elsewhere – has led to the questioning of the conventional 'Islamic movement' formulation of the relationship between Islam and the state. The idea that Islam should be the basis of the state, that Shari'ah should be adopted as a constitution for the state; that political sovereignty rests in the hands of the Divine (by which is meant religious leaders, or the *ulema*); and that the principles of consultation (*shura*) are inimical to the notion of democracy, has now been discredited. Certain segments of the 'Islamic movement' – most notably Pakistan's Jamat Islami and the Muslim Brotherhood of Egypt – still hang on desperately to these ideas, but the majority of Muslims know from experience that this is a recipe for totalitarianism.

Similarly, many thinking Muslims have begun to question the traditional wisdom that all interpretative authority in Islam should belong to a particular class of people – the *ulema* – and the vast majority of believers can be nothing but empty vessels who have to follow the dictates of a select few. Efforts to reframe Islamic Law, both theoretically and practically, have already begun. In works such as

Mawil Izzi Dien's *Islamic Law*,[16] the Shari'ah is being historicised in an attempt to rethink its current purpose.

In the United States, attempts are being made to develop an Islamic jurisprudence (*fiqh*) aimed specifically at Muslims who find themselves as minorities. Taha Jabir al-Alwani, for example, has suggested that minority *fiqh* can be formulated by a 'combined reading' of the 'Revelation for an understanding of the physical world and its laws and principles, and a reading of the physical world to appreciate and recognize the value of Revelation'.[17] Al-Awani also calls for a review of the relationship between the Qur'an and the *sunnah* and insists that the questions we ask of the Shari'ah are contextual. Each minority has to consider the political system it is living under, the kind of majority it is living with, what kinds of rights and protections it enjoys, what kind of common ground it shares with other cultures, and so on. The end product is thus not some 'universal' legal framework but law that is specific to the minority that undertakes the exercise to reformulate the Shari'ah according to its own needs and circumstances.

By far the most radical and practical changes to Islamic law have been undertaken in Morocco. Over a decade of agitation by women's rights groups as well as reform-minded organisations has produced a radically new Islamic family law. Introduced in February 2004, it sweeps away centuries of bigotry and blatant bias against women. Morocco retained much of the legal system France left behind, but followed traditional Islamic family law, known (in Morocco) as *Moudouana*, which regulated marriage, divorce, inheritance, polygamy and child custody. *Moudouana* encouraged a long list of abuses against women, including domestic violence, sexual harassment, polygamy, biased divorce rights, inequality at work and in education, and denial of inheritance. The new law reformulates the conventional notions of the Shari'ah.

Thus, the traditional idea of husband as head of the family is no more. Moroccan families are now the joint responsibility of both spouses. The debasing language previously used in reference to women has been replaced with gender-sensitive terminology. So, women become men's partners in rights and obligation rather than in need of guidance and protection from men. The minimum age for marriage for women has been raised from 15 to 18 – the same age for men. Women and men now have the right to contract their own marriage without the legal approval of a third party, usually a parent or guardian. Women have the right to initiate a divorce; and the previous right of men to a unilateral divorce has been taken away. Men now require prior authorisation from a court before they can obtain a divorce. Verbal divorce (where a man can divorce his wife by repeating the words 'I divorce you') has been outlawed.

Moreover, husbands are required to pay all monies owed to the wife and children in full, before divorce can be duly registered. Polygamy has been all but abolished. Men can take second wives only with the full consent of the first wife and only if they can prove, in a court of law, that they can treat them both with absolute justice – a condition that is all but impossible to meet. Women can now claim alimony and can be granted custody of their children even if they remarry. Indeed, a woman can even regain custody of her children if the courts initially ruled in favour of the husband but the husband failed to fulfil his responsibilities.

For the first time, the new family laws also enhance the rights of children of divorced parents. For example, children can claim suitable accommodation consistent with living conditions prior to the parents' divorce. The new law also protects the child's right to acknowledgement of paternity in case the marriage has not been officially registered or the child was born outside wedlock. Moreover, the new law requires that husbands and wives share the property acquired during marriage. Husbands and wives can have separate estates but the law makes it possible for the couple to agree, in a document other than the marriage contract, on how to manage and develop assets acquired during marriage. The traditional tribal custom of favouring male heirs in the sharing of inherited land has also been dropped making it possible for the grandchildren on the daughter's side to inherit from their grandfather, just like the grandchildren on the son's side.

The new family law also assigns a key role to the judiciary. Public prosecutors must now be involved in every legal action involving family affairs. New family courts have been set up and a family mutual assistance fund has been established to ensure that the new code is effectively enforced. The new law also enshrines the principle that minorities should be allowed to follow their own laws. So Morocco's Jews will now be governed by the provisions of the Hebraic Moroccan Family Law.

Its radical nature notwithstanding, every change in the law is justified – chapter and verse – from the Qur'an; and the examples and traditions of the Prophet Muhammad. What the new Moroccan

Islamic Family Law demonstrates most vividly is that Shari'ah is not *a priori* given; it can be changed, interoperated and reformulated according to contemporary needs.

Similar radical transformations are taking place in the relationship between Islam and the state. Here, Indonesia is providing a lead. The new Islamic intellectualism in Indonesia, which has evolved over the last two decades, is based on a three-point agenda: to (1) re-examine the theological and philosophical underpinnings of political Islam; (2) redefine the political objectives of Islam; and (3) reassess the ways in which these political objectives can be effectively realised.[18] Through an intense debate and lengthy discussions, Islamic organisations such as the Muhammadiyah and Nahdattul Ulama, which have a combined following of over 80 million people, have used this agenda to reassert several important propositions and packaged these propositions into a new Islamic perspective on the relationship between Islam and the state.

Thus, Indonesian intellectuals like Amien Rais and Nurcholish Madjid, reject the notion that the Qur'an and *sunnah* provide a clear-cut directive for Muslims to establish an 'Islamic state'. Moreover, they recognise that Islam does not contain a set of political principles and cannot be viewed as an ideology. Therefore, there is no such thing as an 'Islamic ideology'. Furthermore, they believe that absolute truth is possessed by Allah alone. As such, our comprehension of Islam's religious doctrine is essentially relative and subject to change and multiple interpretations. When we combine this realisation with the fact that Islam does not recognise priesthood, we cannot but reach the conclusion that no individual has the authority to claim that his interpretation is truer or more authoritative than those of others – so the *ulema* have no real authority over the masses.

Using these fundamental principles, the new Islamic intellectual movement in Indonesia has campaigned for substantial, rather than symbolic, change in the political system, focusing their attention, for example, on corruption and more accountable and transparent forms of governance. They have also fought to separate the Shari'ah from the political realms, arguing that Islamic law cannot be imposed from the above and has to evolve from below.

All these developments – various agenda-setting attempts to reform Islam, efforts to reformulate the Shari'ah, and articulations of a new relationship between Islam and the state – are trends that one way or another will have an impact on the future of Islam. When thinking about Islamic futures, we need to be aware of trends already set in motion that could act as a catalyst for ushering more desirable futures for the Muslim *ummah*.

ISLAMIC FUTURES IN THE COMING DECADES

In today's globalised world, what may appear to be a small, insignificant trend can actually contain seeds of radical shifts. So while changes in law in Morocco or politics in Indonesia, or ideas buried in obscure scholarly journals or learned books, may appear to be rather inconsequential, they can, under certain circumstances, lead to transformative change. To understand how this can happen, we need to appreciate the true nature of globalisation.

Whatever the pros and cons of globalisation itself, we need to grasp the fact that it has connected the world in numerous ways. Everything is now connected, as I noted earlier, to everything else; and everyone is connected to some sort of network. Hence the potential for feedback, for things to multiply, for ideas to spread rapidly, is enormous. And these are ideal conditions for chaos: the theory that tells us that apparently insignificant changes can trigger major perturbations, that order can emerge from apparent disorder, and social and political systems can spontaneously self-organise. This insight has a particular significance for Muslims.

At present, the Muslim world looks fragmented, disordered, driven by internal strife, being torn apart by sectarian and political violence. The absence of an overall charismatic, dominant, leader – or, as some would call him, a Caliph – means that no one has overall authority; and Muslim societies, like the clouds, look the same from all perspectives – disordered, confused, panic ridden. Yet, at the same time the Muslim world is totally connected – thanks to phones, the Internet, satellite television, 24-hour news channels – and behaves like a network. Moreover, the *ummah* is a complex system – a network of numerous cultures, truly astonishing diversity and plurality, spread across the globe, incorporating around 1.3 billion people. And, all kinds of feedback loops are being established in this complex network. In other words, the Muslim world is at the 'edge of chaos': the entire system is in a kind of suspended animation between stability and total dissolution into anarchy.[19]

So the Muslim world is at a point where any factor, however small, can push it towards one or other direction. Further acts of terrorism, undertaken in the name of Islam, can lead to total collapse. But positive trends and ideas can equally transform it: like any complex system, the *ummah* has the ability to spontaneously self-organise and 'evolves' impulsively into a new mode of existence. Think of a flock of birds taking off in a haphazard manner: they adjust and adapt to their neighbours and unconsciously organise themselves into a patterned flock. So order emerges from disorder. Similarly, changes in Islamic law or political organisation in one or two Muslim countries can lead to major transformations throughout the *ummah*.

However, for such transformations to occur, it is necessary for us to understand the chaotic nature of the globalised world. So we have to seek actively to be connected to all sorts of networks, Muslim and non-Muslim alike, to learn to think of ourselves as connected to numerous networks, and behave as a truly globalised community with a global system. We have to appreciate that apparent insignificant individual actions can make all the difference in the world. To actively transform chaotic life to our advantage, we have to understand that our problems are interconnected and have to learn to recognise joined-up problems. Thinking chaotically means seeing the connections and searching for joined-up answers. That's the moral of chaos. It requires new thinking, but old Islamic morals and virtues remain intact.

The coming decades will witness minor as well as profound changes both within the Muslim world and at global levels – and any, or a combination, of them can lead to transformative chaotic shifts. Muslim societies would do well to anticipate these changes and to prepare for them.

The first change we can anticipate will be ushered when Turkey joins the European Union (EU). Turkey is part of Europe even though conventionally both Europeans and Muslims have seen it as part of the Muslim world. While we can expect considerable resistance and opposition from many in Europe to Turkey's membership of the EU – particularly in France and Germany – eventually Turkey would be accepted as a full member. It may not happen for at least a decade or two, but it will happen. Europeans know that Turkey cannot be kept out of the Union indefinitely; and, in the end, it is to the advantage of the EU that Turkey is included.

Turkey's inclusion will change both the Muslim perception of Europe; and European perceptions of Islam. Muslims will begin to see that European values are not alien to Islam; indeed, many cherished

European values – its liberal humanism, its concern for accountable governance, its emphasis on research and development – have their origins in Islam, especially Islamic philosophy and literature that Europe acquired through Ottoman Turkey. Europe will notice that Islam is not inimical to European concerns; and a Muslim republic can be just as European as any other European nation. The newly enlarged European Union, with a quarter of its population now Muslim, aligns itself increasingly with its thriving Muslim neighbours, rather than with America. New checks and balances may emerge in a world solely dominated by America.

But we should not take American domination of the globe for granted. American pre-eminence and its staying power are both greatly exaggerated. The power of America rests largely in its advanced technology, which is increasingly available to the rest of the world. Economically, America is a crippled power kept afloat largely by Japanese and German credit. Soon, it will face incurable balance-of-payments problems, made worse by permanent loss of manufacturing and difficulties in maintaining oil imports. Meanwhile, both China and India are emerging as major, global economic powers – the economies of both China and India are likely to overtake the US economy in size in the next few decades.[20] It is likely, as Paul Kennedy predicts, that the US will go the way of the British Empire in the next few decades and we will return to a multi-polar world.[21] The emergence of China will undoubtedly usher serious changes in international relations; and if India joins the Security Council of the United Nations a new era of international relations will emerge. Thus, within the next two decades, no major power, or centres of power, will be able to establish its hegemony over the whole world, not even over large parts of it. We will, instead, see a world of competing civilisations.

At the same time, authoritarian structures within Muslim societies will begin to crumble. States such as Saudi Arabia and theocracies like Iran cannot survive the future. The breakdown of such states will undoubtedly cause a great deal of havoc; and the pendulum may swing from one extreme to another in the initial stages. But in the long run, models of accountable and participatory governance will emerge. Nothing succeeds like success; and successful democracies such as Turkey and Indonesia may become the prototype for the rest of the Muslim world to follow.

Thus, both locally and globally the world is set to change. How Muslims meet the coming challenges depends largely on what steps they take – as individuals, communities and states – now; what note they take of the early warning signals and how they inform their present decision making with the anticipation of things to come. The future is always shaped in the present!

MOVING ON

The ideas embedded in Islamic futures, and its basic principles, serve to empower the Muslim people and to encourage them – as states, communities and individuals – to engage with their problems on a broad front. This engagement must begin with an unreserved confidence in their own ability to determine a pragmatic, sustainable path towards desirable change and empowerment. Without empowerment Muslims can only react to initiatives derived from elsewhere – as they have been doing for the past few centuries. A reacting civilisation is a civilisation whose future has been colonised and systematically confined to the contours of dependency and utter helplessness. An empowered civilisation, on the other hand, is in control of its own destiny.

The essential *problématique* set out here is not that Muslims should engage in concerted futures studies. From the analysis of contemporary problems that beset Muslims everywhere it is clear that commitment to effective futures planning is the only path to empowerment, the only true self-determined trajectory open to them. The real problem we face is how, given the current imbalance of resources within and between nations and the lack of genuinely effective organisation and cooperation at the level of the *ummah*, the appropriate infrastructure and resources to undertake futures thought and planning can be amassed and set to work. Here, the first and most enduring challenge is creating the political and civilisational will to take responsibility for changing things. Such commitment cannot be rhetorical, it must be based on the allocation of real resources and the patient building of resilient mechanisms that have the support and confidence of national authorities as well as ordinary citizens, for undertaking study and dissemination of futures ideas and action.

The utility of futures studies, of envisioning and shaping futures, as I have argued, is how it informs present actions and creates the sense of empowerment to choose between various responses to contemporary problems. But no responsible choice can be made without a strong sense of civilisational identity. A prerequisite of taking responsibility for the continuity of Muslim identity is reforging our own understanding of what it means to be a Muslim. Simple piety and diligent observance of rituals is not enough. We need to activate the concepts and values that define the Muslim personality and use them to shape viable and desirable futures by engaging not just with our own problems but the problems of the whole world. There are no isolated problems and no isolated answers that can be confined to a special reserve set aside for Muslims. The Muslim ethical sense is the prime ingredient in constructing the link between individual piety and civilisational action, the main elements in creating alternative futures where Muslims can be at home with their identity and sanity intact, and the main feature for operating as contributory members of the global community that strives for human betterment.

The basic concepts and principles of the Qur'an are the building blocks of Islamic futures. However, the Islamic worldview cannot be a creative tool through approximation, we can no longer afford to allow imported patterns of modernity, or relativism of postmodernism, to set the agenda of understanding or interpretation of our worldview. Islamic concepts and principles are enduring yet dynamic, their meaning has to be unfolded through intellectual effort and practical endeavour. Our concepts have to be articulated and disseminated through education and our media; there must be widespread discussion and debate that enables contemporary implications to be defined and refined so that the precepts of our most personal and deeply rooted identity become handholds on solutions to the problems we face. Just as we need to devise a language for Islamic futures so we have to incorporate this into a new language of discourse on Islam and an Islamic worldview in the contemporary world. This search for an Islamic discourse cannot be seen as a battle for authority or authoritative interpretations, unless Muslims everywhere participate and unless they seek to regain the open mindedness, tolerance and participatory spirit of the early Muslim community, they will foreclose on their future prospects and resign themselves to being the unwilling instruments of change they neither desire nor choose in perpetuity.

The future will always remain an undiscovered country where none of us can exist. Yet creating confidence in the future potential of Muslim states, communities and peoples – integrated into a dynamic, thriving civilisation – is the only viable means to exert a refined Islamic influence on present circumstances. To be responsible Muslims today means balancing the reverence for the enduring importance of the Prophetic model, the guiding example set in the defining moments of Islamic history, with commitment to envisioning futures where the central concepts and principles of the model find new ways to shape possibilities, choices and actions. The essential link between our past and our future is to take a responsibility for informed changes in the present.

Part II

Science and Knowledge

6
Guardians of the Planet: Muslims and the Environment

Humanity's future is intrinsically linked to its attitude towards the environment. It is to attitudes, which are ultimately shaped by our worldviews, that we must look to discover the underlying causes of our current environmental predicament.

Western scholars of the contemporary human situation have traced the roots of our environmental crisis to the Judaeo-Christian attitude towards nature. It is this attitude, and the accompanying traditional and intellectual heritage, which is responsible for the seven impersonal threats that the human future now faces: a runaway, production-orientated technology; depletion of the earth's natural resources; pressure on land and environment; ever-increasing output of wastes; stockpiles of enough nuclear, chemical and biological weapons to destroy the earth several times; the massive growth in human population and its accumulation in vast urban conurbations; and the alienation of man from his environment and from nature. Each one of these trends represents a major threat to our collective well-being and survival. Scholars like Fraser Darling, Theodore Roszak, Jerome Ravetz, Geoffrey Vickers and Lynn White Jr argue that these threats are a product of the western ethical system. The roots of our ecological crisis are axiomatic: they lie in our beliefs and value structures, which shape our relationship with nature, with each other and the lifestyles we lead.

The chief spokesman of this analysis is Lynn White Jr who argues that this sort of mechanism for self-destruction is inherent in monotheistic religions. He sees the Judaeo-Christian tradition as the source of all ecological evil. This worldview is centred on a divine being who is 'above all and beyond all' and who created man to have dominion over all the animals and the rest of creation. Some contemporary Christian scholars have argued that 'dominion' can mean responsible stewardship. But White asserts that no matter

First published as 'Towards an Islamic Theory of Environment', in Islamic Futures: The Shape of Ideas to Come, Mansell, London, 1985, chapter 10.

how one interprets the concepts of 'dominion', it is difficult to argue that it does not imply the right to exercise power and control over nature. He writes:

Christianity is the most anthropocentric religion the world has seen. As early as the Second century both Tertrillian and Sain Irenaeous of Lyons were insisting that when God shaped Adam he was foreshadowing the image of the incarnate Christ, the Second Adam. Man shares, in great measure, God's transcendence of nature. Christianity, in absolute contrast to ancient paganism and Asia's great religions (except, perhaps, Zoroastrianism), not only established a dualism of man and nature but also insisted that it is God's will that man exploit nature for his proper ends.[1]

For White, the present increasing disruption of the global environment is the product of a dynamic science and technology, which has its origins in the ethical base of Christianity. He considers modern science to be an extrapolation of Christian theology; and technology to be 'an Occidental, voluntarist realization of the Christian dogma of man's transcendence of, and rightful mastery over, nature'. White also believes that as 'science and our technology are so tinctured with orthodox Christian arrogance toward nature that no solution for our economical crisis can be expected from them alone'. Moreover, White asserts, as 'Islam, like Marxism, is a Judaeo-Christian heresy, it is equally responsible for the 'monotheistic debasement of nature'.

White made these pronouncements in 1967. Since then these assertions have been repeated by scholar after scholar so that now they have become part of the western paradigm of the contemporary ecological crisis. This situation has arisen largely because Muslim scholars have never concerned themselves with ecological issues or formulated a coherent Islamic theory of environment. Recently, however, a number of studies have been published which when examined collectively lead us towards a systematic exposition of Islam's position towards contemporary ecological concerns.

What concerns a growing number of western scholars is the clear dichotomy between our behaviour and lifestyles, including the behaviour and lifestyles of most Muslim societies, and what ecology teaches us. The earth's ecosystems are governed by a number of principles, which we have come to appreciate only recently. If our lifestyle is in harmony with these principles, the argument goes, then we can develop an inherent resilience, which will ensure our survival, allow our ecosystems to heal, replenish and begin the long road to restoration. Collectively, these principles provide an ethical framework for our attitudes towards nature and environment – an imperative for a sane future of mankind.

What are the ethical principles of ecology? There are seven such principles, which have been derived from the study of living systems. The first and primary principle is that of holistic environment, with everything affecting everything else – directly or indirectly. Nothing operates in isolation: everything connects with everything else to perform the cosmic symphony of life. 'This principle of holocentric environment', writes Beatrice Willard, 'leads us to certain criteria for guiding human activities. It leads us to the practice of looking before we leap, and inculcates the need for each individual and group to engage consciously or otherwise in "ecological reconnaissance".'2 This involves analysing ahead of time the ramifications of potential activities upon our immediate habitat or our ecosystem, upon present and successive generations of the human race, and upon living resources of all kinds.

The 'living resources' of the earth provide us with the second principle of ecology. The earth exhibits an incredible range of biological diversity as manifested in an almost limitless range of morphological and physiological variations in the plant and animal kingdom. This biological diversity is the most precious for it ensures the perpetuity of life on earth. Within this vast array of ecosystems, each organism has a role to play – a 'niche' to occupy – no matter how insignificant it may seem to us. Our management and use of living resources should be based on a thorough understanding and appreciation of this.

Recycling and redistribution of resources constitutes the third great principle of ecological behaviour. All ecosystems continuously recycle waste, materials are used, discarded and picked up by other ecosystems for their use – on and on, in infinite cycles. Making recycling an essential part of human behaviour will have profound consequences. We will have to learn to use materials in a new way, which does not deprive the future generations of their use while also allowing the present generations a reasonable possibility of disposition. We need to foster the flow of materials rather than their sinking and destruction. Willard gives an interesting example of how this principle would change our mining activities:

We are mining nitrate and phosphate deposits that took many millennia to form. We are distributing them to agricultural lands, increasing run-offs of nitrogen and phosphates into rivers, reaping crops and distributing them to people who use them for human food, etc., the waste of which in many Western countries goes into lakes, rivers and eventually the oceans. Thus it may be removed from ecosystem benefits for millennia, as much of it will not be recycled until new phosphate and nitrate deposits are formed on the ocean floors and ultimately elevated in continent rebuilding millions of years from now. We can assist the operation of ecosystems by facilitating recycling and avoiding those semi-dead-end pathways that keep materials cooped up for longer periods.

But recycling is not limited to grand activities like mining; it has to be introduced in almost every aspect of our lives from daily living to our way of thinking about the future. The next two principles of ecological ethics have not been properly understood in terms of human behaviour. The fourth principle is that of limiting factors: certain environmental factors limit the functioning of living organisms within all ecosystems. These factors define the operating parameters of ecosystems and the living organisms within them. Often, it is not one but a host of physical and chemical factors in the environment which are interacting with a group of species to describe the limiting factors of the system. Associated with this principle is the capacity of the vast majority of the living systems to reproduce in excess of the support capability of the ecosystem in which they live.

A possible reason for this, the fifth principle of ecological behaviour, is the fact that overpopulation ensures that some individuals survive to reproduce the species. But the two principles act together to keep the population of a particular species in equilibrium. We do not really understand and appreciate the interconnection of these two principles and frequently we are unaware of the fact that we may have significantly altered the equilibrium by a seemingly innocent action.

For example, in the United States grazing sheep have been protected by poisoning or shooting coyotes. The effect of this action on the decline of grain crops is not obvious at first sight. But the drop in coyote population produced a sharp rise in rodent and bird population that in turn had its effect on grain crops. Thus isolated actions that ignore the principles of limiting factors and the prolific nature of biological reproduction can have serious consequences. How we shape human behaviour in the light of these two principles is a question that needs to be examined with some urgency. But it is obvious that the impact of these principles on our norms and behaviour can be profound.

All ecosystems have a definite capability of sustaining a given amount of life. This capability is often referred to as 'carrying capacity'. This carrying capacity, the sixth principle of ecology, has its counterparts in engineering systems and organisational behaviour. However, it has a more sophisticated aspect in ecology. Because of the greater diversity of living systems, their strong capability of reproduction, complexity and resilience, the carrying capacity of ecosystems is not easy to determine. Often the fact that carrying capacity of an ecosystem has been exceeded only comes to the fore when the actual point has been far exceeded in time, numbers and equilibrium. But a kind of 'domino' effect may have already been set in motion resulting in a chain reaction, which produces dire consequences for the ecosystem.

That carrying capacity has ethical lessons for human thought and action has been ignored by us for a long time. Yet, we have been well aware of this principle for decades; its importance for us extends to our urban, rural and agricultural activities alike. It even extends to the earth as a whole: it is now being forcefully argued, by James Lovelock and others, that the earth behaves as a single organism, even a living creature; and as a living system the earth has a definite carrying capacity. The biosphere is put together by the totality of living systems to carry out certain necessary control and survival functions. The living matter, the air, the oceans, the land surface, are parts of a gain system which is able to control temperature, the composition of the air and sea, the pH of the soil etc. so as to be optimum for survival of the biosphere. All this means that the earth – or *Gaia* as it is called in this hypothesis – is a finite system with a limited carrying capacity, which cannot be exceeded without introducing serious imbalances. The sub-systems of Gaia, including man as its central nervous system, have to perform a supportive role within this carrying capacity. Urban areas, grazing lands, forests, parks, open spaces, roads, all have upper limits to their capacity for providing services and desired resources and maintaining the delicate balances of Gaia and supporting life. Our thought and action, planning and building, use of resources and materials have to be dictated by this insight.[3]

The seventh and final principle of ecological ethics concerns the development and stability of ecosystems. Ecosystems have developed over a long span of time, starting from simple systems and progressing to more complex, highly interconnected systems, which are in equilibrium and stable. In this progression, natural processes have come into being which ensure the permanency of the system and protect it from disruption, which may be caused by such events as fire, landslide and insect infestations. These processes are slow but nevertheless ensure that the system meets various perturbations and survives. However, if processes that are opposed to these natural processes are introduced in the system, they can have a toxic effect on the ecosystem. Criteria for human behaviour evolving from ecosystem development and stability are not obvious at first sight. But the ethic begins to surface when we realise the value of time in the development of an ecosystem. Soil, water and natural resources like oil have taken millions of years to develop; a rain forest takes tens of thousands of years to reach maturity. The emerging ethic guides us not to destroy natural systems by deforestation, mining, pollution and other human activities, and to spend considerable time and profits to restore viable ecosystems.

All the principles outlined above define and dictate the choice of our activities; and limit our options for full benefit of all human beings and living systems into the distant future. Proponents of ecological ethics argue that human behaviour based on these principles would distinguish between human needs which have to be met for the entire population of the globe and human desires most of which need to be checked. It also distinguishes between what man *can* do to the environment; and what he *should* do. In directing man's action in meeting basic needs and ensuring the survival of all living systems, the argument goes, the ecological ethic forces us to rid ourselves of nineteenth-century technocratic thinking and to reject the idea that human existence is necessarily a battle against nature. Spelled out in detail, the ethics of ecological behaviour form a new philosophy: eco-philosophy. The idea of eco-philosphy offers a new paradigm for our comprehension of reality, for our way of thinking and our norms and behaviour. If the vast array of human societies that inhabit the earth could achieve a consensus on this ethic, the survival of our environment and its ability to sustain life will be ensured.

Well, where should Muslims stand on these principles?

Within the traditional and intellectual heritage of Islam, reverence and respect for ecological principles is total. But the ethical system of Islam is not based solely on environmental criteria. Islam is concerned with the complete human being and, as such, it expresses the state of being characteristic of humans by offering an impressive repertoire of values: instrumental, ethical, aesthetic, eschatological – all of which reflect and recapitulate the variety of aspects of man's existence.

Some of these values are codified in the Shari'ah (Islamic law) while others are inherent in a rich reservoir of concepts to be found in the Qur'an. When understood in an environmental sense, the Shari'ah and Qur'anic concepts provide a very effective ethical and pragmatic answer to our environmental crisis.

The fact that these values, in their environmental aspects, are nowhere to be seen in the Muslim world, where the environmental situation is just as acute as in the west, can be attributed to a very simple fact. Nowhere in Muslim societies is the Shari'ah adhered to in its totality or the Islamic way of life forms the basis of human action. Moreover, Islamic concepts and ethical precepts have been divorced from a pragmatic, living, dynamic form for the last 300 or 400 years, since the decline of the Muslim civilisation and its eventual colonisation by the Occident. It is because the dominant patterns of behaviour, development and thought in the Muslim world are western that we see this environmental degradation and exploitative way of life. Muslim societies themselves need to appreciate the ecological principles of Islam and find practical routes for adopting and establishing them.

So, what is the environment ethic of Islam?

Any discussion of ethics in Islam must, of necessity, start with an exposition of the concept of *tawheed* that exemplifies the unity of God: the recognition that there is one, absolute, transcendent Creator of the universe and all that it contains. Man is ultimately responsible for all his actions to Him. As an ethical rule, *tawheed* dictates the acceptance of God as the only source of all values: not to do this would lead to *shirk*, the negation of *tawheed*, which is a cardinal sin in Islam. As such, *tawheed* is the matrix for human thought and action; it is all-pervasive and penetrates every aspect of our endeavour. In the words of Ali Shariati:

In the world-view of *tawheed*, man fears only one power, and is answerable before only one judge. He turns to only one *qibla*, and directs his hopes and fears to only one source. And the corollary is that all else is false and pointless – all the diverse and variegated tendencies, strivings, fears, desires and hopes of man are vain and fruitless. *Tawheed* bestows upon man independence and dignity. Submission to Him alone – the supreme norm of all being – impels man to revolt against all lying powers, all the humiliating fetters of fear and greed.[4]

Thus conceived, *tawheed* becomes all-pervasive, penetrating all aspects of human thought and behaviour. It is the guiding principle of religion and ethics, politics and social behaviour, epistemology and science, and at the centre of Muslim curiosity regarding nature.

From *tawheed* emerge the concepts of *khilafa* and *amana*. The entire rationale of an Islamic environmental ethics is based on the Qur'anic concept of *khilafa:* man's viceregency or trusteeship. Gaia is an *amana* trust from God and man is the trustee who has the responsibility of looking after the vast panorama of God's creation. Man can use the trust for his benefit but has no absolute right to anything: the trust must be preserved and handed back to its rightful owner. Man is accountable for the misuse of his trust and is liable to pay a price both in this world and the *akhira* (hereafter). This denial of absolute sovereignty to man, writes Parvez Manzoor,

Is tantamount to investing him with moral responsibility. As any kind of responsibility can, in the last analysis, only be personal, it is a natural corollary of man's acceptance of trust that he be born free and innocent. Man is thus in the Islamic tradition a creature unsullied by any ontological flaws. He bears no stigma of any 'original sin' that would make him a victim of his own humanity. From the Muslim standpoint, a 'fallen' humanity is commensurable neither with divine justice nor with human dignity.[5]

Within this framework, nature becomes man's testing ground. Man is enjoined to read its 'signs', which reflect both man's position in creation and the glory of God. As such, nature is created orderly and knowable. Were it unruly, capricious and erratic, morality would be impossible. It would be both oppressive and degrading for man who would humble himself before its slightest whim. Quite apart from praising God, an unruly and disorderly nature would hide the manifestations of God. Man would thus be left in darkness. As such, the orderliness of nature and its amenability to rational enquiry are an essential prerequisite for morality.

The concept that regulates the reading of 'signs' of nature is *ilm* (knowledge). In Islam, the pursuit of knowledge cannot be separated from the concerns of morality. *Ilm* operates through the agency of *tawheed*: knowledge is pursued for the glorification of Allah and to fulfil man's responsibility towards His trust. It follows then that the pursuit of that knowledge which gives man false notions of absolute sovereignty, or which harm God's trust, the terrestrial environment, is not permitted in Islam. The concepts of *tawheed*, *khilafa* and *ilm* are interconnected and shape the concerns and direction of rational enquiry. Islamic epistemology is therefore 'unreservedly and uncompromisingly holistic' and within this context 'fragmented knowledge or reductionist epistemology would be a contradiction in terms'.

The Islamic notion of environment is controlled by two concepts: *halal* (that which is beneficial) and *haram* (that which is harmful). When closely examined, *haram* includes all that which is destructive for man as an individual, his immediate environment and the environment at large. The word destructive should be understood in the physical, mental and spiritual sense. All that is beneficial for an individual, his society and his environment is *halal*. Thus an action that is *halal* brings all-round benefits. The environment, therefore, plays a dominant part in the Islamic scheme of things: an action that may bring benefits to an individual may produce harmful effects on society or the environment. The environment, in all its kaleidoscopic richness, must be preserved.

Combine the concepts of *tawheed*, *khilafa*, *amana*, *halal* and *haram* with the words for justice (*adl*) and moderation, temperance, balance, equilibrium, harmony (*itidal*) and the concepts of *istihsan* (preference for the better) and *istislah* (public welfare) and one has the most sophisticated framework for an environmental ethic that one can possibly desire. 'Muslim societal ethic, nay the very basis of society itself, is but a quest for equilibrium, and hence felicity with God, nature and history. It entails submitting oneself to the will of God, accepting the mandate of trusteeship and striving to be a moderate community (*ummah wasah*)', writes Parvez Manzoor. The goals of justice, public interest, environmental equilibrium and harmony with nature, Muslim consciousness affirms, is reached by treading the path of moderation.

The matrix of this conceptual framework – *tawheed*, *khilafa*, *amana*, *halal*, *haram*, *adl*, *itidal*, *istihsan* and *istislah* – constitutes a paradigm for an Islamic theory of environment. If this framework was fully operationalised in the Muslim *ummah* (community) it would revolutionise the behaviour and thinking of Muslim people. For incorporated in these concepts is a deep respect for nature, an appreciation of interconnectedness of all life, recognition of the unity of creation and the brotherhood of all beings, and that concerns of morality and other living systems must form the basis of any rational enquiry. It was a consideration of these concepts from an ecological perspective that led Parvez Manzoor to dismiss as 'irreverent nonsense' Lynn White Jr's assertion that 'Islam, like Marxism, is a Judeo-Christian heresy' and, as such, is equally responsible for the 'monotheistic debasement of nature'. Indeed, to assume that Islam, like Christianity, marshals an ethic of environmental domination is either simple ignorance or the height of arrogance.

But the conceptual framework is only the tip of the iceberg. The ecological concerns of Islam are given a practical shape in the Shari'ah, or Islamic law, which incorporates a whole body of environmental legislation. There is no division of ethics and law in Islam: once again, the framework of key Qur'anic concepts synthesises the two aspects of human life which in the Western intellectual and religious tradition are isolated in separated water-tight compartments. The ultimate consequence of man's acceptance of trusteeship is the arbitration of his conduct by divine judgement. To be a Muslim is to accept and practise the injunctions of the Shari'ah. Thus, Shari'ah is both a consequence of one's acceptance of *tawheed* and a *path*. 'It is simultaneously a manifestation of divine will and that of human resolve to be an agent of that will.' But Shari'ah is also a methodology for solving problems. To quote Parvez Manzoor again:

By its application temporal contingencies are judged by eternal imperatives, moral choices are transformed into options for concrete action and ethical sentiment is objectified into law. It is in fact that *problem-solving* methodology par excellence of Islam. Any theoretical Muslim thinking, as for instance our search for an environmental ethic, must pass through the objective framework of Shari'ah in order to become operative and be part of Muslim history. Shari'ah thus provides both the ethical norms and the legal structure within which Muslim states may make actual decisions pertaining to concrete ecological issues. And not only is Shari'ah indispensable for decision making in an Islamic context, its moral realism also provides excellent paradigms for theoretical discussion of Islamic ecological philosophy.

Shari'ah, then, is a value-centred system; it exists to realise the values inherent in such key Islamic concepts as *tawheed*, *khilafah*, *istislah*, *halal* and *haram*. The ultimate objective of this system is the universal common good of all created beings, encompassing both our immediate welfare and out future in the Hereafter. The importance of the ultimate future dimension of the Shari'ah cannot be overstated for many immediate benefits could be ultimately unethical. The objective of universal common good is a distinctive characteristic of the Shari'ah and an important implication of the concept of *tawheed*: one can only serve the one Creator of all life by working for the universal common good of all beings.

Consider, for example, the injunctions of the Shari'ah concerning land. If land is a gift from God, how is a Muslim entitled to use this gift? While Islam allows the ownership of land, it is limited to that which can be cultivated by human skills and labour. There are four ramifications of this *amana* from God:

1. That ownership signifies only the right to *use* and this ownership can be transferred.
2. That the owner is entitled to 'private ownership' *only* as long as he uses it.
3. That the owner who ceases to use his gift is induced, and in some cases even forced, to part with idle possessions.
4. That in no case is the owner allowed to charge rent for a free gift of God from another person who, in fact, has the equal right to its use.

These limitations on the use of land are enforced by a number of principles developed by Muslim jurists over the centuries. One of the most basic principles of the Shari'ah is the declaration of the Prophet Muhammad that 'there shall be no injury, and no perpetuation of injury'. Using this principle, Othman Llewellyn points out:

[The Muslim jurists] Malik and Abu Hanifah formulated the principles that the exercise of a right is permitted only for the achievement of the purpose for which the right was created, that the exercise of a right is illegal where it results in excessive harm, and that the exercise of a right is illegal if used to bring injury to others rather than for benefit. Malik restrained land owners from any use of their property resulting in injury. [Another Muslim scholar] Abu Yusuf restricted both the individuals' and the authorities' cases concerning neighbourly relationship, placement of windows, divisions of tenancy in common property, and ownership of uncultivated land, he imposed restrictions if necessary to prevent excessive injury. Abu Yusuf restricted both the individuals' and the authorities' rights in cultivating virgin land where its exercise would result in excessive injury. Jurists [of the Hanbali school] reasoned likewise that since Allah is the real owner of all property, human rights of beneficial title must not be abused.[6]

These principles prohibiting undue injury and abuse of rights form the basis of a large part of Islamic resource law. Invaluable resources such as pasture, woodland, wildlife, certain minerals and especially water cannot be privately owned in their natural state or monopolised in Islamic law. They are managed publicly for the common good of all, and everyone has equal access to them.

Accordingly, writes Llewellyn:

A farm beside a stream is forbidden to monopolise its water. After withholding a reasonable amount of water for his crops, the farmer must release the rest to those downstream. Furthermore, if the water is insufficient for all of the farms along a stream, the needs of the older farms are to be satisfied before a newer farm is permitted to irrigate. This precept safeguards from future injury the previous farmers' investment of labour and wealth in the reclamation of their lands. Moreover, it allows a limited number of farms in one watershed to flourish, rather than encouraging a number beyond its carrying capacity, which would result in an injury to all alike, and a general failure of reclamation. According to jurists such as Malik and Ibn Qudamah, these same principles apply to the extraction of groundwater for a person has no right to adversely affect his neighbour's well by lowering the water table or polluting the aquifer.[7]

The Prophet Muhammad himself emphasised the importance of land reclamation in a number of his traditions. For example: 'Whosoever brings dead land to life, for him is a reward in it, and whatever any creature seeking food eats of it shall be reckoned as charity from him.' He adds: 'There is no Muslim who plants a tree or sows a field for a human, bird, or animal eats from it, but it shall be reckoned as charity from him.' And: 'If anyone plants a tree, no human nor any of the creatures of Allah will eat from it without its being reckoned as charity from him.'

The Prophet also prohibited his followers from harming animals and asked them to ensure that the rights of animals are fulfilled. It is a distinctive characteristic of the Shari'ah that all animals have legal rights which must be enforced by the state. Othman Llewellyn even argues that Islamic law has mechanisms for the full repair of injuries suffered by non-human creatures including their representation in court, assessment of injuries and awarding of relief to them. The classical Muslim jurist Izz ad-Din ibn Abd as-Salam, who lived in the thirteenth century, formulated the following statement in support of animal rights in Islam:

The rights of livestock and animals upon man: these are that he spend on them the provision that their kinds require, even if they have aged or sickened such that no benefit comes from them; that he not burden them beyond what they can bear; that he not put them together with anything by which they would be injured, whether of their own kind or other species, and whether by breaking their bones or butting or wounding; that he slaughters them with kindness when he slaughters them, and neither flay their skins nor break their bones until their bodies have become cold and their lives have passed away; that he not slaughter their young within their sight, but that he isolate them; that he makes comfortable their resting places and watering places; that he puts their males and females together during their mating seasons; that he not discard those which he takes as game; and neither shoots them with anything that breaks their bones nor brings about their destruction by any means that renders their meat unlawful to eat.[8]

Wildlife and natural resources too have rights in Islam. The Prophet Muhammad established inviolate zones bordering water-courses, utilities and towns. Within what are called *haram* (forbidden) zones, the Shari'ah restricts or prohibits development to ensure that invaluable resources are protected. Thus such zones are maintained around wells to protect the well or aquifer from impairment, to provide room for the well's operation and maintenance, to safeguard its water from pollution, and to provide a resting area for livestock and space for irrigation facilities; around canals and natural water-courses to prevent their pollution; and around towns and cities to ensure that their energy needs – forage and firewood – are fulfilled, their carrying capacity is not exceeded and to provide habitat for wildlife. Wildlife and forest come under the dictates of what is called *hima* in the Shari'ah. *Hima* is a reserve that safeguards their rights: it is established solely for the conservation of wildlife and forest. The Prophet Muhammad reserved the surroundings of Medina as a *hima* for the protection of vegetation and wildlife. And he declared that private reserves for the exclusive use of individuals are forbidden. Thus reserves in Islam are public property and are managed by the state. Following the Prophet Muhammad, a number of caliphs established public reserves. The second Caliph Umar Ibn al-Khattab, for example, established the *hima* of ash-Sharaf and the extensive *hima* of ar-Rabdath near Dariyah. The third Caliph Uthman Ibn Affan extended the second *hima*, which is reported to have carried forth 1,000 animals every year. A number of the *hima* established in western Arabia have been grazed responsibly since early Islam and are considered by the Food and Agriculture Organization of the United Nations (FAO) to be the most longstanding examples of wise grazing management known in the world. There are five types of *hima* to be found in the Arabian peninsula today.

These are reserves:

- where grazing is prohibited;
- for forest trees in which woodcutting is prohibited or restricted;

- in which grazing is restricted to certain seasons;
- that contain certain species and numbers of livestock;
- for beekeeping, in which grazing is prohibited during flowering;
- managed for the welfare of a particular village or tribe.

These injunctions concerning the use of land, the protection of water from pollution, the conservation of wildlife and forests are among the few ecological principles codified in the Shari'ah. They demonstrate the environmental awareness of the worldview of Islam, which provides not just an ethic based on ecological concerns but also a body of legislation to give practical shape to ethical issues. But more than that: the legislative structure of the Shari'ah can be extended to cover new problems. And the conceptual framework of key Qur'anic concepts can be used to develop new theories and models of the Muslim environment.

This is exactly what Gulzar Haider has done in his conceptual formulation of an Islamic city and the design principles for an Islamic environment. What is 'Islamic' about Islamic architecture and Islamic environment? This question is being hotly debated among Muslim intellectual circles – not least because in the name of Islam hideous structures have been erected and alienating environments have been created. However, in defining the Islamic nature of Islamic architecture and Islamic environment, much of the attention has been focused on form and structure. A mosque is a mosque because it has a minaret and a dome and wonderful mosaics and calligraphy inside. The geometrical form of Islamic architecture, for example, has been made an end in itself: the arches, which conform to the 'square and root two system' and the 'golden ratio' and the geometric methods based on the circle and so on. Airports, universities and even city enclaves have been built using these rules and there is nothing, as all those who use them confirm, 'Islamic' about them. The manic concern with the forms and structures of Islamic architecture is a great fallacy; it is propagated largely by western architects, planners and consultants, not to mention scholars whose thinking is dominated by linear logic and outward forms. The fact that some of them build mosques, 'Islamic universities' and judge awards for Islamic architecture only adds insult to injury.

What is Islamic about Islamic architecture and Islamic environment is the atmosphere they create: an atmosphere that encourages the remembrance of Allah, motivates behaviour according to the dictates of Shari'ah and promotes the values inherent in the matrix of key Qur'anic concepts. Such an atmosphere is a living, dynamic entity whose force is felt and experienced by those who come within its purview. This atmosphere is created not just by outward forms, though they are important. It is created by the *totality* of the system that produces the built environment: the principles of design, the methodology of architecture, the materials used in the construction, the form and architecture, the materials used in the construction, the form and structure of the buildings and their relationship with the natural environment, and the attitudes, motives and the worldview of the people involved in the system. As such, Islamic environment cannot become a contemporary reality, if one were to rely on principles, methodologies and building technologies, which have created the urban dystopias in the Occident and whose growing reflection one sees in Muslim cities. This system, as Alison Ravetz argues so forcefully in *Remaking Cities*,[9] is completely bankrupt. We need to reconceive and recreate the principles, methodologies and building technologies which will combine to produce an atmosphere which is instantly and instinctively recognised as Islamic.

Gulzar Haider's formulation of an Islamic city is based on the concepts of *tawheed, khilafa, khilqat* (nature), jihad (directed struggle), *adl, ibadahh* (worship), *ilm* and *jamal* (beauty). *Tawheed* and *khilafa* dictate that the Islamic city be a city of trusteeship and accountability: 'there is individual freedom contained by responsibility to the collective (*ummah*)' and 'there is trust with answerability to God'. All this is done within the parameters of the Shari'ah:

Islamic environment is to provide the support structure for Shari'ah and in turn be formed by it. There is to be a delicate equilibrium between the rights of the collective against those of the individual such that one is not antagonistic to the other. Such an environment will provide security and protection not so much by imposed controls as by social responsibility and mutual accountability.[10]

It is a city that nurtures the attitude that every act has consequences, which could be harmful or beneficial, and it produces an environment that both by its morphology and institutions establishes *adl* in all aspects of human endeavour without imposing grey uniformity. It is a city of ecological harmony that reflects the beauty (*jamal*) of nature and promotes the awareness of nature (*khilqat*) as portents and signs (*ayat*) of God for man to reflect upon and enhance his faith (*iman*), as a book of knowledge (*ilm*) to be understood and appreciated, and as a benevolent trust (*amana*) whose value is in its utilisation towards the enhancement of the art of life within the coordinates of Islamic norms and values. Islamic city creates an environment that 'values simplicity as economy of means towards generosity of ends', promotes problem-solving attitudes and values skills, hard work and ingenuity, and where 'creativity and craft are a manner of worship, a homage by the believer to the Creator of all the man's abilities'. Islamic environment is 'a sense of order that inspires aesthetic response, a beauty that is hidden, elusive, transcendental – a beauty beyond our sense bound and fashion dependent normative tastes'. And finally, Islamic city promotes an active, dynamic, goal-orientated environment which maintains a sustained struggle (jihad) for values inherent in the matrix of concepts that give it its unique character.

Identifying the basic characteristics of an Islamic city is the first step in constructing a viable theory of Islamic urban environment. These ethical coordinates not only delineate the principles of design and development but also describe the options available – in terms of materials, technologies, building techniques, forms, structure and limits to growth – for achieving the final goal. Gulzar Haider argues that the design principles, which amalgamate the ideals of an Islamic environment, are based on three formative values: environmental sensibility, morphological integrity and symbolic clarity.

Environmental sensibility implies that the design of Islamic environment must show respect for natural topography such as land form, water bodies and woodlands and climate to which it must respond in the same manner as 'sand dunes respond to wind'. It must not deprive the human psyche of the experience of nature and it must ensure a balance between the organic and the inert. And it must be sensitive to the nature of tools and materials: building technology is far from value-free and requires a strict value discipline within which it is selected, developed and deployed.

Morphological integrity requires a sensitivity towards size, scale and quality, maintenance of private and public intimacy and an appreciation of human scale both in social systems and physical environment. Moreover, it dictates spatial integrity, 'form follows space and space is adopted to function'; and it should show a labyrinthine continuity in both its purpose and form: while physically bounded, the Islamic environment must give an impression of infinite continuity. And, finally, morphological integrity dictates that Islamic architecture achieves its integratedness and ultimate sense of unity and purpose 'through the search for mutually sympathetic orders of function, meaning, symbol, geometry, gravity, energy, light, water, movement' and by characterising 'parts to whole and whole to parts relationship – simultaneously differentiated and integrated'.

Symbolic clarity requires respect for tradition and culture as well as for traditional metaphors, allegories and symbols without which Islamic architecture cannot 'encourage full expression of selfhood and identity without damaging the pervasive unity of *umma*'. It also requires the creation of a relevant language of elements as well as exploration of their compositional rules which achieve an environmental syntax with a socially relevant meaning. It therefore constitutes a challenge to create an urban environment that 'provokes experiences and phenomena that constitute an Islamic expression of life'.

Implementing such a sophisticated set of design principles would not be easy. It requires the development of a whole set of new methodologies and building technologies as well as rediscovering traditional techniques and crafts. More generally, the environmental dictates of the Shari'ah need to be given a living form and extended to cover contemporary and future problems. The work of Gulzar Haider, Othman Llewellyn and Parvez Manzoor has demonstrated that the most viable solution to our ecological crisis is to be found within the worldview of Islam. Drawing from a purely conceptual matrix of Islamic concepts, the rich legal inheritance of Shari'ah, and the history of Islamic architecture and urban planning, they have laid the basic foundations of a comprehensive Islamic theory of environment. It is an exciting challenge for other scholars to develop this theory further and demonstrate how it provides pragmatic solutions to today's and tomorrow's problems. The challenge of conceiving and creating methodologies and technologies and adopting appropriate Islamic legislation to meet the contemporary environmental crisis lies with Muslim societies. It is a challenge that has to be met, for the only other option is to permit our natural and built environment to lead to an ecological catastrophe.

7
Muslims and Philosophy of Science

Islam attempts to synthesise reason and revelation, knowledge and values, in its approach to the study of nature. Knowledge acquired through rational human efforts and through the Qur'an is seen as complementary: a sign of God that enables humanity to study and understand nature. Between the seventh and the fourteenth centuries, when Muslim civilisation was at its zenith, metaphysics, epistemology and empirical studies of nature fused to produce an explosion of what can be called the 'scientific spirit'. Scientists and scholars, like Ibn al-Haytham, ar-Razi, Ibn Tufayl, Ibn Sina and al-Biruni, superimposed Plato's and Aristotle's ideas of reason and objectivity, on their Muslim faith, thus producing a unique synthesis of religion and philosophy.[1] They also placed great emphasis on scientific methodology giving importance to systematic observation, experimentation and theory building.

Initially, scientific inquiry was directed by everyday practices of Islam. For example, developments in astronomy were influenced by the fact that the times of Muslim prayer were defined astronomically and its direction was defined geographically.[2] In the later stage, the quest for truth for its own sake became the norm leading to numerous new discoveries and innovations. Muslim scientists did not recognise disciplinary boundaries between the 'two cultures' of science and humanities, and individual scholars tended, as a general rule, to be polymaths. Recently, Muslim scholars have started to develop a contemporary Islamic philosophy of science by combining such basic Islamic concepts as *ilm* (distributive knowledge), *khilafa* (human trusteeship of the earth's natural resources) and *istislah* (public interest) in an integrated science policy framework.

The Muslim inspiration for the study of nature comes straight from the Qur'an. The Qur'an specifically and repeatedly asks Muslims to systematically investigate natural phenomena, not simply as a vehicle for understanding nature but also as a means for getting close to God. In Chapter 10, verses 5 and 6, for example, we read:

First published in the *Routledge Encyclopedia of Philosophy* Routledge, 1997.

He it is who has made the sun a (source of) radiant light and the moon a light (reflected), and has determined for its phases so that you might know how to compute years and to measure (time) ... in the alternating of night and day, and in all that God has created in the heavens and on earth, there are messages indeed for people who are conscious of Him.

The Qur'an also devotes about one-third of its verses to describing the virtues of reason.[3] Scientific inquiry, based on reason, is thus seen in Islam as a form of worship. Reason and revelation are complementary, and integrated, methods for the pursuit of truth.

The philosophy of science in classical Islam is a product of the fusion of this metaphysics with Greek philosophy. Nowhere is it more apparent than in Ibn Sina's (d. 1037) theory of human knowledge, which following al-Farabi (d. 950), transfers the Qur'anic scheme of revelation to Greek philosophy. In the Qur'an, the Creator addresses one man – the Prophet – through the agency of the archangel Jibreel (Gabriel); in Ibn Sina's neo-Platonic scheme, the divine word is transmitted through reason and understanding to any, and every, person who cares to listen. The result is an amalgam of rationalism and ethics. For Muslim scholars and scientists, who, like Ibn Sina, subscribed to the philosophy of Mutazalism, values are objective; and good and evil are descriptive characteristics of reality which are no less 'there' in things than their other qualities such as shape and size. In this framework, all knowledge, including the knowledge of God, can be acquired by reason alone. Humanity has the power to know as well as to act and is thus responsible for its just and unjust actions. What this philosophy entailed both in terms of the study of nature and shaping human behaviour was illustrated by Ibn Tufayl (d. 1185) in his intellectual novel, *Hayy Ibn Yaqzan*. Hayy is a spontaneously generated human who is isolated on an island. Through his power of observation and the use of his intellect, Hayy discovers general and particular facts about the structure of the material and spiritual universe, deduces the existence of God and arrives at a theological and political system.

While Mutazilah scholars had serious philosophical differences with their main opponents, the Asharite theologians, both schools agreed on the rational study of nature. In his *al-Tamhid*, Abu Bakr al-Baqillani (d. 1013), the theologian who is credited with refining the methods of Kalam and giving the first systematic statement of the Asharite doctrine, defines science as 'the knowledge of the object, as it really is'. While reacting to the Mutazilite infringement on the domains of faith, the Asharites conceded the need for objective and systematic study of nature. Indeed, some of the greatest scientists in Islam, like Ibn al-Haytham (d. 1039), who discovered the basic laws of optics, and al-Biruni (d. 1048), who measured the circumference of the earth and discussed the rotation of the earth on its axis, were supporters of Asharite theology.[4]

The overall concern of Muslim scientists was the delineation of truth. As Ibn al-Haytham declared: 'Truth is sought for its own sake'; and al-Biruni confirmed in the introduction to his *al-Qanun al-Masudi*: 'I do not shun the truth from whatever source it comes.' But there were disputes about the best way to rational truth. For Ibn Sina, for example, general and universal questions came first and led to experimental work. He starts his *al-Qanun fi Tibb* (Canons of Medicine), which was a standard text in the west up till the eighteenth century, with a general discussion on the theory of drugs. But for al-Biruni, universals came out of practical, experimental work; theories are formulated after discoveries. But either way, criticism was the key to progress towards truth. As Ibn al-Haytham wrote: 'It is natural for everyone to regard scientists favorably ... God, however, has not preserved the scientist from error and has not safeguarded science from shortcomings and faults'; this is why scientists so often disagree amongst themselves. Those concerned with science and truth, Ibn al-Haytham continued, 'should turn themselves into hostile critics' and should criticise 'from every point of view and in all aspects'. In particular, the flaws in the work of one's predecessors should be ruthlessly exposed. The ideas of Ibn al-Haytham, al-Biruni and Ibn Sina, along with numerous other Muslim scientists, laid the foundations of the 'scientific spirit' within the worldview of Islam as we have come to know it.

METHODOLOGY

The 'scientific method', as it is understood today, was first developed by Muslim scientists. The supporters of both Mutazalism as well as Asharism, placed a great deal of emphasis on systematic observation and experimentation. The insistence on accurate observation is amply demonstrated in the literature of astronomical handbooks and tables. These were constantly updated with scientists checking and correcting the work of previous scholars. In medicine, ar-Razi's (d. 925) detailed and highly accurate clinical observations provide us with a universal model; he was the first to accurately observe the symptoms of smallpox and described many new diseases. However, it was not just accurate observation that was important; equally significant was the clarity and precision by which the observations are described – as demonstrated by Ibn Sina in his writings.

The emphasis on model construction and theory building can be seen in Islamic astronomical literature, which consists of general exposition of principles underlying astronomical theory. It was on the strength of both accurate observation and model construction, that Islamic astronomy launched a rigorous attack on what was perceived to be a set of imperfections in Ptolemaic astronomy. Ibn al-Haytham, for example, was the first to declare that 'the arrangements proposed for planetary motions in the Almagest were "false"'. Ibn Shatir (d. 1375) and the astronomers at the famous observatory in Azerbaijan, built in the thirteenth century by Nasir al-Din al-Tusi (d. 1274), developed the Tusi Couple and a theorem for the transformation of eccentric models into epicyclic ones. It was this mathematical model that Copernicus used to develop his notion of heliocentricity thus ushering the European scientific revolution.

Apart from the exact sciences, the most appropriate and interesting area in which theoretical work was essential was medicine. Muslim physicians attempted to improve the quality of *materia medica* and therapeutic uses through continued theoretical development; emphasis was also placed on developing a precise terminology and ensuring the purity of drugs – a concern that led to relevant early chemical and physical procedures. Since Muslim writers were excellent organisers of knowledge, their purely pharmacological texts were themselves a source for the development of theories. Evolution of theories and discovery of new drugs linked the growth of Islamic medicine to chemistry, botany, zoology, geology and law and led to extensive elaborations of Greek classifications. Pharmacological knowledge thus became more numerous and diversified, producing new types of pharmacological literature. Since this literature considered its subject from a number of different disciplinary perspectives and a great variety of new directions, there resulted new ways of looking at pharmacology, and new lines opened up for further exploration and more detailed investigations. Paper making made publication more extensive and cheaper than use of parchment and papyrus, making scientific knowledge much more accessible to students.

While Muslim scientists placed considerable faith on the scientific method, they were also aware of its limitations. Even a strong believer in mathematical realism such as al-Biruni argued that this method of inquiry was a function of the nature of investigation: different methods, all equally valid, were required to answer different types of questions. Al-Biruni himself had recourse to a number of methods. In his treatise on mineralogy, *Kitab al-Jamahir fi Maarifah al-Jawahir*, he is the most exact of experimental scientists. But in the introduction to his ground-breaking study of India he declares that: 'To execute our project, it has not been possible to follow the geometric method.' Instead, he resorts to comparative sociology. In *Ifrad al-Maqal fi Amr az-Zilal*, a treatise devoted to the question of shadows, he differentiates between mathematical and philosophical methods.

The works of a scholar of the calibre of al-Biruni inevitably defy simple classification. There is, for example, his treatise called *al-Qanun al-Masudi* and the recently rediscovered *Kitab Maqalid al-Hayah* on the rules of spherical trigonometry and their application to spherical geometry. There is also his magnificent chronology *Athar al-Baquiyah anil-Quran al-Khaliyah*, which provides a mine of information on eras and festivals of various nations and religions. He also wrote a medical treatise, *Kitab as-Saydanah*, and an astrological treatise *at-Tafhim*. Al-Biruni's work is a specific product of a philosophy of science that integrates metaphysics with physics, does not attribute to either a superior or inferior position, and insists that both are worthy of study and equally valid. Moreover, the methods of studying the vast creation of God – from the movement of the stars and planets, to the nature of diseases, the sting of an ant, the character of madness, the beauty of justice, the spiritual yearning of humanity, the ecstasy of a mystic – are all equally valid and shape understanding in their respective areas of inquiry. In both its philosophy and methodology Islam has sought a complete synthesis of science and religion.

Polymaths, like al-Biruni, al-Jahiz (d. 868), al-Kindi (d. 873), ar-Razi, Ibn Sina, al-Idrisi (b. 1166), Ibn Bajjah (d. 1138), Omar Khayyam (d. 1123), Ibn Zuhr (d. 1162), Ibn Tufayl, Ibn Rushd (d. 1198), as-Suyuti (d. 1505), and thousands of other scholars are not an exception but the general rule in Muslim civilisation. The Islamic civilisation of the classical period was remarkable for the number of polymaths it produced. This is seen as a testimony to the homogeneity of Islamic philosophy of science and its emphasis on synthesis, interdisciplinary investigations and multiplicity of methods.

REVIVING MUSLIM PHILOSOPHY OF SCIENCE

Scholars, scientists and philosophers throughout the Muslim world are today trying to formulate a contemporary version of the Islamic philosophy of science. Two dominant movements have emerged. The first draws its inspiration from Sufi mysticism and argues that the notions of 'tradition' and the 'sacred' should constitute the central core of an Islamic approach to science. The second argues that issues of science and values in Islam must be treated within a framework of concepts that shape the goals of a Muslim society. Ten fundamental Islamic concepts are identified as constituting the framework within which scientific inquiry should be carried out, four standing alone and three opposing pairs. They are:

- Unity of God (*tawheed*)
- Human trusteeship of the earth's resources (*khilafa*)
- Worship (*ibadahh*)
- Knowledge (*ilm*)
- Worthy of praise (*halal*)
- Worthy of blame (*haram*)
- Justice (*adl*)
- Tyranny (*zulm*)
- Public interest (*istislah*)
- Waste (*dhiya*).

When translated into values, this system of Islamic concepts embraces the nature of scientific inquiry in its totality; it integrates facts and values and institutionalises a system of knowing that is based on accountability and social responsibility. It is too early to say whether either of these movements will bear any real fruit.

8
Dewey Departs:
Ideas on Classifying Knowledge

Ilm (knowledge) is one of the most powerful and fundamental concepts of Islam. During the Golden Age of Islam its influence permeated all aspects of Muslim individual and societal behaviour. For the early Muslims a civilisation of Islam was unimaginable without the concept of *ilm*. For a Muslim civilisation of the future it is even more so.

It is not surprising, therefore, to note that the definition, classification and exposition of the concept of knowledge was the prime occupation for many Muslim scholars of medieval times. Witness the numerous definitions of knowledge gathered together by Ibn Sabin of Spain (d. 1270) in his *Budd al-Arif*. In his paper 'Muslim Definitions of Knowledge', Franz Rosenthal lists more than 100 definitions from *Budd al-Arif*; and provides an even more extensive survey in his book *Knowledge Triumphant*. No less extensive are the expositions and classifications of knowledge produced by early Muslim scholars and scientists.

The classification of knowledge under Islam had a religious as well as an etymological beginning. The word *ilm* was reserved for religious elementary knowledge and it was classified under two categories: elementary knowledge, or that relating to the words and sentences of the Qur'an and the *hadith* (traditions of the Prophet Muhammad); and revealed knowledge, or a light, which shines into the hearts of the pious Muslims, whereby they gain enlightenment as to the truths of religion.

However, the word *ilm* was eventually broadened in meaning and became the general Islamic term for knowledge. It came to signify 'science' (*al-ulum* being the plural of science, or 'the sciences'); and *alim* came to mean scholar, and especially one using intellectual processes.

Although the concept of knowledge (*ilm*) was analysed by many Muslim scholars, all agreed with its basic characteristics. Muslim

First published in *Islam: Outlines of a classification scheme*, Clive Bingley/Library Association, London, 1979.

scholars saw values as an integral part of all knowledge. Knowledge was not to be separated from the sophisticated framework of Islamic values. This synthesis of knowledge and values had a natural corollary: within the framework of *ilm* – that is the epistemology of Islam – there is a place for both the objective and the subjective, the worldly and the spiritual. Furthermore, knowledge could be praiseworthy as well as blameworthy, and at a certain stage in its development it is possible for a praiseworthy science to become a blameworthy one. The distinction is of considerable importance for understanding the development of science and technology under Islam. The Muslim scholars saw the whole body of knowledge in a unified sense and within this unified framework there was rich diversity due to the various branches of knowledge. The use of the phrase 'branches of knowledge' was common and important in describing various sciences, for knowledge was considered an organic, holistic concept, with 'living' qualities.

For Muslim scholars the problem of classification of knowledge was not just how to arrange books on shelves but also how to organise knowledge so that it could be transferred in a systematic manner to coming generations. They therefore devised a vast array of hierarchical classification schemes which, over the centuries, formed the matrix and background of the Muslim educational system. The living, organic character of knowledge was compared to a tree, and various sciences were regarded as so many branches of this single tree, which grows and sends forth leaves and fruits in conformity with the nature of the tree itself. To stay with the tree analogy, branches of a tree do not grow indefinitely; and so a discipline is not to be pursued beyond a certain limit. Indeed, should a branch of a tree grow indefinitely it could potentially end up by destroying the tree as a whole. Knowledge cannot be pursued for the sake of knowledge: it must have an enlightened social function.

SOME EARLY MUSLIM CLASSIFICATION SCHEMES: AL-FARABI

One of the first attempts to classify knowledge was made in the ninth century by al-Kindi (801–873). However, it was al-Farabi (d. 950), who produced one of the most used and widely influential schemes. This scheme is described in his *Enumeration of Sciences*, which is known to the west from the Latin translation by Gerard Cremona as *De*

Scientiis. Seyyed Hossein Nasr has summarised al-Farabi's classification scheme as follows:

Science of language:
Syntax, grammar, pronunciation and speech, poetry.

Logic:
The division, definition and composition of simple ideas (drawn in large part from Aristotelian logic and including defining syllogisms; discovering dialectical proofs; examining errors in proofs; reasoning; oratory).

The propaedutic sciences:
Arithmetic and geometry (both practical and theoretical); optics; astronomy; music; science of weights and measures; science of tool-making (engineering).

Sciences of nature:
Physics; metaphysics (science concerned with the Divine and the essence of being); knowledge of principles, which underlie natural bodies (mechanics); knowledge of the nature and character of elements, and of the principle by which they combine to form bodies; science of compound bodies formed of the four elements and their properties (chemistry); science of the generation and corruption of bodies; science of the reactions which the elements undergo in order to form compounds; science of materials; science of plants.

Metaphysics:
Knowledge of the essence of being; knowledge of the principles of the particular and observational sciences; knowledge of beings, their qualities and characteristics, which can lead to knowledge of the Truth, that is, of God, one of whose names is Truth.

Science of society:
Although al-Farabi wrote a massive treatise on alchemy, dreams and related exoteric sciences he does not seem to have included these in his scheme. In his *The Book of Healing* and *The Classification of Intellectual Sciences*, Ibn Sina (980–1111), a professor at the Nizamiyyah Academy at Baghdad, considered to be one of the most original and encyclopaedic minds, further extended al-Farabi's scheme.

CLASSIFICATION ACCORDING TO AL-GHAZALI

Al-Ghazali analysed knowledge on the basis of the following three criteria:

Individually requisite knowledge:
Knowledge, which is essential for individuals to survive, e.g. social ethics, morality, civil law.

Socially requisite knowledge:
Knowledge that is essential for the survival of the community as a whole, e.g. agriculture, jurisprudence, medicine, etc.

Revealed knowledge:
Acquired from the prophets and which is not arrived at either by reason, like arithmetic, or by experimentation, like medicine, or by hearing, like languages.

Al Ghazali then categorised knowledge according to the following sources:

Non-revealed sciences:
Primary sources of these sciences are reason, observation, experimentation, and acculturation.

Praiseworthy sciences:
These are useful and indispensable sciences 'on whose knowledge the activities of this life depend, such as medicine and arithmetic'.

Blameworthy sciences:
These include astrology, magic, warfare sciences, etc.

Using the criteria of al-Ghazali, a tenth-century philosopher, Fakhr al-Din ar-Razi (864–925) in his *The Book of 60 Sciences*, expounded the classification of knowledge to 60 individual branches. However, it was not until the fourteenth century that a complete and more detailed study of sciences and their classification appeared.

CLASSIFICATION ACCORDING TO IBN KHALDUN

In his celebrated work *Introduction to History*, Ibn Khaldun (1332–1406) outlined a classification scheme according to which arts and sciences were, in fact, studied in the Muslim world till the seventeenth century. The basic distinction made by Ibn Khaldun is between Shari'ah sciences and philosophical sciences. Shari'ah sciences deal primarily with Islamic law and religion; philosophical sciences were considered to be those acquired by reflection, experimentation, experience and observation. The overall infrastructure of Ibn Khaldun's scheme can be briefly summarised as follows:

Shar'iah sciences:
(Qur'an, its interpretation and recitation; *hadith*, the traditions of the Prophet and their chain of transmission.)

Theology

Sufism

Linguistic sciences:
(Including lexicography and literature.)

Philosophical sciences

Logic

Natural sciences:
(Physics, medicine, mechanics, agriculture, alchemy.)

Sciences dealing with quantity:
(Geometry (plain and spherical optics), arithmetic (including algebra), music, astronomy.)

Paranormal sciences:
(Magic, occult etc.)

Ibn Khaldun, like al-Biruni (937–1048) and hundreds of other celebrated Muslim scholars, tried to keep a proper distinction between the 'revealed' and experimental sciences, objective and subjective knowledge, physics and metaphysics, values and facts. This was essential not only to save the sciences from magic and miracles, and true Islam from credulity, superstition, and pseudo-religious obscurantism, but also to give science and technology a human face. The post-medieval decline of Muslim idealistic rationalism and the civilisation of Islam began only when the distinction between these two classes of knowledge was lost.

THE NEED FOR A CONTEMPORARY CLASSIFICATION SCHEME ON ISLAM

In our times, conceptual analysis and classification of knowledge as a subject of study have been virtually shelved by Muslim scholars.

Classification of books, articles, papers and reports on Islam and Muslims is carried out using well-known general classification schemes – such as the Dewey Decimal Classification (DDC), Universal Decimal Classification (UDC), Library of Congress Classification (LC), Bibliographical Classification of Bliss (BC) and Colon Classification (CC) of Ranganathan. There are, however, at least two difficulties associated with these systems when it comes to classifying knowledge on or about Muslims.

Firstly, there is the problem of 'physical limitation'. Most of these classifications do not give adequate details for accurate subject specifications. The ideology of Islam endeavours to regulate man's behaviour in every aspect of life by determining standards, laying down codes and laws and by setting concrete examples. Islam provides guidance for its followers in the field of politics and economics, social behaviour and education, art and design, science and technology – in every sphere of human activity. Furthermore, the followers of Islam, fast approaching a billion, live on almost half of the globe's solid surface: from Morocco in the west to Indonesia in the far east; from Canada in the north to the Fiji Islands in the south. Now to squeeze this vast cosmos of the world and religion of Islam under the minute 'other religions' schedule is no easy task.

Secondly, there is the problem of political and cultural orientation of the general classification schemes. Any classification of knowledge can be influenced by the political and cultural philosophy of the individual(s) who first structured the scheme. The most commonly used classification schemes, DDC, UDC, and LC, all suffer from the inherent influence of the ideology of the Christian west. In the pre-Cold War Soviet Union, the ideological dimension of knowledge was well recognised; and Russians, who up to the October Revolution used UDC, were forced to develop the Bibliotechus-Bibliograficerishoy Klamifikatory (BBK) based on Marxist-Leninist classification of sciences and published in 25 volumes between 1960 and 1969. Even CC, which contains a few Hindu elements, is essentially a western classification of knowledge. Thus bibliographical classification of Islam using these schemes amounts to forcing Islamic literature into a shape and form that was designed for a different worldview. There are, of course, mental and intellectual counterparts too for this exercise.

We can safely say, then, that the available general classification schemes do not meet the special needs, acquirements and viewpoints of a library devoted entirely to works on Islam and the Muslim world.

Those classifications, which do vary in viewpoint, do not provide flexible combinations of terms which highly specific subject handling demands, and even when they are flexible, the flexibility is achieved by ridiculously lengthy means.

I am inclined to think that a general, universal classification scheme is not *really* a viable proposition. Knowledge can be treated as a unity within a single worldview: as we have seen above, Muslim scholars constructed many hierarchical classification schemes based on this assumption. But we cannot assume that there is compatibility between the bodies of knowledge produced by the great civilisations of the world. Knowledge – at least from the Muslim point of view – is a function of worldview. And even within a single worldview there may be incompatibility between epochs; indeed, even within the western civilisation there is no compatibility between the various epochs of western culture. How, then, can we justify a universal classification for the many diverse worldviews of the inhabitants of the globe?

It is necessary, I think, for the Muslim world to break out of the confinements of the western worldview; to see the illusions of 'universal' classification schemes in their true perspective; to rediscover their rich heritage in definitions, classifications and expositions of knowledge; to be a little more original and tackle their unique needs, requirements and problems in their own particular way.

9
Arguments for an Islamic Science

Whether Islamic science can be accepted as the 'normal' science of the future, at least by the majority of Muslims, depends to a large extent on the arguments proponents of Islamic science can produce to justify the whole enterprise. Of course, it also depends on the practical utility of such a science; but at this stage of the debate, there are numerous theoretical issues that need to be settled and cogent arguments produced to show that the contemporary realisation of Islamic science is both theoretically necessary and practically possible.

Here, I intend to produce four arguments to justify the need for a contemporary Islamic science, which is a true embodiment of the values, culture and worldview of Islam. I intend to show that science has had a different identity and has played a specific role in various civilisations, including that of Islam. Moreover, I argue that western science is inherently destructive and does not – cannot – fulfil the needs of Muslim societies.

ARGUMENT ONE

Different civilisations have produced distinctively different sciences

A civilisation is an embodiment of its total spiritual and material culture. It is an open, and to some extent, self-perpetuating interchange between man, the values and norms inherent in his worldview and cosmology in their numerous dimensions and orders. Human history has seen a number of civilisations each seeking the realisation of its own values within the framework of its worldview. Behind each civilisation there is a vision of man's place in creation, which motivates its attitude towards nature and promotes the search for its specific problems and needs. Whitehead regards this vision, or worldview, as the central element that shapes the main characteristic of a civilisation, 'in each age of the world distinguished by high activity, there will be found at its culmination, and among the

First published in *Explorations in Islamic Science*, Mansell, London, 1989, chapter 4.

agencies leading to that culmination, some profound consmological outlook, implicitly accepted, impressing its own type on the current springs of action'.[1] It is this cosmological outlook, or *Weltanschauung*, that shapes the value structure of a society and political, social and problem-solving activities of a civilisation.

Thus, at the centre of any civilisation is a worldview that acts as a fulcrum on which the society flourishes or falls. The other parameters of a civilisation – namely, culture, values and norms, social and political organisation and science and technology – derive their legitimacy from the worldview (Figure 9.1). The way society is organised, the dominant values, which shape its political structure and social organisation, how its material problems are solved, and how the individual members, as well as the society as a whole, seek its cultural aspirations all stem from the worldview.

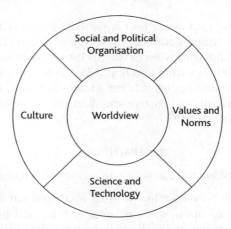

Figure 9.1   Components of a Civilisation

As the worldview of different civilisations tends to be different, the associated parameters also tend to be different. For example, the Chinese worldview based on Confucianism, which dominated China for centuries, has produced a civilisation distinctively different from Greek civilisation. In essence, the worldview of Confucianism, which was later developed by Mencius and Hsun Tzu, is characterised by humanism, occupying itself mainly with human relations subtleties and the supernatural. The bases of Chinese worldview are the concepts of *jen*, humanity, *tao*, the doctrine of harmony, and *Yin* and *Yang*, the cosmic principles of male and female. *Jen* ethics, the politics, the social organisation of the Chinese civilisation all flow from the doctrine of *jen*.

Jen is definied as the 'perfect virtue' and expresses the Chinese ideal of cultivating human relations, developing human faculties, sublimating one's personality and upholding human rights. Its basis is to be found first in one's duties towards one's parents and brothers. In the *Analects*, two other concepts, *hsiao*, filial piety, and *ti*, fraternal love, express the idea of *jen*: *hsiao* signifies a state of spiritual communion with the eternity of time, and *ti* signifies a state of spiritual communion in the infinity of space. Hence, these virtues have become the foundations of Chinese social structure. Mencius claimed that for the cultivation of virtue, *jen* should be supplemented with *yi*. 'What one upholds in one's heart is *jen*: what one upholds in one's conduct is *yi*.' Thus *yi* is the virtuous principle for guiding external conduct. Hsun Tzu recommends *li* as the norm of social conduct. *Li*, a code of ritual embodied in ancient Chinese culture, is also a set of general rules of propriety, the regulating principle in a well-ordered society. It has often been translated as 'social order', 'social institutions and conventions' or 'all regulations that arise from the man-to-man relations'.

The worldview of *jen* is a major force in unifying China and shaping the temperament of the Chinese people. The major characteristic of the Chinese people is that everyone, rich or poor, educated or illiterate, male or female, has profound respect for life. There is an insistence in Chinese culture that in order to live well, one must try to get the best out of life and enjoy what one has. The passionate love of life, the national characteristic of Chinese people, is coupled with a corresponding notion of rational happiness. 'Rational happiness', a unique characteristic of the worldview of *jen*, is not based on worldly riches or external, circumstances, but on one's own virtues. As Confucius said, 'the wise are free from doubts; the virtuous from concerns; the courageous from fear' . . . 'The noble man is completely at ease; the common man is always on edge.'[2] Virtue lies in living with total harmony, in developing a sense of justice and fairness, a spirit of tolerance, a readiness to compromise, and a firm determination to enforce the observance of these virtues against egoism and altruism. Exaggeration, or total absence of *jen*, would upset the social order, and both altruism and egoism are too extreme and could lead to calamities. The way of *jen* is a way of action that avoids extremes, and leads to a state of mind that combines human reasoning and feeling to reach perfect harmony. Only harmony can bring about balance, and only balance can lead to progress. Harmony is obtained by fulfilling one's duties in one's relationships with oneself, with one's family, with the community, with the nation and with the world. Hsun Tzu symbolised *li* with five characters – Heaven, Earth, Emperor, Ancestors and Tutors. The ethics of *jen*, *yi* and *li* stresses the moral importance of human relationships in politics. In the last analysis, virtue alone constitutes the ultimate goal of man.[3]

In contrast, the Greek worldview saw rational knowledge as the ultimate goal of man. Formal religion in Greece revolved around Olympian gods under their leader, Zeus. Although Zeus was supreme, the Greeks did not regard him as the creator of the world but only as a ruler. Indeed, his supremacy was qualified by the fact that the other gods had independent wills and functions. Important among them was Apollo, whose concerns covered medicine, the care of animals, music, and the Delphic Oracle; Hera, Zeus's consort and protectress of marriage; Poseidon, the seagod and bringer of earthquakes; Athene, patron of Athens and of the arts; and Aphrodite, goddess of love. Dionysus gained importance over time as a vegetation deity and as the focus of ecstatic cults. The gods spent most of their time in conflicts with each other and, in particular, with Titans, the gods of evil. Greek religion was at its most personal and ecstatic in the worship of Dionysus who gained a mystical significance when Orphism, a movement that became influential in the fifth and sixth centuries BC, adopted his worship. The legend was that Dionysus, under the name of Zagreus, was a son of Zeus by the Earth goddess Semele, but was eaten by the Titans. Zeus, in anger, burned up the Titans with thunderbolts and from their ashes the human race was formed. Hence, man is a combination of evil (he is Titanic) and good (for he contains an element of the divine Zagreus). The Orphics believed that the body was a tomb that imprisoned the soul; they taught reincarnation and in this and other ways influenced the thinking of Plato and other philosopher-scientists.

As the city-state developed, religion was increasingly integrated into political and civic life. The cult of the hero or patron of the city expressed the unity of the state as an expanded form of the clan or family. The former Greek religions shunned mystical cults such as those of the Orphics who practised their rituals in secret. From the worldview of many gods looking after different aspects of the world emerges the central political notion of a city-state; the Greek civilisation consisted of many city-states that, like the gods, had individual outlooks. The Greeks could seldom agree to act in common.

Order was the main notion of the Greek worldview. A measured balance of forces in society produced a well-ordered state. Order in society meant that everyone knew his or her position and the task to be performed. Order was to be found in rational knowledge. In ethical order, goodness comes from the pursuit of reason, and evil from ignorance. The Greek way of life was mainly secular, dividing functions into various compartments – indeed, reductionism was the cornerstone of the Greek worldview and culture.

For example, Socrates, the father of Greek philosophy, believed that the soul has, in descending order, a rational part, an emotional part, and an acquisitive part. In the just soul these are properly ordered, each attending its own business and obeying the parts above it. Reason, at the top, rules emotion. Emotion, in turn, helps to inspire the actions that reason dictates. When the parts are so ordered that a subordinate part gains an upper hand, the soul is sick. Because the soul is ruled by reason, it is akin to the realm of Form – the eternal, unblemished objects of knowledge over which the Form of the Good is supreme. Similarly, Socrates divided the city-state into three types of citizens: first, common people, the workers, the artisans and the merchants; second, the military, whose task was to protect the city-state from outside dangers and keep order within; third, the rulers and the guardians, who govern and legislate. To ensure the stability of this kind of system, the three orders are kept separate, and each is given training in its appropriate function: the people in their various skills, the soldiers in the art of war and the rulers in government.

As in the Chinese worldview, the Greeks considered that a good life is attained by conforming to the goal or purpose of human existence. But here the purpose of life is seen not as the pursuit of *jen*, *yi* and *li* but as the pursuit of reason. Aristotle, for example, sees the principal occupation for a man who would aim at goodness as the virtuous exercise of reason. Happiness is a virtue called reason.

If happiness is activity in accordance with virtue, it is reasonable that it should be in accordance with the highest virtue; and this will be that of the best thing in us. Whether it be reason or something else that is this element which is thought to be our natural ruler and guide and to take thought of things noble and divine, whether it be itself also divine or only the most divine element in us, the activity of this in accordance with its proper virtue will be perfect happiness.[4]

We see from this brief description, that the worldviews of Chinese and Greek civilisations are distinctively different: for Greeks reason is the supreme, almost divine, virtue; for the Chinese *jen*, the Confucian ideal of cultivation of human relations, developing human faculties, sublimating one's personality, and upholding human rights are the supreme virtues. While the Greeks emphasise individualism, separation of function and roles in society and the religious from the rational; the Chinese stress synthesis, a balance in inner and outer life. In the Greek framework, order comes from Form and separating the individuals and various aspects of social and political life; in Chinese thought, people are interrelated so that order may be maintained. Needless to say, the two worldviews produced two distinct cultures, values and norms, and social and political organisations.

The key question is: did the two civilisations also produce two distinct and unique systems of science and technology? Or, if science and technology is a neutral, value-free and universal system, as conventional wisdom would lead us to believe, are the Chinese and Greek sciences identical? Even a casual examination of Chinese and Greek sciences reveals that they are two distinct ways of knowing and solving problems.

In Chinese science, as indeed in the worldview of *jen*, unity of man and nature is a predominant positive value. The Chinese way of thinking and knowing is organic where the interconnections between various facts of material reality and spiritual needs are emphasised. The fundamental ideas and theories of Chinese science revolve around the theory of Five Elements (*wu hsing*) and the Two Fundamental Forces (*Yin and Yang*). The theory of Five Elements goes back to Tsou Yen, the real founder of Chinese scientific thought, who flourished around 350 and 270 BC. While basically naturalistic and scientific, the theory of Five Elements also served a political function, as it frightened the feudal masters and kept them on an appropriate path. Tsou Yen describes the theory in the following words:

The Five Elements dominate alternately. [Successive emperors choose the colour of their] official vestments following the directions [so that the colour may agree with the dominant element].

Each of the Five Virtues [Elements] is followed by the one it cannot conquer. The dynasty of Shun ruled by the virtue of Earth, the Hsia dynasty ruled by the virtue of Wood, the Shang dynasty ruled by the virtue of Metal, and the Chou dynasty ruled by the virtue of Fire.

When some new dynasty is going to arise, Heaven exhibits auspicious signs to the people. During the rise of Hyuang Ti [the Yellow Emperor] large earthworms and large ants appeared. He said, 'This indicates that the element Earth is in the ascendant, so our colour must be yellow, and our affairs must be placed under the sign of Earth.' During the rise of Yu the Great, Heaven produced plants and trees which did not wither in autumn and winter. He said: 'This indicates that the element Wood is in the ascendant, so our colour must be green, and our affairs must be placed under the sign of Wood . . .' During the rise of the High King Wen of the Chou, Heaven exhibited fire, and many red birds holding documents written in red flocked to the altar of the dynasty. He said, 'This indicates that the element Fire is in the ascendant, so our colour must be red and our affairs must be placed under the sign of Fire.' Following Fire there will come Water. Heaven will show when the time comes for the *chhi* of Water to dominate. Then the colour will have to be black, and affairs will have to be placed under the sign of Water. And that dispensation will in turn come to an end, and at the appointed time, all will revert once again to Earth. But when that time will be we do not know.[5]

The Chinese conception of the elements was not so much in terms of fundamental matter but more in terms of fundamental processes. The theory was an attempt to classify the basic properties of material things when they undergo change. But the significant point is that by concentrating on relation rather than substance, Chinese thought emphasised the interconnectedness of man and nature as well as individual and society. Consider, for example, this passage from the *Ta Tai Li Chi* (Record of Rites of the Elder Tai), a compilation made between 85 and 105 CE, where the insistence of seeing man and nature in a unified framework is so clear:

Tseng Tzu said, That to which Heaven gives birth has its head on the upper side: that to which Earth gives birth has its head on the under side. The former is called round, the latter is called square. If heavens were really round and the Earth really square the four corners of the Earth would not be properly covered. Come nearer and I will tell you what I learnt from the Master [Confucius]. He said that the Tao of Heaven was round and that of the Earth square. The square is dark and the round is bright. The bright radiates *chhi*, therefore there is light outside it. The dark imbibes *chhi*, therefore there is light within it. Thus it is that Fire and Sun have an external brightness, while Metal and Water have an internal brightness. That which irradiates is active and that which imbibes radiations is reactive. Thus the Yang is active and the Yin reactive.

The seminal essence (*ching*) of the Yang is called *shen*. The germinal essence of the Yin is called *ling*. The *shen* and *ling* (vital forces) are the root of all living creatures; and the ancestors of [such high developments as] rites and music, human-heartedness and righteousness; and the makers of good and evil, as well as of social order and disorder.

When the Yin and Yang keep precisely to their proper positions, then there is quiet and peace . . .

Hairy animals acquire their coats before coming into the world, feathered ones similarly first acquire their feathers. Both are born of the power of Yang. Animals with carapaces and scales on their bodies likewise come into the world with them; they are born by the power of Yin. Man alone comes naked into the world; [this is because] he has the [balance] essence of both Yang and Yin.

The essence [or most representative example] of hairy animals is the unicorn, that of feathered ones is the phoenix [or pheasant;] that of the carapace-animals is the tortoise, and that of the scaly ones is the dragon. That of the naked ones is the Sage.[6]

Yin and *Yang*, the two fundamental forces of Chinese scientific thought are ever present in the Heavens as well as in man, each one dominating the other in a wave-like succession. The Chinese classic, *I Ching* (The Book of Change), contains a mathematical exposition of the *Yin* and *Yang* theory. The book contains a series of 64 symbolic hexagrams, each of which is composed of six lines, whole or broken, corresponding to the *Yang* and the *Yin*. Each hexagram is primarily *Yin* or primarily *Yang*, and by a judicious arrangement it was found possible to derive all the 64 in such a way as to produce alternating *Yin* and *Yang*, while the *Yin* and *Yang* components never become completely fragmented and separated; however, at any given stage, in any given fragment, only one is manifested. In one respect, the *I Ching* provides a practical demonstration of the principle of *Yin* and *Yang*.

Within this theoretical framework, Chinese science achieved tremendous heights. While at first sight it may appear that empirical and pragmatic work is not possible in such a framework, it would be a very misleading conclusion. Even in contemporary terms, the Chinese theoretical framework has many parallels: the Yin and Yang principle in genetics and the theory of Five Elements correspond to what might be called the five fundamental states of matter – 'one could think of Water as implying all liquid, and Fire all gaseous states; similarly, Metal could cover all metals and semi-metals, and Earth all earth elements, while Wood could stand for the whole realm of the carbon compounds, that is, organic chemistry'. However, to look at Chinese science with the perspective of western science is to miss the point:

Chinese science was aimed at meeting the practical and spiritual needs of the Chinese civilisation and not of western society.

Within its framework, Chinese science was as empirical as was demanded by Chinese society. The Chinese produced major achievements in hydraulic science and engineering. They excelled in mathematics: the earliest indication of the abacus arithmetic (*suan-p'an*) appears in the work of Hsu Yo who lived around 150–200 CE. Much Chinese arithmetic originates from the classic treatise of Chang Ts'ang (d. 152 BC), entitled *Chiu Chang Suan Shu* (The Arithmetical Rules in Nine Sections) in which there is the earliest-known mention of the negative quantity (*fu*), and the tradition was maintained through several centuries, being noticeable in the Arithmetical Classic of Hsia-Hou Yang (600 CE). In the second century CE, the solution of indeterminate equations of the first degree, and a decimal system appear in the work of Sun-Tzu; and elaborate treatment of fractions and further work on indeterminate equations occurs in the Arithmetical Classic of Chang Chiu-chien (650 CE); and by the early seventh century Wand Hsiao-tung had solved simple cubic equations in connection with the volumes of solids, to be followed by further contributions to the study of indeterminate equations by Ihsing (683–727); so that the body of knowledge in the *Chiu Chang Suan Shu* was gradually augmented. Medicine too was a major science in China and the Chang Chung-ching, the Chinese Galen, led the field at the end of the second century with treatises, one on dietetics and the other on fevers. It had many branches, including theoretical studies of health and disease; macrobiotics or the theory and practice of longevity techniques; pharmacognosy, the study of *materia medica* veterinary medicine; and acupuncture, a minor branch of therapeutics. Because Chinese science clearly incorporated value considerations it has been assumed to be somewhat less scientific. For example, Joseph Needham classifies geomancy – the science of wind and water, which decides the auspicious placement of houses and tombs – a 'pseudo-science' simply because empirical and precise work has been made subservient to value and aesthetic judgement. Experiments and theory-building were an important part of Chinese science although they did not have paramount importance as in western science. Consider the probability of sticking pins in a human body randomly, without a theory, and hitting all the acupuncture points and the absurdity of the suggestion that Chinese science lacked a theoretical and experimental base becomes all too obvious. Indeed,

Chinese experimental work led to the discovery of the three great inventions which became crucial to the transformation of European society from the Dark Ages to the industrial age: the magnetic compass, gun-powder, and the printing-press.

From this rather brief and sketchy description of Chinese science, it can be seen that it not only has a Chinese flavour but a distinct Chinese identity. Within its given framework, it was objective and rational and met the needs and solved the problems of Chinese society. Its priorities reflected the value of the Chinese worldview and its products enhanced Chinese culture.

In contrast to Chinese science, which showed the overwhelming tendency to argue and analyse phenomena in terms of dialectical logic where rigid 'A or not-A' categorisations were avoided, Greek science was based on a linear logic and emphasised reduction. The foundation of Greek science is Aristotelian logic: here two general principles of proof are recognised – the law of contradiction (nothing can both have and not have a given characteristic) and the law of the excluded middle (everything must either have or not have a given characteristic). The Greeks, in particular the Pythagoreans, saw the world as a vast mathematical pattern; and to seek mastery of this world one had to seek the numbers in things. Hence the emphasis in Greek science on mathematics and deductive logic.

The Greek emphasis on mathematics is personified by Pythagorean thought. Pythagoras blended his science with his religious worldview and his politics. The Pythagorean community was a religious brotherhood for the practice of asceticism and the study of mathematics. The sect practised a severe discipline, which included secrecy, respect for the authority of the master, ritual purification, memory exercises, examination of conscience, and various taboos concerning food. Pythagoras taught a cosmology that gave a special place to numbers, which were represented by points juxtaposed to form square, triangular and rectangular figures. 'Things are numbers' was the Pythagorean motto. Pythagoras himself discovered the relation of simple numbers (2/1, 3/2, 4/3), which determine the principal intervals of the musical scale (fourth, fifth, octave), and thought that the distances separating the heavenly bodies observed the same proportions.[7]

Many Greek philosopher-scientists were concerned with questions of life and ethics. Thus Aristotle's interest in the natural and human world led him to biology and a taxonomy of a 'scale of nature'. Aristotle considered mathematics as an abstraction from natural reality, which for him was a complex, self-regulating system. He saw natural phenomena in terms of cause and effect and introduced the principle of teleology, which led his biological studies to the problem of generation and the transmission of form between separate bodies. Aristotle explained why animals and plants grow into whatever they happen to become as though growing was like pursuing a goal. In physics and astronomy, he explained the first cause of all phenomena, through the realisation of its purpose in the celestial cycles.

The Aristotelian doctrine that first principles are required for rational science was challenged by the Sceptic philosophers like Pyrrho of Elis (fourth century BC) who made doubt the central theme of their philosophy. Pyrrho's follower, Timon, criticised the logicians because of their inability to arrive at sound points for their deductions. Sextus Empiricus (second century BC) attacked the doctrine of syllogism for being empty since it is based on circular argument: the conclusion is presupposed in the premise. He also dismissed the theory of causality, arguing that only events that happen at the same time can be linked, whereas causes precede effects. The causal relation is thus merely a mental construction. Sceptics did not believe in divine providence and tried to be detached, refraining both from judgement and action.

Despite the various stances of Greek philosopher-scientists, on the whole Greek science is deeply entrenched in linear mathematical logic and the supremacy of deduction. Despite the powerful influence of the Pythagorean cult, it is thoroughly secular and exhibits a certain degree of rational arrogance. The Greeks were generally irreverent and had a high opinion of themselves. All those outside their city-states were regarded as barbarians. Thus it was the Greeks who coined the name *pyramids* for Egypt's funeral monuments. Pyramid is Greek for 'wheatcake'. Greek scientists were preoccupied with theory and pure mathematics, and largely shunned experimental and empirical work because they had a prosperous economy and a comparatively simple political structure, which gave them a certain amount of stability. Indeed, when they were faced with a social problem, it immediately reflected in their scientific thought. Thus, faced with an ever increasing number of beggars in Greece, Isocrates made a special study of the problem and suggested that they should be enlisted, drilled and hurled against the Persian Empire. If they could not conquer it outright, they could at least tear enough off its territory to provide living-space for themselves. The alternative was unthinkable: 'If we cannot check the growing strength of these vagabonds', wrote

Isocrates, 'by providing them with a satisfactory life, before we know where we are they will be so numerous that they will constitute as great a danger to the Greeks as do the Barbarians.' Isocrates's social remedies are reflected in the scientific thinking of his contemporary, Plato. Just as Isocrates sought to liquidate the vagabonds in Greece, Plato set out to liquidate the five disorderly vagabonds (planets) in the heavens. He set a problem to all earnest students to find 'what are the uniform and ordered movements by the assumption of which the apparent movements of the planet can be accounted for?' This problem had to be solved if Plato's astronomical ideas were to work, especially when he had turned it into a theology by which he wanted to reconstruct society.[8]

Greek science, it can be seen, is different from Chinese science. Not only are the emphases of the two sciences different, but also the nature, characteristics and, indeed, the logic and methodologies. Now, can one generalise from this and argue that all civilisations have their distinct, unique styles of doing science that give them particular characteristics and shapes their contents according to the culture and value structure of their specific worldview?

On the basis of pure logic, it seems unreasonable to assume that two civilisations with different societal problems and perceptions of reality should produce identical systems for solving problems. Schematically, the logical inconsistency in the conventional view that science is the same for all mankind can be demonstrated quite clearly. Figure 9.2 represents two distinct civilisations, A and B; and W, C, V, PS and S represent worldview, culture, values and norms, political and social organisation and science, respectively. Now if W_A / W_B, C_A / C_B, V_A / V_B, and PS_A / PS_B, what logic is there which suggests that $S_A = S_B$?

As I have tried to show in the case of Chinese and Greek sciences, the two are different yet equally valid ways of looking at reality and solving problems. If we look at other civilisations, such as the Romans, the Hindus, the Aztecs or the Mayans, we see that these civilisations, too, had their individual ways of knowing and solving problems. As an activity of human beings, science manifests itself as a process, which occurs in time and space and involves human actors. These actors live not only in science, but in wider cultures, societies and civilisations. And each civilisation stamps the unique characteristics of its worldview on the nature, style and content of the science of that civilisation.

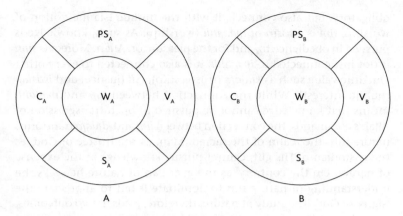

Figure 9.2   Two Civilisations

ARGUMENT TWO

Islamic science in history has a distinctive identity expressed in its unique nature and characteristic style

Islamic science flourished during the zenith of Muslim civilisation, a period of some seven hundred years from 700 to 1500 CE. The science that evolved has a distinct Islamic identity, manifested in terms of an epistemology that shaped the outlook and the goals of science, and in terms of methods that affected the ways of doing, as well as the content of, science.

The epistemology of Islam emphasises the totality of experience and promotes not one but a number of diverse ways of studying nature. The Islamic concept of knowledge, *ilm*, incorporates almost every form of knowledge from pure observation to the highest metaphysics. Thus *ilm* can be acquired from revelation as well as reason, from observation as well as intuition, from tradition as well as theoretical speculation. While the various ways of studying nature are equally valid in Islam, all are subservient to the eternal values of Qur'anic revelation. As such, Islamic epistemology emphasises the pursuit of all forms of knowledge within the framework of eternal values which are the cornerstone of the Islamic civilisation.

Besides diversity, the epistemology of Islam also emphasises interconnectedness. All forms of knowledge are interconnected and organically related by the ever-present spirit of the Qur'anic revelation. Thus Islam not only makes the pursuit of knowledge obligatory, but also connects it with the unique Islamic notion of worship: *ilm* is a form of *ibadahh* (worship). As such, knowledge is pursued in obedience to, and for the pleasure of, Allah. Moreover, *ilm* is not just connected to *ibadahh*; it is also connected to every other Qur'anic value such as *khilafa* (trusteeship), *adl* (justice) and *istislah* (public interest). While the connection between *ilm* and *ibadahh* means that knowledge cannot be pursued in open transgression of Allah's commands, the connection between *ilm* and *khilafa* transforms nature into the realm of the sacred. Man, as the trustee of God, as the custodian of His gift, cannot pursue knowledge at the expense of nature. On the contrary, as the guardian of nature he seeks the understanding of nature not to dominate it but to appreciate the 'signs' of God. The study of nature, therefore, leads to two outcomes: an understanding of the material world as well as reflection of spiritual realities. The interconnection between *ilm* and *istislah* ensures the knowledge is pursued to promote equality, social justice and values that enhance the well-being of Muslim society and culture.

Its emphasis on diversity and interconnectedness gives a very unique character to the epistemology of Islam. It provides a middle path for the pursuit of knowledge, ensuring that no individual form of knowledge or method of knowing becomes the sole criteria of truth or is pursued to the exclusion of all others. It is for this reason that a predilection for systematic classification of knowledge is so noticeable in Muslim civilisation, which was the prime occupation of many Muslim scholars of the classical age.[9] It provided a method indispensable to genuine scholarship and proved extremely fertile in the history of Muslim intellectual endeavour. Moreover, the insistence of Islamic epistemology on giving equal status to all forms of knowledge within a single matrix of values meant that Muslim scholars were able to accept the existing sciences of various civilisations which they inherited. Once it became part of the framework of eternal Islamic values, it was transformed into a new substance. However, while Islamic science, like Greek and Chinese science before it, had its own unique identity, unlike them, it was truly international because of the geographical spread and the cosmopolitan nature of Muslim civilisation.

It was their concern with the classification of knowledge that enabled Muslim scholars, first, to appreciate the intellectual output of other civilisations and then to synthesise it with the worldview of Islam. Thus, right from the beginning, Muslim scholars agreed on the fundamental division of science into Arabic (that is indigenous) and foreign (that is, predominantly Greek) sciences. However, as the process of synthesis proceeded, knowledge was classified on more sophisticated bases that reflected the worldview of Islam. Thus, al-Farabi's (d. 950) classification of knowledge follows the Aristotelian pattern but gives more emphasis to the linguistic science and to *fiqh* (jurisprudence) and *kalam* (speculative theology). But his younger contemporary, al-Khwarizmi (writing c. 976) already offers a classification that is more adequate and incorporates a hierarchy giving prominence to religious knowledge which provides the value structure within which all other forms of knowledge are sought. In the *Rasail Ikhwan as-Safa*, an encyclopaedia compiled in the tenth century by a group of scholars who called themselves the 'faithful friends', metaphysics is placed on the same level as mathematics, logic and natural sciences. In Ibn Hazm's treatise *The Categories of Sciences* (*Maratib al-Ulum*) we find a perfect fusion of knowledge and values. While establishing a hierarchy of science, Ibn Hazm also insists on their interdependence. For Ibn Hazm knowledge is the certainty (*tayaqqun*) of a thing as it is. He associates knowledge with four cardinal virtues: justice (*adl*), understanding (*fahm*), courage (*najdah*), and generosity (*jud*). This brings the intellect and knowledge close to each other in the pursuit of virtue. Knowledge is a multi-faceted thing, but the noblest knowledge is that which brings the individual closer to his maker. A. G. Chejne summarises Ibn Hazm's perception of knowledge, 'Knowledge, like faith, is a passport to happiness in this life and in the hereafter. As depositories of knowledge, faith and reason – although differing in nature – have an identical aim in ibn Hazm's thinking, that is, the attainment of virtue (*fadail*)'.[10] This approximation with faith and reason becomes more evident in his broad conception of knowledge. In as much as knowledge is related to the state of individual happiness on earth as well as in heaven, it should be sought incessantly and disseminated; its seeker, however, should not boast about it, because it is a gift from God.

He should always be humble with whatever knowledge he may have, because someone else could have more knowledge than he. Finally, knowledge should be put into practice, otherwise the ignorant person would appear better off than the scholar. In fact, knowledge and action (*al-ilm wa-l-amal*) are inseparable, particulary with regard to the performance of religious duties. In consequence, the greatest virtue along with the practice of goodness is to teach and implement knowledge.

Ibn Hazm emphasised the middle path in the pursuit of knowledge in numerous statements found throughout his *Akhlaq*. For example:

The one who is greedy with his knowledge is more blameworthy than the one who is greedy with his money.

Intellectual inquiry will be useless if it is not supported by the good fortune of religion and that of (the sciences of) the world.

Recondite sciences are like strong medicine; they help people with strong constitutions, but destroy those with weak bodies. Similarly, they will greatly enrich and purify the vigorous intellect, but they will destroy the weak one.

True science unveils the ignorance concerning the attributes of God – may He be glorified and exalted.

The utility of knowledge in the practice of virtue is enormous, for through it one will be able to know the beauty of virtue which will never escape him; he will also be able to know the ugliness of vices, avoiding them except on rare occasions; he will take heed of nice praise and will wish something like it for himself; he will also take heed of damnation and will attempt to avoid it. On these grounds, it is necessary to conclude that knowledge has a great deal to do with every virtue, and that ignorance has its share in every vice. Moreover, no one will ever achieve virtue without learning the sciences, excepting those who possess pure natures and virtuous constitutions. To this category belong the prophets (may God's prayer and peace be upon them); this is so because God Almighty has taught them all goodness (*khayr*) without the intervention of man.[11]

The concern of such classical Muslim scholars as Ibn Hazm to synthesise values with knowledge, and knowledge with action and virtue led to the classification of certain branches of knowledge as 'blameworthy'. It was clear to scholars and scientists of the 'Golden Age of Islam' that the pursuit of all knowledge did not necessarily lead to virtue; that not all *ilm* can be connected with *ibadahh* and the pleasure of Allah. The basis of the distinction is clearly set forth by Hujwiri:

Knowledge is obligatory only in so far as it is requisite for acting rightly. God condemns those who learn useless knowledge, and the Prophet said, 'I take refuge with Thee from knowledge that profiteth naught'. Much may be done by means of a little knowledge and knowledge should not be separated from action. The Prophet said, 'The devotee without divinity is like a donkey turning a mill' because the donkey goes round and round on its own tracks and never makes any advances.[12]

Much has been said by orientalists and contemporary Muslim scholars of how such a distinction limits inquiry and suffocates science.[13] The subtlety in the Muslim classification of knowledge and divisions of knowledge into those which promote human welfare and eternal values, and those which squander resources or promote injustice and myths, cannot really be appreciated by those who measure the achievements of Islamic civilisation by alien scales and by methods designed to show the almighty supremacy of reason. Only when one appreciates the value of synthesis, the connection between reason and revelation, can one really appreciate the deep insight shown by Hujwiri and other Muslim philosophers. Behind the division of knowledge of al-Ghazali, for example, into individually and socially requisite, and praiseworthy and blameworthy, is a deep commitment to maintain a social balance in society and promote the values of the worldview of Islam. The classical scholars of Islam were concerned that in the pursuit of knowledge the needs of the community should not be lost sight of, that *ilm* should not create undesirable social effects, that it should not tend to such a level of abstraction that it leads to the estrangement of man from his world and his fellow men, or to confusion rather the enlightenment. In this framework science is guided towards a middle path. While it should be socially relevant, the idea of a purely utilitarian science is rejected. Moreover, there is no such thing as science for science's sake; yet the pursuit of pure knowledge for the perfection of man is encouraged. Science, far from being enjoyed as an end in itself, must be instrumental to the attainment of a higher goal.

These special features of the epistemology of Islam gave rise to a unique tradition of science. For the classical Muslim scientists all experiences are real and therefore worthy of investigation. To exclude any one of them is to exclude reality itself. Thus, Muslim scientists did not believe in a single, all-encompassing method of inquiry, but used a number of methods in conformity with the object of study. This is a major feature of the style of Islamic science. Consequently, we find scientists in the classical period working with different methodologies, each as rigorous as the other, and accepting all methods as invaluable in themselves. They defined a particular method or sets of methods for each clearly defined discipline and considered these methods not as contradictory but as complementary. Of course, there were incidences of tension, philosophers arguing with theologians, each accusing the method of the other as being unreliable, but by and large harmony prevailed and the principles of diversity and interconectedness of

Islamic epistemology ensured that the multiplicity of methods were integrated into a totality. Thus it was possible to have several sciences dealing with the same subject, each using its particular methods. A tree, for example, could be studied from the point of view of botany, hence observed and described; or medicine, hence its products tested and turned into drugs, or physics, hence its form and matter analysed; or even Sufism, hence contemplated.[14] Indeed, it was not uncommon for an individual scientist, for example al-Biruni, to have access to all these methods, which he used to arrive at coherent interpretation of reality. In all this he is always *partial* to the truth and never loses sight of the worldview and the framework of values in his working – a practical demonstration of the pragmatic epistemology of Islam.

The hallmark of Islamic science in history is partiality to truth in all its multidimensional manifestations: Muslim scientists were well aware that objectivity reveals only part of the truth, that truth can also be found by other modes of inquiry. We can well illustrate this point by looking at the work of such a representative of Islamic science as al-Biruni.

In al-Biruni we find a scientist who has integrated a number of methods in his very being; there is no such dichotomy as the 'two cultures' of C. P. Snow here. Al-Biruni never fails to remind his readers that there is more than one method of reaching the truth. He starts one of his treatises with the words, 'I pray for God's favour and spacious bounty to make me fit for adopting the right course and help me in perceiving and realizing the truth and facilitate its pursuit and enlighten its courses (methods) and remove all impediments in achieving noble objects.' Thus for al-Biruni there are a number of courses towards the truth, a vital, living assimilative force which permeates every aspect of his scholarly outlook. Al-Biruni derives his emphasis on the truth from the Qur'an, which he quoted often. In his preface to *India* he quotes, 'Speak the truth, even if it were against yourselves.' And it is in the pursuit of truth, not of reason, that al-Biruni uses a number of methods.

Mathematics is central to al-Biruni's scientific research. He considers it natural that man should count the objects around him and establish a quantitative correlation among them. But he also repeatedly stresses usefulness of knowledge as an important motive for his own research and promotion of science in general. In a purely technical book, *The Determination of Co-ordinates of Positions for the Correction of Distances between Cities*, he gives the following reason for pursuing knowledge:

We look around and we see that man's efforts are directed only towards earning a living, and for this purpose he endures hardships and fears, though he needs food only once or twice a day for his life in this world. But he pretends ignorance and neglects what he must not fail to do for his soul in the hereafter, five times in every day and night, thinking that his ignorance is a valid excuse, though he has the opportunity and the power to know it (what is good for his soul).

The Jews also need a direction, because they turn in their prayers to the Temple in Jerusalem which is of known longitude and latitude . . . The Christians need the (direction of) true east because their elders, whom they call fathers, prescribed to them that they should turn to Paradise in their prayers.[15]

Yet he is not a complete utilitarian. Truth, in itself, is also beautiful for al-Biruni: 'It is knowledge, in general, which is pursued solely by man, and which is pursued for the sake of knowledge itself, because its acquisition is truly delightful, and is unlike the pleasures desirable from other pursuits.'[16]

It is the synthesis of the approaches to knowledge into a middle path which is the hallmark of al-Biruni's science. It was this outlook that led to his theory of solar apogee, considered to be one of the most original accomplishments in the history of science. In his *al-Qanun al-Masudi* al-Biruni starts his investigations by recounting the work of previous scientists and then presents and evaluates the results of his own observation. He finds the solar apogee to be situated at degrees 84 59' 51", 9". But his results are arrived at by applying a method of his own, consisting of three essentially different variants, all three of which he shows to lead to the same numerical result. He bases his investigation, on a theorem set forth first by Archimedes of which al-Biruni provides 20 different proofs. Briefly stated, the theorem reads: if a broken line is inscribed in a circular arc, and if the perpendicular is drawn from the point bisecting the arc on the (major part of the) broken line, then the broken line too is bisected by the perpendicular. Of course others before al-Biruni introduced new concepts and methods into astronomy, but what is unique to al-Biruni is the systematic consideration of the criteria according to which preference is to be given to one method over another. His investigation leads him to infer that there undoubtedly exists a continual motion of the apogee in the direction of increasing longitudes. He goes further to demonstrate that the apogee and perigee are the points at which the apparent velocity reaches its extreme values and that, in passing from one to the other, a continual increase or decrease of velocity will be observed – thus, making for the first time, the concept of accelerated motion the subject of mathematical analysis. All this leads him to establish a value subject of mathematical analysis. All this leads him to establish a value for the motion of procession: he states that the longitudes increase by one degree in 68 years and 11 months (the modern values is c.71m 7.5m).[17]

Al-Biruni was aware of the limitations of the methods he used to develop his theory of solar apogee. For one thing it could not be used to equal effect in his study of India: 'To execute our project, it has not been possible to follow the geometrical method which consists in referring back to what has been said before and not what has been said later.'[18] In *India* al-Biruni uses methods nearer to those developed by Muslim jurists and the scholars of *hadith*. The truth here demands a different method but one which is just as systematic, rigorous and critical as the 'geometric method'. The methodology used in *India* is field work and is based on three cardinal principles: 'hearsay does not equal eye witness', 'written tradition is the most preferable', and 'the tradition regarding an event which in itself does not contradict either logical or physical laws will invariably depend for its character as true or false upon the character of the reporters'. Combining these principles with field work and partiality towards truth, al-Biruni was able to produce one of the first and most detailed sociological analyses of India – an achievement that alone would have placed him among the great scholars of the world.

The ability to synthesise different methods in his work was not unique to al-Biruni. It was a general rule, rather than an exception. Ibn Sina, for example, was a master of integrating scientific research in a logical and metaphysical framework and developing different methods for different disciplines. In his *al-Qanun fi Tibb* (Canons of Medicine), Ibn Sina argues that both speculative method as well as empirical observation and practice have a role in medicine. The *Canons* is a monumental work which shows Ibn Sina's power of observation and ability for empirical work. Just the breakdown of the canons reveals the scope of his medical researches: the first book presents a general introduction, dealing with physiology, nosology, aetiology, symptomatology and the principles of therapy. In the second book, the samples from the three realms of nature are presented, the strength, effect and use being given exactly. Special pathology covers the whole of the third book, with diseases enumerated in the order of where they occur in the body. Illness involving the whole body – fevers, ulcers, fractures and poisonings – are covered in the fourth book. The final fifth book deals with the mixing of drugs. In the *Canons*, Ibn Sina also developed a method for discovering whether a particular drug has curative properties. A clear descriptioin of this method is given by Abul-Barakat al-Baghdadi who followed Ibn Sina's lead in this matter.

As for experience, an example is provided by the following judgement: scammony purges human bodies of yellow bile. In this [example] the frequency of the phenomenon puts out of court [the notion] that it might be due to chance. Because of the frequency of the experience these judgements may be regarded as certain, even without our knowing the reason [for the phenomenon]. For there is certain knowledge that the effect in question is not due to chance. It must accordingly be supposed that it is due to nature or to some modality thereof. Thus the cause qua cause, though not its species or mode of operation, is known. For experimental science is also constituted by a knowledge of the cause and by an induction based on all the data of sensation; whereby a general science is reached. . . . But in the cases in which the experiment has not been completed, because of its not having been repeated in such a way that the persons, the time and the circumstances varied in everything that did not concern the determining cause, whereas this cause [remained invariable], the experiment does not prove certain knowledge, but only probable opinion.[19]

Despite the fact that Ibn Sina formulates a similar method in a more abstract form in some of his philosophical treatises, he is well aware of its limitation. It is in fact a close description of the experimental method which, Ibn Sina believed, was more suitable to medicine and did not constitute an all-embracing method of intellectual inquiry. Empirical observation and experimentation was only one method of knowing which method had its uses in particular disciplines.

Consider, for example, Ibn Sina's method of providing evidence for prophecy. In answer to someone afflicted with doubts about prophecy, he writes:

You have asked – may God set you right – that I sum up for you the substance of what I said to you for the purpose of eliminating your misgivings about accepting prophecy. You were confirmed in these misgivings because the claims of the advocates of prophecy are either logically possible assertions that have been treated as the necessary without the benefit of demonstrative argument or even dialectical proof, or else, impossible assertions on the order of fairy tales, such that the very attempt on the part of their advocates to expound them deserves derision.[20]

What follows is not an empirical demonstration of prophecy, but a carefully constructed, elaborated *physiological* proof of prophecy. Despite its inherent difficulties, the philosophical method is just as valid for Ibn Sina as empirical observation. Similarly, in his work on linguistics, law, philosophy, astronomy and Qur'anic exegesis, Ibn Sina had recourse to different methodologies, all of which were considered by him to be equally valid.

Even when a Muslim scientist, for example Ibn al-Haytham, placed a high level of confidence on observation, experimentation, and empirical analysis, he did not lose sight of philosophical and metaphysical methods. Ibn al-Haytham has been described by many western historians of science as the most secular of Muslim scientists because of his unquestioned commitment to science for science's sake. For example, his programme of methodological criticism has been compared to that of Descartes:

Truth is sought for its own sake. And those who are engaged upon the quest for anything that is sought for its own sake are not interested in other things. Finding the truth is difficult, and the road to it is rough. For the truths are plunged in obscurity. It is natural to everyone to regard scientists favourably. Consequently, a person who studies their books, giving a free rein to his natural disposition and making it his object to understand what they say and to possess himself of what they put forward, comes (to consider) as truth the notions which they had in mind and the ends which they indicate. God, however, has not preserved the scientist from error and has not safeguarded science from shortcomings and faults. If this had been the case, scientists would not have disagreed upon any point of science, and their opinions upon any (question) concerning the truth of things would not have diverged. The real state of affairs is however quite different.

Accordingly, it is not the person who studies the books of his predecessors and gives a free rein to his natural disposition to regard them favourably who is the (real) seeker after truth. But rather the person who is thinking about them is filled with doubts, who holds back with his judgement with respect to what he has understood of what they say, who follows proof and demonstration rather than the assertions of a man whose natural disposition is characterized by all kinds of defects and shortcomings. A person, who studies scientific books with a view of knowing the truth, ought to turn himself into a hostile critic of everything that he studies . . . He should criticize it from every point of view and in all its aspects. And while thus engaged in criticism he should also be suspicious of himself and not allow himself to be easy-going and indulgent with regard to (the object of his criticism). If he takes this course, the truth will be revealed to him and the flaws . . . in the writings of his predecessors will stand out clearly.[21]

But presenting al-Haytham's partiality for truth in a secular mould is a gross injustice to the celebrated scientist.[22] The fact that he demands an exacting standard of criticism is not particularly original to al-Haytham; it simply reflects the methodological concerns of Muslim jurists and scholars of *hadith*. Where al-Haytham emphasised the pursuit of science for its own sake, he also emphasised the fact that it should be pursued within a framework of philosophy and theology. Al-Haytham's reputation undoubtedly rests on his mathematics and physics – in particular his vast researches on optics which make Newton's achievements look decidedly pale – but he was equally versed in metaphysics, philosophy, medicine and Islamic theology. Science and theology played an equal part in his philosophy; moreover, despite his belief in science *per se* he sought to serve his society. In a letter dated some 13 years before his death, al-Haytham wrote:

There are three disciplines which go to make philosophy: mathematics, physical sciences, and theology. I (have) discovered that duality and controversy are natural to human beings, and man is mortal; so that, while in his youth man can ponder over these three disciplines which govern his existence on earth, he cannot do so when he grows old. So I thought over these three philosophical disciplines so far as my ratiocinative and intellectual faculties could allow me and summarized and explained them and their branches. . . . I have three objects in adopting this view: first, to be of service to those who are in search of truth; second, that the disciplines which I have been able to understand to some extent should be extended and studied; and, third, the knowledge that I possess may turn out to be the wherewithal of my old age.[23]

Thus, for al-Haytham theology was just as real as science. He believed that reality was a unitary entity which could be studied by both objective and subjective methods. For him knowledge and wisdom went hand in hand: 'I have always been haunted by the desire to seek knowledge and wisdom, and it has also dawned on me that there is nothing better than these two things to bring man closer to God', he writes.[24]

For al-Haytham the pursuit of science without an ethical framework is inconceivable. And ethics, for al-Haytham, is a pragmatic concern not some abstract philosophical notion. He equates every action with accountability on the Day of Judgement. His ethical system is based on three main points: (1) beautification and perfection of morality are not possible without the quest for knowledge; (2) truth, knowledge, and realisation of self depend for their acquisition on (a) a clear and thorough understanding of theology, (b) acquirement of good through noble deeds, and (c) avoidance of evil; and (3) the main object of beautification and perfection of morals is to enjoy a happy, eternal life in paradise in the Hereafter. It is this ethic that forms the base of al-Haytham's works.[25]

Here then in al-Haytham is a scientist from the classical period of Islam who introduced the inductive method and who is an arch believer in rationality – a belief that has led many orientalists and western historians to dub him a secularist, and Aristotelian, even a scientist in the tradition of the Enlightenment, but whose rationality is subservient to his ethical system, so much so that al-Haytham was against the Mutazilites, the founders of the rational school of thought in Islam, and wrote several treatises against them. It is in fact an irony of fate that Basra, where the Mutazilah movement had its origins, was also the birth place of one of the greatest physicists of Islam, indeed, of entire mankind, whose other major field of interest was the refutation of the rationalist doctrine of the Mutazilites.

Al-Haytham, Ibn Sina and al-Biruni are just three classical Muslim scientists in whose works we can show a synthesis of knowledge and values in operation. Modern Muslim historians have tended to study these and other scholars of early Islam largely from the perspective of their achievements and their intellectual and scientific output, and all too readily have accepted the interpretation of western historians that their contributions neatly fit the linear progress of science from the days of the city-states of Greece. Yet, even a casual examination of their methodologies reveals an entirely different system of science: a system which believes not in a single, all-pervasive method but in methods, giving due importance to all; a system that believes in rationality but in a rationality that is subservient to an ethical code; a system that is based more on synthesis and integration than on reduction and isolation; a system that is essentially interdisciplinary, that refuses to place different disciplines in watertight compartments; a system that draws its legitimacy from a worldview based on social and personal accountability; a system that draws its strength from a matrix of Qur'anic concepts and values which it seeks to promote. How can such a system fit an imagined slot in the 'linear progress of science'?

It was its emphasis on synthesis and interdisciplinary investigations, multiplicity of methods and social function and accountability before

God, which produced an institution that is largely unique to Islam and is unparalleled by any other civilisation: polymathy. The Islamic civilisation of the classical period was remarkable for the number of polymaths it produced, a natural outcome of the nature of Islamic science. The emphasis of Islamic science on a whole array of methods meant that Muslim scholars were led by the system to study, write about and contribute to many, if not all, of the different branches of learning recognised in their day. They sought to master, if not the whole field of knowledge in all its details, at least the principles of every branch of learning which then existed. One can fill volumes with the names of Muslim polymaths of early Islam; the fact that al-Jahiz (d. 868), al-Kindi (d. 873), ar-Razi (d. 925), al-Idrisi (b. 1166), Ibn Bajjah (d. 1138), Omar Khayyam (d. 517), Ibn Zuhr (d. 1162), Ibn Tufayl (d. 1185), Ibn Rushd (d. 1198), al-Suyuti (d. 1505) and thousands of other scholars of this period were polymaths is not an accident; it is a clear demonstration of the unique nature of Islamic science.

The existence of the polymath as a permanent feature of classical Islam is an indication of an intellectual attitude radically different from the dominant attitude of western civilisation. As M. J. L. Young points out,

what a contrast between this (Western) disconcerting prospect of two mutually incomprehensible areas of human experience, and the possibility of being literate in one and totally illiterate in the other, with the homogeneity of culture which we find symbolized in the career of an Avicenna (ibn Sina), who, among his many other books, wrote a concise survey of the science of medicine in verse, consisting of 1,326 stanzas; or which we find in perhaps its most striking form in Omar Khayyam, whose immortal quatrains have, at any rate in the West, overshadowed his achievements in the very different field of mathematics.[26]

The motives and the driving force behind polymathy was the paradigm that the physical universe was not inferior to the spiritual, that both, as manifestations of Allah's bounty and mercy, were worthy of study and equally valid. Moreover, the methods of studying the vast creation of God – from the mystic's ecstasy to a mother's love, to the flight of an arrow, the circumference of the earth, the plague that destroys an entire nation, the sting of a mosquito, the nature of madness, the beauty of justice, the metaphysical yearning of man – were all equally valid and shaped understanding in their respective areas of inquiry. Every creation of God is equally important as the subject of study, and each step forward in understanding and appreciating His creation brings man closer to God. In no other civilisation does His creation bring man closer to God. In no other civilisation has there been a more complete synthesis of science and religion.

It is this all-embracing emphasis on the unity of science and religion, knowledge and values, physics and metaphysics, which gives Islamic science its unique character. And, it is its insistence on multiplicity of methods which gives it a characteristic style with synthesis as its main feature. This unique nature and characteristic style means that while Islamic science values a systematic, rigorous search for truth, it is not 'objective' in a clinical sense – it does not kill off all it touches. Concern for social welfare and public interest, promotion of beauty and a healthy natural environment, as well as systematic observation and experimentation and rigorous mathematical analysis are hallmarks of Islamic science in history. As such, Islamic science is *subjectively objective*; that is, it seeks subjective goals within an objective framework. The subjective, normative goals include seeking the pleasure of Allah, the interests of the community, promotion of such eternal Islamic values as *adl* (justice), *ibadahh* (worship) and *khilafa* (man's trusteeship). This contrasts sharply with naive inquiry that is based on emotions, dogma and prejudices. Islamic science has nothing to do with the magic and the occult: it does not seek to introduce anarchy and dogmatism into the pursuit of knowledge, and neither does it seek to impose the method of one discipline on to another. It simply seeks to give equality to all methods of inquiry, and promote research and development within a framework of ethics and values which by nature are subjective. It therefore also contrasts radically with western science which excludes all other branches of knowledge and is based on a single method which is considered to be outside human values and societal concerns. Islamic science, on the other hand, seeks a *total understanding of reality*. It is thus a very holistic enterprise.

Our brief historical analysis shows Islamic science to have an entity different from that of science as it is practised today. We can summarise the nature and style of science of classical Islam as a set of norms. Table 9.1 gives this summary and also compares it with the idealised norms of 'conventional science' as developed by Ian Mitroff.[27]

Table 9.1   A comparision between western and Islamic science

Norms of western science	Norms of Islamic science
1. Faith in rationality.	Faith in revelation.
2. Science for science's sake.	Science is a means for seeking the pleasure of Allah; it is a form of worship, which has a spiritual and a social function.
3. One all-powerful method the only way of knowing reality.	Many methods based on reason as well as revelation, objective and subjective, all equally valid.
4. Emotional neutrality as the key condition for achieving rationality.	Emotional commitment is essential for a spiritual and socially uplifting scientific enterprise.
5. Impartiality – a scientist must concern himself only with the production of new knowledge and with the consequences of its use.	Partiality towards the truth: that is, as if science is a form of worship a scientist has to concern himself as much with the consequences of his discoveries as with their production; worship is a moral act and its consequences must be morally good; to do any less is to make a scientist into an immoral agent.
6. Absence of bias – the validity of scientific statements depends only on the operations by which evidence for it was obtained, and not upon the person who makes it.	Presence of subjectivity: the direction of science is shaped by subjective criteria: the validity of a scientific statement depends both on the operation by which evidence for it was obtained and on the intent and the worldview of the person who obtained it; the acknowledgement of subjective choices in the emphasis and direction of science forces the scientist to appreciate his limitations.
7. Suspension of judgement – scientific statements are made only on the basis of conclusive statements.	Exercise of judgement – scientific statements are always made in the face of inconclusive evidence; to be a scientist is to make expert, as well as moral judgement, on the face of inconclusive evidence; by the time conclusive evidence has been gathered it may be too late to do anything about the destructive consequences of one's activities.
8. Reductionism – the dominant way of achieving scientific progress.	Synthesis – the dominant way of achieving scientific progress, including the synthesis of science and values.
9. Fragmentation – science is too complex an activity and therefore has to be divided into disciplines, sub-disciplines and sub sub-disciplines.	Holistic – science is too complex an activity to be divorced and isolated into smaller and smaller segments; it is a multi-disciplinary, interdisciplinary and holistic enterprise.
10. Universalism – although science is universal, its primary fruits are for those who can afford to pay, hence secrecy is justified.	Universalism – the fruits of science are for the whole of humanity, and knowledge and wisdom cannot be bartered or sold; secrecy is immoral.

Table 9.1   continued

Norms of western science	Norms of Islamic science
11. Individualism – which ensures that the scientist keeps his distance from social, political and ideological concerns.	Community orientation; the pursuit of science is a social obligation (*fard kifaya*); both the scientist and the community have rights and obligations on each other, which ensure interdependence of both.
12. Neutrality – science is neither good nor bad.	Value orientation – science, like all human activity is value-laden; it can be good or evil, 'blameworthy', or 'praiseworthy', science of germ warfare is not neutral, it is evil.
13. Group loyalty – production of new knowledge by research is the most important of all activities and is to be supported as such.	Loyalty to God and his creations – the production of new knowledge is a way of understanding the 'signs' of God and should lead to improving the lot of His creation – man, wildlife and legitimacy for this endeavour and therefore it must be supported as a general activity and not as an elitist enterprise.
14. Absolute freedom – all restraint or control of scientific investigation is to be resisted.	Management of science: science is an invaluable resource and cannot be allowed to be wasted and go towards an evil direction; it must be carefully managed and planned for, and it should be subjected to ethical and moral constraints.
15. Ends justify the means – because scientific investigations are inherently virtuous and important for the well-being of mankind, any and all means – including the use of live animals, human beings and foetuses – are justified in the quest for knowledge.	Ends do not justify the means – there is no distinction between the ends and means of science, both must be *halal* (permitted), that is, within the boundaries of ethics and morality.

We now move on to my third argument for Islamic science; that western science carries within it seeds of its own and global destruction; and unless it is replaced by a more enlightened mode of knowing, mankind willl throw itself into an infinite abyss. Let us then look at the inherent nature of modern science.

ARGUMENT THREE

Western science is inherently destructive and is a threat to the well-being of humanity

It is a common belief, aggressively perpetuated by western historians and apologetic Muslim scholars, that today's scientists stand on the shoulders of their predecessors, especially on Greek and Muslim scientists, to place new bricks on the pyramid of knowledge. To some extent this is true: Newton did build on the work of al-Haytham, Harvey plagiarised Ibn Nafis, and Kepler drew heavily from the studies of al-Battani, al-Biruni and other noted Muslim astronomers. But, as I have just argued, Muslim scientists operated within an entirely different worldview: the nature and style of their science was different from the way science is practised today, even if some of their results became cornerstones for the development of western science. The major difference is in the belief system: while Muslim scientists believed in revelation and regarded reason as one instrument for moving toward God, western scientists believe in rationality and dismiss all other forms of knowing as nonsense.

Western science is a product of this belief. In the Islamic perspective, science is one tool for the realisation of religious goals; in the western purview, science itself is a universal religion. Thus David Landes in his classic book, *The Unbound Prometheus*, makes the point explicit: 'This world, which has never before been ready to accept universally any of the universal faiths offered for its salvation, is apparently prepared to embrace the religion of science and technology without reservation.'[28] When science passed from Islam to western Europe in the Middle Ages, the Christian ethos and the Protestant ethic, with its concern for industrial and mercantile enterprises, its military rivalries and expansive tendencies, was able subtly to transform science. The rather pathetic and sometimes violent conflict that ensued between science and religion led to the old authorities – largely the dominant irrationality of an institutionalised Church – being challenged and ultimately replaced by a cynical view of authority in all its forms. The traditional, cyclic view of life was replaced by a linear sense of time and a belief in progress. And in the advance towards ever-greater achievements it became axiomatic that Man could and would win an Empire over Nature, as Francis Bacon graphically expressed it. Science now became a quest for domination, a search for new social institutions and new meanings, and for more aesthetic and orderly structures of cognition. In its early days it was science which predominated. In sixteenth- and seventeenth-century Europe, the scientist was claiming the right to search for another truth and adopt another mode of self-realisation. But that was left-over romanticism from the classical period; by the end of the nineteenth century, science had developed a formidable organisational base and the romantic goals had given way to more pragmatic objectives of domination and control. Western science had now become an ideology.

The idea of domination has a distinguished lineage in western civilisation, and its deepest roots are to be found in the dominant religious tradition of that civilisation.[29] Only in the modern period, however, was this idea transformed into a socially significant ideology, that is, a conscious principle of legitimacy for a particular phase of western civilisation – capitalism. Science became an ideology when its method became an exclusive way of knowing reality, the only valid entry into the entire realm of objective understanding, and when it assumed the character of instrumental rationality with an exclusive focus on the rationality of means, that it is techniques for attaining a given objective in the most efficient manner. It thus, in a multitude of conceptual forms, promoted the interests of a part of society, a particular class, as the interests of the whole society.

The ideology of instrumental rationality treats its object of study (both human and non-human) as mere stuff that can be exploited, manipulated, dissected and generally abused in the pursuit of scientific progress. Thus, in the attitudes of such champions of western science as Descartes and Boyle that animals are automata are the origins of the revolting experiments that take place in modern laboratories. Once again, the legitimacy for such dehumanising actions of modern science are derived from Christian theology where, in medieval times, the idea of beast-machine was well established. It was simply carried over into the western philosophy of science because, in ontological terms, the relation between spirit and nature in the dominant Judaeo-Christian theology is analogous to the Cartesian conception of the relation between ego cognito and the realm of matter.

The inherent logic of instrumental rationality has reduced Western science into a problem-solving enterprise. It is an endless process of solving problems, of freezing or 'fixing' a subject for study, and of placing it at a 'distance' to evaluate. In its more extreme form, for example in biological reductionism, it has become what Fromm calls necrophilia, the passion to kill so as to freeze and love. Munawar Ahmad Anees summarises the inherent destructive logic of reductionism:

Reductionism, by virtue of its technique and approach, invariably leads to the disappearance of certain attributes peculiar to a given form of life. As a corollary of this, the inter-relationship established through a value structure may crumble. This is precisely what seems to be happening with modern science. Its alleged objectivity and neutrality spring from its adherence to the dictates of reductionism wherein it creates an illusion that at micro level the observations are the same as those at the macro level. It is at this critical point that the organismic holistic attributes are sacrificed at the altar of 'objectivity'. The net products of reductionism are, therefore, a methodological illusion that blurs the social significance of human science and technology, and a 'picture' of life without attributes of life is developed.

The havocs caused by the pursuit of reductionist science in the recent past are only beginning to make their impact on our lives. For example, for the first time in history, we are losing control of human reproduction. Birth control has become a misnomer, for genetic engineering has reached a state where life at its molecular level can be tampered with. Motherhood has now become a saleable commodity for we can buy eggs or even rent a uterus. In its euphoria for 'perfection' of techniques or celebration for the recombinant DNA technology, reductionists have utterly neglected the social upheavals that will certainly be triggered by such hot pursuits of mindless scientific activity.

Is there an end to reductionism? And is there an alternative to reductionism? The argument that reductionism should be allowed to take its logical course is now dangerously untenable. Moreover, the stand that reductionism is by itself a good thing because the pursuit of knowledge can only bear beneficial fruits for mankind is naive – there is no indigenous self-correcting methodology in reductionism that will stop it from the path of oblivion.[30]

The logic of reductionism reduces objectivity to objectification. Behaviourists such as J. B. Watson and B. F. Skinner have only taken to its logical conclusion this process of objectification. How far they derive their legitimacy from the promise of scientific control over human fate is obvious from the fact that behaviourism remains the official ideology of both western modernism and Soviet Marxism.

The objectification of a phenomenon yields a mythical illusion of progress. This illusion has been used to justify blatant injustice and authoritarianism: western science, as it is widely believed, is not an *ally against* authoritarianism; on the contrary, it has an in-built tendency to be an ally of authoritarianism. It is in science that justification of oppression and domination is sought. The excesses of western civilisation, colonialism and racism, class hatred and sexism, and a host of social problems that have been generated by western society are now attributed, by the magical processes of objectification, to the fixed interaction of humanity's biological nature. Inequalities of wealth and power, violence and aggression, competitiveness and xenophobia, it is claimed, far from being socially and politically determined, are being reduced to being merely the inevitable products of the human genome and the process of biological evolution.[31]

It is noteworthy how authoritarian ideologues of the new Right, from Reaganite militarists to Thatcherite monetarists to the fascists of France, Britain and Israel, have seized upon and reiterated scientific ideologies which emphasise the fixity and 'naturalness' of human nature: for instance, see the works of such sociobiologists and proponents of I.Q. theory as Robert Ardrey, Desmond Morris, Edward Wilson, Richard Dawkins, Hans Eysenck and Arthur Jensen.

These are not accidental developments: they are a logical outcome of the nature and style of western science. Most scientists, particularly in the Muslim world, have a textbook, fairy-tale image of how science works. Most textbooks which have a chapter on scientific method have various ideas about what this includes, but all of them are equally dogmatic about the three or four points they mention: observation, hypothesis, experimentation, conclusion and the like. This storybook image is taken further by presenting a linear model of 'autonomous science':

Research ⟶ Fact ⟶ Application

At best the textbook version falsifies science. In real science one works to propagate a particular hypothesis and does not start with it. Observations are often selective; experiments are carried out to support conclusions; it is often considered highly praiseworthy to be unwilling to change one's opinion in the light of latest evidence; lack of humility is highly valued; often the application of results have already been worked out; bias is freely acknowledged; and there is a great deal of emphasis on the importance of intuitive judgement.

Therefore, research activity does not always produce results leading to the true and the good. Of course, we know at least that there are other factors that play a part in the process of scientific research: curiosity and social need. Sometimes a perceived social need stimulates research, which produces results that satisfy the need. The process may throw up new problems which excite curiosity and the process repeats itself.

Curiosity ⟵ (satisfy) Fact ⟶ Application / Need ⟵ (Satisfy)

It is to the credit of some social critics of science who argue that both motivations are necessary for a healthy growth of science: pure curiosity leads to 'ivory tower' science with only haphazard application to social needs; and excessive concentration on application leads to the trivialisation of research.

To this largely dominant, but somewhat simplistic picture of how western science works, Marxist philosophers of science, most notably J. D. Bernal, have added the elements that most distort the picture. First of all scientific curiosity can be clocked by dogma and superstition. Up to the end of the nineteenth century, this dogma and superstition was generated by the institutionalised Church; today it is produced by secular institutions and the various ideologies of domination. More simply, applications of science can be distorted by commercial greed. Or science can be distorted by applications which are deformed and evil: the worst being war. War science now employs over half the scientists worldwide: all the major powers of the world spend a disproportionately large percentage of their natural resources on military science.

But this is as far as Marxist analysis of science takes us. Being a progeny of the Judaeo-Christian heritage, Marxism's faith in science as the ultimate value and the arch force for goodness and truth is unshakeable – hence the role of 'scientific' revolutions and 'scientific' socialism in Marxist theory. Marx, as opposed to many latterday Marxists and champions of the New Left, was a complete prisoner of nineteenth-century scientism and instrumental rationalilty. As Ashis Nandy has put it:

in spite of his seminal contribution to the demystification of the industrial society, he did not have a clue to the role modern science had played in the legitimation of such a society. The product of a more optimistic age, he faithfully put science outside history. That is why Stalin is not an accidental entry in the history of Marxism. He remains the brain-child of Marx, even if, when considered in the context of Marx's total vision, an illegitimate one.[32]

Recent critics of western science, including J. R. Ravetz, Theodore Roszak and Ian Mitroff, have added four more factors to the picture of how western science operates in the real world. First, is unfulfilled promises; that is, no matter how much research is done to find a solution for a pressing social need, the research remains ineffective. No matter what quantity of financial resources is poured into research, the Promethean promise remains unfulfilled. Perhaps the most obvious example here is the ever increasing, indeed maddening pursuit to conquer cancer.

Unfulfilled promises and misplaced optimism only lead to disappointments. But now we must face an even more serious outcome of the contemporary practice of western science: the ever-present shadow of ecological catastrophe. We have learned recently that science not only has an intended outcome, but it can also have many unintended, unplanned, side-effects. Indeed, beyond the first order effect of science lies a whole minefield of second and third order consequences which a scientist never imagines. As Ravetz points out, most well-meaning scientists have been

victims of what we can now see as an illusion, from which we only now are recovering; that is, that the conscious benevolent applications of science cannot do harm. This assumption, or rather faith, has a long history, back indeed to the seventeenth century. We can see it in Francis Bacon, who really believed that magic and the idea of 'power too great to be revealed' were not merely sinful, because you were getting something for nothing, but also implausible, because things do not *really* happen like that. As the vision of the world (for European peoples) lost its quality of enchantment, it became commonsense that science was really safe – effects could only be proportionate to their (material) causes. The idea of a trigger reaction, of non-linear, synergistic reaction, of an ecological system, was effectively absent from mainline scientific thinking . . . until well into the post-war period. In the absence of such ideas, one cannot imagine blunders, and cannot imagine some things with which we are now confronted as urgent problems of survival.[33]

One can plead innocence for the unforeseen outcome of one's research, however serious it may be. But one can also consciously conduct research into unethical areas and inhuman domains all in the name of curiosity. The lack of ethical control is a major factor in the destructive nature of western science. If one considers science to be a pure, virtuous activity, it is only a short step to the illusion that scientists themselves are somehow purified by the activity of research. Western science refuses to treat the scientist as a human being with weaknesses and imperfections. Rather, it claims a special status for scientists as far as the goals of science are concerned. Yet, it refuses to acknowledge that the scientist may have a vested interest in science. When one considers that science refuses to allow criticism from the outside or admit ethical constraints, one can truly appreciate how the domineering presence of science in our society has made the whole of society the prisoner of a small group of professionals who, unlike the political elite in their position, are relatively exempt from the criticism, checks and values of society.

It is, however, always possible for an individual scientist to work according to his own conscience. However, much of western science is 'big science' requiring organisations that are large scale, complex and have a tendency to take on a life of their own. There is not much scope here for an individual scientist to preserve his individuality. 'Big science' consists of hierarchically organised laboratories in which the individual scientist seeks solutions to minute segments of problems, often unaware of a connection between the overall jigsaw and the puzzle they are solving. Institutionalised science has now managed to do the impossible: it has become simultaneously a market place and vested interest. It has an organisational logic of its own; independent of the creativity of the individual scientist but dependent on, and observing, his material interest. It is this hierarchical organisation of science, with its priests and clergy, which has pre-empted basic internal criticism in science. No scientist can now say anything about science policy and scientific choices, which is not uncoloured by organisational interests of science or can be taken at its face value.

When we incorporate such factors as unrealism, the possibility of ecological blunders, the acute questions of ethics and the organisational structure of science into our picture of western science, an altogether new beast makes an appearance. This system of science has its own internal dynamic, which transforms every society it touches: indeed, the society of science cannot survive as an uncontaminated heaven of non-material values. If it continues on its present journey, its relentless logic will inevitably lead to the total destruction of man's terrestrial abode – the Promethean fire, stolen from Heaven by Man's quest for knowledge and power, burns just as fiercely as ever.

ARGUMENT FOUR

Western science cannot meet the physical, cultural and spiritual needs and requirements of Muslim societies

It is easy for us to overlook the inherent destructive nature of Western science for one very strong reason: it works. The glittering successes of Western science are many and diverse: it has enabled western civilisation to amass unimagined power and wealth; it has even relieved ordinary people of discomfort, pain, deprivation and squalor to a degree; it has made it easier for us to travel, communicate and manipulate information. These are by no means small achievements.

But the point is not that western science works. The point is that it works in a particular way that is designed to fulfil the needs and requirements of a society and culture with a specific worldview. It is designed to fashion the image of the western civilisation wherever it operates. That's why, wherever and whenever its problem-solving techniques or its products are applied, the end result is an inferior reproduction of some segment of Western society. Thus promoting the myth that both western science and western civilisation – implicitly implying their values and culture – are universal.

The prime concern of the system of western science is its own survival and extension. To do that it must give absolute priority to itself, its own societal and civilisational roots. This it does in some straightforward, mechanical way. The process, in fact, is very subtle. Glyn Ford describes the main mechanical of the process:

Science and technology depends heavily upon state finance and there is always more waiting to be done than resources available. That which is undertaken is done at the expense of alternative choices. Those who arbitrate between options do so on the basis of their own ideological presuppositions. To expect otherwise is naive. Thus the choice of the trajectory of science and technology is partisan, although this is not to suggest that the work of contemporary scientists and technologists always neatly meshes with the requirements of contemporary Western society. Developments within science and technology emerge from an adversary process in which hypotheses compete for dominance. But the judging is rigged.

New scientific laws, for example, are not brought to society like the tablets from the mountain. They emerge from a field of competing alternatives, all of which reflect, to a greater or lesser extent, aspects of the multidimensional world of nature. The determination of which is to be the victor is not a simple one. It is not determined purely on grounds of truth, content or to suit the implicit wishes of those in positions of authority. Rather it comes from a continuous and multiple series of interactions between science, scientists and society. Nevertheless, the choices that can be made are extremely limited. For mental slavery is as coercive as its physical counterpart. The values science and technology must always reflect are those material values of acquistion, unchecked and uncontrolled growth, and Darwinian competition. Spirit and compassion become marginal at best and ornamental at worst. There is an inevitability about the creation of technologies that are intensive, large-scale and highly centralized; in a word 'inhuman'.[34]

As the style and packaging of western science reflects the needs and priorities of an alien system, it can never meet the requirements of Muslim culture and society. This is largely why western science has not taken social root in Muslim countries. And this is why, in the Muslim world today, science is sporadic, isolated, largely unconnected with local needs and interests and quite incapable of self-sustenance. Most proponents of science decry the poor spending on science in the Muslim countries: but that is only an external symptom of a very deep malaise. And that malaise lies not just with Muslim societies but also with the nature and style of science that is backed and promoted.

One of the most common examples of the wide gulf between what is needed in Muslim societies and what science offers, relates to capital and labour: much of western science is geared to producing labour-saving, capital-intensive final products; yet, in the major part of the Muslim world there is an excess of labour and shortage of capital. What most Muslim people need are simple solutions to their basic problems of everyday living; what western science is geared to is producing sophisticated solutions requiring massive inputs of energy. The most common killers in the Muslim world are diarrhoea and schistosomiasis but much of science-based modern medicine is looking for cures to lung cancer, heart disease and concentrating on transplanting various bits of anatomy from one individual to another. Health problems in Muslim societies cannot be more basic: over-crowded and insanitary city life kills a high number of children and nurtures diseases such as cholera and malaria. Yet western medicine is too preoccupied with herpes and AIDS, test tube conception and cryogenic freezing. In most Muslim countries obtaining energy to cook could be a major problem for a family; while western science concerns itself with fast breeder reactors and development of nuclear missiles.

But it is not just a question of wrong priorities and emphasis, Muslim societies also have spiritual, cultural and environmental needs that western science can never fulfil. Indeed, it can only aggravate such needs. The most blatant example of this is the imposition of solutions derived from western science and technology on the Hajj environment. On the face of it the problem of the Hajj environment is simple: meeting the accommodation, transport and material needs of pilgrims visiting Makkah and Medina every year, while preserving the ecological and spiritual character of the holy areas. Since the early 1970s, almost every solution that modern technology can produce has been tried. The problems have not only become worse, but the very environment for which these solutions were sought has been destroyed. The entire environment has been turned into an extension of western society.

The methodology of reduction cannot take into consideration cultural and spiritual needs. Neither can it grapple with social complexities. Schistosomiasis has been isolated from society and has been studied in Egypt and the Sudan for over 50 years, yet a solution to this problem is not in sight because its connection with irrigation, education, the play needs of children and rural development have not been taken into account. Reductive science approaches agriculture as though it were a problem and not a way of life: that is why agricultural research in Muslim countries has not borne much fruit; it has concentrated on crop yields, developing new strains of seeds, and the use of pesticide and high yield fertiliser. The social aspects of agriculture are beyond its scope.

One can go on listing the dichotomy between the physical, social, cultural and spiritual needs of Muslim societies and what modern science has and can deliver. But the record of western science in Third World countries – including those which have developed a sophisticated infrastructure such as India and Brazil, and those which have tried to buy western science and technology such as Saudi Arabia, Libya and pre-revolutionary Iran – speaks for itself. I have documented and analysed it in considerable detail elsewhere.[35]

A WAY FORWARD

The only true way of meeting the multidimensional needs of Muslim societies is to develop a science which draws its inspiration from the cultural and spiritual ethos of the worldview of Islam and is specially geared to meeting these needs. I have argued in this essay that different civilisations had different sciences reflecting their particular worldview. I have also tried to show that Islamic science in history has a unique nature and style and that western science today also embodies within itself the Judaeo-Christian intellectual heritage. Furthermore, I have argued that western science is intrinsically destructive: the application of western science and technology in Muslim societies is playing havoc with our values and culture and is not meeting our needs and requirements. Given this backdrop, the need for a contemporary Islamic science becomes imperative.

I have argued that the worldview of Islam maintains a unified structure through a matrix of eternal values and concepts which have to be lived and which give Islam its unique character. Because Islam is a total system, these concepts permeate every aspect of human life. Nothing is left untouched: whether political structures or social organisations, economic concerns or educational curricula, environmental outlook or framework for scientific inquiry and technological pursuits. These values shape the parameters of Muslim society and guide the civilisation of Islam towards its manifest destiny.

Within the cordon of such values and concepts as *tawheed* (unity of God), *khilafa* (man's trusteeship of God's creation), *akhira* (man's accountability in the hereafter), *ibadahh* (worship of one God), *ilm* (the pursuit of knowledge), *adl* (social justice) and *istislah* (public interest), Muslim individuals and societies are free to express their individuality and meet their needs according to their wishes and resources. And indeed, throughout the history of Islam, different Muslim societies have realised these values and concerns in different ways according to their time and place. It is by this mechanism that the Islamic civilisation adjusts to change, yet retains its unique and eternal characteristics.

Contemporary Muslim societies have particular needs which have to be met within the purview of Islam. Some of these needs, like food and shelter, are common to all men. Others, such as the need to overcome dependency and technological exploitation, are a product of the particular historic situations of Muslim societies. Still others are an outcome of Muslim culture: the type of dwellings that are most suited for an Islamic way of life, cities that express the cultural and aesthetic concern of Islam, and a natural environment that exhibits the Islamic relationship between man and nature. All these needs have to be fulfilled within the value structure of Islam. They have to be fulfilled with the full realisation that Islam is a total system in which everything is interlinked, nothing compartmentalised or treated as an isolated problem. Such methods, processes and tools for meeting these needs and solving the problems of contemporary Muslim societies must be an embodiment of the culture and values of Islam. And this applies also to science, one of the most powerful tools for solving man's problems and meeting his needs.

As the history of Islamic science teaches us, a science that operates within an Islamic value structure has a unique nature and style. It is essentially a *subjectively objective* enterprise: objective solutions to normative goals and problems are sought within an area mapped out by the eternal values and concepts of Islam. In Islamic science, both the ends and means of science are dictated by the ethical system of Islam: thus, both the objectives of science as well as its tools, processes and methods have to conform to Islamic dictates. These dictates have nothing to do with dogma; but everything to do with ethics. Islamic science is beyond dogma and does not degenerate to the level of naive inquiry. It is a systematic, rigorous pursuit of truth, a rational and objective problem-solving enterprise that seeks to understand the whole of reality. It is holistic and is founded on synthesis. It seeks to understand and preserve the object of its study. It treats scientists as human beings who have weaknesses and who are part of the community and not outside it. It seeks to fulfil the needs of the vast majority and not a select few. It reflects the hopes and aspirations of the entire Muslim *ummah*. We need Islamic science because Muslims are a community of people who 'do good and forbid evil', and to show that science can be a positive force in society. We need Islamic science because the needs, the priorities and emphasis of Muslim societies are different from those that science has incorporated in Western civilisation. And, finally, we need Islamic science because a civilisation is not complete without an objective problem-solving system that operates within its own paradigms. Without Islamic science, Muslim societies will only be an appendage to western culture and civilisation. In short, we have no viable future without Islamic science.

10
Islamic Science: The Way Ahead

What is science? The definition of science is becoming increasingly difficult to pin down. In western tradition, up to quite recently, science was seen as the quest for objective knowledge of nature and reality and scientists were regarded as quasi-religious supermen, heroically battling against all odds to discover the truth. And the truths they wrestled out of nature were said to be absolute: objective, value-free and universal. As a sociologist in the 1940s described it, science reflects the character of nature: 'The stars have no sentiments, the atoms no anxieties which have to be taken into account. Observation is objective with little effort on the part of the scientist to make it so.'[1] This classical view of science as 'natural' contrasts sharply with those of Lewis Wolpert who, while arguing that science is objective and value-free, describes it as 'unnatural'. Science is special: it is counter-intuitive; scientific knowledge is beyond common sense, everyday experience and is unique and universal.[2] J. D. Bernal suggested that science is all about 'rationality, universalism' and 'disinterestedness'.[3] Lord Rutherford settled for a more elegant definition: 'science', he has been widely reported to have said, is simply 'what scientists do'.

But what do scientists *actually* do? The picture of truth-loving and truth-seeking scientists working for the benefit of humanity is rather at odds with the public conception of science and scientists. Consider, for example, what we have been reading in the serious press, over the last few months, about what scientists have been doing:

- In Porton Down research establishment in England scientists have been using live animals to test body armour. 'The animals were strapped on to trolleys and subjected to blasts at either 600 or 750mm from the mouth of the explosively driven shock tube', wrote Tom Wilkie the science editor of the *Independent*. Initially, monkeys were used in these experiments but scientists

This is the text of a public lecture at the International Conference on Science in Islamic Polity in the 21st Century, Islamabad, Pakistan, 26–30 March 1995. Organised by OIC Standing Committee on Scientific and Technological Cooperation (COMMSTECH).

later switched to shooting pigs. 'The animals were shot just above the eye to investigate the effects of high-velocity missiles on brain tissue.'[4] In the United States, in the late 1940s, teenage boys were fed radioactive breakfast cereal, middle-aged mothers were injected with radioactive plutonium and prisoners had their testicles irradiated – all in the name of science, progress and national security reported *Time* magazine. These experiments were conducted from the 1940s through to 1970s.[5]

- During the 1950s to 1970s, the *New York Times* revealed, it was mandatory for all new students of both sexes at Harvard, Yale and other elite universities of the United States, to have themselves photographed naked for a huge project designed to demonstrate that 'a person's body, measured and analyzed, could tell much about intelligence, temperament, moral worth and probable future achievements. The inspiration came from the founder of Social Darwinism, Francis Golton, who proposed such a photo archive for the British population.' From the outset, disclosed the paper, 'the purpose of these "posture photographs" was eugenic'. The accumulated data would be used for a proposal to 'control and limit the production of inferior and useless organisms'. 'Some of the latter would be penalized for reproducing ... or would be sterilised. But the real solution is enforced better breeding – getting those Exeter and Harvard men together with their corresponding Wellesley, Vasser and Radcliffe girls.' The biologist responsible for the project, W. H. Sheldon of Harvard, used the photographs to publish the *Atlas of Men*.[6]

- Scientists have discovered a gene responsible for criminal behaviour, reported the *Independent*. A few months earlier, we read that scientists had isolated a gene for homosexuality. The implication being that criminals and homosexuals are born not influenced by social or environmental factors.[7]

These revelations cast science in a radically different perspective.

What scientists actually do has been extensively examined by historians of science and sociologists of knowledge, producing a different set of definitions and explanations for science and challenging the view of science as an heroic objective adventure, above all concerns of culture and values. Thus, according to the historian Thomas S. Kuhn, science is nothing more than problem solving within a paradigm: a set of dogmas, beliefs and values. This is what most scientists do when they do 'normal science'. When the paradigm is challenged and overturned, 'revolutionary science' comes into being.[8] Paul Feyerabend, the noted philosopher of science, thinks that there is nothing special about science; indeed, there is no fundamental difference between art and science, for both lack a bed-rock of well-founded theory, practice or empirical certainty. There are no epistemological or methodological foundations for science, Feyerabend has argued and tried to demonstrate, that can command universal consent. Thus we can never hope to discover truth by scientific investigation.[9] For historian and philosopher of science Jerome R. Ravetz, science is an industry in which knowledge and power have coalesced, knowledge has been corrupted and become an instrument of control and domination.[10] The proponents of the 'strong programme', a group of historians, sociologists and philosophers of science, located at the University of Edinburgh, describe science as a distinctively western, imperialist phenomenon, concerned largely with social, political and cultural domination.[11] Robert Young, the Marxist critic of science, considers science to have nothing do with objectivity and neutrality: it is purely socially constructed. His classic essay is simply entitled 'science *is* social relations'.[12] For the sociologists Harry Collins and Trevor Pinch, 'science is a golem':

A golem is a creature of Jewish mythology. It is a humanoid made by man from clay and water, with incantations and spells. It is powerful. It grows a little more powerful every day. It will follow orders, do your work, and protect you from the ever-threatening enemy. But it is clumsy and dangerous. Without control, a golem may destroy its masters with its failing vigour ... since we are using a golem as a metaphor for science, it is also worth noting that in the mediaeval tradition the creature of clay was animated by having the Hebrew 'EMETH', meaning truth, inscribed on its forehead – it is truth that drives it on. But this does not mean it understands the truth – far from it.[13]

Feminist scholar Sandra Harding[14] considers science to be a sexist and chauvinist enterprise that promotes the values of white, middle-class males. Ashis Nandy, one of the most respected Indian thinkers, has described science as a theology of violence.[15] It performs violence against the subject of knowledge, against the object of knowledge, against the beneficiary of knowledge and against knowledge itself. To noted Indian science journalist and traditional philosopher, Claude Alvares, science is a recognisable 'ethnic (western) and culture-specific (culturally *entombed*) project, one that is a politically directed, artificially induced stream of consciousness invading and distorting, and often attempting to take over, the larger, more stable canvas of human perceptions and experience'.[16] It is as universal as toothpaste manufactured in the west, just as exploitative in its economic imperialism, it can be used, and is often used, but can be replaced with a *miswak* twig from the neem tree, or dispensed with altogether at any time because it is still largely irrelevant to *life*.

All of these different definitions and perceptions of science tell us one thing for certain: *science is a contested territory*. The various contesting claims and counter-claims about the nature of science, all containing some aspect of truth, reveal science to be a highly complex and multilayered activity. No single and simple description of science can reveal its true nature; no romantic ideal can describe its real character; no sweeping generalisation can uncover its authentic dimensions. In particular, both the extreme positions of scientific fundamentalism and fundamentalist relativism are untenable.

The idea of scientists as dedicated hermit-like lone researchers is now dangerously obsolete. Nowadays, science is an organised, institutionalised and industrialised venture. The days when individual scientists, working on their own, and often in their garden sheds, made original discoveries are really history. Virtually all science today is big science requiring huge funding, large, sophisticated and expensive equipment and hundreds of scientists working on minute problems. As such, science has become a unified system of research and application, with funding at one end of the spectrum and the end-product of science, often technology, at the other. In this system, it is not always possible for us to see where the so-called 'pure' science ends and technology begins. Moreover, in the huge and complex system that is science, it is equally impossible to say where politics and social values cease and experience mediated by nature, hence some resemblance of objectivity, takes over. The whole system is one gigantic continuum with countless feedback loops. The puritan scientists argue that while science may exist within social frameworks and depend on funding from government or political institutions, the actual cognitive formation is independent of all social and political considerations and depends exclusively on what can be seen in nature. Moreover, empiricism, the rules of evidence, testing for falsification and peer review distil out all value contents leaving pure objective reality for us all to perceive. This Weberian ideal, the requirement of *wertfreiheit* – the freedom from values or ethical neutrality – leading to separation of science and politics, just does not stand up to empirical evidence. Despite the brave attempts by the logical positivists of the Vienna Circle, most notably Popper, historians and sociologists of science have demonstrated that almost from its inception in the heydays of Robert Boyle and the English Revolution, science has been embroiled with religion, politics and capitalism. Ironically, Popper's idealised portrayal of experimenting – which is itself now seen as an ideological construct – opened science to the inspection of history of science and sociology of knowledge. Thus, there is hardly an area of modern scientific inquiry that has not been shown to have an ideological, social and cultural content. Postcolonial writers have shown the intimate connection between the emergence of modern science in the west and the rise of the empire, the evolution of scientific knowledge and the subjugation of the non-western cultures and people.[17] Furthermore, anthropologists of science, like Knorr-Cetina[18] and Bruno Latour,[19] have revealed that laws and facts of science are not so much objectively discovered as 'manufactured'. While we ought to be cautious about accepting the totally relativist position that nothing of particular significance happens in a laboratory except the social relationship of the scientists, we cannot altogether ignore the evidence from sociology and anthropology of science.

So where does this leave the heroic model of pure, value-free science? Totally discredited and in shambles. Despite this a large number of scientists, like Wolpert and Richard Dawkins,[20] and our own Abdus Salam,[21] zealously hold on to it. In contrast, the philosophical, historical, sociological and anthropological study of science has become highly sophisticated while, at the same time, becoming ever more deeply entrenched in extreme relativism. The epistemological and moral relativism of postmodern studies of science not only takes us towards absolute chaos but also leaves a few important questions unanswered.[22] Why has science been so successful in bringing prosperity to western civilisation? How is it possible for its results to be repeated across cultures? And the converse: why have different cultures, with different metaphysical axioms and social perceptions, produced universally valid scientific projects? The truth (however we describe it), as always, lies somewhere in the middle.

Considering that the modern world is largely a product of modern science and that science touches everyone's life, it is necessary for us all to understand how modern science is shaped, how its agenda is set, and how deeply (western) values are embedded in it. We need to get involved with science and make it work for us: for our needs and requirements, reflecting our concerns and values, promoting the distributive justice and equality that we cherish. As Margaret Jacob points out,

if more women and non-Western people had been involved in science at any given moment, its agenda would have been set quite differently. Most of its methods and practices and capacity for truth might look much like they do today, but the knowledge generated would have been on very different subjects, been expressed in quite different language, and in some cases been put into the service of very different (although not necessarily better) interests. Not least permitting greater access to science would further democratise its practices and generate more, not less, usable knowledge.[23]

The question is not simply of 'greater access' but actually shaping science based on different values and perceptions. From the Muslim viewpoint, it means shaping a science that is based on the values and metaphysical assumptions of Islam: what many of us have called 'Islamic science'. The first step towards a meaningful discussion of contemporary Islamic science is an appreciation of the part played by ideological and political concerns as well as values in the defining characteristics and development of modern science.

SCIENCE AND VALUES

Values enter the system of science in a number of ways. The first point of entry is the selection of the problem to be investigated. The choice of the problem, who makes the choice and on what grounds, is the principal point of influence of society, political realities of power, prejudice and value systems on even the 'purest' science. Often, it is the source of funding that defines what problem is to be investigated. If the funding is coming from government sources than it will reflect the priorities of the government – whether space exploration is more important than health problems of inner city poor, or whether nuclear power should be developed further than solar. The private sector funding, mainly from multinationals, is naturally geared towards research that would eventually bring dividends in terms of hard cash. Some 80 per cent of research in the United States is funded by what is called the 'military-industrial complex' and is geared towards producing both military and industrial applications. In the former Soviet Union, all research was funded and directed by the state.

Thus the practice of science, by and large, is regulated by the state. In some cases this can lead to obvious and transparent abuse: in the Third Reich, science was literally constructed and developed within the Nazi ideology. Our abhorrence of fascism leads us to dismiss the Nazi construction of science as inherently inferior. But as Alan Beyerchen has shown, German science under Hitler was more than a match for science anywhere in Europe and North America.[24] It not only promoted scientists of the stature of Heisenberg but also led him to ethical conduct that was diametrically opposite from the notion of science as a tool for betterment of humanity.[25] Similarly, Soviet science too was ideologically constructed. In its most extreme form, it produced Lysenkoism in genetics; but on the whole, the ideological concern for big technologies meant an emphasis on the exact sciences. Both in the case of Nazi Germany and the Soviet Union, it is easy for us to see how state ideology directed and shaped science. However, the role of ideology in shaping science in the free and democratic world is not so apparent.

But here too the link between ideology and science is just as strong. American science, for example, is tightly controlled by an alliance of the military, powerful multinationals and research universities. American militarism directs American science while American science propels American militarism: they define each other. 'Just as the technologies of the empire', writes Stuart W. Leslie,

defined the relevant research programs and conceptual categories for Victorian scientists and engineers, so the military-driven technologies of the cold war redefined the critical problems for the postwar generation of American scientists and engineers. Indeed, those technologies virtually redefined what it meant to be a scientist or an engineer. Whereas Vannevar Bush's differential analyser – a pioneer analogue computer – provided a tangible expression of the engineering values, educational practices, and critical problems of early twentieth-century science and engineering, another set of instrumental archetypes – including masers and lasers (for amplifying microwave and visible radiation), missile guidance systems, numerically or computer-controlled machine tools, and microwave radar – provides the texts for understanding the orientations of postwar science ...[26]

Devices and other equipment developed for the military not only provide new instruments for science but also shape the conceptual categories and toolkits of scientists. The computer, rocket launchers, the laser, microwave communication technologies and satellites were all developed for the 'security interest' of the United States and then became key research instruments in shaping and directing science. Instruments which appear to have purely scientific interests usually emerge from the 'Strategic Defense Initiative'. Leslie provides the following list of instruments that were a direct outcome of military research: the Hubble Space Telescope, the supersonic wind tunnels that were used in the design of successive generations of high-speed aircraft and ballistic missiles; the high-power klystrons that fuelled physics at Stanford; MIT's Whirlwind computer; the Gravity Probe B, which owed as much to military interests as in confirming Einstein's theory of general relativity; and transistor and integrated circuits.[27] When the priority of the military shifts, the direction of science changes. Thus when the Pentagon decided to shift its emphasis from radio-controlled to guided missiles, science's model of the ionosphere altered from one envisioning it as a two-dimensional mirror to one viewing it as a three-dimensional medium. Often the discussion of an emerging field is framed within the discourse of war. Just as quantum physics emerged from the concern for war, defeat, rationality, and 'the decline of the West' in Weimar Germany, so, too, the discourse of Cold War shaped American physics, aeronautics, materials science, electrical engineering and other academic fields. Electrical engineering provides an example of how power politics shapes the character of scientific knowledge. Military funding of research laboratories, such as MIT's Research Laboratory of Electronics and the Stanford Electronics Laboratories, ensured that they made defence electronics the leading edge of academic research; in the process, writes Leslie, 'they blurred conventional distinctions between science and engineering, basic and applied research, unclassified and classified material, sponsored research and education'.[28] As a result, the emphasis shifted from the pre-war curriculum of alternating current, radio, and high-voltage power transmission to problems in microwave and solid-state electronics, communications theory and plasma physics. Military orientated research and teaching feed each other, engendering a system that is totally geared towards military goals: 'Professors teach what they know. They write textbooks about what they teach. What they know that's new comes mainly from their own research. It is hardly surprising, then, that military research in the university leads to military-centred undergraduate curricula.'[29] Thus American science, which dominates the world and can be considered to be the practice of science everywhere, is deeply linked to a military culture. Its disciplinary paradigms, its experimental practices, its research and teaching programmes, reflect the security interests of the United States. Considerations of the deep involvement of science with the military ideology of nation-states had led Ashis Nandy to describe 'science as reason of state'.[30]

Ideological concerns are also sometimes brought to bear on the interpretation of scientific discoveries. Scientific findings often raise moral questions. The moral debate around Social Darwinism provides one example of how science is put in the service of a particular ideology. In the nineteenth century, social philosophers developed their ideas from the disconcerting revelations of Wallace and Darwin projecting their own views of class, wealth, race, sex, social justice and progress on their theories:

Spencer justified laissez-faire capitalism by equating economic competition with natural selection, and he drew upon a revised Malthusianism to explain why poverty was unavoidable. Engels fought the trend by pointing out how economic activity intervenes in selection, and how, as Darwin himself had recognized, cooperative behaviour can enhance survivability. Comte represented himself as siring sociology out of the biological sciences. And later, on an openly Darwinian theme, Galton founded the eugenics movement.[31]

However, ideological and political influences enter science not just in terms of funding, which defines the areas selected for research, or in the interpretation of discoveries, but also in what is actually seen as a problem, what questions are asked and how they are answered. For example, cancer rather than diabetes may be seen as a problem even though they may both claim the same number of victims. Here both political and ideological concerns, as well as public pressure, can make one problem invisible while focusing attention on another. Moreover, if for example the problem of cancer is defined as finding a cure, then the benefits of the scientific research accrue to certain groups, particularly the pharmaceutical companies. But if the function of scientific research is seen as eliminating the problems of cancer from society, then another group benefits from the efforts of research: the emphasis here shifts to investigating diet, smoking, polluting industries and the like. Similarly, if the problems of the developing countries are seen in terms of population, then research is focused on reproductive systems of Third World women, methods of sterilisation and new methods of contraception. However, if poverty is identified as the main cause of the population explosion then research would take a totally different direction: the emphasis would have to shift to investigating ways and means of eliminating poverty, developing low cost housing, basic and cheap health delivery systems and producing employment-generating (rather than profit-producing) technologies. The benefits of scientific research would go to the Third World poor rather then western institutions working on developing new methods of contraception and companies selling these contraceptives to developing countries. Thus not just the selection of problems but also framing of problems in a particular way are based on value criteria.

It can be argued that the ideological and political factors are external to science. That within science, the scientific method ensures neutrality and objectivity by following a strict logic – observation, experimentation, deduction and value-free conclusion. But scientists do not make observations in isolation. All observations take place within a well-defined theory. The observations, and the data collection that goes with them, are designed either to refute a theory or provide support for it. And theories themselves are not plucked out of the air. Theories exist within paradigms – that is, a set of beliefs and dogmas. The paradigms provide a grand framework within which theories are developed and make sense, and observations themselves have validity only within specific theories. Thus, all observations are theory laden, theories themselves are based on paradigms which in turn are burdened with a culture baggage. All of which raises the question: can there ever be such things as value-neutral, 'objective facts'? The notion that scientific 'facts' are a reflection of some reality out there is now being increasingly questioned: it is not clear whether a mere mathematical description of a phenomenon actually corresponds to some reality. Does the recently discovered subatomic particle, the top quark, which 'exists' for a mere hundredth of a billionth of a billionth of a second (long enough for 900 hundred scientists working on the problem to measure its existence) after protons are smashed together at high speed in a particle accelerator, actually exist in reality or is it simply an elegant mathematical construction that works in certain models? Similar questions have been raised about the 'truth' of scientific laws. Science uses two types of laws: phenomenological and theoretical; the distinction is rooted in epistemology. Phenomenological laws are things which we can, at least in principle, observe directly, whereas theoretical laws can be known by inference. Theoretical laws are supposed to explain phenomenological laws; and physicists have transformed theoretical laws to fundamental laws, the assumption being that they describe some basic reality in nature. In science, phenomenological laws are meant to describe and they succeed reasonably well; but fundamental equations are meant to explain, and paradoxically enough, the cost of explanatory power is descriptive adequacy. Really powerful explanatory laws of the sort found in theoretical physics do not state the truth. They are arrived at by a series of approximations: whenever theory tests reality, a host of approximation and adjustment is required. And as Nancy Cartwright, the Stanford physicist and philosopher has argued, 'the application of laws to reality by a series of *ad verum* approximation argues for their falsehood, not their truth'.[32] The fundamental laws of science do not govern objects in reality, they govern only objects in models – and the models themselves are artificial construction for the sake of convenience.

Value judgements are also at the very heart of a common element of scientific technique: statistical inference. When it comes to measuring risks, scientists can never give a firm answer. Statistical inferences cannot be stated in terms of 'true' or 'false' statements. When statisticians test a scientific hypothesis they have to go for a level of 'confidence'. Different problems are conventionally investigated to different confidence-limits. Whether the limit is 95 or 99.9 per cent depends on the values defining the investigations, the costs and weight placed on social, environmental or cultural consequences.[33] In most cases, the importance given to social and environmental factors determines the limits of confidence and the risks involved in a hazardous scientific endeavour. For example, when a dangerous chemical plant is placed in an area with an aware and politically active citizenry the risks are worked out to a high level of confidence. However, when toxic chemical plants are located in a region where the citizens themselves are ignorant of the dangers and do not command political power, the confidence levels are much more relaxed. The people of Bhopal and Chernobyl know this to their cost. Most scientists make expert value-laden decisions for and in the name of the public. Consider, for example, geologists: what could be less social and value-free then rocks? But geologists have to make seismic assessments and take decisions for locating hydroelectric or nuclear power plants, advise on beach protection, municipal building codes, transnational water resources, seabed mining, and strategic minerals supply, and lead projects on causes of acidification of lakes and on underground disposal of radioactive water. The confidence limits of each decision would be largely based on value criteria.

But it is not just in its institutions and method that science is value laden. The very assumptions of science about nature, universe, time and logic are ethnocentric. In modern science, nature is seen as hostile, something to be dominated. The western 'disenchantment of nature' was a crucial element in the shift from the medieval to the modern mentality, from feudalism to capitalism, from Ptolemaic to Galilean astronomy, and from Aristotelian to Newtonian physics. In this picture, 'Men' stand apart from nature, on a higher level, ready to subjugate and 'torture' her, as Francis Bacon declared, in order to wrestle out her secrets. This view of nature contrasts sharply with how nature is seen in other cultures and civilisations. In Chinese culture, for example, nature is seen as an autonomous self-organising entity which includes humanity as an integral part. In Islam, nature is a trust, something to be respected and cultivated and where people and environment are a continuum – an integrated whole. The conception of laws of nature in modern science drew on both Judaeo-Christian religious beliefs and the increasing familiarity in early modern Europe with centralised royal authority, with royal absolutism. The idea that the universe is a great empire, ruled by a divine logos, is, for example, quite incomprehensible both to the Chinese and the Hindus. In these traditions the universe is a cosmos to which humans relate directly and which echoes their concerns. Similarly, while modern science sees time as linear, other cultures view it as cyclic as in Hinduism or as a tapestry weaving the present with eternal time in the Hereafter as in Islam. While modern science operates on the basis of either/or Aristotelian logic (X is either A or non-A), in Hinduism logic can be four-fold or even seven-fold. The four-fold Hindu logic (X is neither A, nor non-A, nor both A and non-A, nor neither A nor non-A) is both symbolic as well as a logic of cognition and can achieve a precise and unambiguous formulation of universal statements without quantification. Thus the metaphysical assumptions of modern science make it specifically western in its main characteristics.

The metaphysical assumptions of modern science are reflected in its contents. For example, certain laws of science, as Indian physicists have begun to demonstrate, are formulated in an ethnocentric and racist way. The Second Law of Thermodynamics, so central to classical physics, is a case in point: due to its industrial origins, argues C. V. Seshadri, the Second Law presents a definition of efficiency that favours high temperatures and the allocation of resources to big industry.[34] Work done at ordinary temperature is by definition inefficient. Both nature and the non-western world become losers in this new definition. For example, the monsoon, transporting millions of tons of water across a subcontinent is 'inefficient' since it does its work at ordinary temperatures. Similarly, traditional crafts and technologies are designated as inefficient and marginalised. In biology, social Darwinism is a direct product of the laws of evolutionary theories. Genetic research appears to be obsessed with how variations in genes account for difference among people. Although we share between 99.7 and 99.9 per cent of our genes with everyone, genetic research has been targeted towards the minute percentage of genes that are different in order to discover correlations between genes and skin colour, sex or 'troublesome' behaviour. Enlightened societal pressures often push the racist elements of science to the sidelines. But the inherent metaphysics of science ensures that they reappear in new disguise. Witness how eugenics keeps reappearing with persistent regularity. The rise of IQ tests, behavioural conditioning, foetal research and sociobiology are all an indication of the racial bias inherent in modern science.

Given the Eurocentric assumptions of modern science, it is not surprising that the way in which its benefits are distributed and its consequences are accounted for are themselves ethnocentric. As Sandra Harding has argued, when scientific research improves the military, agriculture, manufacturing, health or even the environment, the benefits and expanded opportunities science makes possible are distributed predominantly to already privileged people of European descent, while the costs are dumped on the poor, racial and ethnic minorities, women, and people located at the periphery of global economic and political networks: this is the racial economy of science.[35] Science in developing countries has persistently reflected the priorities of the west, emphasising the needs and requirements of middle-class western society, rather than the wants and conditions of their own society. In over five decades of science development, most of the Third World countries have nothing to show for it. The benefits of science just refuse to trickle down to the poor.

But modern science is not only culturally biased towards the west: it represents the values of a particular class and gender in western societies. As feminist scholars have shown, science in the west has systematically marginalised women. Women, on the whole, are not interested in research geared towards military ends, or torturing animals in the name of progress or working on machines that put one's sisters out of work. But more than that, even the least likely fields and aspects of science bear the fingerprints of androcentric projects. Physics and logic, the prioritising of mathematics and abstract thought, the so-called standards of objectivity, good method and rationality – feminist critique has revealed androcentric fingerprints in all! For example, in the mechanistic model of early modern astronomy and physics, in modern particle physics, and in the coding of reason as part of ideal masculinity. The focus on quantitative measurements, variable analysis, impersonal and excessively abstract conceptual schemes is both a distinctively masculine tendency and one that serves to hide its own gendered character. Science has tried to hide its own masculine nature in other ways, by, for example, making women themselves objects in scientific investigation. It wasn't entirely accidental that sexology became a major science at the same time as women in the west were fighting for the vote and equal rights in education and employment! A number of studies have shown that scientific work done by women is invisible to men even when it is objectively indistinguishable from men's work.[36] Thus, it appears that neither social status within science nor the results of research are actually meant to be neutral or socially impartial. Instead, the discourse of value-neutrality, objectivity, social impartiality appears to serve projects of domination and control.

The history of science bears this out. The evolution of western science can be traced back to the period when Europe began its imperial adventure. Science and empire developed and grew together, each enhancing and sustaining the other. In India, for example, European science served as a handmaiden to colonialism. The British needed better navigation so they built observatories and kept systematic records of their voyages. The first sciences to be established in India were, not surprisingly, geography and botany. Western science progressed primarily because of the military, economic and political power of Europe, focusing on describing and explaining those aspects of nature that promoted European power, particularly the power of the upper classes. The disinterested commitment of European scientists to the pursuit of truths had little to do with the development of science. The subordination of blacks in the ideology of the black 'child/savage' and the confinement of white women in the cult of 'true womanhood' emerged in this period and are both a byproduct of the Empire. While the blacks were assigned animal and brutish qualities, the white women were elevated and praised for their morality. While the blacks were segregated and enslaved, the women were placed in narrow circles of domestic life and in conditions of dependency. Racist and androcentric evolutionary theories were developed to explain human behaviour and canonised in the history of human evolution. The origins of western, middle-class social life, where men go out to do what men have to do, and women look after the babies and work in the kitchen, are to be found in the bonding of 'man-the-hunter'; in the early phases of evolution women were the gatherers and men went out to bring in the beef. Now this theory is based on little more than the discovery of chipped stones that are said to provide evidence for the male invention of tools for use in the hunting and preparation of animals. However, if one looks at the same stones with different cultural perceptions, say one where women are seen as the main providers of the group – and we know that such cultures exist even today – you can argue that these stones were used by women to kill animals, cut corpses, dig up roots, break down seed pods, or hammer and soften tough roots to prepare them for consumption. A totally different hypothesis emerges and the course of the whole evolutionary theory changes.

Thus the cultural, racial and gender bias of modern science can be easily distinguished when it is seen from the perspective of non-western cultures, marginalised minorities and women. The kind of questions science asks when seeking to explain nature's regularities and underlying causal tendencies, the kind of data it generates and appeals to as evidence for different types of questions, the hypothesis that it offers as answers to these questions, the distance between evidence and the hypothesis in each category, and how these distances are traversed – all have the values of the white, middle-class men embedded in them. Put simply, this implies a relativism in science as in any other sphere of human knowledge.

Given the truly monumental evidence for deep ideological, political and cultural fingerprints in modern science, why do scientists still insist on the neutrality for their enterprise? Indeed, some scientists have even suggested that all the evidence gathered from historical, philosophical, sociological and anthropological studies of science is nothing more than a conspiracy against science of left-wing academics![37] The myth of neutral science not only ensures the power and prestige of science in society but enables it to perform an omnipotent function in shaping the modern world. The idolisation and mystification of science, the insistence on its value-neutrality and objectivity, is an attempt not only to direct our attention away from its subjective nature but also from the social and hierarchical structure of science. Whenever we think of 'the scientists' we imagine white men in white coats: the sort of chaps we see in advertisements for washing powder and skin care preparations, standing in a busy laboratory behind a Bunsen burner and distillation equipment telling us how the appliance of science has led to a new and improved soap or cold cream. This view of the scientists is not far from reality. True power in science belongs to white, middle-aged men of upper classes. Everyone else working in science – women, minorities, and Third World researchers, even white men of lower classes are actually basically rank and file laboratory workers. The social hierarchy within science by and large preserves absolute social status, the social status scientific workers hold in the larger society. The people who make decisions in science, who decide what research is to be done, what questions are going to be asked, and how the research is going to be done are a highly selective, tiny minority. These folks have the right Ivy League background, the contacts to get the necessary appointments and then further contacts to secure funding for their research projects. The actual execution of scientific research, the grinding and repetitive laboratory work, is rarely done by the same person who conceptualises that research and even the knowledge of how to conduct research is rarely possessed by those who actually do it. This is why the dominant (western) social policy agendas and the conception of what is significant among scientific problems are so similar. This is why the values and agendas important to white, middle-class men pass through the scientific process to emerge intact in the results of research as implicit and explicit policy recommendations. This is why, modern science has become an instrument of control and manipulation of non-western cultures, marginalised minorities and women.

To appreciate the social structure of science, consider the fact that science in Britain is controlled by less then 400 men. Or the fact that scientists at the National Research Centre in Cairo, the largest research establishment in Africa, work largely on American projects for which Egypt is paid in kind by wheat! Both China and India have huge scientific manpower yet they are totally on the margins of global science. India, with its relatively well-developed scientific infrastructure, including scientific laboratories, universities, a network of scientific journals, and large number of scientists and researchers, is the Third World's scientific superpower. Both countries have a long history of scientific research and both have achieved considerable success: both have advanced physics facilities, a growing high-tech industrial base and universities of international standards. But both are located firmly on the periphery of science because science is highly centralised and those who control and manage it are concentrated in a small number of industrialised countries. The scientific communications system is also centralised and controlled by the major research-producing nations. While there are between 60,000 and 100,000 scientific journals worldwide, only about 3,000 are indexed by the Institute for Scientific Information (ISI), which keeps track of 'significant', internationally circulated science: most of the science that happens in non-western countries is considered irrelevant and unworthy of attention. It is publications that are indexed by institutions like ISI that communicate the major findings of scientific disciplines, that are read by scientists throughout the world, and that are cited and used by other scientists for their own work. Most of these journals are edited by senior scientists in America and Europe who guard their territory jealously and ruthlessly. It is these individuals who define what is science and what is of interest globally. Scientists with different interests or concerns find it almost impossible to be published in these journals. Databases and information systems, so important for scientific work, are also located in the industrialised countries who own the information as well as control access to it. This system not only ensures that science in non-western countries remains on the periphery but actually transforms it into an appendage of the western system of science. Much of the science in the Third World is led by scientists who were educated in the west. For example, in the early 1990s, more than 10,000 scientists from China and about 60,000 from India obtained their doctorates from the United States. When these scientists return to their homelands, having imbibed particular models of science and research, they promote the same research with the same priorities and emphasis. Thus, science in the Third World serves the needs and goals of industrial societies – albeit in a rather subservient and marginal role. The social structure of science even kept the Soviet Union, despite the fact that it built the world's largest scientific and technical establishment, firmly on the margins.

So, wherever we look in science, from its funding to its methodology, facts and laws to its control and management, we see values in action. In fact, even if we were to ignore all other arguments and evidence, the very claim of modern science to be value-free and neutral would itself mark it an ethnocentric and a distinctively western enterprise. Both claiming and maximising cultural neutrality is itself a specific western cultural value: non-western cultures do not value neutrality for its own sake but emphasise and encourage the connection between knowledge and values. By deliberately trying to hide its values under the carpet, by pretending to be neutral, by attempting to monopolise the notion of absolute truth, Western science has transformed itself into a dominant and dominating ideology.

To believe, to pretend, to insist in the neutrality of science is to be a dupe and a victim of western domination and control. To break free from the suffocating hold of the western scientific knowledge system, and to make science work for ourselves, we need to consciously strive towards shaping a science that is an embodiment of our norms and values. The function of the debate on a contemporary Islamic science is to explore how this can be done.

ISLAMIC SCIENCE

The debate on meaning, nature and characteristics of a contemporary Islamic science really started when I first published a cover story on science in the Muslim world in *Nature*.[38] In the 1970s, the rise of OPEC, the Iranian revolution and a growing consciousness in Muslim societies of their cultural identity led many scientists and academics as well as institutions to emphasise the distinctive scientific heritage of Islam. I discovered this when I systematically went around the Muslim world, from Morocco to Indonesia, visiting scientific institutions, looking at research and evaluating the problems and potentials of Muslim countries: the results emerged as *Science, Technology and Development in the Muslim World*.[39] The reflections on the history of Islamic science generated a question of contemporary relevance: how can modern Muslim societies rediscover the spirit of Islamic science as it was practised and developed in history? I put this question, on behalf of *Nature*, to Muslim scientists in several countries. A year later, in 1980, I travelled, once again, throughout the Muslim world with the support of *New Scientist* and wrote another cover story, followed by a number of essays exploring and extending the theme of Islamic science.[40] These articles and essays led to a number of international seminars and conferences – most notably the series of seminars on 'Science and Technology in Islam and the West: A Synthesis' held under the auspices of the International Federation of Institutes of Advance Studies in Stockholm (24–27 September 1981) and Granada (31 May-2 June 1982);[41] the 'International Conference on Science in Islamic Polity – Its Past, Present and Future' backed by the Organization of the Islamic Conference and held in Islamabad, Pakistan (19–24 November 1983);[42] and 'The Quest for a New Science' conference organised by the Muslim Association for the Advancement of Science (MAAS), in Aligarh, India (8–11 April 1984)[43]

– where ideas relating to Islam and science were explored further. The conferences provided a launchpad for the debate and revealed a great deal of confusion around the whole notion of Islamic science and its meaning and relevance to contemporary times.

That the idea of a contemporary Islamic science is fraught with difficulties was recognised by all those who participated in the early discussions. Even the meaning and relevance of the term itself came into question. As Ravetz has pointed out, the term 'science' has come to mean a specifically modern, European and secular view of the world. Thus, 'Islamic science' appears as a self-contradictory concept. But

this would be the case with any sort of science with a religious description; thus even though modern science was created with a Christian culture, the term 'Christian science' is now firmly associated with a belief system that all scientists would strenuously reject. Those whose priority is to Islam rather than to the scientific worldview must therefore reckon with the consequences of a half millennium of history in this sphere as in others. The result of this heritage is that a double difficulty faces anyone who would construct, or reconstruct, a characteristically Islamic science. First, science as we now understand it is historically rooted in Christianity; and second, its practical consequences in the spheres of ideas have been to render all religion irrelevant.[44]

These problems were anticipated; as were the objections of conventional positivists like the Nobel laureate, Abdus Salam. Relativism in science is, of course, anathema to positivists who have both an image and a myth to maintain. However, positivist defence of the purity of western science has now turned into scientific fundamentalism, as illustrated by the semi-literate diatribe of Pervez Hoodbhoy.[45] Perhaps, recent developments in eugenics, patenting of genes as a result of the Human Genome Project, and the efforts in theoretical physics to produce a Theory of Everything that can be proudly displayed on a T-shirt and the emergence of complexity, would change the perceptions of the positivists. Anyhow, how long can the positivists ignore the advances in philosophy and history of science and sociology and anthropology of knowledge?

What came as a total surprise was the influence of the ontological tendency on the debate. For many Muslim scientists and scholars, Islamic science amounted to little more than the study of the nature of things in an ontological sense. Two main strands emerged from this approach: the mystical and the apologetic, the latter I have dubbed 'Bucaillism'. In the mystical perception, the material universe is studied as an integral and subordinate part of the higher levels of existence, consciousness and modes of knowing. Thus, here we are talking about science not as a problem-solving enterprise, but more as a mystical quest for understanding the Absolute. In this universe, conjecture and hypothesis have no real place; all inquiry must be subordinate to the mystical experience. This school of thought, led by Seyyed Hossein Nasr, Iranian scholar and follower of the esoteric sect of Frithjof Schuon, has a hypnotic effect on the minds of many proponents of Islamic science.[46] Nasr also has a very specific position on Islamic science in history. For him, all science in the Muslim civilisation was 'sacred science', a product of a particular mystical tradition – namely the tradition of gnosis, stripped of its sectarian connotations and going back to the Greek neo-platonists.[47] In his historical works, Nasr has concentrated exclusively on such matters as the occult, alchemy and astrology at the expense of vast amounts of work done on exact sciences in an attempt to show that Islamic science in history was largely 'sacred science'. (Not surprisingly, Nasr's rewriting on the Islamic history of science has been strongly refuted not just by Muslim historians of science like Fuat Sezgin and Ahmad al-Hassan but also by a string of western historians such as David King and Donald Hill.) To Nasr and his followers, like Osman Bakr, 'traditional science' does not mean science as it has existed in Muslim tradition and history, but esoteric products produced within the tradition of Islamic mysticism or Sufism. Traditional science is *science sacra*, the Science of Ultimate Reality, as thought by Sufi masters and mystics of other traditions. The goal of Islamic science today, they argue, is to rediscover the classical Islamic esoteric traditions and its sacred nature.

Bucaillism is a highly toxic combination of religious and scientific fundamentalism. Bucaillists try to legitimise modern science by equating it with the Qur'an or to prove the divine origins of the Qur'an by showing that it contains scientifically valid facts. Bucaillism grew out of *The Bible, the Qur'an and Science* by Maurice Bucaille, an eccentric and authoritarian French surgeon.[48] Bucaille examines the holy scriptures in the light of modern science to discover what they have to say about astronomy, the earth, animal and vegetable kingdoms. He finds that the Bible does not meet the stringent criteria of modern knowledge. The Qur'an, on the other hand, does not contain a single proposition at variance with the most firmly established modern knowledge, nor does it contain any of the ideas current at the time on the subjects it describes. Furthermore, the

Qur'an contains a large number of facts which were not discovered until modern times. Bucaille's book, translated into almost every Muslim language from the original French, has spouted a whole genre of apologetic literature (books, papers, journals) looking at the scientific content of the Qur'an. From relativity, quantum mechanics, big bang theory to the entire field of embryology and much of modern geology has been discovered in the Qur'an. Conversely, 'scientific' experiments have been devised to discover what is mentioned in the Qur'an but not known to science – for example, the programme to harness the energy of the *jinn*; or the project backed by the World Muslim League to prove the validity of the famous fly 'hadith' which states that if one wing of a fly falls into something you are drinking dip the other one in as well for it may contain the antidote. This sort of attempt to put science in the service of ontological causes is based on an acute inferiority complex which demands that the superiority of the Qur'an must be demonstrated by scientific validity and on the mistaken understanding of the ability and power of science. Unfortunately, this is the dominant perception of the relationship between science and Islam in the Muslim world.

So what do we actually mean by Islamic science? The science part of the term here emphasises the fact that we are talking about *science*: as an organised, systematic and disciplined mode of inquiry based on experimentation and empiricism that produces repeatable and applicable results universally, across all cultures. Although science, in our perspective, incorporates the rich heritage of Muslim civilisation, we are essentially talking about contemporary science. Where work, theories and results of earlier Muslim scientists are incorporated in the contemporary venture, they have to be updated to the level of current thought. The Islamic element of the terms suggests that values and assumption shaping this science are those of the worldview of Islam. However, we are not talking about 'Islamisation' of science as though Islam was some sort of boot polish which is used to put an Islamic gloss on science. What we are concerned with are the universal values of Islam that emphasise justice, unity of thought and ideas, a holistic approach to the study of nature and social relevance of intellectual and scientific endeavour. In this framework, fragmentation, meaningless and endless reduction and appropriation of god-like powers, or monopoly of truth and marginalisation and suppression of other forms of knowledge are shunned. At this juncture, the nature of what is meant by Islamic science would be further clarified by restating Munawar Ahmad Anees' categories of what it is *not*:

1. Islamised science, for its epistemology and methodology are the products of Islamic worldview that is irreducible to the parochial western worldview.
2. Reductive, because the absolute macroparadigm of *tawheed* links all knowledge in an organic unity.
3. Anachronistic, because it is equipped with future-consciousness that is mediated through means and ends of science.
4. Methodologically dominant, since it allows an absolute free-flowering of method with the universal norms of Islam.
5. Fragmented, for it promotes polymathy in contrast with narrow disciplinary specialisation.
6. Unjust, because its epistemology and methodology stand for distributive justice with an exacting societal context.
7. Parochial, because the immutable values of Islamic science are the mirror images of the values of Islam.
8. Socially irrelevant, for it is 'subjectively objective' in thrashing out the social context of scientific work.
9. Bucaillism, since it is a logical fallacy.
10. Cultish, for it does not make an epistemic endorsement of Occult, Astrology, mysticism and the like.[49]

To begin with this perspective changes our approach to science from the conventional secular to an Islamic attitude. The Islamic approach to science is to recognise the limitations of human reason and human mind and acknowledge that all knowledge comes from God. This was the goal of the 'science in Islamic polity' debate that began with the First International Conference on Science in Islamic Polity (19–24 November 1983). Within an Islamic polity – that is, an idealised 'Islamic state' – the principles and injunctions of Islam which are the basis of the state, it was argued, would automatically guide science in the direction of Islamic values. Individual Muslim scientists would also bring their own values to bear on their work. The 'Statement on scientific knowledge seen from Islamic perspective', issued by the Conference states that science is one way in which humanity seeks 'to serve the Supreme Being by studying, knowing, preserving and beautifying His creation'. The Islamic framework seeks a 'unifying perspective, combining the pursuit of science and the pursuit of virtue in one and the same individual'. The 'Islamabad Declaration' also called for the creation of 'the Islamic science and technology system' by the end of the century.[50] Although this is the essential first step, there are a number of problems with this perspective. Perhaps the major problem is the definition of an Islamic polity: we do not really know what constitutes a contemporary Islamic polity. The examples before us of states that claim to be 'Islamic' hardly provide us with confidence: Saudi Arabia, Iran, the Sudan and Pakistan. It seems that the label Islamic is being used here to justify authoritarianism, naked oppression, suppression of dissent and criticism, and state violence against the people. How can science, any science, develop in such states? Moreover: apart from the fact that the emphasis on Islamic values in this perspective has remained largely at the level of rhetoric, science is still seen in similar terms to those of the western paradigm as neutral and value-free. Not surprisingly, much of the work done at the national and international level within the framework of the Standing Committee on Scientific and Technological Cooperation (COMSTECH) of the Organization of the Islamic Conference, has been very conventional and concerned largely with nuclear physics, biotechnology and electronics. There is, for example, no real concern with building indigenous science, identifying areas of national concerns and needs, or changing the direction of science towards the principles of Islam or the societal needs of Muslims. Replacing 'nature' with Allah in science textbooks may provide a psychological balm for our inferiority complex but it does not solve any real problems.[51]

In contrast, both the Ijmalis, a group of independent scholars and thinkers who have championed a future-orientated critique of contemporary Muslim thought, and the Aligarh school, which has evolved around the Center for Studies on Science in Aligarh, India, have argued that the practice of science must change in Muslim countries if a contemporary Islamic approach to science is to have any meaning. The Ijmalis emphasise the 'repulsive facade' of the metaphysical trappings of western science, the arrogance and violence inherent in its methodology, and the ideology of domination and control which has become its hallmark. These things are inherent both in the assumptions of western science as well as its methodology. Thus attempts to rediscover Islamic science must begin by a rejection of both the axioms about nature, universe, time and humanity as well as the goals and direction of western science and the methodology which has made meaningless reductionism, objectification of nature and torture of animals its basic approach. But science in this framework is not an attempt to reinvent the wheel; it amounts to a careful delineation of norms and values within which scientific research and activity is undertaken. At the

Stockholm Seminar in 1981, Muslim scientists identified a set of fundamental concepts of Islam which should shape the science policies and scientific activity of Muslim societies.[52] The concepts generate the basic values of Islamic culture and form a parameter within which an ideal Islamic society progresses. There are ten such concepts, four standing alone and three opposing pairs: *tawheed* (unity), *khalifa* (trusteeship), *ibadahh* (worship), *ilm* (knowledge), *halal* (praiseworthy) and *haram* (blameworthy), *adl* (social justice) and *zulm* (tyranny), and *istislah* (public interest) and *dhiya* (waste). When translated into values, this system of concepts embraces the nature of scientific inquiry in its totality: they integrate facts and values and institutionalise a system of knowing that is based on accountability and social responsibility. How do these values shape scientific and technological activity? Usually, the concept of *tawheed* is translated as unity of God. It becomes an all-embracing value when this unity is asserted in the unity of humanity, unity of person and nature and the unity of knowledge and values. From *tawheed* emerges the concept of *khilafa*: that mortals are not independent of God but are responsible and accountable to God for their scientific and technological activities. The trusteeship implies that 'man' has no exclusive right to anything and that we are responsible for maintaining and preserving the integrity of the abode of our terrestrial journey. But just because knowledge cannot be sought for the outright exploitation of nature, one is not reduced to being a passive observer. On the contrary, contemplation (*ibadahh*) is an obligation, for it leads to an awareness of *tawheed* and *khilafa*; and it is this contemplation that serves as an integrating factor for scientific activity and a system of Islamic values. *Ibadahh*, or the contemplation of the unity of God, has many manifestations, of which the pursuit of knowledge is the major one. If scientific enterprise is an act of contemplation, a form of worship, it goes without saying that it cannot involve any acts of violence towards nature or the creation nor, indeed, could it lead to waste (*dhiya*), any form of violence, oppression or tyranny (*zulm*) or be pursued for unworthy goals (*haram*); it could only be based on praiseworthy goals (*halal*) on behalf of public good (*istislah*) and overall promotion of social, economic and cultural justice (*adl*). Such a framework, argue the Ijmalis, propelled Islamic science in history towards it zenith without restricting freedom of inquiry or producing adverse effects on society. When scientific activity was guided by the conceptual matrix of Islam, it generated a unique blend of ethics and knowledge. It is this blend – which produces a distinctive philosophy and methodology of science – that distinguishes Islamic science from other scientific endeavours. Rediscovering a contemporary Islamic science, argue the Ijmalis, requires using the conceptual framework to shape science policies, develop methodologies, and identify and prioritise areas for research and development.[53] Of course, other concepts and values must be brought into play in shaping a contemporary Islamic science: the ten concepts suggested are not meant to be exhaustive; they provide a minimal framework within which scientific inquiry must take place. The Aligarh school has added a number of other concepts to this framework, for example, *akhira* (accountability in the Hereafter), and has explored the relationship between *iman* (acceptance of belief) and *ilm* at length.[54] However, the point is that Islamic concepts and values lead to a radical change in the direction and methods of science from the dominant style and practice of science. Imagine a biology without vivisection or animal experimentation; or physics based on synthesis rather than reduction; materials research based on local and traditional materials; medicine incorporating the wealth of indigenous traditions; research and development focused on indigenous problems rather than prestige science and on empowering the populace rather then marginalising or victimising them. Only by developing science policies within the framework of the fundamental concepts of Islam, bringing these values to the level of the laboratory, and recognising the complexity of the issues and the difficulties involved in solving the problems generated by western science, can we develop a contemporary relationship between Islam and science.

Both Buciallism and the mystical fundamentalism has fragmented the debate on Islamic science, drawing it away from pragmatic and practical concerns. As Andrew Jamison has pointed out, the attempts to develop an Islamic science during the last 15 years have repeated the same process and mistakes as the efforts to develop a 'science for the people' went through in the early 1970s: 'in both cases, a critical identification of problems leads to an overly ambitious formulation of an alternative that has proved impossible to realize in practice. While the alternative becomes ever more extreme and absolute in terms of rhetoric, it thus fails to solve the particular problems that were initially attributed to Western science'.[55] While there is dire need for more thorough explorations on the theoretical framework for Islamic science, it is also necessary for those concerned with Islamic science to turn their attention towards pragmatic policy and methodological work. So, how do we proceed from here?

THE WAY AHEAD

Perhaps, the most immediate need that the Islamic science movement faces is that of defragmentation. Without some theoretical consistency the Islamic science project will continue to be trapped in meaningless ontological discussions that have no real solutions. We need to separate the thought of Islamic science from what Parvez Manzoor has described as its 'unthought':

One of the great unthoughts of our discourse is the relationship between the traditional Sufi metaphysics and the knowledge-generating societal activity that we mean by Islamic science. Given the fact that the task of delineating the metaphysics of Islamic science has been appropriated by the mystically-minded Muslim intellectuals, something which, perhaps, has been instrumental in stifling growth of a societal and empirical outlook – the *sine qua non* of any 'scientific' perception – our discourse cannot be sustained by this ahistorical, asocietal epistemology any longer.[56]

A similar break is needed from the unthought of modern science: all pretense to the neutrality of science, along with the notion that science is the pursuit of some romantic truth, must now be abandoned. There were always problems with the assertion that the goal of science is to generate truth since one of the hallmarks of science – its claims to scientific objectivity – is that results of its inquiry must always be seen to be open to revisions in the face of new, contradictory empirical evidence. In post-Popper days, it was accepted that no empirical observation could prove a hypothesis true; it could only prove it false. But the ideal of falsification too is now in shambles. Both historians and sociologists have shown that scientific establishment tends to be stubborn when faced with evidence that refutes dominant theories: 'young theories must be retained in the face of occasional or even frequent falsifying observations: favoured older theories are usually retained until they are forced into retirement by the scientific community's shift in allegiance to an alternative; any theory can be retained as long as its defenders hold enough institutional power to explain away potential threats to it'.[57] When the ideal of falsification has itself been shown to be false, what use is the concept of truth in science? The whole notion of truth in science is

inextricably linked to objectivism and its absolutist standards. 'Less false' claims are all the procedures of the sciences (at best) can generate: the hypothesis passing empirical and theoretical tests is less false than all the alternatives considered. This gap between the best procedures humans have come up with for weighing evidence and the unachievable procedures that a truth standard requires (e.g., testing all possible alternative hypotheses) gives more reason for thinking past objectivism and relativism. Nostalgia for the possibility of certain foundations for our knowledge claims can more easily be left behind us as part of the safety net we no longer need in order to make the best judgments we can about nature and social relations. Who needs truth in science? Only those who are still wedded to the neutrality ideal.[58]

Thus renouncing the chimera of neutrality also means relinquishing the idyllic notion of science as the pursuit of truth. However, abandoning neutrality does not mean giving up the ideal of objectivity. When values are brought into play in shaping science, objectivity does not suddenly evaporate – only *objectivism* is knocked out. In shaping science with Islamic values, we are openly acknowledging the roles that values play in science. This is why in *Explorations in Islamic Science*, I described Islamic science as 'subjectively objective'; Sandra Harding, more appropriately, calls the same process 'strong objectivity' – that is, an objectivity that honestly declares its values and subjective elements up front. From the alleged neutrality and objectivism of science, we thus have to move forward towards strong objectivity.

Strong objectivity is the basis on which we need to develop models of Islamic science policies. Using the matrix of the fundamental concepts of Islam, Islamic science policies have to be developed both at the level of Muslim countries as well as the transnational level of Muslim community: the *ummah*. The problems and potentials of Muslim countries are complex and varied; not all Muslim countries have the potential to solve many, or indeed any, of their problems within the limits of their own resources. But collectively, the Muslim world possesses enough resources to solve most of its problems. Thus national weaknesses in scientific research have to be tackled at regional levels by joint research endeavours. At present, most Muslim countries either have no science policy at all or have policies that make science subservient to economic or military policy or give some notional lip service to science in national development plans. We therefore need to develop mechanisms by which Islamic science, as is dictated by the notion of *ilm*, is moved to the centre of Muslim cultural, social and economic life. In other words, Islamic science, as pursuit of objective knowledge and as *ibadahh*, occupies the same place in Muslim everyday concerns as prayer, fasting and other forms of worship. However, given the current status of Muslim societies this is a tall order.

If the discourse of Islamic science is to move from the pages of scholarly books and journals into the real world, it must receive serious support from Muslim states. Conventionally, it has been argued that a country must spend at least 1 per cent of its gross national product on science to give science its due. But most Muslim countries have not even managed that. However, as the newly industrialised states of South-East Asia have shown, those who are really serious about science, and hence viable development, have to devote far greater amounts to science. Malaysia, for example, has poured as much as 10 per cent of its GNP into science and education: the results can be seen in the level of its achievements from almost 100 per cent literacy to its scientific infrastructure to its high-technology manufacturing base. Transforming Muslim societies to knowledge-based societies requires an even greater level of commitment. A science policy that is justified with the adjective 'Islamic', or a state that claims to be an 'Islamic state', must be committed totally to the endeavour of knowledge generation. Islam and ignorance are antonyms: even though the two seem to be bosom pals in contemporary times!

However, the development of Islamic science policies cannot be left only to states: administrative services, experts, ministries and faceless bureaucracies. It has to reflect both *istislah*, that is public interest, as well as public participation. Thus any science policy that is worthy of the label 'Islamic' must actively involve the citizens in its formation. The participation of the citizens in decisions of science policy assumes an aware and well-informed public which itself requires the transformation of scientific activities into social institutions. Here, the recognition by the state that science plays an important part not just in the modern world, but also in creating an informed, tolerant, socially aware and enlightened Islamic society, has to be the first and necessary step. But individuals and communities themselves cannot be passive on this issue: scientific *ilm* has a direct bearing on our individual and communal lives and it is an obligation that we have to meet, whatever the sacrifices. We thus need to discover how we can redirect the religious energies of our communities, which are currently being used largely for destructive purposes, towards creating *ilm*-based societies.

Both at the national level and the level of *ummah*, Islamic science policies have to identify specific areas for target research – research geared to solving the most pressing and urgent problems of our societies – and the place with the best potential for conducting this research. Thus at a national level, major material, health, environmental and social problems must all have designated research centres devoted to target-orientated research. Here, both public as well as private sectors must play an equal role in financing and promoting research and development activities. In each area of public concern, careful choices of institutions, fields and foci has to be made. Similarly, we need to identify areas of research at the level of the *ummah* which reflect its current problems and needs. Consider, for example, that almost three-quarters of all the political refugees in the world are Muslims. There ought to be a centre of excellence somewhere in the Muslim world devoted exclusively to the problems of refugees: developing materials for quick and clean temporary housing, efficient and cheap methods for supplying emergency water, mechanisms for providing basic health care and preventing the spread of diseases and other systems for reducing the hardship and relieving the misery of the helpless and innocent victims of political turmoil. Certain essential areas of research which would be too much of a burden on individual Muslim countries, for example advanced computer systems or molecular biology, need to be promoted at the level of the Muslim world. Here, we need to identify areas of research that could become crucial for the survival of Muslim societies in the future as well as develop mechanisms for joint finance and management of a string of international centres of excellence located in the major centres of the Muslim world. Some thought to developing long-term linkages between scientific and research institutions within the Muslim world is also essential. Some Muslim countries like Malaysia, Turkey and Egypt have reasonably well-developed scientific infrastructures: their experience in knowledge production needs to be passed on to other Muslim states and contacts and linkages have to be established so that resources can be pooled and common problems tackled more effectively.

Science that is actively shaped and directed by an open set of values, will, of course, be resisted by the puritan strand of Muslim scientists arguing that 'pure' and 'fundamental' research cannot be interfered with. This research has to be done for its own sake. However, we have to vigorously resist any notion that scientists and researchers are helpless to make choices among envisionable future lines of research and development, or that they are totally dependent on the science of the industrialised countries. Whatever view we may hold of research already undertaken, it is wrong to think that not-yet-accomplished research, which cannot be undertaken without commitment of will and resources, is anything other than value-laden. And, given the complexity of scientific work and the rate of contemporary changes, it would be simple-minded not to recognise that at the moment of its emergence new knowledge could have beneficent as well as maleficent potential that demands our constant attention: 'questions of practical ethics always lie in *what to do next*'.[59]

In our attempts to rediscover Islamic science we have to allow ample space for the growth and development of traditional knowledge. Muslim countries have a valuable, although largely untapped reservoir of indigenous knowledge and experience on medicine, agriculture and natural resources. Islamic medicine, for example, is a highly sophisticated system of medicine and health care that led the world for some eight centuries. There is a very good reason why it appears a little outmoded: during the colonial period, it was systematically suppressed, outlawed and marginalised so that western medicine could take its place. Originally, Islamic medicine was a system that progressed by continuous research. However, both due to the decline of Muslim civilisation and the fact that research on and teaching of Islamic medicine was prohibited by colonial powers, its development ceased around the middle of the eighteenth century. So what we have is a system that reflects the contents of the medicine of that period. However, if research on Islamic medicine was appropriately promoted, it would develop and bloom into a fully-fledged alternative system of medicine that could easily be better than the system of modern, Western medicine. Similarly, traditional agricultural and water management systems have proved to be highly effective and ecologically sound. For example, the traditional 'chain wells', known as *karez* in Persian and *qanat* in Arabic, have been shown to be superior to modern irrigation schemes.[60] These ingenious systems consist of one or more mother wells drained through a network of tunnels. For centuries before the arrival of the tubewells, the ecologically sound and the exceptionally durable *qanats* served as the principal means for supplying water for irrigation to villages and towns. Research on indigenous knowledge has revealed that valuable traditional science is available in such fields as ecology, soil science, veterinary medicine, forestry, human health, aquatic resource management, botany, zoology, agronomy, agricultural economics, rural sociology, mathematics, fisheries, range management, information science, wildlife management and water resource management.[61] This knowledge is an important resource that we cannot overlook. It needs to be tapped, upgraded where necessary, made an important part of science policies of Muslim countries, integrated into the national system of science and used in designing development projects.

Undoubtedly one of the most formidable tasks that faces those who wish to shape science with Islamic values is the question of methodology. An obvious candidate for replacement is vivisection which has become the dominant methodology of modern biology. Our ethical concerns here lead to some tough questions: what happens to much of contemporary biological research if we are to shun torture of innocent animals in the name of progress? How can we ensure that research on such areas as cancer continues? What alternatives to vivisection can we develop? Similarly overwhelming questions arise when we argue for replacing perpetual, and often meaningless reduction, with synthesis. What methods would encourage synthesis and bring it to the level of the laboratory? How can synthesis become the dominant paradigm of science? We need to tackle these questions seriously if we are to take the discourse of Islamic science beyond its present impasse.

Finally, there are fundamental axiomatic questions just waiting to be addressed. What happens to modern science if its basic metaphysical assumptions about nature, time, universe, logic and the nature of our humanity are replaced with those of the worldview of Islam? How do we actually perform the task? How will it transform physics and what would the new physics look like? What new disciplines will be generated? How will the new axioms change mathematics? And what new directions about our understanding of the material universe and reality will be opened up?

It took modern, western, science over three centuries, and all the resources of colonialism and neo-colonialism, to reach its present level of complexity and sophistication. Discovering alternatives to and in modern science, leading to its eventual dethronement, will thus not be a simple or easy exercise. It will require sustained and prolonged intellectual and financial commitment to even begin to highlight the contours of a viable Islamic alternative. To become meaningful and engage more seriously with the challenge, the discourse of Islamic science must lift itself from its current obsession with feel-good rhetoric and ontology. Only pragmatic policies, conscientious empirical labour and sober theoretical and methodological work, can move the Islamic science discourse forward – and lead, eventually, to a more just and humane future for us all.

11
Science Wars: A Postcolonial Reading

Just as America existed before Columbus, science wars have existed for much longer than the nascent discipline of sociology of knowledge. Surprisingly, Columbus and science wars have a great deal in common. Columbus globalised a worldview: the worldview of modernity. Science wars, in their current manifestations, represent a last ditch effort to defend that worldview. But the science wars themselves have their origins in the formative phase of modernity. The first, pre- and post-Columbus, science wars have two strands – one visible and one invisible. The visible strand is the post-Columbus warfare of science and Christian theology in western civilisation; the invisible strand is the war of modern science against the sciences of all other civilisations and all other notions of science. The new science wars are a consequence, in a dialectical fashion, of the victory of science in that earlier conflict.

The sciences that existed before the emergence of western civilisation were not all that different from science as it exists today. The sciences that thrived in such civilisations as China, India and Islam were, within their own framework, just as 'rational', 'objective' and 'universal' as contemporary science claims to be. The mathematics of Brahmagupta (c. 568) in India, acupuncture in Chinese science, and the experiments of Ibn al-Haytham's in optics or ar-Razi's observations of smallpox, are all empirically verifiable and are equally valid across time and cultures. What is different between sciences of non-western civilisation and modern science is that non-western sciences are a product of cultures and civilisations which emphasise the unity of knowledge. Physics is not separated from metaphysics, and science is seen both in terms of a social function and as an integral part of the value structure of the culture within which it thrives. Thus, science and religion, or science and values, were/are perceived as two sides of the same coin of knowledge. In other words, the metaphysical assumptions of the culture and civilisations within which non-

First published as 'Above, Beyond and at the Centre of the Science Wars: A Postcolonial Reading', in Keith M. Ashman and Philip S. Bringer (eds), *After the Science Wars*, Routledge, London, 2001, pp. 120–39.

western science flourished were openly acknowledged. Of course, these assumptions shaped the style and emphasis of these sciences; sometimes they even shaped the contents of these sciences leading to culturally specific, or tacit, knowledge. However, the emphasis on the unity of all knowledge did not mean, as is sometimes suggested, that all differences of opinions or plural perspectives were precluded. It would be much too simplistic to assume that civilisations like Islam or India or China contain only one, single point of view and that scientific activity and its products were not contested within each civilisation. But in the history of these civilisations, there has been no such thing as a pitched battle between science on the one hand, and religion on the other. In Islam, for example, such a war would be inconceivable given the emphasis placed in the Qur'an on reason and empiricism and the praise heaped on scientific knowledge by the Prophet Muhammad. The nearest thing we have is the long-running debate between Greek philosophy and classical scholasticism in Islam; a controversy that lasted over 400 years and ended with the victory of traditional Islamic thought.

The Europe of Columbus owed most of its science and learning to Islam. From Islam, Europe learned how to reason logically, acquired the experimental method, discovered the idea of medicine and rediscovered Greek philosophy. Most of algebra, basic geometry and trigonometry, spherical astronomy, mechanics, optics, chemistry and biology – the very foundation of the scientific renaissance in Europe, came from Islam.[1] But while Islam furnished Europe with its intellectual apparatus, it also presented a series of problems. The main one, which dates back to the very origins of Islam, was the theological problem of the very existence of Islam as a new post-Christ religion. What need was there for a new Arabian Prophet when God's own son had died on the Cross to redeem all humanity? The rapid expansion of Islam also presented a military problem. The cultural and scientific advancements of Islamic civilisation were perceived as an intellectual problem. Western civilisation solved the 'problem' of Islam not just by war and conquest, going back to the Crusades, but also by a very specific representation of Islam as the 'darker' side of Europe. Islam was the evil, infidel Other that was forever menacing Christendom and that personified everything that Europe was not. While Europe was civilised, Islam was barbaric; while Christianity was peaceful, Islam was inherently violent; while Europe was clean, orderly and law-abiding, Muslim lands were unclean and inferior, lawless and chaotic. It followed that Islamic science and

Muslim learning, that Europe borrowed, plagiarised and otherwise appropriated freely for over seven centuries, was more than tainted with unsavoury colours.

The Islamic intellectual inheritance was a pervasive presence in Europe right till the end of the sixteenth century. Clearly, a Europe perceived to be far superior to Islam could not admit a deep intellectual debt to the inferior, barbaric civilisation of Islam any more than it could acknowledge the existence of an Islamic science that was at par with anything that Europe produced. Thus began the first and the original science wars: the war of European science against the science and learning of Islam. This war had three main functions. First, to sever the Islamic roots of European science and learning. Second, to make the history of Islamic science all but invisible. Third, to deny the very existence of science in Islam. In the initial stage, this was done consciously as an integral part of the Orientalist scholarship. Orientalism, as I have stated elsewhere, is 'the scholarship of the politics of desire: it codifies western desires into academic disciplines and then projects its desires onto its study of the Orient'.[2] When the sixteenth- and seventeenth-century Orientalists looked at Islamic science they found it to be trivial and, in many cases, to be not science at all, but simply a rag-bag of superstitions and dogma. The fiction was created that Muslims did little more than translate the works of Greeks and were themselves unable to add anything original to them. Thus was born what I call the 'conveyer belt' theory: the Muslims preserved the heritage of Greece and, like a conveyer belt, simply passed it on to its rightful heir: the western civilisation. Islam was by-passed, and the intellectual roots of the West were reconnected to Greece. The 700-year history of Islamic science became a dark, blank hole. At later stages, the denial became so total and so pervasive at every level, that it became unconscious; and it was extended to other civilisations. Indian and Chinese science also came to be seen as non-science, insignificant and irrelevant when compared to the European achievements. This was the invisible strand of early science wars.

The visible struggle for the domination of science took place in Europe itself. The myth that relegated non-western sciences to the dark ages and edges of Europe had a corollary: true science was created by and belonged to the West. But this true science had to be radically different from non-sciences of other civilisations. In non-western cultures, several different sources of knowledge are recognised and respected equally. Islam, for example, gives equal emphasis to empirical as well as intuitive knowledge; reason and revelation are legitimate sources of knowledge and truth. Moreover, new knowledge comes about from the interaction between a whole array of different branches of knowledge, and the society itself plays an important part in both shaping and directing that knowledge. Since all cultures and civilisations have equal access to reason and revelation, knowledge can come from anywhere, any civilisation, any methodology – no particular culture or civilisation has a monopoly over knowledge. Such ideas of science were the un-thought of Europe: perceived as dark and unworthy notions but ever present though deeply suppressed in European consciousness. The reconstruction of science in Europe, as *the* science and *the* only way to Truth, during the seventeenth and eighteenth centuries, was partly an outcome of this un-thought and partly a product of the European colonial project. The un-thought found its expression in science's war against Christianity.

If we look at the writings of the founders of the Scientific Revolution, the militant proclamation of the Truths of science is quite clear. Galileo has a classic quote, which established the hubris of science for centuries afterwards:

If this point of which we dispute were some point of law, or other part of the studies called the humanities, wherein there is neither truth nor falsehood, we might give sufficient credit to the acuteness of wit, readiness of answers, and the greater accomplishment of writers, and hope that he who is most proficient in these will make his reason more probable and plausible. But the conclusions of natural science are true and necessary, and the judgement of man has nothing to do with them.[3]

Galileo's stance contrasts sharply with the position of a Muslim scholar like Ibn Hazm who saw law, science and humanities as equally valid modes of inquiry and truth and accorded them equal respect. 'Intellectual inquiry', Ibn Hazm suggested, is 'useless if it is not supported by the good fortune of religion and by that of sciences of the world.'[4] Ethics and empiricism go hand in hand, argued Ibn Hazm, for whom the conclusion of science had no meaning without the judgement of community. Prudently, Galileo chose not to include Christian theology in his attack; but Descartes was more direct. In speaking of his humanistic education, in which he first praised and then murdered the whole syllabus, he commented:

Our theology I revered, and was as eager as anyone else to gain heaven; but having learned that the way thither is open to the most ignorant no less than to the most learned, and that the revealed truths, which guide us on our way, are above our understanding, I should not have dared to submit them to the weakness of my understanding. Indeed, a man who undertook to investigate these truths and who succeeded in his task, would need, in my judgement, to be favoured with some special aid from heaven, and to be himself more than a man.[5]

In other words, theology declares itself to be impossible as a learned discipline. This, despite the fact that both Descartes and Galileo were (to all intents and purposes) believers. Indeed, the humanism that Descartes was so proud of was itself based on a theology – the theology of Islam. Europe did not invent humanism; as George Makdisi demonstrates so powerfully in *The Rise of Humanism in Classical Islam and the Christian West*, humanism began in Islam and was transferred, almost intact, to Europe.[6]

The self-confidence of natural science, in the tradition of Galileo and Descartes, increased steadily after their lives. Criticisms of its claims to truth came only from outside. The first serious attempt was by Bishop Berkeley, who attacked the mechanics of Newton (who was a not-very-secret Unitarian), and (with greater success) the foundations of mathematics. As a committed defender of the truths of religion, he was outraged by the pretensions of the irreligious scientists to be the bearers of clarity and enlightenment. Ironically, Berkeley became a freethinker in his criticism not of Newton's mechanics but the calculus. He was concerned with the reasoning whereby the differential calculus is explained, raising the question, 'Does the increment actually reach zero, or not?' The answers he received were totally unsatisfactory, and in his reply he produced this classic analysis of dogmatism in science:

Men learn the elements of science from others; and every learner hath a deference more or less to authority, especially the young learners, few of that kind caring to dwell long upon principles, but inclining rather to take them on trust; And things early admitted by repetition eventually become familiar; And this familiarity at length passeth for evidence.[7]

With these words, he explained the phenomenon of explanation by the principle of 'every schoolboy knows' that something is obvious, when in fact it is totally obscure. The pamphlet in which he published this was entitled *A Defence of Freethinking in Mathematics*, an ironical accusation that the mathematicians themselves were the dogmatists, who treat any criticism as scandalous. But in the eighteenth century

Berkeley was a lonely voice; and even those mathematicians who took his criticisms seriously were sure that there was a simple answer to something so clear as the calculus.

There were later attacks on mechanistic science from what is called the 'Romantic' school, which for a while was quite influential in chemistry. This flourished most strongly in Germany, as in Goethe's (unsuccessful) theory of colours and the (successful) drive by the 'Naturphilosoph' scientists to demonstrate the unity of electricity and magnetism. But we had to wait till the end of the nineteenth century before the first genuine self-conscious criticisms of basic science emerged from within. It is to be found in the works of Ernst Mach, who was a physicist of some distinction. Mach demonstrated that Newton's Laws of Motion, hitherto accepted as very nearly 'synthetic *a priori*' truths, were in fact quite confused. Their concepts were unclear and their scientific status obscure. Mach went on to analyse the foundations of scientific knowledge, including truth and error, and came up with his own solution to the problem of how scientific knowledge can be considered as genuine: a principle of economy of effort.

After Mach, others made similar critical analyses, notably Karl Pearson in Britain and Pierre Duhem in France. But in all cases the intent was to find a more secure basis for the scientific knowledge which all knew to be genuine. This was a large part of the motivation of the Vienna Circle, which flourished through the 1920s and 1930s until dispersed by the victory of fascism in Austria. For the Circle, there was an overt political dimension to the struggle between a secular, progressive Science and the reactionary theology and metaphysics of the Catholic Church in Austria. Its leader, Moritz Schlick, was assassinated by a student, who, although doubtless mad, did also make the political point that Schlick's teachings were undermining traditional certainties.

The end of the First World War ushered in the second science wars, where the 'academic left' initially makes its presence felt. The war exposed the technological weaknesses of the British Empire and led to direct government intervention in the management of science. The monopoly of universities as research institutions was broken as new research institutions were established with public and private funding. To many intellectuals and scholars, particularly of Marxist persuasion, a relationship between science and economics became plainly evident. It led to the formation, in 1918, of the National Union of Scientific Workers (later Association of Scientific Workers) with a categorically socialist agenda for science. Increased expenditure on science, along with centralised planning, it was argued, would release the liberating potentials of science.

The connection between science and ideology was made explicit in 1931 when a conference on the history of science in London played host to a delegation from the (then) Soviet Union. The key event at the conference was a paper by Boris Hessen on 'The Social and Economic Roots of Newton's *Principia*'.[8] Hessen argued that Newton's major work was not so much a product of scientific genius or a result of the internal logic of science, but rather a consequence of social and economic forces in seventeenth-century Britain. It fulfilled the needs of the British bourgeoisie. The young British left-wing scientists and historians of science attending the conference took a few years to grasp the full import of Hessen's arguments. But with the publication of J. D. Bernal's *The Social Function of Science* in 1939, the radical science movement had truly arrived. Bernal saw science as a natural ally of socialism: its function was to serve the people and liberate them from capitalism. Bernal combined his Marxist humanitarianism with technocratic and reductionist motives. Despite all its problems, Bernal held on to his faith in science as an objective, neutral mode of inquiry that could produce peace and plenty for all were it not for the corruption of science under capitalism.

The idea of a 'socialist science', first suggested in the Soviet Union, also gained currency in Britain. But its realisation in the Soviet Union came to be seen as a crude and opportunistic exercise. The Lysenko affair of the 1940s and 1950s, which involved the Soviet geneticists in arguing that heredity can be transformed by means of environmental manipulation and grafting, did great harm to the idea of a socialist science. Later, the avowedly radical British Society for Social Responsibility in Science did manage to organise a conference on the question 'Is there a socialist science?', but the outcome remained definitely inconclusive.

In the popular perception of science, the Second World War completed what the First World War had started. This time, science was seen to be running the show in the battlefield, as well as moving into government. Scientists were responsible not just for developing new and deadlier forms of chemical and biological weapons but for conceiving, producing and finally unleashing the Bomb. The mushroom clouds of the atomic weapons dropped on Hiroshima and Nagasaki declared the end of the era of scientific innocence. Now the connection between science and war was all too evident, the complicit relationship between science and politics had came to the fore, and all notions of scientific autonomy had evaporated. The public, which had hitherto concerned itself largely with the benefits of science, suddenly became concerned with its devastating downside.

The protest against militarised science, starting with the launching of the dissident journal *Bulletin of the Atomic Scientists* by nuclear physicists totally disenchanted by the Manhattan Project in the US, was consolidated by the emergence of CND (Campaign for Nuclear Disarmament) in the later 1950s. Many scientists were concerned that the Bomb should not be seen as an inescapable consequence of physics. This would discourage bright young scientists with ethical concerns about the Bomb from a career in physics. The ploy was to claim that science is neutral: it is neither good nor bad; it is society that puts it to good or bad use. The neutrality argument became a dominant defence of science during the 1950s and the 1960s; and it enabled many scientists to work in atomic physics, even accepting grants from defence establishments, while professing to be politically radical.

The neutrality argument also played a very important part in the evolution of development theory. When development first became a catch-word in international politics, in the early 1960s, most of the newly independent countries of the Third World were seen as 'underdeveloped'.[9] Some, however, were viewed as 'developing' along a model similar to the industrial development in Europe. At the foundation of this ethnocentric view of the world – a manifestation of the social Darwinist ideas of the Victorian era, which produced such notions as 'white man's burden' and 'manifest destiny' – was the belief that science and technology could transform the developed and developing countries into carbon copies of European industrialised states. Science was seen as something that has to be acquired from the West; and technology had to be 'transferred'. Many Third World scientists totally embraced the ideology of neutrality of science, and spent their entire career on problems that were conceived in the West and had no relations to their society in the hope that their efforts would bring economic benefits to their countries.

While the radical science movement questioned the neutrality of science, debated its social function, and campaigned against the Bomb, it still saw science very much as a western concern. Thus, while radical historians of science were eager to show how social forces shaped the development of science, they remained largely silent on the role non-western cultures played in shaping science.

So, Bernal for example, explains his reasons for writing *Science in History* as follows:

In the last thirty years, largely owing to the impact of Marxist thought, the idea has grown that not only the means used by natural scientists in their researches but also the very guiding ideas of their theoretical approach are conditioned by the events and pressures of society. This idea has been violently opposed and as energetically supported; but in the controversy the earlier view of the direct impact of science on society has become overshadowed. It is my purpose to emphasise once more to what extent the advance of natural science has helped to determine that of society itself; not only in the economic changes brought about by the application of scientific discoveries, but also by the effect on the general frame of thought of the impact of new scientific discoveries.[10]

But Bernal perceived 'society' largely as an autonomous western society; and civilisation (always in the singular) for him is essentially western civilisation which starts with the Greeks and progresses linearly to 'our time'. In a four-volume study, he devoted less than ten pages to Islamic science. China and India do not even get a mention.

However, the historiography of science was about to change quite radically. The foundation for this change had been established by two truly monumental studies. The first was George Sarton's *Introduction to the History of Science*, published between 1927 and 1948. What is surprising about Sarton's study is that the first three volumes of the four-volume chronological study are largely devoted to science in Islam. Sarton not only made it clear that western science is inconceivable without Islam, but suggested that the sheer scientific contribution of Islam, both in terms of quantity and quality, should concern those who see science purely as a western enterprise. Perhaps the reason for Sarton's influence was that his work was little more than a list of names and references with hardly any synthesis. The second study, Joseph Needham's massive multi-volume *Science and Civilisation in China*, published from 1954 onwards, performed the same function for China, even more effectively.

Both Sarton and Needham showed that science was not limited to western societies; non-western societies also had highly developed and sophisticated cultures of science. But for them this did not mean that there could be different sciences; or indeed different definitions of science. Indeed, Needham was able to isolate the 'problematic' bits of Chinese science such as acupuncture and label it 'non-science'. Science may be tainted with politics, and embroiled with the military, but it was still largely seen as a neutral, objective, universal, pursuit of truth.

Thus, the history of science still presented science as a linear pursuit of progress, where the sciences of other civilisations were so many tributaries – in some cases, as Islam and China, rather large tributaries but tributaries nevertheless – which merged into the great universal river of Western Science. The philosophy of science, as well as the broader public image of science, also promoted the assumption that Science gives Truth, is the only way to Truth, and the Truth accumulates as a single, universal perspective of Western Civilisation. And this was imbibed, most strongly of all, by students of science itself.

In this picture, science had been almost universally seen in heroic terms. The lone scientists struggled against all odds for the sake of Truth. Science was a pure, autonomous activity, separate from technology and industry and above society. The purity of scientific research was particularly enshrined in universities where research was pursued for the sake of Knowledge and future generations of scientists were trained. The scientist was someone engaged in a unique social role who required protection and had autonomous existence from the rest of the society. The scientists, particularly Great Scientists, were the object of inquiry for historians and philosophers of science. Thus the emphasis of the history of science was on discoveries by great scientists and the justification of these discoveries in the unique objectivity, impartiality and universality of science.

But there was a contradiction lurking in this beautiful picture. If science is always true, and also always progressive, how do we account for the changes in theories and explanations? One way is to deny that the changes are real, and to see progress as simple discovery of new things. But that does not hold; thus even Newton espoused a theory, which in the nineteenth century was considered incorrect, namely that light travels as particles rather than waves. So the history books fell back on another explanation: when new truths were discovered, or errors exposed, it was the good scientists who went along with progress. Those who opposed what we now know to be True, were somehow bad scientists, who were not following Scientific Method. The historians then had their work defined: to show that science is always 'true', and when it isn't, that the good scientists were right.

The unravelling of the triumphalist, dogmatic ideology of science is associated with the exposure of the contradiction between infallible truth and permanent progress. The first move was made by Karl Popper.

While Popper was loosely associated with the Vienna Circle in the 1920s, he was not a member of it, being highly critical of some aspects of its philosophical position. The Circle asserted that metaphysics and theology were meaningless, for they consisted of propositions that could not be verified. By contrast, Popper hit upon 'falsification' or 'falsifiability' as the real demarcation criterion between scientific knowledge and the other sorts (which he did not altogether dismiss). He argued that there is no final truth in science, and that scientific progress is achieved by 'conjectures and refutations'.[11] By positing the self-critical spirit as the essence of science, Popper shifted the defence of science from its achieving the Truth of objective knowledge, to its embodying the Good of the values of a liberal society. He can be seen as the last of the defenders of the traditional ideology of science. But he had already given away too much. The arrival of Thomas Kuhn, who was the true philosophical revolutionary, however reluctant and inconsistent he was in his attitudes to what he had wrought, spelled the beginning of the end of science as we had known it.

Kuhn reduced scientists from bold adventurers discovering new truths to simple puzzle solvers within an established worldview. Instead of worldview, Kuhn used the term 'paradigm'. By using the term paradigm, he writes,

I mean to suggest some accepted examples of actual scientific practice – examples which include law, theory, application, and instrumentation together – provide models from which spring particular coherent traditions of scientific research. These are traditions which history describes under such rubrics as 'Ptolemaic Astronomy' (or 'Copernican'), 'Aristotelian dynamics' (or 'Newtonian'), 'corpuscular optics' (or 'wave optics') and so on.[12]

In the Kuhnian scheme, the term paradigm is closely related to 'normal science': those who work within a dogmatic, shared paradigm use its resources to refine theories, explain puzzling data, establish increasingly precise measures of standards, and do other necessary work to expand the boundaries of normal science. This dogmatic stability is punctuated by occasional revolutions. Kuhn describes the onset of revolutionary science in vivid terms. 'Normal science', he suggests, 'often suppresses fundamental novelties because they are necessarily subversive of its basic commitments ... (but) when the profession can no longer evade anomalies that subvert the existing tradition of scientific practice...',[13] then extraordinary investigations begin. A point is reached when the crisis can only be solved by revolution in which the old paradigm gives way to the formulation of a new paradigm. Thus 'revolutionary science' takes over; but what was once revolutionary itself settles down to become the new orthodoxy: the new normal science. So science progresses, argues Kuhn, through cycles: normal science, which is the science we find in the textbooks, is followed by revolution which is followed again by normal science and then again by revolution. Each paradigm may produce a particular work that defines and shapes the paradigm: Aristotle's *Physica*, Newton's *Principia* and *Optiks* and Lyell's *Geology* are examples of works that defined the paradigms of particular branches of science at particular times.

In the publication of *The Structure of Scientific Revolutions* and the debate that followed we find the genesis of the third – and current – science wars. The right-wing Kuhn was a radical departure from the left-wing radical critique of science which was concerned more with tinkering with the periphery rather than changing the centre. The post-war academic left still held on to the belief in a science that gradually progressed to cumulative acquisition of knowledge – all that was necessary was to purge it of its bourgeois influence and bring it into the service of the working classes. In sharp contrast, Kuhn presented 'normal' science as a dogmatic enterprise. If we regard outmoded scientific theories such as Aristotelian dynamics, phlogistic chemistry, or caloric thermodynamics as myths, he argued, then we can just as logically consider the current theories to be irrational and dogmatic. After Kuhn, the understanding of science could never be the same again.

The developments that followed after Kuhn – the debate between Paul Feyerabend and Imre Lakatos,[14] the emergence of sociology of knowledge, the evolution of the feminist critique of science, right down to the Sokal hoax[15] – have been documented, debated and discussed quite thoroughly elsewhere. But what has been happening over the past three decades besides the science war – away from the centre where defenders of the purity of science and its critics amongst the 'academic left' and the feminist movement – is far more interesting. The last three decades have seen the emergence of what we can describe as postcolonial science studies. The rubric 'postcolonial' does not mean 'after colonialism'. Rather it signifies how the colonising nature of contemporary science continues to shape the relationship between western and non-western science, how the dominating tendencies of western science are resisted, and what is being done to replace the grand narrative of western science and give voice to non-western discourses of science and learning. The postcolonial enterprise of science will probably have far greater impact on the future of science than the current phase of science wars.

Kuhn's analysis shows how science works in one civilisation: the western civilisation. His insights are hardly news for postcolonial writers on science: the very premise of all non-western sciences is that science operates and progresses within a worldview. Kuhn does, however, provide (western) legitimacy for the existence of science in other, non-western, paradigms. Other civilisations, such as Islam, China and India, and other cultures, such as those of the Pacific Isles, Sub-Saharan Africa and the Native Americans, can now be recognised as having different practices and different kinds of sciences based on their own paradigms. One of the primary goals of postcolonial science studies is to show that this in fact is the case. What makes western science distinctively western is its metaphysical assumptions about nature, universe, time and logic. The idea that nature is there only for the benefit of man (sic) and, as Bacon put it, has to be 'tortured' to reveal its secrets, is totally alien to most non-western cultures. Islam and China, for example, do not look at nature as an object. In Islam, nature is a sacred trust that has to be nurtured and studied with due respect and appreciation. In Chinese tradition, nature is seen as a self-governing web of relationships with a weaver, with which humans interfere at their own peril. Similarly, the western ideas of universe and time are culturally based. The western idea of universe as 'a great empire, ruled by a divine logos', owes more to centralised royal authority in Europe than to any universal notion – it is totally incomprehensible to the Chinese and Indians. Similarly, while western science sees time as linear, other cultures view it as cyclic as in Hinduism or as a tapestry weaving the present with eternal time in the Hereafter as in Islam. While modern science operates on the basis of either/or Aristotelian logic (X is either A or non-A), in Hinduism logic can be four-fold or even seven-fold. The four-fold Hindu logic (with the extra forms: X is neither A nor non-A; nor both A and non-A; nor neither A nor non-A) is both a symbolic logic as well as a logic of cognition. It can achieve a precise and unambiguous formulation of universal statements without using the 'for all' formula. Thus the metaphysical assumptions underpinning modern science make it specifically western in its main characteristics. A science that is based on different notions of nature, universe, time and logic would therefore be a totally different enterprise from western science.[16]

The conventional (western) history of science, however, does not recognise different types of civilisational or cultural sciences. It has represented western science as the apex of science; and maintained its monopoly in four basic ways. First, it denied the achievements of non-western cultures and civilisations as real science, dismissing them as superstition, myth and folklore. This dismissal is undertaken by a tautological argument where western culture is defined as superior to all other cultures; by analogy the science, technologies and medicines of inferior cultures are, well, inferior. William Henry III provides the most recent example of this kind of shameful thinking in his book, *In Defense of Elitism*. Henry defines superior cultures in terms of certain basic criteria. 'A superior culture', he writes, 'preserves the liberty of its citizens', 'provides a comfortable life, relatively free from want', and 'expands, by trade or cultural imperialism or conquest'. Now, since non-western cultures are seen as authoritarian, unable to fulfil the basic needs of their people and were colonised by the west, they are by definition inferior. So, Henry has no problem in reaching his conclusion that 'superior culture promotes modern science (and) western medicine'.[17] It was this kind of analysis that led to ruthless suppression, during colonialism, of Islamic and Indian medicine. In India, for example, these systems were dismissed as mere mumbo jumbo and their practice banned. In Tunisia the French actually instituted a death penalty and killed numerous practitioners of Islamic medicine. Only recently have these systems been recognised by the World Health Organization as legitimate medical systems at par with western medicine – after their use by and benefits to rural populations were amply demonstrated.

Second, the histories of non-western sciences were largely written out of the general history of science. So wide is this practice that it has become an integral part of western consciousness. For example, in Floyd Bloom's timeline of discovery, published 'to help readers negotiate *Science* magazine's yearlong series, Pathways to Discovery', nothing exists between 131–200 (when Galen wrote his textbook on anatomy) and 1285–1349 (when William of Ockham produced his razor, the logical implement he wielded to trim absurdities out of arguments).[18] This despite that Galen was rewritten by Ibn Sina whose *Canon of Medicine* was a standard medical text in Europe for over 600 years; and William of Ockham learned all his logic from Muslim philosophers. As Don Ihde points out in his comments on *Science*'s 'Timeline', this is a 'traditional and parochial display of Eurocentrism regarding the history of science and technology'.[19]

We know, at least, that Su Sung's heavenly clockwork, a mechanical clockwork, was operating in China by 1090. Gutenberg may have developed moveable type in 1454, but metal (copper) moveable type was invented in Korea two centuries earlier. However, the point here is not who did what first, but a mindset that sees the period between Greek sciences and the emergence of European science as a dark era where nothing worthy ever happened.

Third, Europe rewrote the history of the origins of European civilisation to make it self-generating. Many notable scientists, Newton in the late seventeenth century and Kelvin in the late nineteenth century amongst them, were involved in creating and disseminating the revisionist history of the origins of modern European civilisation and the creation of the Aryan model. This model introduced the idea that Greek culture was predominantly European, and that Africans and Semites had nothing to do with the creation of the classical Greek civilisation. But the identification of Greek culture as European is questionable on several grounds. For one thing, the idea of 'Europe' and the social relations such an idea made possible, came centuries later – some would date it to Charlemagne's achievements, others to the fifteenth century (Greece and Rome were civilisations of the Mediterranean). Moreover, it was Islam that introduced Greece to Europe; and due to the spread of Islam, the diverse cultures of Africa and Asia can also claim Greek culture as their legacy.

Fourth, through conquest and colonisation, Europe appropriated the sciences of other civilisations, suppressed the knowledge of their origins, and recycled them as western. We know that many scientific traditions were appropriated and fully integrated into western sciences without acknowledgement. Thus the pre-Columbian agriculture that provided potatoes and many other food crops was absorbed into European agricultural practice and science. Mathematical achievements from Arabic and Indian cultures provide another example. Francis Bacon's three great inventions that made modern Europe – printing, gunpowder and the magnetic compass – are now admitted to have all come from China. Knowledge of local geographies, geologies, botany, zoology, classification schemes, medicines, pharmacologies, agriculture, navigational techniques were provided by the knowledge traditions of non-Europeans.

The emergence of postcolonial science studies is an attempt to expose this Eurocentrism, reclaim the history of non-western sciences and rediscover the modes and styles of doing non-western sciences today. Postcolonial science studies began with empirical work in the history of Islamic, Indian and Chinese sciences. For example, Fuat Sezgin's monumental work on Islamic science, *Gesichte des Arabischen Schrifttums*[20] and the work of scholars in France working with Roshdi Rashed,[21] reveals how truly awesome, both in depth and breadth, was the scientific achievements of Muslim civilisation. Ekmeleddin Ihsanoglu's work on Ottoman science has revealed it to be far from 'insignificant' as it is often projected.[22] Similarly, D. M. Bose, S. N. Sen, P. V. Sharma and numerous other historians have shown that Indian science cannot be easily dismissed.[23]

While the western camp has been forced to acknowledge the new historical reality, its counterattack has been based on the argument that great scientists of Islam, for example, were all secularists. Thus, their achievements owe little to Islam but everything to secularism and they can be represented as a part of the Great History of Western Science.[24] This is a patently absurd suggestion. We are talking about highly religious men before the age of secularism; the separation of the sacred and the profane was beyond their wildest imagination. They were all, even the most unorthodox ones, Muslim first and anything else second. For them, science without values was profane. Many of them were indeed also humanists; but their humanism was derived from their own worldview and was a product of their Islamic commitment. So everything they did had an Islamic subscript: this is why they spend so much time establishing the direction of Makkah from every point on the globe (*qibla*), developing a mathematics for the Islamic laws of inheritance, studying the heavens, establishing hospitals and developing medicine and generally pursuing learning.

But postcolonial scholarship of science goes much further than empirical historical undertaking. It also seeks to establish the connection between colonialism, including neo-colonialism, and the progress of western science. For example, in his several books, Deepak Kumar,[25] the Indian historian and philosopher of science, has sought to demonstrate that British colonialism in India played a major part in how European science developed. The British needed better navigation, so they built observatories, funded astronomers and kept systematic records of their voyages. The first European sciences to be established in India were, not surprisingly, geography and botany. Throughout the Raj, British science progressed primarily because of military, economic and political demands of the British, and not because of the purported greater rationality of science or the alleged commitment of scientists to the pursuit of disinterested truths. Moreover, postcolonial science critics seek to develop a specific position on western science as demonstrated by the work of Indian scholars Ashis Nandy[26] and Claude Alvares[27] and a string of young Muslim scholars, including my own output.[28] Finally, postcolonial scholarship of science seeks to re-establish the practice of Islamic, Indian or Chinese science in contemporary times. There is, for example, a whole discourse of contemporary Islamic science devoted to exploring how a science based on the Islamic notions of nature, unity of knowledge and values, public interest and so on, could be shaped.[29] A similar discourse on Indian science has also emerged in the last decade.[30]

The main parties to the science war have ignored much of the postcolonial scholarship. The same fate has fallen on Jerome Ravetz's seminal work *Scientific Knowledge and Its Social Problems*[31] which has played a key, though underlying, role in shaping a great deal of postcolonial science criticism. Ravetz's identification of the social problems of science could be easily witnessed by postcolonial writers in their own societies. His four problematic categories of science – shoddy science, entrepreneurial science (where securing grants is the name of the game), reckless science, and dirty science – may have been somewhat shrouded in the west but they were all too visible in countries like India, Pakistan, Egypt and Malaysia. Moreover, Ravetz's contention that we need to abandon the idea that 'science discovers facts', or it is 'true or false' – presented much before sociology of knowledge became a fashion – in favour of a broad interpretation of science as a craft takes us back, or rather forward, to a common notion of science in non-western societies. If science is seen as craft, then 'truth' is replaced by the idea of 'quality' in the evaluation of scientific output. Quality firmly places both the social and ethical aspects of science, as well as scientific uncertainty, on the agenda. All this was evident at a famous conference on 'The Crisis in Modern Science', organised by the Consumer Association of Penang and held during 21–26 November 1986 in Penang, Malaysia.[32] The Penang conference, which produced a famous declaration on science and technology, was a key event in the development of postcolonial science discourse: it was here that the possibility of contemporary non-western discourses of science was first established.

With the emergence of postcolonial science, defenders of scientific purity encounter a contradiction all of their own. Should they refuse to engage in dialogue with these new enemies of (western) reason – declaring them, as Popper had declared Kuhn a few decades earlier, to be the enemies of civilisation? If so, then they would be exposed as not belonging to the polity where all different opinions short of those engaging in violence should be debated. But engagement brings its own risks. For no one can deny that western civilisation has operated a totally closed system where the only true knowledge is western knowledge and the only true science is western science thus marginalising, suppressing and rendering invisible sciences of all other civilisations. But now that this science is exposed as a social activity, where choices have to made, errors in scientific judgement and social behaviour occur, the clearly identifiable difference between western and non-western science evaporates. The superiority of western science cannot be defended anymore.

To a large extent, postcolonial science studies make 'science wars' quite irrelevant. Moreover, the rapid change in circumstances will also gradually deflate science wars. One is an ironic twist in the relations of science and religion, which may well overturn the whole ideology laid down by Galileo and Descartes. For while science still claims exclusive possession of truth about Nature, in the matter of ethical judgements about the consequences of scientific advance, no one can claim that science has all the answers. The recent decision by Craig Venter to consult with clergymen before going ahead to construct a virus from its parts, puts a completely different perspective on the traditional debate. But this is only a particularly salient point in the general transformation of the social and ethical situation of science. Science is simply not what the new realists and old idealists claim it to be. Its ideological and value-laden character has been exposed beyond doubt. But it is not simply a question of how political realities of power, sources of funding, the choice of problems, the criteria through which problems are chosen, as well as prejudice and value systems, influence even the 'purest' science. Or that burden of proof, in terms of statistical inference, can be found at the heart of scientific method. Or that most of the metaphysical assumptions of science are those of the European civilisation. It is more an issue of how science is now associated with uncertainties and risks. A great deal of the most important contemporary science is no longer normal science in Kuhnian terms. As can be seen from a string of recent controversies from the BSE ('mad cow disease') affair in Britain to the issues of genetically modified foods, science cannot deliver hard and fast answers to a host of contemporary issues. The old paradigm of science, which provided certainty and assurance is no longer valid.

And the paradox mentioned above, that western 'neutral science' can affect social and economic affairs in the developing countries, has returned in a new form, with a vengeance. For it is precisely that same reductionist, abstracted science which shapes the new intensive technologies like genetically modified organisms. And these are now fully identified with neo-colonialism through such products as 'terminator' crops. Moreover, the close link of such technologies with biopiracy is beyond doubt. It is Kuhnian 'normal scientists' who go out to sample the biological heritage of the non-western world, so that their multinational bosses can then steal it by patenting it as their own.

Many working scientists could regard this triumphalist view of western science as somewhat exaggerated. The initial reaction could be: this view of western science has a lot more to do with western historians and philosophers of science, particularly those with imperialist agendas, rather than the scientists themselves. Well, dogmatism in science has certainly existed in past epochs; one only has to read the first few paragraphs of Kuhn to see what the history of science had been. While the historians and philosophers perpetuated an imperialist view of science, the scientists themselves participated in shaping it. For example: it was scientists at the forefront of medical research in the colonies who sought and participated in the ruthless suppression of non-western medical systems. A more considered view could be: science may have been dogmatic in the past, but western science just isn't like that anymore. Now most western scientists regard science as a tool. But if that had been the attitude just 50 years ago, we would not have had Kuhn. And had this attitude existed only a decade ago, we would not have had science wars. It was only a few years ago that distinguished American scientists confidently looked forward to discovering the genes for violence and homelessness. And there are still some prominent scientists who believe and proclaim that genetic engineering is a precise technique, giving us just the properties we want and no others. The recent Darwin versus Creationism controversy also illustrates how much dogmatism still persists in science. As Steve Fuller notes, the American science establishment considers

the treatment of Darwinian evolution and Creation science as mutually exclusive options in the American public school curriculum. Although two-thirds of Americans who believe in evolution also believe that it reflects divine intelligence, such compatibility has yet to be seen as a philosophically respectable option, and consequently has no legal import. But what exactly would be wrong with teachers trying to render findings compatible with the Creationist commitments of most of their students? One common answer is that the presupposition of a divine intelligence or teleology has retarded biological inquiry in the past and has not contributed to evolutionary theory since time of Darwin's original formulation. Yet, the contrary presuppositions of mechanistic reduction and random genetic variation have equally led to error.[33]

Science teaching remains as dogmatic as ever. But this does not mean that many working scientists do not realise that scientific knowledge is always contingent, the next experiment or observation may cast doubt on what has gone before. However, this increasing common-sense amongst working scientists is very recent, partial and differentiated. It is a product of the radical transformation in science itself, which has ceased to be science as we know it. Now it has become what Funtowicz and Ravetz call 'post-normal science':

We are now witnessing a growing awareness among all those concerned with global issues that no single cultural tradition, no matter how successful in the past, can supply all the answers for the problems of the planet. Closely connected with the emergence of these changed attitudes is a new methodology that reflects and helps us guide the development of a new scientific approach to problem solving for global environment issues. In this, uncertainty is not banished but is managed, and values are not presupposed but are made explicit. The model for scientific argument is changing from a formalised deduction to an interactive dialogue. The paradigmatic science is no longer one whose explanations are unrelated to space, time and process: the historical dimension, including human reflection on past and future change, is now becoming an integral part of a scientific characterisation of nature and our place in it.[34]

In other words, science is returning to its non-western roots in Islam, India and China. Funtowicz and Ravetz's studies, over the last decade, of the emergence of post-normal science leads them to believe that the scientific community would no longer be limited simply to scientists. In situations where 'facts are uncertain, values in dispute, stakes high, and decisions urgent',[35] the questions of quality in science, along with issues of policy, will become paramount. They would lead to an 'extended peer community' which would use 'extended facts' which would include even anecdotal evidence and statistics gathered by a community. Lay persons, journalists, campaigners, housewives and theologians will join scientists in making decisions of science policy and shaping and directing scientific research. Science would thus be democratised and values of multiculturalism would play an increasing role in shaping its character. So: out goes the supremacy of western culture and in come the very ethics and values that bring terror to the heart of alleged Neutral Objectivists. This is the essence of the moral panic in a large segment of the scientific community – a panic that produced the science wars. This manifestation of the uncertainties inherent in science is a mark of nostalgia for a secure and simple world that will never return.

Part III

Cultural Relations

12
Coming Home:
Sex, Lies and all the 'I's in India

It is raining outside. Inside his home, Randhir, motionless next to his new bride, feeling lonely and isolated, thinks of another rainy night. Equally lonely and depressed, he had asked a mountain girl, seeking refuge from rain under a tamarind tree to come shelter in his house. He offered her a fresh change of clothes. And was overwhelmed with desire for her. But what attracted Randhir to the mountain girl? Her beauty? Her elegant simplicity? It was her smell: the compelling odour that emanated from her, drew him towards her, united him to her, reached out to the depths of his soul, stirred the most profound emotions. It was both a becoming and a quest. That *bu*.

Bu – 'Smell' – is undoubtedly the most controversial and the most intense short story in the oeuvre of Saadat Hassan Manto. It has received both lavish praise and condemnation: it has been described as a masterpiece and has been a subject of an obscenity trial; it has been attacked as pornography and presented as *the* model for imitation for all aspiring Urdu short story writers. Devastatingly precise and written in the simplest of prose, *Bu* is concerned largely with Randhir's feelings, his inner and outer quest for rediscovery of the smell of the mountain girl: the smell that led to his fathomless experience of ecstasy and unity. He cannot duplicate this experience with his college-educated bride. He found the smell of her perfume and henna sour and unwholesome: 'sad, colourless, without vitality' – no counterpart to his experience on that rainy night. The Anglo-Indian prostitutes he visited before his marriage produced trembling of his knees – that's all. But the dirt and sweat of the mountain girl was another story.

The stark sexual imagery of *Bu* distracts from its real essence. The obvious presence of the Hindu metaphors – where females are identified with the earth, the males with wandering clouds, the rain with sexual encounters and the smell with sexual pleasure – also

This paper was presented as the first Saadat Hassan Manto Lecture at the Nehru Memorial Museum and Library, New Delhi on 4 September 1996.

cover the story in purdah. Both the imagery and the metaphors of *Bu* have ensured that it is seen and interpreted almost exclusively in sexual terms. Thus, Leslie Felmming suggests that Manto is essentially writing about the nature of sexual experience:

In portraying Randhir's experience with the Ghatan as being more moving than that with either the prostitutes or his new bride, Manto suggests that the sexual relationship, at its most fundamental level, stripped of the artifice of both commercial transaction and socially acceptable commitment, is an intensely moving experience, perhaps the most profound human experience. Moreover, as the imagery used to describe Randhir's experience with the Ghatan suggests, it is also ultimately a mystical experience .... In short, the point in this story is that the sexual relationship, in its essence, is the most profound human experience, one that partakes of mystical, even cosmic, elements.[1]

But this is only a surface reading of *Bu* for *Bu* has as much to do with sex as *Animal Farm* has to do with pigs, donkeys and chickens.

THE SCENT OF AUTHENTICITY

In Manto's stories mountain girls serve a particular function. There are a number of stories with mountain girls, such as *Mausam ki Shararat* ('The Naughtiness of the Season'), *Lalten* ('Lantern'), *Namukmal Tahrir* ('Unfinished Writing') and others which have appeared in his various anthologies, that essentially tell the same story. A young traveller meets a young mountain girl and feels an intense attraction towards her; but for one reason or other, the relationship remains unfulfilled. In contrast to Manto's urban women, who tend to be old, passive, dependent and victims, the mountain girls are young, dynamic, independent, full of life and live in nature. However, while they live with nature, they are not pure: in the Indian context, they could hardly be said to be 'pure' if they are willing to contemplate an encounter with a 'traveller'. Manto's mountain girls do not represent a mystical sexual transport, they are cultural authenticity. Just as cultural authenticity addresses the deepest hopes and desires of a people and articulates ways and means by which these hopes and desires can be realised, so Manto's mountain girls awaken the innermost longing of world-weary 'travellers'. Manto was not entertaining some romanticised, fixed and unchanging notion of the past – he is as far removed from the European notion of pure, idolised nature lovers as possible. So his mountain girls, as the representatives of cultural authenticity, are more than simple products of the soil:

they are dynamic, independent, confident about themselves and their environment, willing to engage with outsiders, make mistakes and are thus fully human. They have innocence, but not some absolute kind of purity; they have recognisable ('brown') contours, but not eternally fixed masks of beauty; they are assimilated in their environment but totally free; they are playful but live meaningful lives.

And this is what they pass on to the 'travellers' they encounter. But the 'travellers' are not just any old travellers: they are young, confused and unsure of their destination: they are India. Randhir is India. And what he discovers in his encounter with the mountain girl is cultural authenticity: what he actually experiences is not sexual ecstasy but meaning. The *bu* of the mountain girl is a smell that was generated without 'external effort', that Randhir recognised and 'understood' 'even though he could not analyse it'. Hence Randhir's experience is transformed into a search: a quest for meaning, for cultural authenticity.

Whereas the mountain girl represents cultural authenticity, the bride personifies ossified tradition. In describing the bride, Manto deliberately uses all the terms that we find in the standard criticism of ossified tradition: lifeless, decaying, dying ... Like ossified tradition, the smell of a bride's henna is taken for granted: it does not have the 'sensation of having been smelt', it simply goes 'into his nose by itself and reached its proper level'. Once ossified, tradition becomes meaningless. Randhir's existence with his wife is devoid of all meaning; just as fossilised, life-denying tradition has become meaningless for the vast majority of Indians.

And what about those 'Anglo-Indian prostitutes'? It is worth noting that Manto gives a particular 'Anglo' character to the 'fair' prostitutes: they represent young India's flirtations with western ideologies – nationalism, modernity, secularism, fascism. Just as the prostitutes generate a sense of momentary excitement in Randhir, so western ideologies have produced a thrill, a quiver of expectation for India. But the end product in both cases is the same – the encounter is guilt-ridden and physically, emotionally and financially destructive.

Like Randhir, India cannot find peace. Having experienced meaning, both now search constantly and restlessly, beyond the fading aroma of henna and petrified tradition, beyond the seduction of Anglo-Indian prostitutes and western ideologies, for the life-enhancing odour of the mountain girl: the aroma of genuine Self.

And this is where violence – psychological, domestic, ethnic and national – enters the equation.

In Manto's universe, violence is often the result of a distorted self that is either generated by meaninglessness or leads to total loss of meaning. Trapped in a meaningless marriage, Randhir himself could easily be transformed into the characters in other Manto stories, men leading meaningless lives who perform meaningless violence on others either to get away from their boredom or to give some sort of contorted expression to their distorted selves. In *Khuni Thuk* ('Bloody spit') for example, a completely callous rich individual kicks a hard-working coolie to death. Moreover, to prove he is superior to the honest coolie, he bribes the judge and is acquitted of murder. In *Taqat ka Imtahan'* ('Test of Strength'), two idle youths seek amusement by betting on the ability of a starving labourer to carry a very heavy beam for them. The labourer dies in the attempt: but no one is moved, only the pavement is soiled by his blood. In *Tamasha* ('Entertainment'), the 1919 massacre of civilians in Jalianwala Bagh in Amritsar is depicted as a product of the distorted British self. The very name of the story suggests that the violence that is taking place is as meaningless as a *tamasha* one sees in a bazaar. But here British imperialism has a particularly distorted and superior notion of itself: a notion that is amply brought out by presenting the massacre through the innocent eyes of an infant. Even when violence is sought for meaningful purposes, Manto argues, it is an insane proposition. The hero of *Inqilab Pasand* ('The Revolutionary'), a young student, who is slowly transformed from a witty individual to a revolutionary thinker, ends up in a lunatic asylum. India needs to change, Manto seems to be saying, but bloody revolution is not the way: violence is *the* route to all round alienation.

The India of *Inqilab Pasand* and *Tamasha*, as seen and experienced by Manto, was a civilisation. A civilisation under siege from British imperialism. A civilisation caught between cultural authenticity, that it was rapidly losing, and ossified tradition that was not only becoming the norm but perpetuating and heightening all forms of oppression and violence – particularly towards women. A civilisation that, as Manto saw so clearly, was tearing itself apart with the emergence of new forms of violence that he could only chronicle but not comprehend. Nevertheless, for Manto 'India' signified a civilisation; and the quest for India's true Self was a quest for the realisation of its civilisational values in the contemporary world.

A civilisation – any civilisation – is an embodiment of its total spiritual and material cultures. It is a product of open, and to some extent, self-perpetuating interchanges between cultures and individuals and values and norms that are inherent in its basic constituents. Behind each civilisation, there is a vision that glues it together into a coherent unit, motivates it towards its higher goals and promotes the search for the resolution of its specific problems and needs. For India, this vision was always a vision of spiritual plurality: it could not be otherwise for the subcontinent boasts more religions, local cultures and languages than any other region in the world. Thus, India had always been a pluralistic civilisation where a number of different religious and local cultures – 'Hindu, Muslim, Sikh, Issai (Christian)' in the words of the famous song – fused together to produce a thriving, dynamic entity that is perhaps unique in world history.

Manto's angst, and the cause of his insecurity about his identity, was India's coming fall from grace. In all the ethnic riots and the communal violence he witnessed, he could see the civilisational base of India evaporating before his eyes. He had grown up in a confident environment in which he had no reason to question his Indian/ Muslim identity; not even repeated academic failure could shake his confidence. But the emergence of Hindu nationalism, which in turn gave birth to Muslim nationalism, began to change that. Manto witnessed the appearance of a new kind of Indian, one he could not comprehend, but whose exploits he chronicles with all their savagery in his partition stories: the portrayal of Ishar Singh who goes on a six-day spree of murder and looting and ends up raping a dead woman after killing six members of her family in *Thanda Gosht* ('Cold meat'); an old Muslim's search for his daughter who is finally discovered almost dead but even in her near-death state her lifeless hand has become accustomed to opening her *shalwar* (trousers) in *Khol Do* ('Open Up'); and the violence depicted in various stories in the collections *Nimrod ki Khudai* ('The God-like Power of Nimrod') and *Khali Botelen, Khali Dibbe* ('Empty Bottles, Empty Cans') suggests the depth of barbarity into which Manto's homeland was sinking. India's civilisational identity was evaporating fast leaving behind artificially created 'national' and 'ethnic' identities that knew nothing but hostility and inhumanity.

The new identities were created by a stress on definition, a new self-conscious awareness of what it is to be Hindu that must be justified by reassessment of what constitute the salient values of Hindu culture. The self-conscious search must generate points of distinction and difference to substantiate that any special identity exists. The very process of looking for points of separation must submerge and deny other, equally valid and authentic cultural concepts that stress openness, tolerance, interaction and inter-communication. What is falsely constructed is a walled fortress of cultural identity where once a semi-permeable membrane served to keep boundaries malleable, adaptable and the culture it enclosed nourished and alive. Behind the newly built walls all aspects of culture and history must be dragooned into an acceptable martial array – identity becomes something that is no longer self-evident and accepted but a perception of self that must be protected and defended, it seamlessly reconstitutes itself as a battleground, with hierarchically ordered ranks of official arbiters of what is authentic and what is not. Such self-consciousness is subtle, and not so subtle, reordering; not an affirmation of all that is old, original and enduring but a wholesale departure from history through the enforced act of personal redefinition. But the self-definition it insists on to shape a new identity becomes the antithesis of continuity, the very essence of neurotic obsession. Manto's own insecurities about what and who he was were an internalised manifestation of India's lack of self-confidence about its own self-perception. The end of the Raj did not return India to its original status: that of a world civilisation. It brought India down to the station of a nation-state at par with other modern nation-states such as Kenya, Bolivia and Hungary. The reductive violence that India performed on itself was bound to be reflected in the breakdown of civilisational synthesis among and between religions and communities, cultures and customs, friends and neighbours.

Manto saw violence as a necessary product of a distorted Self. This is why, for him, the end of the Raj was not a cause for celebration: he never talked of 'independence' but of 'partition' – of breakdown of a civilisation into mutually hostile and warring nation-states. His deep hatred for nationalism, and the meaningless violence it generates and perpetuates, is well illustrated in *Tay wal ka kutha* ('The Dog of Tay Wal'). In the mountains of Tay Wal, two armies face each other, entrenched not just in their military positions but also their nationalisms. These two 'nationalities' are the tributaries of the same river as is made clear by the fact that both armies are humming and singing the same Urdu and Punjabi poetry. But their encounter in the battlefield is meaningless – neither side understands what they are doing there or why they should be there. Into this no man's land of banal violence wanders a stray dog. But is it an Indian or a Pakistani dog? As a perceptive soldier remarks, 'now the dogs too will have to be either Hindustani or Pakistani'. Both sides look at the dog's identity with suspicion. Each side feeds it and then fires at it forcing the poor animal into a quandary where it doesn't know where to turn. The dog is eventually shot in a pointless act of violence. But each side tries to find significance by interpreting the act in its own terms:

'The poor fellow has died a noble death', Subaidar Himat Khan mumbled sympathetically. Jamadar Harnam Singh gripped the hot muzzle of his gun in his hand and said, 'He's died the death of a dog.'[2]

And that's the point: significance cannot be wrenched out of futility. The killing of the dog in *Tay Wal ka Kutha* is as meaningless as the murder of the coolie in *Khuni Thuk* or the killing of the labourer in *Taqat ka Imtahan*. The difference is that acts of individual violence are now replaced by the violence of the armed forces of nation-states. Whether individual, communal or acts of the collective state, Manto tries to show, violence is meaningless, a product of distorted self-perceptions.

But it is not just nationalism that distorts India's Self. Manto saw that other forms of imported ideology were equally detrimental to India's civilisational identity. Despite the fact that he was courted by 'progressive writers' all his life, he never joined their ranks – a rebuke that was avenged when, later in his life, his work was mercilessly attacked by them. The comedy, *Taraqi Pasand* ('The Progressive'), reflects what Manto thought of those who are easily impressed by 'progressive' western ideas. Juginder Singh, a devout husband and a short story writer, likes to describe himself as 'progressive'. But 'what is *this* "progressive"?', his wife asks him:

With a slight movement of his turbaned head, Juginder Singh said, 'Progressive ... one can't understand the word right away. A "progressive" is a person who believes in progress. It's a Persian word. In English such a person is called "radical". Writers who promote progress are referred to as "progressive writers". At present there are only three or four progressive writers in India, and I am one of them.'[3]

The portrait of Juginder Singh is more than a representation of so-called progressive writers in India during the 1930s and 1940s – it is a composite portrait of all Indians enamoured with modernity and captivated by the west. Hence:

Juginder Singh always made a conscious effort to express his ideas in English; it was a habit now for him to constantly use English words. Indeed, they had become part of his personality. He would go out of his way to use words, sentences and expressions that he noted in the works of famous English novelists. Some 50 per cent of his conversation consisted of English words and sentences selected from books written in English. Aflatoon was referred to as Plato now; Aristoo was Aristotle and Dr Sigmund Freud, Schopenhauer and Nietzsche were often quoted.[4]

We are consciously presented with shift in self-perception. Despite his appearance and long beard (which plays an important part in the story), Juginder Singh has ceased to be an Indian. In so far as language shapes thought, he has moved out of the mental frame of Indian concepts and categories. The transformation of 'Aflatoon' and 'Aristoo' into Plato and Aristotle is particularly significant. Although they refer to the same individual, Aflatoon is not Plato: Aflatoon reflects the Indian understanding of the Greek philosopher; Plato is how Europe saw the same philosopher. The two perceptions are not just different, they are based on different histories, and reflect different values, different ethical and practical potentialities: Juginder Singh's rejection of Aflatoon amounts to a rejection of his own history, the learning and knowledge of his own civilisation, understanding and appreciation of his own culture – hence a negation of his own identity. The embrace of Plato is the grip of western civilisation; thus Juginder Singh is a prototype modernist.

Like most modernists, Juginder Singh is eager to assert his new (distorted) identity, to seek reaffirmation from others who are deemed worthy of appreciating his stature. He thus regularly invites celebrated writers to spend a few days as his guest. His search for notable guests leads him to Harendarnath Tirpathi, 'a poet as well as writer of stories' who is 'immensely popular'. The main cause of Tirpathi's popularity is that he is *awara*: a displaced person who moves from place to place. But Tirpathi's *awara* nature is as much terrestrial as it is mental: as a popular writer Tirpathi inhabits landscapes that are clearly outside the purview of Indian civilisation. Perhaps he has learned his craft, Juginder Singh's wife thinks aloud, 'from an Englishman'.

That Tirpathi is even more of a progressive than Juginder Singh is made obvious in the first encounter of the two writers: Tirpathi's 'thick, black beard' is 'at least 20 times longer' than that of Juginder Singh – which itself is not short by any means! During the first few days of his stay, Tirpathi listens to the stories of Juginder Singh. Then, he starts reading his own stories to Juginder Singh: and he reads, and reads, and reads. Now, while there is no overt violence in *Taraqi*

Pasand, it is in fact a story of sadistic violence – despite its humorous overtones. This violence is generated by Tirpathi's absolute obsession with himself and how he totally takes over Juginder Singh's life. He comes not to visit, but to stay. And he does not come alone; he shifts his whole family to Juginder Singh's house. So:

One day, when Tirpathi had finished reading his latest story, about the sexual relationship between a man and a woman, Juginder was heartbroken to realise that for 21 days he has been sleeping, curled up under the same blanket, with this huge, long-bearded fellow, instead of being with his wife. The thought overwhelmed him and burnt him from the inside. 'What kind of guest is this', he agonised, 'who has become a parasite, who won't budge from here ... and his wife and daughter, I had almost forgotten, the whole family has shifted here without thinking of me, without realising that a poor clerk like me, with a meagre pay of 50 rupees a month, cannot support them for long. I would be pulverised. How much longer can I afford to entertain them? And then there are his stories, unending – after all I am only human, not a steel trunk, I cannot listen to his stories every day ... and how dreadful that I have not slept with my wife in all this time ...'[5]

Taraqi pasand ends with the entrapment of Juginder Singh: all his attempts to get rid of Tirpathi are thwarted; and Tirpathi's presence effectively renders him impotent by practically denying his conjugal relationship with his wife. He is eternally enmeshed listening to never-ending stories of Tirpathi, he cannot return to his own home or restore his home life to himself.

Manto saw the western 'isms' popular in India – progressivism, modernism, nationalism, secularism, fascism – in terms of the character of Tirpathi. We invite them because we are impressed by them and because through them we seek to confirm our distorted identity. They come with their entire cultural baggage. And once they arrive they never leave; they perpetuate themselves with endless productions of new fashions, new trends, new stories.

The 'isms' present us with a linear projection: progressives tend to be modernists who lean towards nationalism who insist on secularism as the only ideology for nation building – and secular nationalism sometimes leads to fascism. Of course, not all progressives follow this linear course; not all nationalists become fascists; but the path is there and there are always those who will, consciously or unconsciously, take it. Manto was shocked, as I am, to notice how many in India chose to follow this path.

VIOLENCE OF THE DISTORTED SELF

Hindu self-perception changed in the quagmire of colonialism. While Britain discovered its racial Self in the Raj, many Indian intellectuals sought cures for their colonially engineered inferiority complex in Germany. While the British tutored their coming generations of colonial administrators in Plato's philosophy, Homer's epics and escapades of Alexander the Great, Indian intellectuals schooled themselves with Max Mueller's ideas of the superiority of the Aryan race and sought audience with a certain Adolf Hitler. The Hindu who was forced to inject the images of himself from the colonial folklore as 'inherently untruthful', 'effeminate' and 'lacking moral courage', sought relief by a reactionary search to establish a macho version of himself. However, identities do not emerge from thin air – they have to be consciously constructed. Moreover, identities, especially distorted ones, need sustenance from history and provisions within contemporary culture to survive and thrive. This is where lies, as an instrument of social engineering, enter Indian history.

As Purushottam Agarwal observes, 'the theoretical construct and the historical narrative of communal nationalism *follows the method* of secular nationalism. It creates its own historical narratives in order to prove the perennial existence of the putative nation and the inevitability of this nation acquiring the modern form of a nation state.'[6] For the chauvinist Hindu Self to exist a new nationalist history for India had to be constructed. Before and during the Raj, both Muslims and the Hindus were perceived as indigenous to Indian civilisation. Hindu nationalism sought to portray the Muslims as 'Outsiders', as the demonic Other who usurped Hindu destiny. Thus the mass uprising of 1857 against the British became a conspiracy to re-establish Muslim rule in India (my childhood heroine, the Rani of Jhansi, obviously died in vain!). For many Hindu nationalists, British rule was not an aberration but as 'blissful' as that of Ram; indeed, Bharatendu Harishchandra (1850–1885), wrote in a poem, it was an act of liberation for Hindus oppressed and suppressed for centuries by Muslims. And, 'such writers as Vishnu Krishna Chiplunkar (1850–1882), Pratapnarayan Misra (1856–1894) and Swami Shraddhananda (1857–1926) could construct a history of Hindu society in which social evils such as sati, child marriage, purdah and the caste system were read as survival mechanisms, reactions to Muslim lechery'.[7] By the end of the First World War, liberal, progressive writers had joined

Hindu nationalist literatis in describing India as distinctively Hindu and Muslims as fundamentally alien.

By the time Manto turned 20, in 1933, Hindu fascism had become quite a fashion in India. Fascist movements, emulating the fascists of Europe, were active throughout the subcontinent. The leaders of the Rashtriya Sawamsevak Sangh (RSS), or National Volunteers, were openly advocating that Hindus should follow the example of the Nazis: treat the Muslims just as the Nazis were treating the Jews.[8] Communal riots were a common occurrence. There was a movement amongst the literati to expunge the Urdu heritage from Hindi. Manto was appalled by it. 'This war between Hindi and Urdu', he wrote, 'no matter how hard I try, I just cannot fathom it.'[9] Reluctantly, Manto began to accept the reality of Hindu chauvinism; like Jinnah and other leaders of the Muslim League, he realised that behind the benign ranks of Hindu nationalism there lurked another troop formation, one whose objective was the realisation of Hindu chauvinism. In a famous speech to the students of Jogeshwari College in Bombay in 1944, he announced: 'If you are not familiar with the time period we are passing through, read my stories. If you cannot bear these stories, that means this is an unbearable time. The evils in me are those of the era.'[10] In *Naya Qanun* ('New Law'), published in 1937, Manto puts his feelings about Indian politics in the mouth of his protagonist, Ustad Mangoo, a socially aware but impatient and simple-minded driver of a one-horse carriage (*tonga*). The India Act of 1935 has just become law and Ustad Mangoo is out in his *tonga* to see what visible changes the new law has ushered in. When he fails to notice any change, Mangoo becomes frustrated and picks a fight with a British soldier. Despite the new law, the soldier freely throws abuse at Mangoo and the police treat him as they always treated the natives. *Naya Qanun* is about change – or rather lack of change in India. 'The Congress wants to free India', Mangoo says. 'I say that they can struggle all they want, for a thousand years, and not much will be achieved. The biggest achievement will be that the British will leave ... but Hindustan will remain enslaved.' Mangoo asks: 'why the Hindus and Muslims are always fighting each other?'. Because, he answers, 'a holy man cast a curse upon the people. I have been told by my elders that Emperor Akbar once upset a learned sage who cursed him. "Go", the sage said, "there will always be strife in your Hindustan".'[11] In an interesting historical twist, Manto traces the origins of Hindu–Muslim discord to Akbar, who is acknowledged as the most accommodating and tolerant of all Mughal kings, thus providing a counter-point to the Hindu extremism he saw all around him. His way of coming to terms with it was to satirise it. In contrast, Jinnah and the Muslim League sought to contain and, if possible, to eradicate it. As Jinnah's biographer Ayesha Jalal has argued and shown so convincingly, Jinnah's strategy to combat the rise and rise of Hindu nationalism, and Hindu fascism, was to *threaten* separation of Hindus and Muslims: it was only a bargaining device in the Muslim League's confrontation with the Congress.[12] The actual partition of India was not the product of this bargaining device but the result of the direct influence that Hindu chauvinism exercised on the Congress – the Muslim League was totally outmanoeuvred. Jinnah is often portrayed as an arid, uncompromising and sinister man in the historical narratives of partition – as for example in Richard Attenborough's public relations job for India, *Gandhi*. In reality, Jinnah was as much a victim of Hindu chauvinism as Manto who was driven out of Bombay, under threats of death, and forced to migrate in January 1948 to Lahore.

The physical and ethnic partition of India were prerequisites for the full flowering of Hindu chauvinism. An ideology that 'celebrates aggression and violence, declares war against other communities, and scorns all legal and democratic norms'[13] needs identifiable enemies both within and without to flourish. Partition was a necessity if the project of modern Hindutva was to continue. It provided those concerned both with acquiring power and keeping and managing power with a readily available instrument whereby the cultural logic of 'them' and 'us', 'insiders' and 'outsiders', the 'native majority' and the 'ethnic minority Other', could be played out to its full potential.

The discourse of 'Othering', the political project of creating sharply defined Outsiders who can be easily painted with all colours black, is based essentially on three elements: a yardstick by which the Others are measured; a conceptual language by which the Others are described; and foolhardy Others who – consciously or unconsciously – accept the process of demonising and then play the assigned roles of the new dynamic: the pincer movement of corresponding reactionary non-encounter.[14] Once the category of Other is in place there are only non-encounters between representatives of artificially constructed identities: 'real' people in all their complexity cease to exist, one deals with character notes that are defined as abstraction, irrespective of the living, breathing individual one happens to meet.

Western civilisation uses a linear projection of history, starting from Greece and ending today with *pax Americana*, as its yardstick to measure all other cultures. All history, in western perception, is western history: history of all non-western cultures are mere tributaries which flow into the Grand History of secularism at the apex of which sits the white Anglo-Saxon male who today is the WASP who symbolises the potency of American power. Just as the WASP is unrepresentative, an actual minority within American society and history, so the linear notion of history is an historically fabricated idea, unrepresentative of the emergence and development of the west. The self-ascribed essentials of character, lifestyle and belief, however unrepresentative they may be of actual practice today or in history, become the norm by which Other cultures are measured, censured and demonised, and must inevitably be found wanting. The irreducible problem of the Other is they are not 'us'. Once virulent self-description becomes the norm it must include description of the Other, a description which stands before and in front of all individuality or community, as the first and last truth that can never be denied or overthrown; for at base, the Other is legitimately and decidedly not 'us', but someone seeking to be his or herself. As problematic as the philosophical conundrum of the chicken and egg, it is impossible to say whether it is the creation of a new sense of self-identity which creates the Other in all its boundary-defining utility, or the presence of those perceived as Other that stirs the self-conscious Self description industry into headlong search for a newly constructed identity. What is obvious is that neither can exist without their Other, the darker shadow that throws into high relief what is valued, best and admired about the Self that has been devised. What does the Othering do for the Other? As the excluded and marginalised in a power equation they always come off second best. But by the very term of the equation they have one thing to hold on to, effectively powerless they may be but they know precisely and exactly that they scare the hell out of the dominant society, they are assured of the frightening capacity on every opportunity, from every manifestation of culture. To be Othered is not fair, just or equitable – but it does have its frisson, its air of intoxicating machismo – 'they have all that and they are still afraid of little old us?' The practice and rhetoric of Othering leave no room for dialogue, it is a logic too rationalistic and formulaic to permit exchange of meaningful opinion, it constructs as the only questions real matters that are not of overriding significance, yet which cannot be denied or disowned in their totality, as the only valid topics for debate – the rest must be silence. So what resort do those who are Othered upon have? They embrace their militant, frightening menace as a bolster to their pride, they become as neurotically delusional as everyone else – and sometimes they learn to play the power game on exactly the same terms as the dominant society.

Islam stubbornly refuses to be a part of the Grand History of Secularism – indeed, it claimed and projected itself as World History, in other words, as a rival, the very means by which it entered into western consciousness.[15] Hindu chauvinism has closely followed this route. Just as Islam has been projected by Europe as a hostile creed at war with the west since the days of the Crusades, so too the Hindu right has structured Indian history on the myth of a continuous, thousand-year-old Muslim hostility against the Hindus. What began in the west is reinforced through the pervasive culture of the west, which affects India as much as any part of the globe. It is the justification built over millennia in the relations between Islam and the west which adds weight to the new process of Othering Islam in India. It is an ironic reflection that 500 years of Hindu chauvinism is indeed completing da Gama's task for him: a prime objective of the European search for a direct route to the Indies was to acquire new allies in the contest with Islam, to outmanoeuvre the rival who could never be one of 'us'. It is certainly the case that Hindu chauvinist conceptions of the 'Muslim threat' in India cannot be delinked from the global media barrage of justificatory material that equates the word Muslim with terrorist and Islam as the source of unrelenting incitement to terror tactics. Every technique of this western media industry can be found reiterated in the Indian media, not by co-incidence but by design, the design enforced by the adaptation of national Self description and the Othering process it gives birth and is heir to.

The western fixed scale of measurement, secularism, is replaced in Hindutva discourse by an equally rigid, and totally fabricated, notion of Ram. Secularism creates an authoritarian structure by placing itself above all other ideologies; it presents itself as an arch ideology that provides the framework within which all other ideologies can exist. Truth thus becomes secular 'truth': other notions of truth must prostrate themselves in front of secular absolutes. Secular man thus not only knows the Truth, he actually owns it. The new Ram of Hindutva politics is a similar linear construction: devoid totally of the multi-layered complexity and richness of the traditional concept of Ram, the newly constructed deity now appears as a flat, singular projection that allows for no deviation, no alternative visions, no compromises. The tender and tolerant Ram of traditional Hindu religiosity, the figure that inhabits the memories of traditional Hindus, is replaced with an intolerant, violent Ram hell-bent on war against Muslims.[16] This Secularist Ram now defines truth solely in terms of his attitudes to the Other: he is the yardstick by which one determines who is an insider and who an outsider in the Indian Nation. But this Ram has not only been secularised; he has also been commodified: those who know Ram, know the truth, also own the truth: Ram is a property, a corporation that can take over the 'disputed sites' of the outsiders. Just as secularism is totally disdainful of all religion, so too Hindu chauvinism is quite contemptuous of Hindu religiosity. This is a direct result, argues Purushottam Agarwal, of the

cultural inferiority complex suffered by the colonial literati. This literati was anxious to replace traditional religiosity (of which it was disdainful) with a muscular 'national' religion capable of embodying the aggressiveness latent in their sense of political and cultural inferiority as a colonised people. Thus popular religiosity became a recurring object of disdain in the writings of Dayanand Saraswati, and in a more subliminal fashion, in the writings of Savarkar and Golwalkar.[17]

But popular religiosity, the Ram of the traditional Hindu memory, cannot be banished totally:

In a television report on the riots in Kanpur in the wake of the demolition of the Babri Masjid, an illiterate woman narrated her nightmarish experience, in a story which is a painful manifestation of unsullied faith. She had given shelter to her frightened neighbours in her own house, when some rioters approached her and asked her to prove her Hindu credentials by uttering the slogan 'Jai Shri Ram' (Victory to Lord Ram). She refused. As she put it later, how could the name of Ram sanctify a murderous assault? The woman was simply differentiating (without articulating in so many words) between Ram as a name given to an idea that permeates the universe and Ram as a name being used to legitimise the politics of murder. This is then the distinction that Hindu communalism consciously seeks to eliminate ...[18]

Before partition, the communalist favourite slogan was *Vande Matram* (Hail, mother country). After partition, the slogan changed to *Jai Sri Ram* (Victory to Ram). But the new Ram needed a new language which in describing the Outsiders could actually construct reality according to the new vision of civil society as a terrain for civil war. Here too Hindu chauvinism found a ready made instrument from the western canons: the language of orientalism. The Hindu nationalist discourse has totally internalised both the language and the perceptions of orientalism. Muslims are typically represented in the literature of Hindu right, as well as in the Indian press and media in general, as violent, intolerant, criminally inclined and sexually depraved – a direct echo of all the orientalist travel literature of the eighteenth and nineteenth century. Just as colonial visitors and administrators saw the Muslims of the Middle East, and their counterparts still see today, as teeming masses, proliferating and multiplying like rabbits, so too Hindu nationalists project Muslims as a polygamous lot, with huge families, multiplying at an exponential rate. When mosques are destroyed they become 'disputed structures' but when temples are destroyed they remain temples; Muslims defending their mosques or their lives and property are 'out looking for blood' but those who perpetuate and participate in chauvinistic terror are simply *kar sevaks* (religious workers) or *ram bhaks* (devotees of Ram); Muslim migrants from Bangladesh become 'infiltrators' but Hindu migrants are simply 'refugees'.

This kind of pathological orientalising is not the sole province of the Hindu nationalist right. It has now become a common perception of the Indian intelligentsia and middle classes – a direct reflection of the deeply ingrained prejudices that are etched out in the subconsciousness of the western middle classes and western intellectuals: a perception that resurfaces periodically as we witnessed during the Rushdie affair and the Gulf War.[19] The notion that Muslims are some sort of violent, social deviants, prone to spontaneous violence is now taken for granted: 'it has become one of the unspoken assumptions of the news framework'.[20] Examine almost any report of communal violence in the Indian press and witness the whole array of the orientalist lore in action. Consider, for example, the terrible riot in Bhagalpur in October–November 1989.

A thousand people were killed. Nine hundred of these were Muslims. According to the recent Sinha-Hasan report on the Bhagalpur riots, 'hordes of Hindus, the number approaching thousands, attacked the localities and villages of Muslim inhabitants, but nobody was arrested while in the process of attacking an area'. And during the subsequent searches and arrests 'reminiscent of the searches in occupied Europe by the Nazis', it was the responsible and respectable members of the Muslim community who were neither involved in political nor in any ideological or religious fanaticism who were subjected to the fascist methods of torture ...'. Yet, during the entire period of Bhagalpur riots, there was an established bias against Muslims in almost all the newspapers. The reports pointed to the Muslims as instigating the riots; claimed the Hindus were tolerant, while Muslims were aggressive; and spotted a fictitious Pakistani hand in the disturbances. In fact, the myth of equal losses by both communities could have been easily shattered by even a cursory visit to the camps.[21]

Indeed, it now seems that Hindu chauvinism has finally claimed most of the Hindu middle class as its mantle. The notion of 'the highest Good as a life of endless devotion to the nation state, and the religious devotion to and celebration of the nation as valorous community', writes Dilip Simeon, is now uncritically accepted by most Indians. 'Homogeneity, a monolithic culture, uniformity (and uniforms) in civil society' are notions that are embraced by 'even those who laid claim to a liberal heritage'.[22] The language of Hindu nationalism is quite in evidence in the press, television, films and judiciary – every Indian institution seems to be singing the same tune. If we are to believe *The Times of India*, for example, little Hindu communalism is not much more than a backlash against the activities of Muslims. According to Girilal Jain,[23] the national daily's ex-editor, only Hindus can form the basis of Indian Nation and nationalism; Hindu secularism is wonderfully tolerant towards other religious beliefs; and 'Hindutva' is a mass movement originating from subaltern depths (so it is all right to kill and mutilate Muslims, destroy their property, go on rampant mass killings of adivasis and harijans, organise mass rapes – for this is what the good people of India want!). That celebrated champion of western humanism, and pathological hater of Muslims, V. S. Naipaul, naturally sees all this violence and savagery as a positive development: he just cannot get himself to describe Hindu chauvinism as fascism or to refer to the Babri Masjid with its proper name but waxes lyrical about 'resurgent' Hinduism.[24] These messages reverberate on television. The most recent rendering of *Ramayana* (shown in Britain on BBC), for example, brings the sacred epic text into the service of chauvinism: it is presented as discourse on the necessity of defending national and racial (Aryan) purity and as a narrative where illuminated patriarchy rescues a romanticised community from a debased present. The hagiographic biography of the militant Hindu nationalist, V. D. Savarkar, broadcast on Doordarshan, the state-run television station, on 28 May 1992, conveniently forgets to mention that he was actually accused of, and was certainly the main conspirator in, the murder of Gandhi. And we can read the same message on the big screen. In films like Mani Ratnam's *Roja*, Islam is portrayed as intrinsically violent, and Muslims as inherently unpatriotic. *Roja* is about the kidnapping of a newly married man by the Kashmiri separatists. In the film's key sequence, the Indian flag is set ablaze by separatists angered at the Indian government's refusal to negotiate with them. While the leader of the separatists offers his prayers, the protagonist leaps on the flag, his hands tied behind his back, in a valorous attempt to extinguish the flames that threaten the ultimate symbol of the Nation. The praying separatist is deliberately inter-cut with our hero's attempt to save the flag in a clear attempt to show that Islam is incontestably against the principles of Indian nationalism and Muslims demonstrably alien to Indian nationhood. In such an atmosphere, it is easy to fix the origins of riots, all riots, upon Muslims and hence justify the course of Hindu nationalistic violence. 'There is thus', note Charu Gupta and Mukul Sharma, 'a common construction of riots as a case of Muslim aggression and Hindu counter-aggression.'[25]

Whereas films like *Roja* both express and provide a rationale for chauvinistic Hindu violence and nationalism, Indian judiciary – that bedrock of Indian secularism and impartiality – protects those who translate this vision into programmes of terror:

In recent years the high organs of the judiciary (with some noteworthy exceptions) have shown themselves to be increasingly pusillanimous in the face of criminal provocation of fascistic movements – witness the retreats of the Supreme Court over the Babri Masjid both in 1990 and 1992, as well as its demonstrable incapacity to punish those politicians and state officials who defied its order to protect the mosque. Moreover, political authority has shown itself to be partisan in the administration of justice: those guilty of the (anti-Sikh) pogroms of 1984 still receive protection; and no action has been taken against Bal Thackeray, the man who openly boasts of his responsibility for the violence in Bombay and tells the international press that Indian Muslims will be treated like the Jews were in Nazi Germany.[26]

Forget action! Instead read how mild-mannered, sophisticated and refined Thackeray really is in *The Times of India* whose pages he graces more than frequently. Or find out how Thackeray makes his favourite meals in the pages of society magazines, discover what he thinks of his favourite cricketers in sports periodicals or which actors he adores in film reviews. We shouldn't call this guy a fascist – V. S. Naipaul would remind us: he is a pop star.

In Manto's *Taraqi Pasand* ('The Progressive'), it was only Juginder Singh's household that was trapped by the invited Tirpathi and his extrinsic ideas. Western ideas behave like western imperialists: as Ustad Mangoo declares in *Naya Qanun* ('New Law'), 'they came to borrow fire, now they've become the masters of the house'. In modern India, the whole nation is entrapped – dare one say enraptured – by an imported ideology that came, like Tirpathi, to stay, and has now become the master of the Indian house. It has generated endless new stories, and refashioned old ones, to keep the traditional inhabitants of India away from their homes and conjugal beds.

The process of Othering is completed when the perceived enemy actually accepts, and begins to behave according to, the chauvinist projections. In other words, the categories of demonisation are internalised by the subject community. Stereotypes and caricatures assume realistic proportions; and those who are projected as outsiders begin to perceive themselves as outsiders. The Sikhs provide us with a good example of this process in action. In the 1960s and 1970s they were considered to be the bulwark of Hinduism. But in the 1980s the perception grew that the state was systematically denying justice to the Sikhs; the Sikh demonstrations, in the early 1980s, many of them quite peaceful, were not seen as legitimate action on the part of a grieved minority. On the contrary, the polity as well as the press and the media began to demonise the Sikhs just as they demonised the Muslims during the destruction of the Babri Masjid[27] and the 1993 riots in Bombay. The Sikh agitation transformed into communal violence: it was not surprising that if the Sikhs are going to be described as a violent, treacherous minority that they actually started moving within the orientalising projections. Worse: no community in India stood up for the Sikhs, or demonstrated with them, thus reinforcing the belief that the entire Indian nation-state saw them as Outsiders. The Sikh communal movement thus acquired secessionist tones and soon became separatist. Both succession and violence becomes legitimate in the eyes of those who are described as 'Outsiders' and who see the nation-state treating them as such.[28] We can see the same process in operation in the case of the Kashmiri militants: the origins of the demand for an independent Kashmir are to be found not in Srinagar but in the conceptualisation of a Ram that is intrinsically anti-Muslim, a nation-state that has legitimised violence against its own people, and an orientalising language that denies the Kashmiris their basic humanity.

Basic humanity: this is what Hinduism loses when it is transformed into Hindu nationalism. And in its turn, this is what Hindu chauvinism denies all Others who inhabit the subcontinent. An 'India' that is solely for the 'Hindu nation', a nation-state of Hindu *sarkar* where non-Hindu people 'entertain no idea but the glorification of the

Hindu nation', or can 'stay in the country wholly subordinated to the Hindu nation, claiming nothing, deserving no privileges ... not even citizen's rights', to use the words of M. S. Golwalkar, is not India.[29] Such an entity has never existed in history. Indeed, it is an impossible entity that cannot exist: there are too many 'cultural nations' in India for it to be the sole domain of a single distorted self-perception. Such a construction cannot accommodate all the 'I's – the cultural identities, the religious outlooks, the ethnic customs, the myriads of traditions – that constitute India.

Hindu nationalism, it seems reasonably clear, is a prescription for the balkanisation of India. If Hindus are a 'nation' so are all the other cultures of India. And they can fight for their 'nationhood' just as violently, and self-righteously, as the dominant group. As Dipankar Gupta notes, 'once such an option to nation statehood has become universally available, both ideologically and pragmatically, there is no holding a good, cultural logic down' and other cultures within the Indian state 'will inevitably force their way out of the unitary structure by delving deep into their respective ascriptive consciousness'.[30]

We need to see communal violence in terms of a cyclical process that eventually returns and consumes the perpetuator. Its origins can be firmly located in the distorted self-perception of a community. The contorted Self is often the product of an externally induced inferiority complex that leads both to lack of confidence in the authentic Self as well as to the construction of a new Self that is designed to undermine extrinsic demonising. If the newly constructed and distorted Self is to have any meaning, a fabricated historic narrative has to be created in which to locate its being; this narrative then becomes the yardstick by which the distorted Self is defined and all Others are measured. But this historical narrative not only defines the distorted Self of the community, it defines a linear Truth: a Truth that is owned by the community that it defines. History, tradition and culture thus cease to be based on common experience but are transformed into a system for concealing conflicts and oppressions – a system that operates by deploying a rhetoric of hatred and destruction. Often our use of terms to describe the violence of the distorted Self itself legitimises this violence. If we describe violence between two communities as ethnic violence than we unwittingly ascribe the roles of insiders and outsiders to each community. For ethnicity 'connotes, above all else, the signification of the primordially constituted "Other" as an "*outsider*"'. The term has its roots in the 'North American provenance where, apart from White Anglo-Saxon Protestants (WASPs), all other communities – Greek, Irish, Catholics, Germans, Jews, Hispanics and so on, have traditionally been, and continue to be, considered as "ethnics". The WASPs alone are the true insiders, the bed-rock of American mainstream culture.'[31] Thus, when we describe communal violence in India as 'ethnic violence' we concede that all minorities are outsiders and Hindu chauvinism is the only true culture of India. The language of demonisation eventually forces the demonised to accept their role as the Outsider. A new distorted Self is thus produced that repeats the cycle. Communal violence therefore is often the violence of the distorted Selves.

THE DERANGED COME HOME!

A distorted Self is a false Self; a Self that is located in a territory that does not and cannot provide the comforts of home; an *awara* (free-spirited) Self that is displaced and wanders aimlessly, like a vagrant, from place to place. For the cycle of communal violence in India to end, the distorted and displaced Selves of all the cultures of the subcontinent must come home. But where is home; and how do we get there?

This is precisely the question that the inmates of a lunatic asylum in Lahore ask in *Toba Tek Singh*, one of Manto's last stories. It is a couple of years after partition and the governments of India and Pakistan have agreed to exchange the inmates of their lunatic asylums: the Muslim lunatics from India are to be sent to Pakistan and Hindu and Sikh lunatics from Pakistan are to be transferred to India. The news of the exchange produces interesting reactions from the inmates of the Lahore asylum. 'What is this Pakistan?' one asks. 'A place in India where they manufacture razors', another replies. A Sikh lunatic asks another Sikh: 'Sardarji, why are we being sent to Hindustan? We can't even speak their language?' When two Anglo-Indian inmates hear that the British have given freedom to India they are devastated. They organise secret meetings to discuss their status in the asylum: will the European ward be retained? Will they continue to get English breakfast? Or will they be forced to eat bloody Indian *chappati* instead of sliced bread? All the inmates are confused: 'they could not figure out whether they were in Pakistan or India, and if they were in Pakistan, then how was it possible that only a short while ago they had been in India when they had not moved from the asylum at all?' No one was more baffled than Bishan Singh, 'a harmless man' who was known amongst the officials and inmates as Toba Tek Singh because he said he was from a place called Toba Tek Singh, where he owned land, and because he constantly uttered long strings of nonsensical words which sometimes ended with 'and Toba Tek Singh'. He did not want to go to India or Pakistan; he wanted to go home to Toba Tek Singh. So he asked one of his inmates, who believed he was God, about the location of Toba Tek Singh. The man replied, laughing: 'It is neither in Pakistan nor Hindustan. Because I haven't yet issued orders where it should be.' So Bishan Singh pleaded with this 'God' to give orders so that the question of Toba Tek Singh could be settled. But the man refused. And Bishan Singh thought that if the man had been a Sikh God instead of a Muslim one, he would have helped him find his home. The inmates were loaded onto a lorry and taken to a border crossing to be transferred. But when Bishan Singh's turn came to cross the border he refused to move. The officials pleaded with him saying, 'Toba Tek Singh is in Hindustan now – and if it is not there yet, we'll send it there immediately.' But Bishan Singh would not budge; and because he was totally harmless he was not forced and allowed to stand in his place while the transfer continued. Then, at dawn:

A piercing cry was emitted by Bishan Singh who had been quiet and unmoving all this time. Several officers and guards ran towards him; they saw that the man who, for 15 years, had stood on his legs day and night, now lay on the ground, prostrate. Beyond a wired fence on one side of him was Hindustan and beyond a wired fence on the other was Pakistan. In the middle, on a stretch of land, which had no name, lay Toba Tek Singh.[32]

Bishan Singh had come home.

   Toba Tek Singh is not a place: it is a state of grace. What Bishan Singh seeks is *toba*, the common Urdu word for forgiveness, but which in its deeper Islamic connotations means return to the original (guiltless) Self. The cure for Bishan Singh's insanity, the recovery of his distorted Self, cannot be found within the boundaries of nation-states, connected together with chains of animosity, and declaring their manhood in the language of nuclear bombs. In a rather subtle way, Manto suggests that the subcontinent itself is like the lunatic asylum in Lahore: he cleverly goes through all the standard subcontinental types and reveals their madness to be symptomatic of their particular obsessions. The cure for our collective insanity, the recovery of the Self, lies in that no man's land which has been abandoned in the mad pursuit of Nationhood. Home is that in-between territory where all the myriads of cultures of the subcontinent co-exist in a state of grace, at ease with their authentic Selves, with all the richness of their diversity intact and in full bloom. Home is the civilisation of India.

There is an alternative India waiting to be recovered by all the religions and cultural communities of the subcontinent, just as there is an alternative dynamic of coexistence waiting dustily in the wings to be brought to bear upon contemporary problems. There are indigenous conceptions of community, religious and ideological plurality, social diversity, of mediation and conciliation that have nothing to learn and much to teach the imported creeds of nation-state and secularism. The attraction of the nation-state and secularism is the allure of power, but the power they possess is malignant, a cancer whose progressive debilitating effects can be seen by careful analysis of the fragmenting social fabric of western society. Gorged on power, consumed by greed, afraid of everyone and trusting in nothing, not even their ability to spin delusional fantasies to give meaningful form to their own lives, this is the postmodern dispensation of the west. It can be purchased by anyone, the price is to accept the necessity of the supremacy of the secular nation-state as an ideology, and as that ideology which has been defined by the west. The journey home to the civilisational reconstruction of India is something quite different.

It must be a journey that embraces the kaleidoscopic plurality, heterogeneity, inclusive diversity of India and genuinely celebrates difference. All these things existed in the Indian past, they developed rationale, a practice, even a reformatory insurgency which could become new traditions at specific moments in history. What has been lost, overlaid, obscured and obliterated is our own knowledge of these things. Not only the future but the past is being made into a foreign country, a country where we were not at home. We need scholarship, and sincere effort to reach back and learn from the past, not to idealise it but to see it in its modes of living and living imperfections so that we can see our way to a different understanding of the present and our future potential. It is not chauvinism, the desire to admire uncritically, but informed critical sensibility and sensitivity that must be our guide. The crucial difference is that chauvinists can never admit to the enormity of past errors. But to build a better future we must be able to see, acknowledge and learn from those errors if we are to accept how fallible we are in contemporary times and thus acquire the courage to opt for an alternative, to change. How we change can never be a return to the past. It can only be a conceptual continuity in tune with our past, one that draws sustenance from the totality of the ideas present in the past, which included the means of sustainable tolerance and operative plurality that denied no one community its identity but did not make narrow identity the be all and end all of who and what we are.

The religious and cultural communities of the subcontinent need to see themselves not as 'nations' but as constituents of a world civilisation: with common histories, similar cultures and hence a common destiny. The reconstruction of India as a world civilisation must be the work of all its cultures and peoples, only such an inclusive endeavour can recover the authentic practice of plurality which was our past. Our alternative must be a leap of faith, founded in confessional consciousness, commitment to the values, ethics and beliefs we each cherish for we will find each of our traditions has not stinted in providing us with the imperatives to do justice, love mercy and walk in humility before our Creator. A confessional identity in a rabidly secular vessel is a nonsense that can only do violence to our sanity and sense of equilibrium. But different faiths can live together only when we have the good sense to follow the clearly enunciated dictates of justice, insight and mutual understanding that are their finest, most spiritual endowments of conscientious commitment, a dispensation incomprehensible to the secular mind. The common, shared love of home, of the places that make the world meaningful and provide our continuity with the ancestors who went before us, bind us together into the world civilisation of India that we must recreate, revitalise and give alternative expression to. The traditions of all the peoples of the subcontinent must come alive, be given contemporary meaning beyond the empty and inappropriate ideologies of nation-state and secularism. A civilisation thrives not on borrowed ideas and ideologies but on what it generates internally from the very fabric of its own vision: we thus have to relearn to see the world through the concepts and ideas that are our own. We have to learn where, in constructive tension with the rest of the world that is and will be, these ideas can take us. The past will not answer our contemporary difficulties but informed by its concepts, values and enduring significance we can make a worthwhile attempt to shape authentic futures for ourselves. A return to cultural authenticity would be a step forward to reconstructing India as a civilisation. Coming home is not easy: to reconstruct a fragmented civilisation is a daunting task. But the scent of Randhir's mountain girl and the short stories of Manto have left a long trail for all of us to follow on our return journey home.

13
The A B C D (and E) of Ashis Nandy

Ashis Nandy's *The Savage Freud* is dedicated to the memory of 'three Indians who symbolise the hundred-and-fifty-year-old attempt to re-engineer the Indian':

Vinayak Damodar Savarkar (1880–1965), unflinching warrior for Hindu nationalism, who spent his life trying to make the Hindu more martial, masculine, cohesive and organised; Damodar Dharmanand Kosambi (1907– 1960), indefatigable rationalist and progressive thinker, who never gave up his effort to make Indians more scientific, objective and historically minded; and Nirad C Chaudhuri (1897–) the last of the great Edwardian modernists of India, who has always thoughtfully shared the white man's burden, especially Europe's educational responsibilities in South Asia.[1]

It would be safe to assume that Nandy himself is not in favour of re-engineering the Indian: there is nothing much wrong with the old fashioned, traditional, but somewhat world weary *hindustani*. After all, the less than 'masculine' and 'scientific' Indian has survived centuries of colonisation and decades of modernity and instrumental development – and survived with his sanity and identity intact. Even now, in the closing years of the western millennium, the *hindustani* seems to demonstrate stubborn resilience in the face of all-embracing postmodernism and 'globalisation' and appears ever ready to preserve his or her Selfhood from whatever else the twenty-first century may throw at him or her. If Nandy stands *for* anything, it is the traditional *hindustani*; that is, someone who is much more than a mere 'Indian', a citizen of a nation-state called 'India'; someone whose Self incorporates a civilisation with its own tradition, history (however defined), life-styles and modes of knowing, being and doing.

It would be simplistic to try and understand Ashis Nandy in relation to others. For one thing, counterpoising the author of *The Intimate Enemy* with others amounts to comparing his thesis (tradition, civilisation, the total Self) with their anti-thesis

First published as the introduction to *Return from Exile* by Ashis Nandy, Oxford University Press, India, 1998.

(nationalism, rationalism, secularism etc.). Nandy is not amenable to this kind of (western) dualistic logic. There are three prerequisites for understanding Ashis Nandy and his thought. First: it is important to appreciate that he operates on a non-dualistic, four-fold logic where relationships of similarity and convergence are more important than cold, instrumental rationality and the universe has more options than simply either/or duality. Second: it is necessary to understand that Nandy functions beyond (rather than outside) the established conventions of western thought. Both the man and his ideas span a different universe, a universe that includes 'the west' but only as one civilisation in a multicivilisational world and then largely – and this may come as a surprise to many – as a victim. Nandy categorically locates himself with the victims of history and the casualties of an array of grand western ideas such as Science, Rationality, Development, Nation-State; but the victims of *zulm* (tyranny) in history and conceptual and ideational oppression in our time are located as much in a geographical, civilisational, intellectual and conceptual space called 'the west' as in the non-west. Nandy seeks both to unite the victims and to increase the awareness of their victimhood. Third: even though he is trained as a psychologist, Nandy has no respect for disciplinary boundaries. Indeed, to accept the disciplinary structure of modern knowledge is to accept the worldview of the west. But Nandy's scholarship is not interdisciplinary or transdisciplinary in the conventional sense; he is no 'Renaissance Man'. He is a polymath in the traditional sense; meaning he operates beyond the disciplinary structure of knowledge *and* regards all sources of knowledge – revelational as well as non-revelational, traditional as well as modern, tacit as well as objective – as equally valid *and* all methods and modes of inquiry as equally useful.

Given these traits, it is clear that Ashis Nandy's thought and scholarship is one long quest for alternatives to the dominant modes of everything! But it would be out of character if Nandy's alternatives were located within prevailing boundaries, or the search itself followed a common path.

ALTERNATIVES, ANDROGYNOUS

Nandy's first book, *Alternative Sciences: Creativity and Authenticity in Two Indian Scientists*, is dedicated to 'the Ramanujans who walk the dusty roads of India undiscovered and the Boses who almost make it but never do'.[2] The book analyses the life and work of Jagadis Chandra Bose, the Indian physicist and botanist, and Srinivasa Ramanujan, the brilliant mathematician. Bose, who tried to give a special Indian perspective to world science, was one of the earliest modern scientists to do interdisciplinary research, and mapped out a philosophy of science, which anticipated a number of major themes in the contemporary philosophy of science. In the west, he was considered a genius and a missionary-scientist; in India, he was a national hero. Unlike Bose, Ramanujan was totally a product of traditional India. Despite the fact that he failed all his academic examinations, Ramanujan emerged as a world-class mathematician: he practised a neat, non-dualistic science that has been the forte of Indian thought since the eighth century. Through an analysis of their lives, Nandy explores how modern and traditional India tried to cope with the culture of modern science, and how their personal search for meaning personified India's search for a new self-definition.

While Bose had a total belief in science, he was concerned with the parochialism of western science and the hostility of western scientists towards India and all things Indian. He suffered, Nandy alleges, from a double bind: on the one hand the perceived hostility of the west led him towards a growing hostility to the west; and, on the other, he felt a sense of inferiority vis-à-vis the west. He loved to have his wife and assistants sing western scientists' eulogies of his work to his visitors. Ramanujan's science relied as much on mysticism, metaphysics and astrology as it did on the abstract ideas of mathematics. He developed his own philosophy of life and his mathematics formed an integrated whole with his metaphysics and astrology. Nandy shows sympathy with both scientists – indeed, he demonstrates an unconditional love towards both – but he finds both their lives as well as their perceived alternatives wanting.

So what exactly is Nandy rejecting in *Alternative Sciences*? He clearly rejects the dominant mode of western science. But he also rejects Bose's attempts to seek an alternative within western science – an Indian Science that is actually an appendage to the 'universal model' of western science. And he rejects too Ramanujan's version of traditional Indian science even though it is rooted in a folk history. Both use a strategy that uses the west as a yardstick and consider their Indianness as a negative identification. And, as such, both alternatives are derived from the western notion of what is science and strive 'to be the exact reverse of what a hypothetical model of western analysis is'.[3] Thus, for Nandy, an alternative that is genuinely an alternative cannot take the west as its reference.

So what is Nandy's alternative an alternative to? To begin with, it is an alternative to a worldview that

believes in the absolute superiority of the human over the nonhuman and the subhuman, the masculine over the feminine, the adult over the child, the historical over the ahistorical, and the modern or progressive over the traditional or the savage and that has its roots in anthropocentric doctrines of secular salvation, in the ideologies of progress, normality and hyper-masculinity, and in theories of cumulative growth of science and technology.[4]

It is also an alternative to 'a fully homogenised, technologically controlled, absolutely hierarchised world' based on a dualistic logic of 'the modern and the primitive, the secular and the non-secular, the scientific and the unscientific, the expert and the layman, the normal and the abnormal, the developed and the underdeveloped, the vanguard and the led, the liberated and the savable'.[5]

But this alternative is not, and cannot be, an alternative to the west *per se*. For Nandy, the west is more than a geographical and temporal entity; it is a psychological category. Now the west is everywhere: within and without the west, in thought processes and actions, in colonial and neo-colonial structures and in the minds of oppressors and the oppressed – the west is part of the oppressive structure as well as in league with the victims. Thus, to be anti-west is itself tantamount to being pro-west; or in Nandy's words 'anti-colonialism, too, could be an apologia for the colonisation of minds'.[6]

Nandy's alternative then is located beyond the west/anti-west dichotomy, even beyond the indigenous constructions of modern and traditional options, in a totally different space. It lies in an entirely new construction: a 'victims' construction of the west, a west which would make sense to the non-west in terms of the non-west's experience of suffering.[7] This construction, both of a 'victims alternative' as well as of alternative west, turns out to be a strategy for survival. Modern oppression, Nandy asserts, is unique in many respects. Unlike traditional oppression – which is an encounter between the self and the enemy, the rulers and the ruled, the believers and the infidels – modern oppression is 'a battle between dehumanised self and the objectified enemy, the technologised bureaucrat and his reified victim, pseudo-rulers and their fearsome other selves projected on to their "subjects"'.[8] This is the difference between the Crusades and the Auschwitz, between Hindu–Muslim riots in India and the

Gulf War. And this is why, Nandy's alternative is the alternative of the victims; and whenever the oppressors make an appearance in this alternative they are revealed to be disguised victims 'at an advanced stage of psychosocial decay'.[9] The construction of their own west allows the victims to live with the alternative west 'while resisting the loving embrace of the west's dominant self.'[10]

India, then, is not the non-west. It is India and it cannot be defined in relation to the west. The ordinary Indian has no reason to seek his/her self-definition in relation to the west or to see himself/herself as a counter player or an anti-thesis of the western man or woman. The strain to be the opposite of the west distorts the priorities of the traditional worldview of India, dissolves the holistic nature of the Indian view of humanity and its place in the universe, and destroys Indian culture's unique *gestalt*. The search for alternatives is not a choice between east and the west or between north and south: 'it is a choice – and a battle – between the Apollonian and the Dionysian *within* India and *within* the west'.[11] Even if such a distinction does not exist in an oppressive culture, Nandy asserts, 'it has to be presumed to exist by its victims for maintaining their own sanity and humanness'.[12] There is thus no need to look elsewhere for ethically sensitive and culturally rooted alternative social knowledge for it is already partly available outside the framework of modern science and social sciences – 'in those who have been the "subjects", consumers or experimentees of these sciences'.[13]

Nandy's search for alternatives beyond the Hegelian thesis anti-thesis dichotomy has an interesting gender dimension. Colonial India, taking cue from the colonisers, went through a radical shift in its gender consciousness. Traditionally, Indian thought has given greater preference to *naritva* (the essence of femininity) and *klibatva* (the essence of androgy or hermaphroditism) in comparison to *purusatva* (the essence of masculinity).

Colonial India came to perceive the notion of *naritva* and *klibatva* as dangerous pathologies that could only lead India to a negation of masculine identity. All forms of androgyny were lumped together as a dangerous anti-thesis of beneficial, undifferentiated masculinity. Nandy leans towards the traditional by carefully choosing the subjects of his inquiry. Thus Ramanujan is deliberately counterpoised against Bose because he resembled his mother and grandmother in looks and had 'a delicate and conspicuously feminine build and appearance' with 'velvety soft palms and long tapering fingers'.[14] The British mathematician George Hardy, who gave Ramanujan the big break that his genius deserved, also turns out to be a 'queer'. Most of the characters in *The Intimate Enemy*, perhaps Nandy's most influential book, have ambiguous sexualities which are deliberately played upon: Gandhi, Oscar Wilde, Kipling, C. F. Andrews (the English priest described by Gandhi as Indian at heart and a true Englishman), Aurobindo ... However, this should not be read as an uncritical endorsement of the feminine principle. Under certain, specific conditions, Nandy argues (thinking perhaps of Mrs Indira Gandhi and Mrs Margaret Thatcher), femininity can be an indication of higher forms of masculinity.

The point here is that traditional Indian society, despite its patriarchal dimensions, does not allow gender, age and other biological differences to be transformed into principles of social stratification. On the contrary, it sees the masculine and the feminine, the infant, adult and the aged as a total continuum. The differences are acknowledged, but the boundaries are open and diffused.

BOUNDARIES, BIOGRAPHY

The dedication in *Science, Hegemony and Violence*, an anthology of essays that deconstruct modern science with devastating power edited by Ashis Nandy, reads: 'For A K Saran, Dharampal, Mohammad Idris who have tried to keep the future open for our generation of South Asians.'[15] Perhaps it is not widely known that Nandy is a futurist – but a futurist of a particular type. His concern, as opposed to those like Daniel Bell and Herman Kahn who would turn future studies into a closed discipline with its own priesthood, sacred texts and formal content, is to keep the boundaries of future studies and the future completely open. In their own way, the three to whom the book is dedicated have tried to do the same: A. K. Saran has spent all his intellectual energies demolishing the positivist boundaries of all Indian social science disciplines;[16] Dharampal tried to rescue the history of Indian science and education from the clutches of western and westernised historians and open it up to new interpretative possibilities;[17] and Mohammad Idris has devoted his life to saving the environment and cultural ecology of South-East Asia and South Asia.[18] Nandy stands for a plural future and much of his thought is concerned with the survival of cultures incompatible with western notions of modernity, science, progress and rationality. The survival, and hence the future, of non-western cultures, he has maintained, depends on pluralising human destiny; and future studies, in its current incoherent form, offers escape routes that history, in its current institutionalised, disciplinary form, does not.

Nandy's concern for ensuring that boundaries – of disciplines, cultures, genders, futures, alternatives – remain open and diffused, combined with his genial but aggressive stance against western grand narratives – Science, Reason, Progress, Nationalism – and his deliberate attempt to dissolve the difference between high and low art and culture, appear to locate him within the domain of postmodernism. But this location is more apparent than real. Nandy's position has some subtle and some serious differences from many of those who belong to the postmodern persuasion. Postmodernism celebrates difference but blurs the boundaries that maintain difference. Under postmodernism, boundaries come crashing down. Nandy celebrates difference but not for its own sake: he wants different cultures to survive, indeed thrive, and remain different with their distinctive traits intact. Thus in his thought, boundaries are still needed so that difference can retain its difference; but one must have an open attitude to boundaries to avoid falling into the trap of 'fundamentalism', 'puritanism' and 'nationalism'. Like so many postmodern writers, Nandy does not recognise a category called 'ethnicity' which demarcates a division between 'true insiders' and the constructed Other, the outsider. All those people who are described as ethnic, whether in the United States – where, apart from the white Anglo-Saxons, all other communities, from the Jews to Greeks, Irish, Hispanics and Asians, are described as ethnic thus confirming their outsider status – or in India, are primordially deemed to be Others. His basic elements of analysis are culture and civilisation (which assumes grand narrative proportions in Nandy's writings); he wants to retain both categories as analytical tools as well as distinctive and different entities. The cultural subjects of difference, the non-western cultures and civilisations, Nandy has argued so forcefully, must be accorded the right and the space to negotiate their own conditions of discursive control and to practise their difference as a rebellion against the hegemonic tendencies of both modernity and postmodernism. The differences and diversities in Indian culture, he writes, are often sought in

The uniqueness of certain cultural themes or in their configuration. This is not a false trail, but it does lead to some half-truths. One of them is the clear line drawn, on behalf of the Indian, between the past and the present, the native and the exogenous, and the Hindu and the non-Hindu. But ... the west that is aggressive is sometimes inside; the earnest, self-declared native, too, is often an exogenous category, and the Hindu who announces himself so, is not that Hindu after all. Probably the uniqueness of Indian culture lies not so much in a unique ideology as in the society's traditional ability to live with cultural ambiguities and to use them to build psychological and even metaphysical defences against cultural invasions. Probably, the culture itself demands that a certain permeability of boundaries be maintained in one's self-image and that the self be not defined too tightly or separated mechanically from the not-self. This is the other side of the strategy of survival – the clue to India's post-colonial worldview.[19]

For non-western cultures and civilisations, as well as for Nandy, relativism cannot be absolute: it must be conditional, critical and concise. Postmodernism notwithstanding.

In postmodern thought and practice, past and future implode into the present. Thus both history and (western) utopia/dystopias become instruments of dominance and techniques of rewriting the life plan of the lesser mortals of the world. For Nandy, all politics of the past, as well as all politics of the future, are attempts to shape the present. And the search for a non-oppressive present or a just and sustainable future often ends with new modes and techniques of oppression. The past is often used to keep the non-western cultures and civilisation in a vice-like grip; and it comes in useful for imposing limits on the visions of the future. The present of the non-west is often projected as the past of the west; and the future of non-west, in such a straitjacket, can only be the present of the west. This linear, progressive and cumulative notion of history, a product of liberal, humanistic ideologies, is used to curb the emergence of genuine alternative worldviews, alternative visions of the future and even alternative self-definitions and self-concepts. This is why, Nandy contends, 'the peripheries of the world often feel that they are victimised not merely by partial, biased or ethnocentric history, but by the idea of history itself'.[20]

How can we ensure that alternative visions of the future do not simply become steps towards the construction of new oppression? Future utopias and visions, Nandy contends, must have in-built ability to account for their legitimate and illegitimate offsprings. The oppressive actions of zealous visionaries in the name of their visions cannot be explained away as simply the actions of misguided adherents or products of misuse or deviations and false interpretations. A vision must take the responsibility of what is undertaken in its name. What this actually means is that the vision itself must have some capacity to liberate the visionaries from its own straitjacket. And, as such, it cannot claim 'a monopoly on compassion and social realism, or presuming itself to be holding the final key to social ethics and experience. Such a mission not merely devalues all heretics and outsiders as morally and cognitively inferior, it defines them as throw-backs to an earlier stage of culture and history, fit to be judged exclusively by the norms of the vision.'[21]

When Nandy uses biography and narrative as a tool of cultural analysis, he deconstructs them using these criteria. In postmodernism, narrative – particularly fiction – has itself become a theory of salvation. For example, Richard Rorty argues that philosophy and theory can no longer function to ground politics and social criticism, only fiction (he is particularly partial towards Nabokhov and Orwell), can give us insight into what sort of cruelty we are capable of, and awaken us to the humiliation of particular social practices.[22] In British cultural studies, biography has acquired a similar role. Our salvation lies in art, argues Fred Inglis, and 'the art-form for each of our ordinary lives is, of course, biography'.[23] Thus, biography makes sense of our experiences and gives meaning to our individual lives: it teaches us how to live and how not to live. And cultural studies, particularly in its British form, is going to be the new theology that will teach the young how to think, what to feel, how to live, and what it is to be good. The assertions, writes Inglis,

Arise distinctly from the structure of feeling and frame of thought which, in small corners of non-elite academies, have formed cultural studies. And elite or not, there is no doubt in my mind that the strong tide of interest running through a generation in the style and preoccupations of cultural studies however named is evidence of the subject's larger timeliness. I will risk declaring that *this is the way the best and brightest of present-day students in the human sciences want to learn to think and feel.* And having learned to think and feel thus, this is how they want to act and live ...There is, as always, a story hidden in these assertions. It is the story of how cultural studies will make you good. (italics in the original)[24]

It is beyond Nandy's intellectual constitution to be so coarse. For him, biography is a ground for mining psychological insights, for understanding how the Indian Self survived, or failed to survive, the onslaught of colonialism, for constructing a politics of awareness – not a new theology of deliverance.

But deliverance is essentially what western thought is all about, Nandy would argue. In modernity, of course, the grand narratives are essentially vehicles of salvation. Having swept all grand narratives aside, postmodern thought generates the illusion that there is nothing for us to do than to live with the horror of meaninglessness. But both modernity and postmodern thought fall back on a single theory of salvation: the secular imagination. It is not by accident that Rorty suggests that the real goal of postmodernist thought is to expunge all traces of religious thought;[25] and Inglis suggests 'that the study of culture, as of nature, teaches atheism'[26] – this is not a conclusion of philosophical or cultural inquiry but a deep-seated assumption that is an essential component of dominant western consciousness. This insistence of western thought to fall back on secularism – disguised as 'liberal humanism' or 'biography' or 'cultural studies' as well as numerous other forms – has led Nandy to argue that the west and its relationship with the non-west has become deeply intertwined with the problem of evil in our time. The only good that the west can see in the non-west is purely in terms of secularism. Thus, Inglis cannot see any good in Islam and is happy to dismiss it as 'angry and vengeful'.[27] He lionises neo-orientalists like V. S. Naipaul (who is described by Nandy as 'ethnocidal') who portray the non-secularist people as puritan savages. Inglis represents the westernised Jawaharlal Nehru as 'India' and sees in his biography the vision of what India should be because 'Nehru took the narratives embodied in the biographies of J S Mill and William Morris, and turned them to Indian account.'[28] The India imagined by Nehru, Inglis asserts, 'would be peaceable, independent, industrialised, united, social-democratic. It would not be Gandhi's peasant homeland with a loom in every cottage and his creaking, cranky ideas about sex, the deity, asceticism and whatnot'.[29] Yet, without Gandhi there would not be an independent India; and with Nehru we have an aggressive, warring nation-state nursing Hindu nationalism and disunited communities perpetually fighting the centre for 'autonomy' or 'independence'! Grand narratives may damage your health, as Inglis suggests, but, Nandy would insist, the secular imagination underlying the dominant western thought of all varieties is pathologically demented and intrinsically, but unconsciously, part of the landscape of evil.

Inglis' perception of Gandhi echoes George Lukacs' criticism of Rabindranath Tagore. Reviewing Tagore's *The Home and the World*, Lukacs makes some bold claims:

Tagore himself is – as imaginative writer and as thinker – a wholly insignificant figure. His creative powers are non-existent; his characters pale stereotypes;

his stories thread-bare and uninteresting; and his sensibility is meagre, insubstantial ...

The intellectual conflict in the novel is concerned with the use of violence ... The hypothesis is that India is an oppressed, enslaved country, yet Mr Tagore shows no interest in this question ....

A pamphlet – and one resorting to the lowest tools of libel – is what Tagore's novel is, in spite of its tediousness and want of spirit.

This stance represents nothing less than the *ideology of the eternal subjection of India* ...

This propagandistic, demagogically one-sided stance renders the novel completely worthless form the artistic angle ...

But Tagore's creative powers do not stretch to a decent pamphlet ...The 'spiritual' aspects of his story, separated from the nuggets of Indian wisdom into which it is tricked out, is a petty bourgeois yarn of the shoddiest kind ... (his) 'wisdom' was put at the intellectual service of the British police.[30]

Lukacs was writing in 1922. Inglis is writing in 1992. Seventy years on, the critical apparatus of western scholarship still sustains a hegemonic cultural discourse. What is it about Tagore and Gandhi that so frightens western intellectuals in general, and cultural critics in particular? Both saw themselves as members of a civilisation that, in the words of Nandy, 'refuses to view politics only as a secularised arena of human initiative. While associating the country with maternity and sacredness, they insisted that the association imposed a responsibility on the individual to maintain that sacredness.'[31] The position taken by both had an intrinsic, in-built critique of nationalism and the whole idea of the 'nation-state'.

In *The Illegitimacy of Nationalism*, Nandy explores the biography of Tagore to reveal how the Bengali poet developed his anti-nationalism views. *The Illegitimacy of Nationalism* is an excellent example both of concise, pithy writing and the use of biography in cultural analysis. Unlike western art criticism, where an artist's work is often seen to be independent of his life – the whole notion of art for art's sake – Nandy insists on looking at Tagore's biography through a pluralistic framework. Tagore's worldview is unfolded through ideological and mythical construction as well as through the examination of his novels and his life. Thus Tagore's divided selves – his modernist upbringing and appreciation of British culture, his innate traditionalism and consequent distaste for British culture – are brought together both through confrontation and synthesis. Tagore was, indeed is, one of the founding fathers of the modern consciousness in India. So it is somewhat of a paradox that he ended up, counter to his own instincts and social upbringing, as an ardent critic of modernity. Nandy explains the paradox by using a technique that is almost a hallmark of his scholarship. Just as he counterbalances, in *Alternative Sciences*, the life of Bose with Ramanujan, in *The Illegitimacy of Nationalism*, he juxtaposes Tagore with what he calls his 'political double': the biography of the writer and activist Brahmabandhab Upadhyay. Both Tagore and Upadhyay were patriots who had great respect for each other. But while Upadhyay used nationalism, both in his life and his fiction, to fight imperialism, Tagore was concerned about nationalism's hidden costs. He saw nationalism as a dualistic counter-ideology of imperialism: both had moorings in a single worldview. Thus the author of the national anthem of India, who has influenced Indian nationalism through his poetry, songs and participation in the struggle against the Raj, could speak of nationalism as 'a *bhougalik apadevata*, a geographical demon, and Shantiniketan, his alternative university, as a temple dedicated to exorcise this demon'.[32]

Tagore's analysis of his own culture and its power to resist physical, mental and spiritual colonisation, leads him to a conclusion diametrically opposed to many of his contemporaries. Nandy's analysis shows that cultural analysis itself can be a tool of dissent and resistance. Thus cultural studies need not take us to atheism, as Inglis contends, it can lead us to belief, and towards strategies for surviving (in the case of the non-west) and curing (in the case of the west) the pathologies of the dominant, and still inherently colonial, modes of western thought. Nandy uses psychological biography to exorcise the demons within the modern nation-state of India and heal its split and disintegrating selves. He shows how cultural studies can be, and must be, about liberating the western and non-western civilisations from the suffocating embrace of the older and newer versions of ever-present colonialism.

COLONIALISM, CIVILISATIONS

The dedication in *The Tao of Cricket* could not be simpler: 'To Uma'.[33] In the preface to *The Intimate Enemy*, Nandy confesses that 'without my wife Uma and my daughter Aditi I would have finished the work earlier but it would not have been the same'.[34] The difference that wives and daughters (and sons!) make to scholarly thought and output is seldom recognised. Traditional societies do not assign different categories of thought to different sexes or to different stages of human biological growth. Men are capable of feminine thoughts, just as children can have 'adult' ideas. Wives and children, as any Sufi manual of a good life will confirm, have a great deal to teach husbands and parents. But in the ideology of colonialism, thought and education flowed only one way: the aggressively masculine coloniser taught the cowardly feminine colonised subject. The subjugated non-west had nothing to teach the imperial west particularly when its cultures were so primitive and child-like. The adult, male and virile western civilisation had a responsibility to husband the weak, docile and passive cultures of the Orient.

This self-image of the colonial powers produced a counter-image in its dissenters. The conventional view holds that the only victims of colonialism were the subject cultures and societies. So colonialism is seen essentially as a political economy designed to ensure one-way flow of goods and benefits with the non-western communities as passive and perpetual losers. But this is a vested view of colonialism propagated by colonialism itself. It suppresses the fact that the colonisers too were devoured by the ideology of colonialism: 'behind all the rhetoric of the European intelligentsia on the evils of colonialism lay their unstated faith that the gains from colonialism to Europe, to the extent that they primarily involved material products, were real, and the losses, to the extent they involved social relations and psychological state, false'.[35]

Colonialism dehumanised the colonisers as much as it brutalised the colonised. The relationship it produced between the colonisers and the colonised was akin to a family headed by an abusing husband and father: the father keeps the family together by sheer force of terror but the more he abuses the family the more he loses his own humanity the more the family as a whole is reduced simply to a group of victims. What the European imperial powers did in the colonies bounced back to the fatherland as a new political and public culture. Colonialism transformed Britain culturally by declaring tenderness, speculation and introspection as feminine and therefore unworthy of public culture and by bringing the most brutish and masculine elements of British colonial life to the fore. It justified a restricted cultural role for women and promoted an instrumental notion of lower classes; both slightly modified versions of the colonial concept of hierarchy. Thus the calamity of colonialism for Britain was the tragedy of the women, the children, the working classes and all those placed at the bottom of the heap by a set of masculine values. Such instrumental values as punishment, discipline, productivity and subjugation, which were used in the colonies to whip the subjects into shape, were used in the fatherland to encourage new forms of institutionalised violence and ruthless social Darwinism.

In George Orwell's classic essay, 'Shooting an Elephant', Nandy finds the most profound description of the trepidation and terror induced by colonialism in the colonisers: 'the reification of social bonds through formal, stereotyped, part-object relationships; an instrumental view of nature; created loneliness of the colonisers in the colony through a theory of cultural stratification and exclusivism; an unending search for masculinity and status before the colonised'.[36] The perception of the subject people as simple children who had to be impressed with 'conspicuous machismo' forced the colonisers into perpetual suppression of their own self for the sake of an imposed imperial identity. Over a period of time this inauthentic and generously murderous identity would be internalised. It is hardly surprising then that all the themes that can be identified with the present cultural crisis of the west are there in Orwell's essay.

The imperial powers also created a self-image for those who were being husbanded by colonialism. In as much as this self-image is a dualistic opposite, it is and remains in essence a western construction. Colonialism replaced the Eurocentric convention of portraying the Other as incomprehensible barbarian with the pathological stereotype of the strange but predictable Oriental. He was now religious but superstitious, clever but devious, chaotically violent but effeminately cowardly. At the same time, a new discourse was developed where the basic mode of breaking out of these stereotypes was to reverse them: superstitious but spiritual, uneducated but wise, womanly but pacific. 'No colonialism could be complete', writes Nandy, 'unless it "universalised" and enriched its ethnic stereotypes by appropriating the language of defiance of its victims. That was why the cry of the victims of colonialism was ultimately the cry to be heard in another language – unknown to the coloniser and the anti-colonial movements that he had bred and then domesticated.'[37]

The victim's language of defiance may be totally different, but the agony caused by centuries of colonialism and the experience of authoritarian imperial rule equally distorted the minds and cultures of both, the imperialists and their prey. Moreover, the mutual bondage of long-term anguish generated strong justifications for this suffering from both sides of colonial divide. The forces that unleashed and maintained this torment shape almost every aspect of our history, our contemporary lives and our imagined futures.

Indeed, institutionalised suffering has acquired its own momentum and has thus become self-perpetuating.

Nandy's perspective on dealing with institutionalised torment is based on three assumptions. First, he asserts, no civilisation has a monopoly on goodness and humane values. All civilisations share certain basic values and cultural traits that derive from our biological self and social experience. What is unique about a given civilisation is not its values but the framework within which these values are actualised and the emphasis and priorities it assigns to these values. Thus certain values, or traditions based on these values, may, at a given point, be receding or acquiring dominance in a civilisation but they are never solely absent or exclusively present: 'what looks like a human potentiality which ought to be actualised in some distant future, is often only a cornered cultural strain waiting to be renewed or rediscovered'.[38] Second:

Human civilisation is constantly trying to alter or expand its awareness of exploitation and oppression. Oppressions which were once outside the span of awareness are no longer so, and it is quite likely that the present awareness of suffering, too, will be found wanting and might change in the future. Who, before the socialists, had thought of class as a unit of repression? How many, before Freud, had sensed that children needed to be protected against their own parents? How many believed, before Gandhi's rebirth after the environmental crisis in the west, that modern technology, the supposed liberator of man, had become his most powerful oppressor? Our limited ethical sensitivity is not a proof of human hypocrisy; it is mostly a product of our limited cognition of the human situation. Oppression is ultimately a matter of definition, and its perception is the product of a worldview. Change the worldview, and what once seemed natural and legitimate becomes an instance of cruelty and sadism.[39]

Third, all civilisations, in as far as they are human, are imperfect; and imperfect civilisations can only produce imperfect solutions for their cultural and social imperfections. Solutions, after all, emerge from exactly the same cultural and social experience as the problem and, as such, the same thought or consciousness as well as the same un-thought, or unconsciousness, informs them.

What, then, are the possible boundaries of a solution? Our release from institutionalised suffering, Nandy argues, must involve both the non-west as well as the west. But this is not an invitation for the masculine, oppressive west to transform itself; it is the recognition that the oppressed and marginalised selves in the west need help and that they can be recognised and used as civilisation allies in the battle against institutionalised suffering. It is the non-western civilisations that must give collective representation to all suffering everywhere – the suffering of the pasts as well as the present to release the bondage of suffering in the future. And, as such, the non-western civilisations have to be aware of both: the outside forces of cruelty and grief as well as the 'inner vectors' that have dislodged their true Selves. The non-western cultures have to do much more than simply resist the west: they have to transform their cultures into cultures of resistance. And they have to rediscover their traditions of reinterpreting traditions to create new traditions – including new traditions of dissent.

DISSENT, DEFINITIONS

'For those who dare to defy the given models of defiance' reads the dedication in *Traditions, Tyranny, and Utopias*, which is subtitled: 'Essays in the Politics of Awareness'.[40] Dissent, in Nandy's thought, is all about awareness. And any attempts at dissent must begin with two realisations. First, 'yesterday's dissent is often today's establishment and, unless resisted, becomes tomorrow's terror'.[41] Second, dissent itself has been colonised. The dissenters, the counterplayers to the game of western imperialism and domination, work *within* the dominant model of universalism and *with* the dominant consciousness. Western categories and systems of knowledge, argues Nandy, have been much more successful in ensuring dominance than naked political and economic power. The true power of the west lies not in its political and technological might, but in its power to define. The west defines what is freedom, history, human rights, dissent – the non-west must accept this definition. This unquestioned, and often unrecognised power of the west to define, and the game of categories the west plays with the non-west, ensures that dissent not only remains docile and confinable but serves as an illustration of its democratic spirit. Witness how easily the dominant academic culture took over 'disciplines' that began as attempts to break out of the straitjacket of conventional knowledge systems. Ecology, feminism and cultural studies have been successfully domesticated and professionalised as new specialisations in the knowledge industry. Thus by subtle but well-organised means, the dominant knowledge industry ensures that the capitals of dissent, along with the capitals of global political economy, are located in the stylish universities, think tanks and other intellectual centres of the First World. Domination is only complete when dissent can be foreseen and managed; and this cannot be done unless definitional criteria have been established to determine what is genuine and sober dissent and these criteria have been systematically institutionalised through the university system. This is what fashionable academic and intellectual trends, such as post-modernism, post-coloniality and post-structuralism, are designed to do. Appreciating how dissent is predicted and controlled, Nandy confesses that it:

Explained to me some of my earlier disappointments with western dissenters, particularly from the left. Many of them are not only eminent scholars in their own right but have brought up, with paternal concern, at least three generations of non-western dissenting scholars, teaching them with loving care the meaning of 'true' dissent and the technology of 'authentic' radicalism. But copious tears shed for the Third World and its exploited masses, I was gradually to find out, rarely went with any respect for the Third World's own understanding of its own plight (as if that understanding had to be hidden like a family scandal from the outside world).[42]

But it is not just in the west that dissent is domesticated; India too has its versions of managed dissent. The Indian public life culture gives voice to all types of non-conformity; indeed there is a culture of in-house dissent that is part of the Indian political scene. The radical Marxist movement, the thundering editorials of the nation's newspapers and magazines, the popularity of the new video newsmagazines – are all examples of dissent that Indian democracy has nurtured and can comfortably contain. However, there is one thing that domesticated dissent can never do; or is never allowed to do: to challenge, compromise or remove the 'core components', the founding pillars of 'India'. Amongst these, writes Nandy,

Are the state (by which is meant the nation-state); nationalism (defined as allegiance to a steam-rolling monocultural concept of India, composed out of the nineteenth-century European concept of nationality); secularism (used not as one possible way of containing religious strife but as a synonym for the promotion of supra-religious allegiances to the now-dominant idea of the Indian state); development (which has now fully colonised the idea of social change); history (paradoxically seen as an ahistorical, linear, scientific enterprise); rationality (as an allegedly non-partisan, contemporary embodiment of the post-Enlightenment theories of progress) and a totally romanticised concept of *realpolitik* that is neither realistic nor truly political in its content.[43]

The ideal western, and hence 'universal' notion, of cultural dissent is well presented by the story of fifteenth-century Aztec priests who were rounded up by their Spanish conquerors and given two choices: to convert or to die. The priests responded that if their gods were dead, as alleged by the Jesuit fathers, then they too would rather die. The Spanish took no time to burn them at the stake. What would, Nandy asks, be the response of Brahman priests if they were given the same choice? They would readily convert to Christianity; some of them would even write treatises praising the ruthless colonisers and their gods. However, their Christianity would soon reveal itself to be a minor variation of Hinduism. Why does the dominant culture regard the Aztec priests as models of courage and the Brahman priests as hypocritical cowards? On one level, the answer is simple. After their last defiant act, the Aztec priests die leaving their killers to continue with their rampage and sing praises to their courage. But the Brahmanic response ensures that 'unheroic cowards' are always there ready to make their presence felt when opportunity arises. The Aztec priests also set a good example, from the perspective of the dominant culture, for all dissenters to follow: die in glorified dissent:

There is also another answer. And it is this:
that the average Indian has always lived with the awareness and possibility of long-term suffering, always seen himself and protecting his deepest faith with the passive, 'feminine' cunning of the weak and the victimized, and surviving outer pressures by refusing to overplay his sense of autonomy and self-respect. At his heroic best, he is a *satyagrahi*, one who forges a partly-coercive weapon called *satyagraha* out of ... 'perfect weakness'. In his non-heroic ordinariness, he is the archetypal survivor. Seemingly he makes all-round compromises, but he refuses to be psychologically swamped, co-opted or penetrated. Defeat, his response seems to say, is a disaster and so are the imposed ways of the victor. But worse is the loss of one's 'soul' and the internalisation of one's victor, because it forces one to fight the victor according to the victor's values, within his model of dissent. Better to be a comical dissenter than to be a powerful, serious but acceptable opponent. Better to be a hated enemy, declared unworthy of any respect whatsoever, than to be a proper opponent, constantly making 'primary adjustments' to the system.[44]

By accepting a violent end to their dissent, the Aztec priests, Nandy seems to be saying, unwittingly collude with the worldview of their oppressors. In some celebrated non-western dissenters, this collusion is much more open and conscious. For example, violence has a central, cleansing role in Frantz Fanon's vision of a post-colonial society. This is why his vision, which is so alien to many Africans and Asians, has been so readily accepted in the west. Fanon argued that the oppressor is often internalised by the oppressed. So it becomes necessary for the oppressor to be confronted in violence not just to liberate oneself from his oppression but also to mark an agonising break with a part of one's own self.[45] But, Nandy argues, if Fanon had more confidence in his culture (this is a problematic assertion as Fanon had no notion of what *his* culture was) he would have realised that his vision ties the victims more deeply to the culture of oppression than straightforward collaboration. By accepting the oppressors' principle of violence, the victims further internalise the basic values of the oppressors. And once violence is given cultural and intrinsic legitimacy, it transforms the battle between two visions and worldviews into a struggle for power and resources between two groups with identical values. Thus those who are sinned against often end up sinning themselves.

The anti-violence stance, however, should not be confused with pacifism. Pacifism, like environmental consumerism, is often a luxury and can be a symbol of status. The rich and well connected dodge the contaminated world of military violence more easily and skilfully. This ensures that those who are sent to fight distant wars to protect 'our national interests' are often the under-privileged and the marginalised. During the Vietnam War, for example, 'conscientious objectors' and draft dodgers were mostly well-to-do whites. Those who were shipped to fight in Vietnam were predominantly blacks and poor whites who 'neither had any respite from the system nor from their progressive, privileged fellow citizens protesting the war and feeling self-righteous'.[46] They were men who had experienced direct and institutionalised violence at home in the form of overt and latent racism, oppressive labour regulations and other discriminatory practices. The stereotyping of the 'commie' Vietcong and the genocidal behaviour of many of these soldiers is hardly surprising: 'the Vietnam war on this plane was a story of one set of victims setting upon another, on behalf of a reified, impersonal system of violence'.[47]

Beyond violence and pacifism, there is a third option: the dissenter as non-player. Here the oppressed, refusing to be a first-class citizen in the world of oppression, is neither a player nor a counter-player: he or she plays another game altogether, a game of building an alternative world where there is some hope of winning his or her humanity. This is a game that someone like Radhabinod Pal knew how to play well. Pal was a member of the International Military Tribunal for the Far East that conducted the Tokyo war crimes trial from 1946 to 1948. He found the Japanese accused of war crimes to be not guilty – the only one of the judges to do so. This is not to say that Pal was unaware of Japanese atrocities – he was simply playing a different game, a game that involved going beyond the dualistic logic of the accused and the accusers. He was, as so elegantly shown by Nandy, playing a game of symbiosis of adversaries. In his dissenting judgement there was a silent summons not for the accused to reflect on their guilt but to the plaintiffs, and the judges, 'to discover the accused in them'.[48] Nandy himself knows how to play this game rather well.

In the final analysis, it is a game of dissenting visions and futures. The future itself is a state of awareness. And the main aim of the game is to transform the future by changing human awareness of the future. By defining what is 'immutable' and 'universal', the west silences the visions of Other peoples and cultures to ensure the continuity of its own linear projections of the past and the present on to the future. By avoiding thinking about the future, Other cultures and societies become prisoners of the past, present and the future of western civilisation. As Thomas Szasz has declared, 'in the animal kingdom, the rule is, eat or be eaten; in the human kingdom, define or be defined'.[49] Non-western cultures must define their own future in terms of their own categories and concepts, articulating their visions in language that is true to their own Self even if not comprehensible 'on the other side of the global fence of academic respectability'.[50] The plurality of dissent can only be ensured if human choices are expanded by 'reconceptualizing political, social and cultural ends; by identifying emerging or previously ignored social pathologies that have to be understood, contained or transcended; by linking up the fates of different polities and societies through envisioning their common fears and hopes'.[51]

ET CETERA

Hope is perhaps the last weapon in the armoury of those who reside outside the 'civilised' world. But hope alone is not enough: 'the meek inherit the earth not by meekness alone'.[52] Nandy seeks to furnish the victims with a host of other tools that have always been there but have either been overlooked or been buried under the mental construction of internalised colonialism and modernity.

While much of Nandy's thought has been directed towards colonialism and modernity, and their disciplinary and intellectual offshoots, its hallmark has been consistency. Ashis Nandy is nothing if not totally consistent. This is not to say that he has not modified his ideas, refined and sharpened them, or that he is not aware of his own failures. For example, in the preface to the second edition of *Alternative Sciences*, he provides a critique of the book pointing out where it has failed, where he has refined his ideas and where it could be improved if he were to rewrite it. He is consistent in two senses. Firstly, he is always true to his own roots. His ideas are a distillation of the plurality of India, they emerge from examinations of all things Indian, and he tends to rely almost exclusively on Indian myths and categories for his analysis as well as Indian examples for his explanation. Anyone who has seen Nandy in action at a seminar or a conference knows that he is totally open to ideas whatever their source and is scintillated by the power of ideas to move people and societies. In particular, and in line with his own position, he relishes the ideas that seek to sabotage his own position. He is ever ready to grant that his ideas may become irrelevant by new readings of traditional visions or by new visions with changed perception of evil. But he measures the quality of ideas by their non-dualistic content and the import they may have on the victims of manufactured oppression. In this respect, he is a true friend of all victims – everywhere.

Secondly, he is consistent in the application of his critique and equally harsh on both the west and the non-west. Unlike the British colonial attitude to Indian culture – which, on the one hand accused the Indians of being this worldly (exceedingly shrewd, greedy, self-centred, money-minded) and on the other hand saw them as overtly other-worldly (too concerned with spirituality, mysticism and transcendence, not fit for the world of modern science and technology, statecraft and productive work) – Nandy sees India as a consistent whole. He is not concerned with romanticising Indian tradition and is equally interested in warts as well as the beauty spots. As such, he is always eager to expose the folly of fossilised, suffocating tradition ('the blood-stained, oppressive heritage of a number of oriental religious ideologies') as well as tradition constructed under the impulse of modernity (so 'immaculate in the hands of their contemporary interpreters'). It is this consistency in Nandy that makes him truer to his own Self.

The qualities of Ashis Nandy's mind are in full evidence in the three books brought together in this omnibus: *Alternative Sciences*, *The Illegitimacy of Nationalism* and *The Savage Freud*. One could see them as three different and distinct books; but they could easily be read as a unified collection of essays. As a writer, Nandy is, above all, an essayist. And, in their own different ways, all of these essays explore, expand, interrogate, a single theme – a theme that could be described as the ultimate ambition of the civilisation that is India: 'to be the cultural epitome of the world and to redefine or convert all passionate self-other debates into self-self debates'.[53] In seeking to reflect India's genuine Self, Nandy seeks only to be true to his own Self.

What more could one possibly ask from a *truly* Indian intellectual?

14
God Bless America!

Millions of people around the world hate America. The terrorist campaign against America in general, and the 9/11 atrocities in particular, are a product of this hatred.

The dreadful pictures of innocent Iraqis being tortured in the Abu Ghraib prison have fuelled this hatred. But it is not just the Iraqis, or the Afghanis, or the terrorists who hate America. Resentment against America is at an all-time high in South Asia, Latin America and South Korea. In many parts of Europe, particularly in France and Germany, revulsion against America is now widespread. In Canada, America's closest neighbour, a junior minister captured the public's sentiment and sympathy, when she described President Bush as 'a moron'. In a world where everything seems to be relative and changing, hatred of America appears to be a universal sentiment and the only constant.

But why is America engendering such strong feelings? Are these feelings rational? I believe that these feelings against America are not simply a product of its foreign policy. Or the way it rides roughshod over the rest of the world. A stronger and deeper motivation for American hatred comes from the fact that America has appropriated the traditional arguments for God.

Whereas these arguments were conventionally used to justify the existence of God, people around the world now see them as providing American validation for American behaviour. There are four such arguments.

In the first, the cosmological argument for God, derived originally from Aristotle, God is described as the cause of everything. Instead of God, America has now become the cause of everything. The presence of the US is felt in every corner of the globe. Its foreign policies affect us all. Nothing seems to move without America's consent. Only America can resolve the conflict between Palestine and Israel; only America's intervention can lead to some sort of resolution between India and Pakistan over Kashmir; and only America can

First published in *Resurgence* magazine, May/June 2003, 19–21.

decide whether 'the world' should or should not attack Iraq. Without American ratification the Kyoto Treaty on carbon dioxide emission is not worth the paper it is written on. If the American economy sneezes, the rest of the world catches an economic cold.

What this means is that America is no longer a conventional superpower. It is the first hyperpower in history: its military might is now greater than all the empires of history put together; its reach is not only global, but it has firm control of all global institutions, such as the IMF and the WTO; its culture has penetrated every minute segment of the globe. America has not only colonised the present, like previous empires – such as the Roman, British and Spanish empires – but, in a very real sense, the US has also colonised the future. The cosmological dominance of America extends to total consumption of all space and time – so America is now engaged in rewriting history, changing the very stuff of life, our genetic structure, shifting weather patterns, colonising outer space, indeed, transforming evolution itself, beyond recognition. Given its cosmological status, it is not surprising that its arrogance has a cosmological dimension too. Recall that the 'war against terrorism' was originally dubbed 'Operation Infinite Mercy'! Quite simply, the rest of the world resents the fact that at the global level America has become both the first cause and the sustaining cause of most things.

The second argument is ontological. The ontological argument for God's existence, attributed to St Anselm, goes something like this: God is the most perfect being, it is more perfect to exist than to not exist, therefore, God exists. Ontological arguments infer that something exists because certain concepts are related in certain ways. Good and evil are related as opposite. So if evil exists there must also be good. America relates to the world through such ontological logic: because 'terrorists' are evil, America is good and virtuous. The 'Axis of Evil' out there implicitly positions the US as the 'Axis of Good'. But this is not simply a binary opposition: the ontological element, the nature of American being, makes America *only* good and virtuous. It is a small step then to assume that you are chosen both by God and History. How often have we heard American leaders proclaim that God is with them; or that History has called on America to act?

The ontological goodness of America is a cornerstone of its founding myths. America is a society of immigrants: what immigrants know is that the country they left behind, for economic, social or political reasons, is a bad place. They escaped an unworthy place to start afresh and create a new society in a barren frontier, 'the last best hope of mankind' in Lincoln's famous phrase, and succeeded. They succeeded because right, virtue, God and History were on their side. The Founding Fathers incorporated the new state's right to possession and appropriation of 'virgin land', its claims to righteousness, its self-image of total innocence, and its use of violence as a redemptive act of justice through which American civilisation is secured and advanced, as integral parts of the very idea of America. So America seems incapable of seeing anything bad in itself, its foreign policy, the behaviour of its corporations or its lifestyle. Even the recent scandals at Enron and Worldcom have not dented this self-belief. And despite the indignity involved in the presidential election, in which George W. Bush came to power, American democracy is still seen as the pinnacle of human achievement.

Ontologically good folks need constant reaffirmation of their goodness. This is why America always needs a demon Other; indeed, it is incomplete without its constructed Other. The current demon is, of course, Islam. But America has constantly generated evil Others to justify its military interventions. If it is not the 'Evil Empire' of the Soviet Union, then it is 'the Communists' in Korea or Vietnam, or the 'left-wing revolutionaries' in Latin America. If it is not Iran or Iraq, then it is the 'Axis of Evil'. And, evil is always 'out there'; never 'in here' in the US.

The third argument is existential. Like God, America exists for, in and by itself. All global life must, willingly or unwillingly, pay total homage to the *de facto* existence of the US. For America, nothing matters except its own interests; the interests, needs, concerns, and desires of all nations, all people, indeed the planet itself, must be subservient to the interests of the US and the comfort and consumption of American lifestyles. This is why Americans are happy to consume most of the resources of the world, insist on exceptionally cheap fuel, and expect to be provided with an endless variety and diversity of cheap, processed food, because for them only their existence matters. If the Kyoto climate treaty imposes too many constraints on US business, it must be ditched. If the Nuclear Non-Proliferation treaty interferes with the US strategic defence initiative, it must be ignored. If an international criminal court might take action against US citizens, it must be subverted. If US farmers need subsidies then who cares about WTO rules and regulations that the US itself imposed on the world!

This hubris is demonstrated by the fact that while the rest of the world was attending the 2002 Earth Summit in Johannesburg, President George Bush was on holiday, playing golf at home in Texas. Yet, even from there he was able to veto one of the least contentious issues in the Summit: that safe drinking water and sanitation should be available to the poor people of the world by 2015. The rest of the world, including all the European states, realised that dirty water and poor sanitation are the biggest killers in the world and were all too willing to sign an agreement. But America's belligerence led to the collapse of the agreement. Similarly, the rest of the world is willing to allow poor countries to develop and use much-needed generic medicines for such diseases as HIV/AIDS, cancer and cholera. But America, unwilling to save billions of lives and the prospect of reduced profits for its pharmaceutical companies, vetoed the proposal at the WTO negotiations.

Thus, America sees itself as the world and the world as America. The domain of God is now the domain of America. Hardly surprising then that most of the God-fearing people of this planet resent this claim.

The fourth and final argument is definitional. In religious thought, the power to define what is good and what is bad, what is virtue and what is not, lies solely in the hands of God. But in the contemporary world, America has become the defining power. America now defines what is 'free market', 'international law', 'human rights' and 'freedom of the press'. It also defines who is a 'fundamentalist', a 'terrorist', or simply 'evil'. The rest of the world, including Europe, must accept these definitions and follow the American lead.

Moreover, the definitions depend on context and change when expediency demands. So the Shari'ah (the so-called 'Islamic law') is barbaric and inhuman in the Sudan, which has a clear anti-American policy, but is humane and acceptable in Saudi Arabia, which is fanatically pro-American. Not all 'terrorists' are terrorists: American ones, like Timothy McVeigh the Atlanta bomber, can be tried in American courts; but non-American terrorists have to be tried in specially established military courts. Similarly, the struggle of the Muslims in East Turkestan against China is a 'human rights issue', but the struggle of Chechen Muslims against Russia has nothing to do with human rights. Muslims happen to be the majority in both Chechnya and East Turkestan and are fighting for independence in both places. The much-vaunted universal precept of 'freedom of the press' gets a similar treatment. When it comes to other countries, it is defined as a universal imperative. When freedom of the press ends up as criticism of America, it becomes a dangerous value. So the US went out of its way to stop Qatar-based Al-Jazeera, the only independent satellite television station in the Arab world, broadcasting from Afghanistan. It placed enormous pressure on Qatar to 'rein in' Al-Jazeera and eventually bombed its office in Kabul.

The definitional power of America has two other vital components. America is the story-teller to the world: through Hollywood films and television shows, America presents a specific self-definition of itself as well as represents the rest of the world to the rest of the world. For the most part the stories it tells are either based on its own experiences, or, if appropriated from other cultures, are given a specific American context. So the rest of the world also sees itself in American films and television as America sees them or the way it wants to project them. Thus, the foreigner in global American media, news as well as popular entertainment, is always a pastiche of hackneyed stereotypes because that's the way America thinks about the rest of the world. But, the stereotypical representation is not limited to Hollywood or the media; it is also an integral part of the knowledge industry. Other peoples and cultures are thus constantly pigeonholed – in newspapers, magazines, television, films, textbooks, learned journals and 'expert opinion' – and their identity and humanity are regularly compromised. This power to define others in terms of American perceptions and interests through representation often leads to the demonisation of entire groups of people. Consider, how all Arabs are seen as 'fundamentalists', all those who question the control of science by American corporations are projected as anti-science, or those who question American foreign policy are dismissed as 'morally bankrupt' or 'nihilist' or 'idiots'.

What all this means is that America now behaves as though it was God. It has a God-like presence in the world, which is awash with American junk food and cultural junk, from McDonald's to Hollywood to pop music. The rest of the world, particularly the non-west, is getting physically and culturally impoverished daily. The places to be different – to be other than America – are shrinking rapidly. And double standards rule the day. No wonder hatred for America is spreading like a forest fire around the globe.

The real question is why abundant evidence fails to stir American public consciousness. Why despite all the evidence Americans refuse to question their lifestyles and refuse to accept responsibility for how their corporations behave and their government operates in their name. Why does criticism fail to dent American policy, shape its public discussion, let alone prompt change? Why have, for example, the pictures from Abu Ghraib prison failed to stir the consciousness of the American public?

This is the real enigma Americans need to ponder – for their own, and everyone else's sake.

15
Managing Diversity: Identity and Rights in Multicultural Europe

Diversity presents us with one of the main challenges of the twenty-first century. Every nation, every community, and every individual on the planet has to come to terms with diversity: the diversity of human communities, the diversity of different ways of being and doing, the diversity of contemporary identities, and the rich diversity of our flora and fauna. Living together in proverbial peace and harmony requires us to acknowledge, appreciate and support diversity; and create space for difference to exist as difference. Diversity thus challenges the very essence of our humanity, while enriching the sheer variety of different ways of being human.

But, what do we actually mean by diversity? Diversity, in relation to European citizens, is the complex pattern of relationships people have to nationality. Conventionally, nationality has been presented as single historic narrative and one uniform identity. This simplistic notion of nationality is now dangerously obsolete. Diversity is the existence of multiple, compound identities within one nation, each with its own, different historic narrative. Thus, citizens are not just individuals but also members of different religious, cultural, linguistic, ethnic and regional communities. And macro communities within a given nationality are further diversified into micro communities. So, for example, the Muslims in Britain are not a monolithic entity: they are divided into Sunnis and Shias as well as numerous other sects; they have various 'national' backgrounds such as Pakistanis, Indians, Bangladeshis, and so on; there are numerous ethnic identities such as Punjabi, Arab and Malay; and within each cultural and ethnic grouping there are liberals, moderates, conservatives and fundamentals. So the Muslims in Britain constitute a multi-layered community of communities. Britain itself is a compound community of communities. Thus, the challenge before any European nation is to develop a cohesive set of values with due regard for diversity, and

This is the text of the keynote address to the Council of Europe colloquium on new global challenges, 24–25 April 2003, Strasbourg, France.

discover ways of nurturing diversity while fostering a shared identity amongst its citizens.

Diversity and identity go hand in hand. In order to come to terms with diversity, we have to understand why identity has become so problematic in postmodern times.

DIVERSITY AND IDENTITY

Philosophically, the concept of identity, as Amartya Sen has pointed out, is based on two basic assumptions. First, the presumption that we must have a single – or at least principal and dominant – identity. Second, the supposition that we discover our identity. The first assumption is plainly wrong: not only do we exist with multiple identities but often invoke different identities in different contexts. So:

the same person can be of Indian origin, a Muslim, a French citizen, a US resident, a woman, a poet, a vegetarian, an anthropologist, a university professor, a Christian, an angler, and an avid believer in extra-terrestrial life and of the propensity of alien creatures to ride around the universe in smartly designed UFOs. Each of these collectives, to all of which this person belongs, gives him or her a particular identity, which are variously important in different contexts.[1]

The second assumption is just as erroneous. We discover our identity, the argument goes, from the community we belong to: it is through the relationships within a community that we discover our identity. This argument suggests that we have no role in choosing our identities. But even though the constraints of community and traditions are always there, reason and choice too have a role to play. The point is not that we can choose any identity at random; but 'whether we do have choices over alternative identities or combinations of identities, and perhaps more importantly, substantial freedom on what priority to give to the various identities that we may simultaneously have'.[2]

It is because we have a problem with pluralistic identities that we are in the midst of a global epidemic of identity crisis. The symptoms of this crisis are everywhere. In Spain, the Basques do not see themselves as 'Spanish' and are willing to use violence to make their point. Britain does not know whether to become more American or more European. For much of the twentieth century, American identity, and its foreign policy, was shaped in opposition to a 'communist bloc'. In a post-Cold War world, America has to create new villains ('Muslim terrorists', rogue states such as bankrupt and starving 'North

Korea', 'the Chinese menace') in an inane attempt to resolve its predicament of self-identity. The collapse of the Soviet Union has produced a plethora of new artificial, national feuding identities, pitting Azerbaijanis against Armenians, Chechens against Russians, Kazakhs of one kind against Kazakhs of another. The Balkans has just gone through one of the most brutal balkanisation of identities in all its history. In the Muslim world, traditionalists and modernists have been engaged in battles over what constitutes true Islamic identity for decades. The very idea of being 'white' has now become so problematic that 'whiteness' is studied as an academic discipline in its own right. In short, identity is being contested everywhere.

To 'know thyself', as Socrates put it, is both a fundamental human urge and a basic question in philosophy. Having some idea of who or what we are helps us to determine how we ought to live and conduct our daily affairs. A little self-knowledge also provides us with a little coherence in our metaphysical and moral outlooks. But in a rapidly globalising world, it is almost impossible to have even a modicum of self-knowledge. All those things that provided us with a sense of confidence in ourselves – such as nation-states with homogeneous populations, well-established local communities, unquestioned allegiance to history and unchanging tradition – have evaporated. The sources of our identity have been rendered meaningless.

Consider, for example, the territory called 'England'. It is not the sole preserve of 'the English' anymore: the population now is much more heterogeneous, with 'Englishness' (however it is defined) as only one segment in a multi-ethnic society. Moreover, the history and tradition that are associated with this 'Englishness' – the Empire, House of Lords, fox hunting, the national anthem – are either questionable or meaningless to the vast majority of new-English who now live in England. Worse: this Englishness becomes quite insignificant when it is seen in relation to a new European identity which itself is an amalgam of countless other cultural identities. Not surprisingly, 'the English' feel threatened.

But it is not just the diversity or the shifting context of identities that are problematic; the very notions and ideas we use to describe our identities are themselves changing radically. What does it mean, for example, to be a 'mother' in a world where in vitro fertilisation and surrogate motherhood is rapidly becoming common? What happens to conventional ideas of parenthood if a baby is 'constructed' from the egg of a 62-year-old woman, sperm from her brother, and 'incubated' in a surrogate mother? What does it mean to be a 'wife' in a homosexual marriage? Or 'old' when you have rebuilt a 65-year-old body through plastic surgery and look like a young starlet?

Thus, identity has become a perilous notion; and with it diversity itself has become deeply perplexing.

To accommodate diversity, we have to come to terms with multiple and changing identities. And the most fundamental change is this: all those other categories through which we in Europe defined and measured ourselves – the 'evil Orientals', the 'fanatic Muslims', the 'inferior races of the colonies', the immigrants, the refugees, the gypsies – are now an integral part of ourselves. It is not just that they are 'here', in Europe as an integral part of the Continent, but their ideas, concepts, lifestyles, food, clothes now play a central part in shaping 'us' and 'our society'. The distinction between 'us' and 'them' is evaporating; and we must adjust to this radical change.

What this means in practice is that we cannot allow European identity to be exclusive. Conventional collective European identity – the British, the French, the Germans, etc. – is based on the selective processes of memory. Let me illustrate how this process works, and how European identity has become exclusive, by dwelling on the notion of British identity. British identity was (is?) the acknowledgement of a common past. Sharing and having been shaped by this common past is what makes the British different from all other identities. The trouble is history is a deliberate human creation, itself another wilful act of power, artificially constructed to support an artificial identity. Europe engineered a cultural identity based on a common descent from the supposed traditions of ancient Greece and Rome and 2,000 years of Christianity. British history books always began with the arrival of the Romans. So British history begins by submerging, barbarising and differentiating itself from Celtic history. Celt and Welsh are words whose linguistic roots, one Greek the other Saxon, mean stranger. The history of Britain, as written in the age of devolution, records not a common shared past but continuous contest and conflict within the British Isles. Whatever Britain is, it is the creation of dominance by kings and barons and upwardly mobile yeoman who practised colonialism at home, and after perfecting the technique, moved abroad.

It was Oliver Cromwell who noted that Britain had its 'Indians' at home in what he called the 'dark corners of Britain'. He referred, of course, to the residual Celtic corners. It makes perfect sense that Margaret Thatcher should propose the solution to the Ulster problem as relocating Catholics to Ireland. It was Cromwell's policy: if they will not reform, be educated and submit, then they have no place within the identity, history and society that is Britain. That no one seriously proposes sending the Union Jack-waving Ulstermen back to where they came from, or removing the Union from them, itself suggests a strong allegiance to a constructed history, the history of irreconcilable difference. As Orangemen so often say, marching with fife and drum to intimidate and demonstrate their dominance is their culture. In an age of the politics of identity, culture has its rights. But how far can you defend the rights of a culture whose only reason for being is to retain dominance?

It really is quite dumbfounding how much of Britishness, and by association Englishness, is based on fabricated history. Consider the whole notion of Anglo-Saxon Britain. Winston Churchill and Rudyard Kipling were devotees of Anglo-Saxon history for a reason. It enabled them to avoid how genuinely European British history has always been. Norman kings hardly ever spent time in Britain, spoke French rather than English, and were most concerned with dominating Europe from their French possessions. Of course, the Saxon bit of the Anglo Saxon has its own problems. After the Welsh Tudors, and Scots Stuarts, a brief *quasi* native interlude, German monarchs were bussed in to reign over Britishness that was to be marked by Englishness alone, and that wanted nothing to do with Europe.

The selectivity of historic memory is part of its inventiveness. History always seeks ancient roots, the better to justify its innovations. Ancient Anglo-Saxon liberties were purposefully invented on a number of occasions to fashion the Mother of Parliaments. This foundational institution was not a true popular democratic institution until 1929, the first election based on universal adult suffrage. The statue of Oliver Cromwell quite properly stands outside Parliament. His insistence that ancient Anglo-Saxon liberties rested on property owning was the novel twist that secured class hierarchy, made the Restoration of monarchy easy, and enabled manufactured history to continue its work. The pomp and ceremony of the British monarchy was a late Victorian invention. The Royal Family as the model for the normative family, an ideal for a nation, is a post-Edwardian invention, Victoria's son Edward hardly being a suitable candidate for model husband and father. And so it goes on.

Thus, the notions of race and class are intrinsic to the self-definition of the English. Without the idea of race there is little left for English identity to hold on to: only being a disadvantaged minority within Britain, the complete inversion of received history. What works well for youthful addicts of street culture does not suit the aspirations of new English identity, and that's why the appeal to the barricades, sending them back, locking them up has to be made.

But diversity demands that we transcend such notions of exclusiveness. European identities have to become much more open and inclusive. Consider, for example, the relationship between Islam and Europe which has been used to define the identities of these respective cultures. Europe has conventionally thought Islam to be an external Other. Muslims, in their turn, have always assumed that Europe had nothing to do with them. Yet, Islam and Europe have been intrinsically linked. Quite simply, there would be no Europe as we know it today without Islam. And Islam without Europe is unimaginable. It is not just that the two civilisations have shaped each other's identities in relation to each other – by defining the Other as the darker side of itself; but the interaction between the two cultures and civilisation also shaped their values and outlooks and hence their identities. Europe acquired much of what it called 'the Renaissance' from Islam. Starting with the basics, Islam taught Europe how to reason, how to differentiate between civilisation and barbarism, and to understand the basic features of a civil society. Islam trained Europe in scholastic and philosophic method, and bequeathed its characteristic institutional forum of learning: the university. Europe acquired wholesale the organisation, structure and even the terminology of the Muslim educational system. Not only did Islam introduce Europe to the experimental method and demonstrate the importance of empirical research, it even had the foresight to work out most of the mathematical theory necessary for Copernicus to launch 'his' revolution! Islam showed Europe the distinction between medicine and magic, drilled it in making surgical instruments and explained how to establish and run hospitals. And then, to cap it all, Islam gave Europe liberal humanism.

The differences between Islam and Europe are often expressed in terms of liberal humanism. Yet, liberal humanism that is the hallmark of post-renaissance Europe has its origins in the *Adab* Movement of classical Islam, which was concerned with the etiquette of being human. Islam developed a sophisticated system of teaching law and humanism that involved not just institutions such as the university, with its faculties of law, theology, medicine and natural philosophy, but also an elaborate method of instruction including work-study courses, a curriculum that included grammar, rhetoric, poetry, history, medicine, and moral philosophy, and mechanisms for the formation of a humanist culture such as academic associations, literary circles, clubs and other coteries that sustain intellectuals and the literati. When Europe adopted this system, including the text-books, the European humanists felt that they had to replace classical Arabic with another classical language, Latin, in spite of its being not quite their own. As a result they replicated the errors that are associated with Islamic humanism: the horror of barbarism and solecism.

Thus, any definition of Europe, let alone an attempt to map out its future, must fully acknowledge its debt to Islam. Indeed it is not possible to conceive of a revitalised Europe, whole and free, without Islam. The suggestion that Islam is alien, somehow un-European, inherent in the belief that Turkish membership of the EU would destroy the European identity, is not merely Eurocentric. Deliberately or not, it purports to justify and perpetuate centuries of cultural hatred. European humanism, however defined, is a product of the same values that shaped Muslim civilisation. By acknowledging its Islamic heritage, Europe would not only be true to itself and its history, it would be initiating a reconciliation transcending all those past and present tensions that divide Europeans and Muslims. In their turn, Europe's Muslim minorities have to appreciate that Europe shares the legacy of Islam; that European values are not very different from those of its classical period. Indeed, without Islam, Europe, as we know it today, would not exist. As such, both European Muslim identities and European national identities become much more inclusive and open. Such open and inclusive identities would lay the foundation of a genuine multiculturalism.

DIVERSITY AND MULTICULTURALISM

Conventionally, we have tried to manage diversity through multiculturalism. Multiculturalism is the recognition that societies are pluralistic and consist of distinct cultures, multiple identities and different ethnic components. This view of multiculturalism is little more than a truism. Most societies are, and have been in history, multicultural. India, for example, has always consisted of a plethora of cultures and ethnicities. Even Britain was multicultural before multiculturalism was invented: the Welsh, the Irish, the Scots are not just different people, they are also different languages, cultures, histories, and ethnicities. A fact now acknowledged by devolution.

A more specific view of multiculturalism describes it as an eclectic mix of races that now live under the same geographical umbrella in

Europe and America. It is assumed that at some point this mix of cultures would synthesise generating hybridised cultural experience, influenced by various strands and practices from all the different mix of races. In some respect, we have already reached this multicultural nirvana. The food we eat, the clothes we wear, the way we furnish our homes show strong influences garnered from immigrant communities. And our art, literature and movies now reflect the many voices and cultures that make up the racial mix of modern European society. Yet, despite all this 'ethnic' influence, racial harmony is conspicuous by its stark absence.

Multiculturalism came chronologically after 'assimilation' and 'integration'. In the 1950s and 1960s, the politics of assimilation aimed at assimilating, and thus wiping out, the cultural identity of the immigrant communities. In the 1970s and the early 1980s, integration policies were designed to transform immigrant groups into indistinguishable 'members' of the dominant culture. Multiculturalism appeared after the failure of such hegemonic exercises and focussed on 'celebrating difference'. Europe actually imported multiculturalism from America where it replaced the 'melting pot' of earlier black and immigrant generations with what David Dinkins, the first African-American Mayor of New York, called 'gorgeous mosaic'. The emphasis, once again, was on racial and ethnic difference. So emphasis on difference became a key component of multiculturalism.

Indeed, champions of multiculturalism have turned difference and ethnicities based on race, into a fetish. The 'vision' of *The Future of Multi-Ethnic Britain*, the so-called Parekh Report, for example, is based squarely on difference. 'The fundamental need, both practical and theoretical', the report says, is to 'treat people with due respect for difference'.[3] Over the past decades, both Conservative and Labour governments in Britain have been insisting that minorities demonstrate and interminably celebrate their difference. Difference is a hot commodity in our art galleries and museums where it is regularly constructed, fabricated and paraded as a sign of enlightened plurality.

The undue emphasis on difference and ethnicity has not only turned multiculturalism into a commodity, it has made true multiculturalism impossible. This is not an accidental result; but a product of initial design. As currently understood, multiculturalism is intrinsically an American construction and incorporates all the assumptions and experiences of American history. To appreciate why multiculturalism has failed in Europe so demonstrably, we need to grasp why America does not work as a pluralistic society.

The United States is a nation conceived, born, reared and nurtured by immigrant communities. The nation was invented from the essence and as the epitome of all that should be learned from the failures of the Old World. Yet, even constitutionally, it is unable to get from '*I pluribus unum*' to '*in unum pluribus*' – from official motto of 'from many, one' to a sustainable acceptable reality of 'in one, many'. Why? Because America is the ultimate product of western colonialism. Whereas colonialism was what European nations did abroad, it is how America came to be on the ground it stole and ethnically cleansed to call home. The ideology of colonialism, with all its assumptions about race, ethnicity and difference, is how Europe looked at the rest of the world; but it is how America looked at itself and forged its self-identity at home.[4]

So, the American notion of multiculturalism is constructed securely behind the walls of colonial structures of power. What it had to say about self-evident truths concerning life, liberty and the pursuit of happiness was the extent of its multiculturalism. The vision of equality before the law and separation of power between church and state were designed specifically to make a multicultural white society possible. These were lessons well learnt from the Old World, where, as Thomas Jefferson so cogently argued, inordinate amounts of blood had been spilled and still failed to make everyone conform and produce uniform orthodoxy. The question avoided rather than overlooked was how the principles of libertarian rights could apply to non-whites – to native peoples seen as savages and blacks owned as property, both, nevertheless, being extant non-persons within the nation-state.

The horrors of America's historic failure to include Native Americans and blacks and then the Chinese within its notion of plurality were addressed during the 1970s and 1980s in two ways. The first option was ethnicity. Ethnic pride was the entitlement the system bestowed on those whites it assimilated but who were not the ideal, the archetypal WASP (white Anglo Saxon Protestant), such as the Irish, the Polish, the Russians, and the Jews. When the question arose of what to do about the excluded ethnicities, the answer was simply to indulge them. So, the hitherto excluded Native Americans and blacks acquired ethnic labels and permission to wear their ethnicity and historic victimhood on their sleeves.

The second option may be called legal individualism. Individualism is the cornerstone of western liberal thought and the basic premise of American constitutional philosophy. The very idea of equality is based on individualism. So, treating the excluded ethnicities as equal meant giving them equal treatment before the law. What this means for true equality turns out to be, in American history, a double-edged sword. One way southern states subverted the abolition of slavery, for example, was by inventing the 'separate but equal' formula that led to separate black schools, lunch counters, drinking fountains and the like. Similarly, equal individualism for Native Americans meant the drive to convert tribal reservations into individually owned plots of land. It also was the impetus behind the 1960s Civil Rights legislation where the law was supposedly 'colour blind', treating each individual citizen equally irrespective of race or ethnicity.

But far from making multiculturalism a reality, mixing equality and ethnicity generates new kinds of problems. Talking up ethnicity leads to fragmentation. And if each individual has equal and immutable rights of attachment to distinct and separate ethnicities with full rights of self-expression, diversity and difference become an unsolvable, enduring problem. Worse: those who are not members of distinct and separate ethnicities – like the youth – then manufacture new ethnicities to show their distinction. The insatiable desire for difference can never be satisfied: it can only lead to perpetual dissatisfaction, frustration, animosity and riots.

When black Americans travel the ethnicity route they have to begin by creative recovery of a diverse identity out of Africa. They face the problem of identity ripped from them and the discovery of an identity that is equally demeaned and disparaged by white, western civilisation. African ethnicity is not one entity, but any African ethnicity, along with any non-European ethnicity, becomes another battleground because of the impossibility of equivalence. The white majority do not see African ethnicity, or various Asian ethnicities, as anything other than completely different and inferior. When American blacks show pride in their ethnicity, by teaching black children their ethnic heritage, howls of protest are raised about diluting the inviolable sanctity of the western canon as the true embodiment of all that is noble in the human heritage. Afrocentric education, far from providing positive reinforcement for black children, centres them in another vortex of marginalisation. Afrocentric ethnicity is not an option for inclusion but proof of why they have been excluded. And it does nothing to combat the social and economic legacy of their marginalisation within America and its history. This is precisely why the ethnic route does not deliver multiculturalism.

The legal route does not fare much better either. The law signals the intentions of society, but is a rather blunt instrument for actually changing the attitudes of society. So equality may be declared through law, but it cannot be delivered by law. At law, black Americans are more likely to be charged, convicted, incarcerated and executed than any other group. As the legal rolls in the famed Florida re-count debacle of the 2000 presidential election proved, blacks are more easily and more likely to be disenfranchised by law. Laws that make everyone equal fail to address enduring disadvantage or redress the issues of communal repression. Perceptions about groups and communities, the weight of history, and the differences of historic experience all affect the reality of what is called equality of opportunity and ensure that the status quo continues to generate inequality. Making the law theoretically colour blind effectively works to keep non-white ethnicities in their place and leaves ample scope for the whites to evade the problem of equality by moving to the suburbs, removing themselves from contact with the non-white underclass.

By following the American model, Europe is repeating the failures and experiences of American history. We promote multiculturalism as an ideology of difference in a legal framework that insists that everyone is the same and makes no allowances for difference. Our courts, police and prison system, as in America, are institutionally biased against non-white ethnicities. Thus, despite the fact that we are proud to call ourselves multicultural societies, racism and lack of respect for diversity continues to be the norm.

All this, however, does not mean that multiculturalism is a bad idea. Critics and distracters of multiculturalism notwithstanding, it is a profound idea, the very thing we actually, in practical reality, genuinely need. Multiculturalism is a necessary quest not just for any self-respecting society, but for human social evolution as such. Multiculturalism is failing simply because the version on offer does not and cannot make concessions on the hierarchical superiority of the western worldview. Multiculturalism has escaped us because it cannot be reconciled with liberal individualism, the cornerstone of western society. Multiculturalism has been so unsuccessful because it is offered as a one-way traffic, something that the white community does for the 'ethnic minorities'. Multiculturalism is coming under attack from all sides, because both the Left and the Right realise that any socially viable version challenges the vindication of their inherent rightness and righteousness. In the final analysis, multiculturalism fails because what is on offer is not *multi*-cultural at all.

Europe needs to develop its own notion of multiculturalism based on the diversity of European society. For multiculturalism to work in Europe as a tool for managing diversity, it must have two unique characteristics. First, multiculturalism must be related to issues of power in all its aspects. Multiculturalism requires diversity to be represented in all dimensions of power; different minorities must have equal access and opportunity in political representation, in education and in the pursuit of economic goals. However, given that citizens have different needs, equal treatment requires that a full account be taken of their differences. As the Parekh Report notes, 'when equality ignores relevant differences and insists on uniformity of treatment, it leads to injustice and inequality; when differences ignore the demands of equality, they result in discrimination. Equality must be defined in a culturally sensitive way and applied in discriminating but not discriminatory manner.'[5]

Second, multiculturalism must be about transformation. Here we are not just talking about transforming the poor inner city blacks and Asians, Moroccans and Algerians, Turks and the Gypsies, by providing them with economic and educational opportunities. But also of transforming European society itself so we move from the irrational premise that 'they' – all the ethnic others – see the errors of their ways and become 'more like 'us' to the humane idea that European culture is as deeply flawed as all other human cultures. Multiculturalism does not require more commitment to liberal values in western societies, as some have argued. Rather, it requires a transformation of liberal values to more inclusive forms.

What we assume to be naturally good and wholesome in liberalism often turns out to be rather limited. For example, the classical, liberal notions of 'freedom', all the way from Mill to Rawls, do not have a place for the marginalised and the poor. In *Essay on Liberty*[6] Mill excludes 'the backward nations', women and children from the rights to liberty; and John Rawls, in his celebrated *Theory of Justice*,[7] acknowledges that societies where the basic needs of the individuals are not fulfilled do not fit in his framework of liberty. There is no way you can build multiculturalism on such exclusivist ideas.

Transformation requires that we move from the simplistic notion of multiculturalism as a tolerated extension of western liberalism to a sophisticated process that aims to transform and transcend liberalism itself. This process has to begin with the realisation that liberalism is neither a European invention nor a European concern; it is, and has always been, part of all traditions. All cultural minorities within Europe have their own liberal traditions, which need to be embraced and appreciated. We also need to transcend the hegemony of such ideas as liberal individualism to realise that groups and communities too have rights. And we have to realise that multiculturalism is a partner project – it requires full and equal partnership with other cultures in shaping modernity, postmodernity and the human future.

DIVERSITY AND RIGHTS

Most of the problems of managing diversity hinge on the notion of individualism. Individualism is *the* absolute of liberal democracy: the notion that society is nothing more than the sum of individuals and that the individual is a self-contained, autonomous and sovereign being who is defined independently of society. This assumption, that the individual is prior to society, is unique to western culture: it is the defining principle of liberal democracy and shapes its metaphysical, epistemological, methodological, moral, legal, economic and political aspects. But in many minority cultures that are now an integral part of Europe, the individual does not define him/herself by separating from others but in relation to a holistic and integrated group: the family or clan, the community or culture, religion or worldview. The Muslims, for example, see the individual as an integrated part of the society which in a local area is defined by the Friday mosque and on an international level by the collectivity of all Muslims: the *ummah*. Society is ontologically prior to the individual and social obligations come before individual dictates. The Chinese community sees the family as an organism linking the past, the ancestors, with the present and the future, the descendants. The individual thus exists not as an autonomous, isolated being but in a living union with his/her ancestors.

For the Hindu community, to give another example, the notion of *dharma*, one of the fundamental concepts of Indian tradition, is a multi-layered concept that incorporates the terms elements, data, quality and origination as well as law, norm of conduct, character of things, right, truth, ritual, morality, justice, righteousness, religion and destiny. In Sikhism, the prime duty of a human being is *sewa*: there is no salvation without *sewa*, the disinterested service of the community without any expectation. The rights of the individual are thus earned by participating in the community's endeavour and thereby seeking *sakti*. That's exactly what the Sikh Gurus did themselves. Thus cultures based on such notions as *dharma* and *sewa* are not concerned with the reductive exercise of defining the 'rights' of one individual against another, or of the individual against the society: the individual is but a single knot in a web of material, social, cultural and spiritual relationships and his/her duty is to find a harmonious place in relation to the society, the cosmos and the transcendent world.

In the western liberal framework, the individual is constantly at war with the community feeling perpetually ontologically threatened. The main concern of the individual is to keep his/her identity intact, separate from all others, to enclose herself/himself inside a protective wall. Whereas in non-western cultures, morality is defined by the community or society, in liberal thought the individuals have to make moral choices for themselves. Thus there can never be substantive agreement between the individual and the community as a whole. Morality becomes a matter of individual behaviour: the emphasis is not on what is of ultimate value and what ends should be sought, but how whatever ends are chosen ought to be pursued. The goals of liberal democracy therefore focus on providing the individual with all possible avenues to pursue whatever is desired, even if it is, and often it is, at the expense of the community. The government can never seek communal social, cultural, economic or political goals such as ensuring equal distribution of wealth, creating a less class-based society or providing equal educational opportunities for all.

Thus the liberal notion of what is a human being is unique and suspicious of communal concerns and values. This notion is not only the defining value of liberal democracy; it is actually built into its conceptual structure. This is why in a liberal democracy, certain representative individuals are elected to ensure that other individuals have all the freedom to pursue their individual interests. So, strictly speaking, liberal democracy is not so much representative democracy as representative government.

Managing diversity requires us to transcend this rather truncated view of liberalism based exclusively on individualism. Given that an individual may have a string of fluid and multiple identities, many of which are related to different communities to which the individual may belong, it makes little sense to see the individual as absolute, discrete, irreducible, separate and ontologically prior to society. The whole person, with a plethora of his or her identities, is much more than the individual who cannot exist without the links between history and community, culture and ethnicity, sex and gender and environment and nature. Thus, the person and the individual are not the same thing. The individual is simply an abstraction, a truncated and selected version of the person for the sake of practical convenience. A person incorporates his/her parents, children, extended family, ancestors, community, friends, enemies, ideas, beliefs, emotions, self-image, perceptions, visions, self-identity. Thus, violence, discrimination and racism inflicted on a person equally damage the whole community.

While the individual is protected through human rights, the person and the community are often left unprotected. It is therefore necessary for European liberal democracies to go beyond the individual and consider the rights of persons and communities. The notion of collective, cultural or group, rights is highly contested. As Will Kymlicka has suggested, for many people, the very idea of '"group rights" is both mysterious and disturbing. For how can groups have rights that are not ultimately reducible to the rights of their individual members? And if groups do have rights, won't these rights inherently conflict with individual rights?'[8] Such concerns are based on a defective reading of what constitutes a human being: humans, as I have argued, are not simply packages of material and psychological needs, wrapped in an atomised microcosm.

If we recognise the extent to which a person's well-being is tied up with the community or groups they belong to, as Darlene Johnston[9] has argued in relation to Native Americans, then it makes sense to talk of group rights, not reducible to individual rights. A community's self-preservation, its ability to survive as a distinct, different community, should be seen as a right by itself. The group rights model makes sense when a society operates on the assumption that it is a collection, or a confederation, of communities. And the traditional way of life of each community has to be protected for the community to exist as a different community.

I would argue that 'positive discrimination', or affirmative action, is a matter of rights for certain minority communities in Europe. The disadvantages of being on the margin cannot be overcome unless special attention is paid to the economic and educational situation of say Pakistanis and Bangladeshis in Britain, or Arabs in France or Turks in Germany. In the garden of multiculturalism, with a host of different communities, these minorities are like fledgling plants. They need care and nourishment to grow. But once they have taken root in their particular states, and the plants have become trees, affirmative action becomes irrelevant. Different minority communities in Europe are in different stages of taking cultural root in their respective countries. As such, each minority has special needs that can only be met with tailor-made and guided affirmative action.

GOING FORWARD WITH DIVERSITY

The real strength of Europe is the sheer cultural diversity of its numerous communities. Coming to terms with this diversity requires us to transcend certain contradictions in liberalism, particularly its obsession with individualism. To reject the demonisation of difference does not require the abandonment of difference. European states need to create space for difference to exist as difference; and for diverse communities to exist within their own parameters.

As such, the question of assimilation does not arise if minority communities are to exist as different and distinct communities. Assimilation was a dubious notion even when it was first suggested in the 1960s. It is an idea based on the modernist notion that there is only one civilisation and all other cultures and civilisations are nothing but small tributaries in this Grand Civilisation of Europe. So it seemed natural for all other cultures, particularly immigrant cultures, to assimilate themselves in the superior culture of Europe. It reminds me of *Star Trek*'s Borg who assimilate all other people to enhance their own power. Assimilation leads to eradication of identity and as such it is a suicidal path for the minority communities of Europe. To remain sane and ethnically alive, minority communities must retain a modicum of their historic and cultural identities.

Similarly, we need to abandon the notion of integration. What shall minority communities integrate with? The class- and race-based English culture? Or French colonial culture? Or the German notions of identity based on superiority? The notion of integration is not only problematic; it assumes there is a dominant culture that is the yardstick of civilisation. The pursuit of integration also undermines true multiculturalism, which demands equal respect for all identities and cultures.

We need to move beyond fake notions of plurality that emphasise cuisine and 'celebration', to a practice of multiculturalism that is specifically aimed at bringing the marginalised into the circles of power. A representative Europe that consists of communities within communities, has to share power equitably among all its people. And giving diversity its due would require affirmative policies for certain minorities and recognition of collective and group rights.

However, diversity does not rule out shared national values. The desire for common European values is not the same thing as the aspiration for homogeneity. Minority communities need to change too; and realise that traditions and customs that do not change cease to be traditions and customs and are transformed into instruments of oppression. Identity has historic anchors but is not fixed to a limited, unchanging set of traditional signs and historic symbols. Identity is not what we buy, or what we choose, or what we impose on others; rather, it is something from which we learn how to live, discover what is worth pursuing, and appreciate what it is to be different. Minority cultures in Europe need to learn to live with majority values and aspirations just as the flora and fauna in a garden learn to live with each other.

Both majority and minority cultures need to abandon the idea that a single truth can be imposed on a plural society. Just as a garden does not function on the basis of a single species, so the single Truth of European culture or Islam or any other creed or ideology that is based on exclusivist notions of truth and seeks redemption by imposing this truth on all others, cannot lead us to viable, multicultural Europe. The Platonic idea that truth is the same for all cultures has no place in a pluralistic Europe.

As Rabbi Jonathan Sacks argues in *The Dignity of Difference*,[10] this notion of truth sets up false oppositions. If all truth is the same for everyone at all times, then if I am right, you must be wrong. And, if I really care for truth, I must convert you to my view. We must move forward from the old recipe that 'truth is supremely important, and therefore all persons must live by a single truth' to the new formula that 'truth is supremely important, and therefore every man and woman must be allowed to live according to how they see the truth'. Ultimately, my notion of pluralistic identities comes down to how we all see the truth differently, according to our historic experiences and perspectives, and how we all live the truth in our lives, as individuals and communities, in our uniquely different and cultural ways of being human.

This means that Europe must recover its confidence in identities as the product of various and diverse traditions. We need to recognise that any identity is the means to synthesise similarity through difference and to see difference as discrete means of expressing basic similarity. We need to move away from the politics of contested identities and ethnicities that heighten artificial differences towards acceptance of the plasticity and possibilities of identities that focus on our common humanity. Living identity, as opposed to the fossilised to die for variety, is always in a constant flux. It is an ever-changing balance, the balance of similarities and differences as a way of locating what it is that makes life worth living and what connects us with the rest of the changing world.

Multicultural Europe must come to terms with a plethora of pluralistic identities. In the future, to be a European would mean being much more than one, rigid thing. Not least, we will have to come to terms with new European identities, which would include European black, European Arab, European Turkish, European Muslim and numerous other identities. The challenge of shaping a multicultural Europe is to transcend difference and thereby enable multiculturalism to fulfil its real purpose – to provide variety and diversity in a continent that cannot exist without it.

16
Beyond Difference:
Cultural Relations in the New Century

Let me begin by saying what a great privilege and pleasure it is to be invited to deliver this lecture to mark the British Council's 70th anniversary. Since its inception the British Council has played an important part in promoting cultural relations, predominantly, according to its remit, abroad but also, as a consequence of its work overseas, here in Britain.

The business of cultural relations is the seminal issue of the new century. But if cultural relations – that is, how we relate to others, how we relate to each other in Britain, how we promote Britain's relationship with the rest of the world – is the big issue of our times it has been made so by history and comes with histories attached. To get beyond the impasses of the present, with their blood-laden consequences, we have to wrestle with not only problematic issues on the ground, but also the ideas in our heads. Cultural relations are all about interconnections. It is as much about the business of managing how we see ourselves as how we see people other than ourselves; it is also about how we conceive of the interconnections between ourselves and those who are not like us. Cultural relations are as much about how we aspire to construct the future according to a specific set of core values as they are about how we understand the past and present of people other than ourselves. Cultural relations are about a kaleidoscope, seeing the world in a diversity of ways – but with a kaleidoscope we have to remember there is one eye and one hand providing the point of perspective and shuffling the patterns into an array of pleasing, delightful colours and configurations. At the end of the day with a kaleidoscope one has to concentrate not on the delightful lights and colours but the hand and eye manipulating the show.

Cultural relations is an industry and as an industry it has a history. It is important to appreciate this history because we need to transcend

This is the text of a public lecture delivered at 'Eye to Eye', a conference held to mark the British Council's 70th anniversary on 2 November 2004.

it. This history has a hold on our thought and does not permit us to go beyond the current impasse to usher a genuine paradigm shift and develop a new agreed consensus. It forces us to hold mutually contradictory views at the same time and will not give precedence to any particular set of ideas. This is the impasse. It is an impasse because the kind of change, the leap of faith, necessary to renounce one set of ideas for another leads to the overthrow of some of the most cherished props of civilisation as we know it in exchange for what, from certain perspectives, appears to be ultimate anarchy.

The history of cultural relations is embedded in two specific concepts that I think we need to transcend: modernity and multiculturalism.

Modernity is the eye through which we look at the kaleidoscope of diversity. Modernity refers to the mode of social and cultural organisation that emerged in Europe after the Enlightenment and came to dominate the world through colonialism and still rules supreme in the postcolonial period. Modernity posits itself as a distinctive and superior mode of existence. Consequently, all other modes of being, doing and knowing are implicitly seen as inferior. Modernity has a particular problem with traditional societies – in other words, with most of humanity – which are seen as trapped in the past, hence lacking modern sensibilities, modern concerns about style and fashion as well as democracy and human rights.

Now, this is not the place to develop yet another critique of modernity. There are numerous critiques of modernity – profound as well as pedestrian.[1] My concern is to highlight how modernity has distorted cultural relations.

In the framework of modernity, non-western cultures can only be minor partners in any cultural interaction. It is always we the modern British, Europeans, Westerners who are dispensing enlightenment to the less fortunate of the Earth. Our aim, conscious and unconscious, is always to supersede the indigenous idea of culture, which we frequently identify with superstition and oppression, and replace it with what we consider to be necessary and important for a traditional society to join the twenty-first century. Meanwhile, the colonial political economy that goes under the rubric of globalisation continues to subvert the life-support systems of those who maintain some semblance of traditional life in the non-western world. This is what my friend Ashis Nandy, the Indian intellectual, has called the 'push factor' in cultural relations.

But there is also the 'pull factor'. The elite in traditional societies – and it is always the elite we deal with when it comes to cultural encounters – have accepted their 'backward' position *vis-à-vis* modernity. This perception is an essential ingredient of their understanding of their own culture, their nationalism, and even their anti-western sentiments. To measure one's 'backwardness' by the standards of an alien, 'modern' culture, and to seek to overcome it by imitating that culture, as Nandy notes, generates a number of contradictions.[2] It is imitative; and hostile to the model it imitates. It leads, quite naturally, to the loss of self-esteem. The redoubled quest for self-esteem, therefore, often takes the form of cultural self-affirmation and attempts to retain the unique features of one's culture. Often, most of the features of one's culture identified as unique turn out to be an impediment to modernity – yet, they have to be cherished and defended as the essence of one's self-identity. One way to overcome these contradictions is to construct a golden past: it is not just Islam and Hinduism that have constructed a romanticised, imagined past – it has been a standard project of most non-western nations. The problem with golden pasts is that they cannot be totally recreated in the present. What can, and is often, retained are some visible symbols of traditional cultures: the quaint ceremonies, rituals plucked out of context, exotic dances and colourful costumes worn on special, 'national', occasions. The end product of this process is that both indigenous culture and modernity are seen with ambivalence and hostility.

The push and pull factors are not amenable to healthy cultural relations. Yet, there is another problem. In many non-western societies, cultural expression is in itself a form of resistance to modernity – indeed, there is cultural resistance and cultures of resistance. Some cultures of resistance – such as certain 'Indian' cultures in Latin America – are only visible on the margins of modernity and expressed by those who are not part of the dominant globalisation process. But others, such as Islamic fundamentalism, have now taken a centre stage. In either case, cultures of resistance not only reject modernity but seek a modernity-free cultural space; yet, paradoxically, they may use the tools of modernity to fight their corner.

If cultural relations is the business of building trust, as is often asserted by its practitioners, then it is difficult to see how that trust can be built within the framework of modernity. Moreover, this framework is not very conducive to mutuality, the current major theme in cultural relations, either. 'The word "mutuality"', write

Martin Rose and Nick Wadham-Smith, 'describes the quality of a
two-way relationship, with overtones of benefit distributed between
the two parties, of ownership shared. There are implications of
equality in the relationship and there is certainly a strong sense of
movement in both directions between the parties'.[3] It is a process
of joint ownership and implies equality and a two way relationship:
'advocating mutuality means understanding that trust arises not
from unequal relationships and conversations based on asymmetrical
distribution of power, but from relationships built on respect,
openness, and a preparedness, where appropriate, to change one's
own mind'.[4] The problem is that while mutuality can make you aware
of and compensate for the 'push factors', it can do nothing about
the 'pull factors'. Mutuality cannot work if a culture has accepted
its 'backwardness' in relation to modernity and is ambivalent and
hostile to both modernity and its own tradition. Mutuality may be
unconditionally 'good in itself' but what good is it when faced with
a culture of resistance whose very reason to be is to disengage itself
from dominant modern forms of cultural expression?

The hand that is manipulating the kaleidoscopic show of cultural
diversity is multiculturalism. Multiculturalism, as we understand
it today, has its origins in the American civil rights movement.
If one were to pinpoint a specific historic event that engendered
multiculturalism, it would be the 1954 *Brown v. Board of Education*
judgement issued by the Supreme Court of the United States.[5] The
case concerned the segregation of white and black children in the
public schools in the State of Kansas; and the judgement swept away
the malign fictions of separate but equal treatment for members of
different races. There are a number of issues behind the judgement,
the most important being the centrality of race as *the* problem of
modern society.

The activism and thinking prompted by *Brown v. Board of Education*
quickly revealed a host of different aspirations and understandings
that tested the central propositions on which the judgement relied.
What is equality in an unequal world? Can simple reliance on
access to civic rights put right a historic legacy of civic wrongs?
And is race really the issue? Is one system of civic thought not the
imposition of a cultural homogeneity on the reality of cultural
difference constructed by history? Is cultural experience constructed
by history not complicit in the existence and continued operation
of inequality? Thus affirmative action was born, the redistributive

programme for the equal but disadvantaged, out of which various ideas of multiculturalism gradually developed.

What is often missed in this familiar history is the substantive issue. And that issue is difference. It was insufficient to offer equality when glaring differences denied the real experience of equal opportunity. To be poor, black, rural or urban and suddenly presented with the right to vote and a place in the same schools and colleges as white people did not guarantee the end of inequality. And to be poor and black and invested with inalienable rights to life, liberty and the pursuit of happiness opened profound questioning about historic identity, the history of one's identity, and loss and recovery of one's identity. Afrocentrism was born and stimulated thinking and activism among other American minority groups such as native Americans and Latinos that was not simply political and economic but essentially cultural. The era of multiculturalism and political correctness was upon us and is part of the impasse in which we are still perplexed.

So the basic premise of equal civic rights opened the whole question of identity. Cultural relations as a field of social management, policy-making and theoretical inquiry is simultaneously a historic discourse about power over identity and a search to operate, enable and empower new thinking about identity. As a question of identity it stands in contrast to the entire history of thought concerned with civic and individual rights, which have worked on the premise of homogeneity. Equality is the management and delivery of sameness. But identity is the perception of difference, a cultural construct of like and not like, us and them. What the achievement of civic rights revealed was that sameness could take people only so far in realising their cultural aspirations for inclusion. For sameness, the kind of homogeneity constructed, was not merely an abstract, impersonal ideal but in a very profound way a cultural, historic artefact of a specific civilisation. This is the real nub of the problem.

The whole movement for civic rights and legislation about race relations was and is a theory and practice for domestic, national use in the US. But it has not remained in the US nor been confined to domestic purposes; it has been globalised and has had profound influence on how we think about cultural relations in the international arena, the relations between different nationalities and civilisations. And the American model for race relations, extracted from its specific national context, proved limited when applied in other nations, such as Britain, whose immigrant population was more diverse, multi ethnic, racial and creedal.

The American model of multiculturalism has a number of intrinsic problems. It fetishises difference – indeed, the very notion of 'ethnicity' has its origins in the American society where everyone except the whites are 'ethnic'. Difference is emphasised and celebrated for its own sake; yet, inequality based on identity is dismissed. According to the dominant ideas of American society civic rights had nothing to do with identity. Equality is seen only as equality before the law and delivery of homogeneity within a capitalist framework.

On the international level, this model of multiculturalism translates as the spread of standardised ideas on democracy, civic society and human rights. So while we emphasise the cultural difference of other nations, we do not tolerate the expression of this very difference either in terms of social and political institutions, or norms and values or rights and responsibilities. Every culture is equal, like different ethnic groups in a nation, before the Law of Humanity as shaped and framed by western culture and civilisation. In other words, we assume that there is only one and the same way of being human. This is why we are happy to impose 'democracy' on other nations; and insist that 'human rights' can only be formulated in one particular way. And, of course, we impose homogeneity on all cultures and cultural values through the standardising forces of our technology, media, consumer products and global western cultural products.

Multicultural relations that emphasise difference and promote sameness are not conducive to mutuality either. Mutuality is not about difference for the sake of difference; or about promoting a western framework of sameness. Mutuality must be about acculturation – where both sides of the cultural relations equation change, transform and transcend their own limitations.

The big question about cultural relations even as mutuality is what it is for. Is it a staging post on the progress to a globalised, homogenised world where the expression of difference will be contained within common adherence to a basic set of principles and institutions that have been extracted from the history and ideas of just one history and civilisation? Is it an agent of acceptance of difference and a movement to equity within plurality? It is my contention that if mutuality is located in the familiar western framework of dichotomy, it is destined to fail. Both modernity and multiculturalism emphasise simplistic polarities and ignore the complex paradoxes of their strange history and contemporary application.

The first function of cultural relations, as far as I am concerned, is to bring parity to and among diverse cultures. That means we must restore confidence in traditional cultures while restraining the excesses of modernity. We have to enable what Unesco has called 'living communities of cultures'[6] to speak in their own terms and we must seek to understand them with their own concepts and notions. This suggests we need to go beyond modernity. The second function of cultural relations is to create space for difference to exist as difference – so that ultimately difference becomes irrelevant; and we can all concentrate on our common humanity. This implies moving beyond multiculturalism.

For cultural relations to have meaning and significance, we need to make two basic transitions: from modernity to transmodernism, and from multiculturalism to mutually assured diversity.

So, what is transmodernism?

To begin with, transmodernism should not be confused with postmodernism. Postmodernism, as I have argued elsewhere,[7] is not a disjuncture in history but a continuation of the culture of western imperialism. Modernity, as I mentioned earlier, frames traditional societies as backward, 'living in the past'. The essential principles of tradition are seen as the cause of 'backwardness', just as it is in the nature of traditional societies to be incapable of change. Thus, traditional societies are a major hurdle to development and 'modernisation'. The classic texts of development all argued that tradition must be abandoned, indeed suppressed where necessary, if 'backward' societies of developing countries were to actually develop and 'catch up with the west'.[8] And, in the name of development, progress and modernity, traditional cultures have been uprooted, displaced, suppressed and annihilated. Postmodernism simply considers tradition to be dangerous; it is often associated with 'essentialism' – that is, harking back to some puritan notion of good society that may or may not have existed in history. Indeed, there are segments of traditional societies that have constructed a romanticised past and seek to recreate it in contemporary times, such as certain varieties of Islamic fundamentalists. But it is important to appreciate that traditional communities on the whole do not see tradition in this way. They do not view tradition as something fixed in history but see it as dynamic; they reinvent and innovate tradition constantly. Indeed, a tradition that does not change ceases to be a tradition. But traditions change in a specific way. They change within their own parameters, at their own speed, and towards their chosen direction. There is good reason for this. If traditions were to vacate the space they occupy they would cease to be meaningful. When tradition is cherished and celebrated the entire content of what is lauded can be changed. Such change is then meaningful because it is integrated and enveloped by the continuing sense of identity that tradition provides. Furthermore, change can be an evaluative process, a sifting of good, better, best as well as under no circumstances, an adaptation that operates according to the values the veneration of tradition has maintained intact. Thus, non-western traditional communities do not think of tradition as something that will take them to pre-modern times; on the contrary, tradition will take them forward, with their identity and core values intact, to a future beyond modernity.

Postmodernism is what comes after modernity; it is 'post' in terms of time; it is a natural culmination of modernity. This is why it is sometimes described as 'the logic of late capitalism'. It represents a linear trajectory that starts with colonialism, continues with modernity and ends with post-modernity, or postmodernism. It is not surprising then that postmodernism and tradition are like two fuming bulls in a ring: they are inimically antagonistic to each other. Postmodernism states that all big ideas that have shaped our society, like Religion, Reason, Science, Tradition, History, Morality, Marxism, do not stand up to philosophical scrutiny. There is no such thing as Truth. Anything that claims to provide us with absolute truth is a sham. It must be abandoned. Moreover, postmodernism suggests, there is no ultimate Reality. We see what we want to see, what our position in time and place allows us to see, what our cultural and historic perceptions focus on. Instead of reality, what we have is an ocean of images; a world where all distinction between image and material reality has been lost. Postmodernism posits the world as a video game: seduced by the allure of the spectacle, we have all become characters in the global video game, zapping our way from here to there, fighting wars in cyberspace, making love to digitised bits of information. We float on an endless sea of images and stories that shape our perception and our individual 'reality'.

While postmodernism provides a valid description of contemporary, globalised times, its basic premises are intrinsically anti-tradition. Religion plays a very important role in non-western societies; and religious morality is central to the norms and values of many traditional cultures – ditto for the idea of Truth and Reality. So far from embracing postmodernism, traditional societies wish to shape a future where these ideas play a predominant role. Their journey is across postmodernism.

So, transmodernism goes beyond modernity and postmodernism: it transcends both and takes us trans – i.e. into another state of being. Thus, unlike postmodernism, transmodernism is not a linear projection. We can best understand it with the aid of chaos theory.[9] In all complex systems – societies, civilisations, ecosystems etc. – many independent variables are interacting with each other in a great many ways. Chaos theory teaches us that complex systems have the ability to create order out of chaos. This happens at a balancing point, called the 'edge of chaos'. At the edge of chaos, the system is in a kind of suspended animation between stability and total dissolution into chaos. At this point, almost any factor can push the system into one or other direction. However, complex systems at the edge of chaos have the ability to spontaneously self-organise themselves into a higher order; in other words the system 'evolves' spontaneously into a new mode of existence. Transmodernism is the transfer of modernity and postmodernism from the edge of chaos into a new order of society. As such, transmoderism and tradition are not two opposing worldviews but a new synthesis of both. Traditional societies use their ability to change and become transmodern while remaining the same! Both sides of the equation are important here: change has to be made and accommodated; but the fundamental tenets of tradition, the sources of its identity and sacredness, remain the same. So we may define a transmodern future as a synthesis between life enhancing tradition – that is amenable to change and transition – and new forms of modernities that are shaped and articulated by traditional cultures themselves.

Transmodernism introduces two major shifts in cultural relations. First, it sees tradition as dynamic, amenable, capable and eager to change; and traditional cultures not as pre-modern but as communities with potential to transcend the dominant model of modernity. This is a profound shift; and its real importance lies in ways of seeing non-western cultures. (But the greatest change happens in the ideas and understanding of western cultures?) Transmodernism forces us to see non-western cultures on their own terms, with their own eyes (ideas, concepts, notions), and as (part of) the common future rather than the past of humanity. Moreover, if one believes that traditional cultures can change, then one looks for signs of change. When traditions change, the change is often invisible to the outsiders. Therefore, observers can go on maintaining their modern or postmodern distaste for tradition irrespective of the counter evidence before their very eyes. The contemporary world does provide opportunity for tradition to go on being what tradition has always been – an adaptive force. The problem is that no amount of adaptation, however much it strengthens traditional societies, actually frees them from the yoke of being marginal, misunderstood and misrepresented. It does nothing to dethrone the concept 'Tradition' as an *idée fixe* of western society. Transmodernism, on the other hand, focuses one's eyes on the signs of change, and attempts to make visible what is often shrouded from the gaze of the outsiders. A good example is contemporary Islam. The west has always seen Islam through the lens of modernity and concluded that it is a negative, static, closed system. Since the basic assumption is that Islam is incapable of change, and is inimically anti-modern, there is little point in looking for change. Yet, from Morocco to Indonesia, Islam has changed profoundly over the last decade, particularly after the events of September 11, 2001. But to notice this change, Islam has to be seen from the perspective of transmodernism and understood through its own concepts and categories.

Second, transmodernism shifts the notions of modernity from being *a priori*, the given and exclusive preserve of the west, to a participatory negotiation of a plethora of (trans)modernities each answering to different histories. Just as there are different ways to be human, there are different ways to be modern. Traditional societies can be (trans)modern too and can shape their own models of modernities based on their own norms, values and worldviews. This shift restores parity to cultural relations. The conventional ideas that it is only 'the west' that modernises 'the east' is turned upside down: 'the east' can just as easily transmodernise 'the west'! The west thus has as much to learn from the east – and I am not referring here to obscurantist ideas on mysticism and 'spirituality' – as it has to teach. Transmodernism thus introduces new ways of listening to non-western cultures. It directs the ear towards the debates that are going on in all cultures and civilisations striving to find contemporary interpretations of their basic values within the complexities of their histories, and contemporary relevance of their cherished ideas. As the sum of learned experience, culture implies a rootedness in ongoing categories, ideas and identities of enduring significance. Transmodernism is all about listening to this experience; and realising that identity as a cultural construct is as much a work in progress in traditional societies as in western ones. In a globalised world, transmodernism attunes cultural relations to new modes of (trans)modernities emerging in the non-west and travelling the unconventional route.

The other transition, from multiculturalism to mutually assured diversity, works within the framework of transmodernism to create cultural space for difference to exist as difference.

What is mutually assured diversity?

Mutually assured diversity is more than mutuality. It is explicitly a definition of what we are being mutual about. Mutually assured diversity is the universal acceptance of the continuity of cultural identity for all as the negotiated, adaptive, meaningful space in which all human beings operate in contemporary circumstances. It is the proposition that identity is the vessel of cultural relations for the individual – and as such is the relational agent through which one perceives, understands and interacts with the self, with members of one's family, community, with other individuals and with groups and collectives of belonging that ripple outward from the self as well as the material universe.

What is mutual is that the human condition is a cultural condition and that culture is an essential relational attribute, an enabling feature of knowing, being and doing. It is the acceptance that identity provides everyone with a hand and eye to manipulate the kaleidoscope of diversity, both within their culture and between cultures. It is the acceptance that for all people everywhere identity is not formed in a vacuum but within a cultural realm that comes with values, history, axes to grind and a variety of perplexities, conundrums and perennial questions.

What has to be transcended to arrive at mutually assured diversity is the idea that culture is ascriptive or prescriptive. It was the long established convention of western social thought and then social science that traditional societies ascribe status, roles and relationships as well as operate through prescriptive rules and therefore, as bounded wholes, operate to maintain stasis, to keep change at bay. History becomes the charter that makes the present work but does so because traditional society fictionalises its history to permit the present to replicate the essential elements of the past. This was, and is, an elegant delusion that fostered the notion that it was western society alone that embraced the future and the concept of change.

What needs to be grasped is that all societies, cultures and civilisations have undergone change and are in a process of negotiating with change. What is significant is what kind of change they accept, find problematic, reject or have mixed feeling about and alternate responses to, and for what reasons. It is the transmission of identity across change that is the cultural reflex par excellence, because identity is the attribute of belonging that grows from knowing oneself so that one has the ability to know others and learn about things.

Martin Rose and Nick Wadham-Smith suggest that we should accept the mutuality that should mature from multiculturalism not as a transactional good but as a good in itself. I would argue the transition we need to make is to the recognition of the good in each culture, or rather the acceptance that culture is the personal relationship with ideas of good and evil, a nexus of values, a system for adherence to values and a praxis for the operation of values in contemporary existence. This relationship is always personal and therefore diverse but the diversity does not preclude commonality, but rather is specifically constructed to encourage communal relations that expand up to and to include the universal. Our historic problem has been the failure to admit the universality of diversity and to insist on the limitations of other peoples' concepts of the universal. Such insistence has made cultures incommensurable competing wholes allied to the even more virulent ideas of exclusivity and superiority that lead the way to xenophobia and all the dehumanisations, antagonisms and combative ills trailing in its wake.

Mutually assured diversity is the sanity that permits an end to contending for the upper hand, the one way that is the only right way by recognising the multiple ways the world's people have of seeking to comprehend values and means of delivering values in daily life.

What does it mean to accept that cultures are systems for seeking good and knowing what is evil, for delivering values? It is to accept that a civilisation with a record of genocide, institutionalisation of chattel slavery and racism, imperialism, fascism, holocaust and Stalinism along with taking the lead in the development of the technologies of mass destruction up to and including nuclear Armageddon, knows as much about savagery, barbarism and outright evil as any other civilisation that has ever existed or currently exists. And yet, this self same western civilisation knows itself only as good. It has had recourse to its concept of good to generate reform, remedial action to countermand its capacity to bring forth horrors. None of the evil and wrongs perpetrated by western civilisation was or is uncontested. Even when wrong was accepted as the dominant organising principle for whole societies there have always been dissenting voices, alternative interpretations and from these in time change at the level of values has been made manifest. The mutuality necessary to arrive at mutually assured diversity is the recognition of this as the common human condition. And the human cultural condition is always caught in the perplexities and confusion of history which comes with its attendant baggage of disparities of power within and without, betwixt and between. With the human condition we, none of us in our diverse identities, are ever in clear water; rather, we are all in our plurality of ways seeking to make sense, to find a point of clarity on the good, better and best as opposed to the bad, worse and worst of what needs to be done – and other people never leave us alone to get on with it and simplify how to make the world a better place.

Multiculturalism is ready to acknowledge we all have histories. Mutually assured diversity is founded on the proposition that all identities have futures; that identity is the cultural aptitude to seek a better future fashioned out of all the possibilities and predicaments offered by contemporary times and circumstances and in the light of histories that shape those circumstances. What is diverse is the means, institutions and social forms of delivering values. To arrive at mutually assured diversity requires learning to see not only the debates, knowledge and distinctness of various different cultures, but to see how within them common values and commensurate ideas enacted in radically different ways.

Multiculturalism is a measure of tolerance for difference, within limits which are neither precise nor openly acknowledged. Multiculturalism is the encouragement of and indulgence in the performance of difference as the optional, private or innocuous communal celebration of ethnicity and its origins. By and large multiculturalism is about niceness, building civic inclusion by controlled learning and general avoidance of difficult or potentially devastating inquiry. It is possible to proceed a long way before encountering the limits, the demarcations of power which demonstrate that multiculturalism is a dispensation only so long as it exists within the parameters of liberalism and acknowledges the superior norms of western civilisation and modernity.

How does mutually assured diversity differ from multiculturalism? Simply put because it is not about niceness but acceptance of necessity and willingness to redistribute the concept of power. When diverse identities are presumptively perpetual the emphasis shifts from toleration to polylogue – multiple dialogues – and the necessity of understanding to make visible what has previously been shrouded in obscurity: the meaning of their particular culture to the bearers of that culture. It is the embrace of polylogue that places self-description first, however destabilising that may be to cherished systems of knowledge, the knowledge accumulated by and through the lens of modernity.

Culture and identity are constantly in flux because they are systems of interpretation. They are also systems of preference for particular ways of knowing, being and doing that have a rationale justified by recourse to values, to history and to material circumstance. Cultural rationale offers a balance sheet that distributes rights, responsibilities and duties in distinctive ways. And any cultural system is open to abuse, misapplication and perversion. Arranged marriage within the network of extended family is a useful case to highlight the shift that has to be made to arrive at mutually assured diversity. It is conventional to see arranged marriage as an oppressive, backward practice that is especially demeaning to women, a violation of the liberation of their individual rights to equality. It can indeed be a system open to abuse, a marriage market manipulated for the enrichment of men at the expense of the rights of women. These familiar critiques, however, are not the whole story. Arranging marriages is the operation of sets of values which in the ideal create not only new family units but also provide compatibility, companionship, love, mutual support and a lifelong enduring bond between the married couple themselves. It offers both parties individual benefits, as well as securing to them benefits from membership of wider networks of family relations which come with responsibilities, obligations and duties but also can have significant material, social, psychological and spiritual utility. It also comes with the usual set of human tensions – the problem of getting along with family. It is a system that is open to amendment, adaptation and evolution in conditions of social change. Asians in Britain have developed a whole host of innovations while accepting the value premises of the institution. And the track record of the system at the very least can be no worse than the various systems of contracting male–female relationships in western society in today's world. Mutually assured diversity is not merely accepting different practices, such as arranged marriage, among other ethnic groups, it is uncovering why, how and in what ways different practices have meaning and serve the values and interests of their practitioners.

A more telling example stands behind this year's Nobel Peace Prize awarded to Wangari Maathai, the first African woman to receive the accolade. The Prize was awarded for 'promoting ecologically viable social, economic and cultural development in Kenya and in Africa'. The Green Belt Movement she heads has planted some 30 million trees and its membership is 90 per cent women. In 1989 Prof Maathai told the *Guardian*, 'We are overwhelmed by experts who sap confidence. People [have been made to] believe they are ignorant, inexperienced, incapable and backward'.[10] And furthermore, it should be noted that for decades across Africa these experts missed a basic fact – across Africa it is predominantly women who are the farmers. Clearing land is man's work, planting and tending crops the province of women. Development education and assistance was geared to men, because it was self-evident to the experts that by universal laws of nature men were farmers. Consequently, the half of the population most intimately concerned with the expertise and practice of farming were eradicated from the equation and had to acquire oppression before they could become pitiable dependants in urgent need of becoming modernised. What was also lost in this mistranslation of cultural realities was the local knowledge of sustainable prudent, ecologically sound, farming strategies. Across the Third World indigenous knowledge of farming, irrigation, crops and much else has been dismissed as backward in favour of modern inappropriate impositions with devastating results that have compounded poverty rather than offered a way out of poverty. The current worldwide competition to examine the horticultural riches of traditional societies for their medicinal benefits not only ignores the vibrancy and capabilities of indigenous knowledge but appropriates them as patented commercial property of multinational corporations, thus blocking the potential for new industries and economic rewards for the true inventors and innovators.

Mutually assured diversity makes cultural relations part of the human condition and opens the way to acculturation, the multiple ways, mutual processes of learning from and exchanging ideas between different identities. This is precisely where modernity and multiculturalism have signally failed. Acculturation is an adaptive process that domesticates influences, translates them into indigenous categories and applies them where they are most productive of benefit. Acculturation is not an imitative process, it is creative, innovative, and endlessly diverse in its outcomes. It can lead to surprising synthesis. Historically, one could site the example of fireworks, invented in China where their function was to frighten away evil spirits, a necessary part of any Chinese festival. Acculturated to European society the explosive agent became an evil spirit in its own right adapted, weaponised, routinely employed in forging new kinds of cultural relations. One must always be open to the possibility that transmission and exchange can have negative as well as positive outcomes – it is a human process. The essence of acculturation is then autonomy, the power to self-determine and control the pace, content and resulting form in which ideas, influence and innovation is accepted. The autonomy to self-determine is the ingredient that enables change to be subjected to the dialogue of values during which it acquires meaning and becomes domesticated, appropriated within the continual flux that is identity. Acculturation as a consequence of cultural relations leads to difference, to parallel or divergent courses or, should people so determine and find conducive, increasing similarity. It is not an homogenising process but a component of mutually assured diversity, the profusion of forms in which the basic necessities and exuberant possibilities of human existence can be met and enduring values delivered as sustainable, meaningful lifeways.

Modernity has not led to acculturation as I have outlined the concept. It has created instability, tension, dissension and profound failure in the shape of failed states, devastated environments rife with poverty, death, disease and rampant injustice. This is not merely a consequence of the inequities of the global system that predetermined the failure of newly independent Third World nations, nor the legacy of underdevelopment under colonial tutelage, nor the ramifications of superpower rivalry that made these new nations surrogates in the Cold War. A major part of the explanation is that so many newly independent states, artificially constructed, were multi-ethnic, composed of a plurality of cultural identities and saddled with the imperative to be modern, a condition where these identities had no legitimate place. Which brings me back to the general proposition that cultural relations always begin at home. It is as much a vital issue within Third World nations as in First World countries.

The pressing question is whether there are any examples of nations that have been prepared to begin the process of realigning their self-definition to move beyond modernity and seek transmodernism with mutually assured diversity? I would argue Canada offers a tantalising example, a prospect potentially in the making. And so near to the United States.

The United States and Canada are both immigrant societies, products of colonial western expansion, settler societies with frontier experience formed through the encounter with the Other, the native peoples who were eradicated and marginalised in both countries. But their modern experience has sharp divergence. Where multiculturalism and cultural, social and political questions of identity, are a source of turmoil for the United States, Canada has embraced multiculturalism as a legislative model, as the basis of its civic formation as a nation.

Canada has become home to novel legislative programmes and policies as well as theorising about multiculturalism.

The American frame of reference is simple and direct: *e pluribus unum*, from many one. Coming to America is the unifying experience of making a people whose identity begins with the reality of migration and consequent construction of a new identity. The remaking of identity is shaped by the declarative constitutional form of citizenship, which is a learned experience. Citizenship classes are required to achieve naturalisation, the very language is expressive of the nature of the project and its goal to generate a united identity – American – commonly held and overarching the hyphenated diversity that is entirely subordinate and secondary. This view of identity, founded on dominance leading to homogeneity, suits a nation that saw itself as the new bastion of western civilisation and drew its immigrants predominantly from European nations. However, that is not the full story since it ignores Native Americans, slavery, remnant Latino populations and Chinese railroad builders before encountering the more recent waves of immigrants from East and South Asia. The distinction shared by these latter minorities of hyphenated Americans is a repertoire of cultural affiliations and premises and therefore histories that do not nestle conveniently and decorously within the broad church of western civilisation.

The Irish, Italians, Poles and Russians can keep on singing their folk songs, romanticising the folk identities retaining smatterings of old languages and eating traditional food without ever stirring any major definitional issues so far as identity is concerned. The interesting question is why this is not true of Latinos. Latino identity is as old as American identity – slightly senior in being the first European transplant to arrive in the Americas actually. The strong language identification is with a European language, Spanish, and overwhelmingly the population is Christian, so why is it problematic? One is tempted to suggest the problem is the central horror and fear underpinning America – the fear of miscegenation. For Latino populations are predominantly mestizo, mixed race. Latin American nations have produced a caste system based not so much on gradations of racial mixing as cultural identification with the dominance of Spanish culture, but even this is not enough. For the embrace of syncretism, the admixture of nativist forms is much more pronounced in Latin American nations and culture, most strongly in Mexico but true throughout most South American nations (Argentina is questionable but leave that aside). Length of historic identification with the land of America is not the question – race and culture are because at base it is the exclusivity of identification with western civilisation as the dominant defining culture and its consequent social and political forms that is the issue.

This has been made abundantly clear in the backlash to multiculturalism in the United States and is best illustrated by the hissing fit of erstwhile liberal historian Arthur Schlesinger Jr who gives explicit vent to the nub of the problem:

whatever the particular crimes of Europe, that continent is also the source – the unique source – of those liberating ideas of individual liberty, political democracy, equality before the law, freedom of worship, human rights, and cultural freedom that constitute our most precious legacy and to which most of the world today aspires. These are *European* ideas, not Asian, nor African, nor Middle Eastern ideas, except by adoption.[11]

The essence of this is that America creates a nation unified by a view of individual rights and has no place for group rights, hence it has only private domestic tolerance for cultural dabbling in the construction of identity. The public space belongs entirely to the dominant identity and if that is white, European and Christian in the most Waspish of ways it is not just because it is so but because it is the best, the terminus of history to which all other identities must eventually aspire to conform. What is to be learnt from other cultures is limited at best and only relevant in so far as they have fed into the great stream of human experience that led up to western civilisation and the apex of that civilisation, America, the manifest destiny of all people as the great nation of futurity.

Canada is different. The history of its settling matches and marches hand in hand with that of America. Both were British colonies, Canada receiving those Tories who declined Independence at the precocious date of 1776 and were content to exist within Dominion status before proclaiming full nationhood and repatriation of all responsibilities including for treaties with its First Nations populations, which interestingly was the very last step in national development. Perhaps Canada is different because it exists around the conundrum of the lack of cordiality that ever underpins the *entente cordiale* – a bilingual nation by virtue of the enduring existence of Quebec, not so much diluting its rootedness in western civilisation as stretching it immeasurably to accommodate dual claims to dominance within the formation of western civilisation.

The perplexed possibilities of Quebec remaining within Canada and the compromises and accommodation necessary to achieve this objective clearly changed the nature of the debate in Canada and with it the definition of identity, as well as national civic formation that resulted. If Canada was a bilingual nation of two traditions (enshrined in the Official Languages Act of 1969) on what grounds did it restrict and de-legitimise other languages and traditions as the basis for enduring identities? The logical answer by another interpretation of equality and civic rights philosophy was it could not and the modern development of multiculturalism in Canada has proceeded on this basis. The Canadian Multiculturalism Act of 1988 states: 'It is hereby declared to be the policy of the Government of Canada to foster recognition and appreciation of the diverse cultures of Canadian society and promote the reflection and evolving expressions of those cultures'.[12] The Act was the culmination of Canada being the first country in the world to adopt a multicultural policy in 1971, and section 27 of the 1982 Charter of Rights and Freedoms which required the courts to interpret the Charter 'in a manner consistent with the preservation and enhancement of the multicultural heritage of Canada'. As a result, to use the words of Canadian Prime Minister, Jean Chretien, 'Canada has become a post-national, multicultural society. It contains the globe within its borders, and Canadians have learned that their two international languages and their diversity are a comparative advantage and a source of continuing creativity and innovation. Canadians are, by virtue of history and necessity open to the world.' Chretien added: 'we have established a distinct Canadian Way, a distinct Canadian model: accommodation of cultures, recognition of diversity, a partnership between citizens and state, a balance that promotes individual freedom and economic prosperity while at the same time sharing risks and benefits'.[13]

The distinctly Canadian framework produced the 1991 Arbitration Act which allowed religious groups to resolve civil family disputes, such as divorce, within their faith. Catholics and Jews were prompt in taking advantage of the legislation. The signature move, however, came at the end of 2003 with the formation of the Islamic Institute for Civil Justice, a 30 member Council that will appoint arbitrators and oversee the application of Shari'ah law to the 1 million strong Canadian Muslim community, a procedure which will be enforced by the local secular Canadian courts.

In one sense the Canadian model is a return to an ancient pattern. It is a truism that cannot be stated too often – there have always been cultural relations. A plurality of models exists in human history; there have been a diversity of ways of managing diversity and operating cultural relations. Specifically, Canada is finding space for the classical, Islamicate model that existed into the modern era only to be eradicated not by colonialism but the triumphalism of the west. The classical world of colonies and colonialism, especially the Roman, had multiple communities which administered themselves under the rubric of Roman law – that is the actual familiar, though I think not often recognised as such, kernel of the New Testament crucifixion narrative repeated each Easter: Jesus convicted under Jewish law and handed over to the Roman authorities for punishment.

Islamic civilisation begins with the 628 Treaty of Hudaibiyah which recognised the cultural diversity of peoples who became part of the polity of Medina, led by the Prophet Muhammad, and provided a modus vivendi for communities following different systems of religious law within its boundaries. The expansion of Muslim power beyond Arabia led to development of this as the characteristic framework, the guarantee of the continuation of diverse identity and the right for various communities to be administered and judged under their own system of religious law, in what remained a multicultural and multi-religious civilisation. This formula was applied throughout the trading communities within and beyond what became the Muslim world.

In time, this was also applied to the European trading posts that were established in the Muslim world, such outposts as Aleppo, Alexandria and Tripoli. In these cities European traders maintained their group identity, appointed their own leadership which administered law based on religious law within the trading community, the leader serving as the negotiator with the officials of the polity within which they traded. The model was common until the end of the nineteenth century in China. British colonialism was clearly informed by this inherited system – with the patchwork of provision for the family and personal law and native land holding arrangements developed not only in the Indian subcontinent but in various forms around the British Empire as a whole.

The history of cultural relations is as long as human history and as diverse and plural as the peoples of the world. Acculturation has always been underway until it was obliterated, swamped by modernity and its narrow strictures. The transmission of ideas, concepts, forms of action, fashion and technology has been swirled around the world throughout history, a factor in the construction of cultural diversity.

There have been few if any hermetically sealed cultural entities. Within 50 years of the Americas being opened to European expansion the technology of tobacco, and the weed itself, were to be found among the indigenous peoples in the interior jungles of Borneo! Modernity has disrupted the creative and adaptive possibilities of cultural relations while seeking to eradicate appreciation of how much western civilisation itself has been a participant and recipient of the process of acculturation and transmission of ideas from other cultures.

What is fascinating is the confusion within Britain today about multiculturalism. Given the colonial experience, having spawned in some senses both America and Canada, Britain is permanently undecided, equivocal and looking in all directions politically, socially and culturally. So we have citizenship classes, fusion food, multicultural education, resentment of immigration, Islamophobia tolerated, acknowledged, studied and reported and inherent in the warp and weft of intellectual thought and street corner perceptions of one's neighbours.

Mutually assured diversity begins at home. It is part of the agenda Britain must address for domestic purposes. As the Canadian example suggests, once the transition is made a whole new world of possibility for cultural relations becomes actual. Identity ceases to be fragile, a source of tension and dissension but emerges robustly to meet the challenges at home and abroad. The challenges are many. There are Canadian Muslims who want nothing to do with Shari'ah arbitration; other Canadian Muslims who see the opportunity to reinterpret, remake Shari'ah in synthesis with their contemporary concerns and circumstances as Canadian citizens. The dynamic of dialogue within Canada as a diverse post-nation has not resolved the misunderstanding, misrepresentations and mutual reticence that shaped its past. But it has constructed a new base on which to aspire to mutually assured diversity in the future. It has embraced its diverse communities within a post-nation as bridges to the world at large. It suggests a path that has to be made into a well-trodden thoroughfare.

Cultural relations in the new century have to ensure that there are other cultures to have a relationship with. The history of the twentieth century suggests that difference cannot exist as difference under the framework of modernity. Multiculturalism can only proceed with the dominant homogeneous structure of liberalism. We need to actively explore new thoroughfares to transmodernism and mutually assured diversity to ensure that the future belongs to all cultures – and, that plurality is persevered in multiple, diverse futures. *The* future is not the realm of a single civilisation or worldview but a domain of multiple potentials with a plethora of alternative futures. For difference to stretch the creative possibilities of humanity we must wake up to the fact that there is more than one way of being human.

Notes

1   JIHAD FOR PEACE

1. Mahathir Muhammad stepped down as Prime Minister of Malaysia shortly after this essay was published. Anwar Ibrahim was freed as a political prisoner and the charges against him were dropped.
2. See for example Ziauddin Sardar, *The Future of Muslim Civilisation*, Cassell, London, 1979 and Ziauddin Sardar, *Islamic Futures: The Shape of Ideas to Come*, Cassell, London, 1985.

2   REREADING THE LIFE OF MUHAMMAD

1. Ibn Ishaq, *The Life of Muhammad*, translated by Alfred Guillaume, Oxford University Press, Oxford, 1955. Guillaume's translation is regarded as unreliable. See the review by A. L. Tibawi, 'The Life of Muhammad: A Critique of Guillaume's English Translation' originally published in the journal *Islamic Quarterly* and reprinted in A. L. Tibawai, *Arabic and Islamic Themes*, Luzac, London, 1974. Tibawi's conclusion: the translation 'cannot be accepted as a reliable reproduction on the received Arabic text of the Sira'.
2. Hafiz Ghulam Sarwar, Muhammad: The Holy Prophet, Sh Muhammad Ashraf, Lahore, 1961. Editor's note: this title is still in print, as is the case with many (much older) biographies of the Prophet.
3. See the searching analysis of A. L. Tibawi, *English Speaking Orientalists*, Islamic Cultural Centre, London, 1965; and Edward W. Said, *Orientalism*, Routledge and Kegan Paul, London, 1978.
4. Shibli Numani, *Seerat un Nabi* (the Life of the Prophet), translated by Tayyib Bakhsh Budayuni, Kazi Publications, Lahore, 1979. The original in Urdu is in six volumes and was published in 1936. Editor's note: Budayuni's translation is in print and available from <www.islamicbookstore.com>. Numani was a rare historian-biographer from within the Islamic tradition. See Mehr Afroz Murad (Professor of History, *Intellectual Modernism of Shibli Nu'amani*, University of Karachi), Kitab Bhavan, India, 1996.
5. Muhammad H. Haykal, *The Life of Muhammad*, translated by Isma'il Raji al-Faruqi, Islamic Book Trust, Kuala Lumpur (1976, reprinted 2003). Editor's note: Haykal is a journalist (still active) and a former spokesman for Egypt's President Gamal Nasser and a former adviser to President Anwar Sadat.
6. Numani, *Seerat un Nabi*, vol. 1, p. 85.
7. Editor's note: William Muir, *The Life of Mahomet*, published by Smith, Elder and Company, London, 1861. The full text of Muir's biography has been scanned onto the Internet and can be found (April 2005) at <http://answering-islam.org.uk/Books/Muir/Life1/index.htm>.

8. Syed Ameer Ali, *The Spirit of Islam*, (reprinted by Islamic Book Trust), India. Editor's note: Ameer Ali (1849–1928) was an Indian-Muslim barrister and Calcutta High Court judge who settled in Britain in 1904 and later became active on the British Muslim scene.

9. Abul Hasan Ali Nadwi, *Muhammad Rasulullah* ('Muhammad, the Prophet of God'), translated from the Urdu by Mohiuddin Ahmad, Academy of Islamic Research and Publications, Lucknow, India, 1979.

10. Martin Lings, *Muhammad: His Life Based on the Earliest Sources*, George Allen and Unwin, London, 1983. Editor's note: Martin Lings, former Keeper of Oriental Manuscripts at the British Museum in London and among the standard-bearers of Traditional Sufi Islam, died in May 2005 aged 96.

11· Muhammad Hamidullah, *Muhammad Rasulullah*, Huzaifa Publications, Karachi, 1979.

12. Tayeb Abedein, 'The Practice of Shura', *The Muslim*, 7: 159–61 (April 1970). Editor's note: *The Muslim* was a periodical published by the principal UK Muslim university students' organisation known as Federation of Student Islamic Societies (FoSIS). FoSIS still exists, though *The Muslim* ceased publication in the 1980s.

3   FAITH AND THE WRITTEN WORD

1. Ruth Stellhorn Mackensen, 'Arabic Books and Libraries in the Umaiyad Period', *American Journal of Semitic Languages and Literature* 52: 245–53 (1935–36).

2. For a detailed look at bookbinding under Muslim civilisation see Gulnar Bosch, John Carswell and Guy Petheridge, *Islamic Bookbinds and Bookmaking*, The Oriental Institute Museum, University of Chicago, 1981.

3. For a detailed look at the art of illumination under Muslims see Martin Lings, *Qur'anic Art and Calligraphy*, World of Islam Festival Trust, London, 1976.

4. F. Rosenthal, *Technique and Approach of Muslim Scholarship*, Pontificium Institutum Biblicum, Rome, 1947, pp. 8–9.

5. George Makdisi, *The Rise of Colleges: Institutions of Learning in Islam and the West*, Edinburgh University Press, 1981, pp. 24–5.

6. Al Nadim's *Fihrist* has been translated in two volumes by Bayard Dodge, Columbia University Press, New York, 1970.

7. Khuda Bukhsh, *The Islamic Libraries*, 'The Nineteenth Century', 52: pp. 125–39, 1902.

8. Islamic Foundation of Bangladesh, Dhaka, 1983, p. 71.

9. This anecdote has been related by many historians of the library in Islam, including Khuda Bukhsh, Ruth Stellhorn Mackensen and Shaikh Inayatullah in 'Bibliophilism in Mediaeval Islam', *Islamic Culture* 12 (2): pp. 154–69, 1938.

10. 'Background to the History of Moslem Libraries', *American Journal of Semitic Languages and Literatures* 51: pp. 112–124, 1935.

4   RESCUING ISLAM'S UNIVERSITIES

1. Hamed Hasan Bilgrami and Syed Ali Ashraf, 'The Concept of an Islamic University', The Islamic Academy, Cambridge, 1985, p. 42. Editor's note: Syed Ali Ashraf (1925–1998) was an influential figure in the Islamic university movement of the 1970s and 1980s, and who later turned his focus on the education of Muslim children in Britain. A professor of English at the University of Karachi, he went on to found the Darul Ihsan University in Dhaka, Bangladesh; and later the Islamic Academy in Cambridge, UK, a Muslim education-policy think-tank. His books include *The Crisis of Muslim Education*; he was also founder of the journal *Muslim Education Quarterly*. Syed Ali Ashraf was also a noted Sufi teacher and had a considerable following in this capacity in South Asia.
2. Muhammad Naguib al-Attas, *Islam, Secularism and the Philosophy of the Future*, Mansell, London, 1985, p. 205.
3. Catalogue of the Islamic Institute of Advanced Studies, Washington, D.C.
4. Sher Muhammad Zaman, *Islamic Studies* 24 (2): 125–38, Summer 1985.
5. Ziauddin Sardar, 'Islamization of Knowledge, or Westernization of Islam?', *Inquiry* 1 (7): 39–45, December 1984.
6. Abraham Edel, *Exploring Fact and Value*, Transaction Books, London, 1980.

5   WHAT DO WE MEAN BY ISLAMIC FUTURES?

1. Ali Mazuri, 'The Resurgence of Islam and the Decline of Communism', *Futures* 23 (3): 273–288 (1991).
2. I am grateful to Richard Slaughter for this insight. The diagram is, in fact, part of his e-mail signature!
3. For a wide ranging discussion of complexity see Roger Lewin, *Complexity: Life at the Edge of Chaos*, Macmillan, New York, 1992; and Mitchell Waldrop, *Complexity: The Emerging Science at the Edge of Order and Chaos*, Simon and Schuster, New York, 1992.
4. For an analysis of complexity from the futures perspective see the special issue of *Futures*, 26 (6) August 1994, 'Complexity: Fad or Future' edited by Ziauddin Sardar and Jerome R. Ravetz.
5. Dennis Meadows et al., *The Limits to Growth*, Potomac Associates, New York, 1972. The Club of Rome was also responsible for other reports on the future of the world, based on different methodologies, such as M. Mesarovic and E. Pestel, *Mankind at the Turning Point*, Hutchinson, London, 1974 and J. Tinbergen, *RIO: Reshaping the International Order*, Hutchinson, London, 1976.
6. Michel Godet, *Scenarios and Strategic Management*, Butterworth, London, 1987, p. 21. Quoted by Elenora Masini, *Why Future Studies?*, Grey Seal, London, 1994, p. 91. Masini provides an excellent introduction to various methodologies of future studies. See also: Richard Slaughter (ed.), 'Futures of Futures Studies', *Futures* 34 (3) 3 April 2002 (Special issue) and Sohail

Inayatullah (ed.), 'Layered Methodologies', *Futures* 34 (5) June 2002 (Special issue).

7. Edward Cornish, *The Study of the Future*, World Future Society, Washington D.C., 1977, p. 99.

8. Samuel P. Huntington, *The Clash of Civilizations and Remaking of the World Order*, Simon and Schuster, New York, 1997.

9. Anwar Ibrahim, 'From "Things Change" to "Changing Things"', in Ziauddin Sardar (ed.), *An Early Crescent: The Future of Knowledge and Environment in Islam*, Mansell, London, 1989, p. 19.

10. S. Parvez Manzoor, 'The Future of Muslim Politics: Critique of the "Fundamentalist" Theory of the Islamic State', *Futures* 23 (3): 289–301 (1991).

11. Anwar Ibrahim, 'The Ummah and Tomorrow', *Futures* 23 (3): 302–310 (1991).

12. For a history of western antagonism towards Islam see Ziauddin Sardar and Merryl Wyn Davies, *Distorted Imagination: Lessons from the Rushdie Affair*, Grey Seal, London, 1990; and Ziauddin Sardar, *Orientalism*, Open University Press, Buckingham, 1999.

13. See their manifesto edited by Omid Safi, *Progressive Muslims*, One World, Oxford, 2003.

14. Ziauddin Sardar, 'Can Islam Change?', *New Statesman*, 13 September 2004, pp. 24–7.

15. 'Rethinking Islam' in Sohail Inayatullah and Gail Boxwell (eds), *Islam, Postmodernism and Other Futures: A Ziauddin Sardar Reader*, Pluto Press, London, 2003.

16. Mawil Izzi Dien, *Islamic Law: From Historical Foundations to Contemporary Practice*, Edinburgh University Press, Edinburgh, 2004.

17. Taha Jabir al-Alwani, *Towards a Fiqh for Minorities*, IIIT, London, 2003, p. 15.

18. For a detailed analysis of the new Islamic intellectualism in Indonesia, see Bahtiar Effendy, *Islam and the State in Indonesia*, Institute of Southeast Asian Studies, Singapore, 2003.

19. For a more analytical explanation of what happens at the 'edge of chaos', see Ziauddin Sardar, *Introducing Chaos*, Icon Books, Cambridge, 1998.

20. Jeffrey Sachs, 'Welcome to the Asian century: by 2050, China and maybe India will overtake the US economy in size', *Fortune*, 12 January 2004, pp. 53–54.

21. Paul Kennedy, *The Rise and Fall of the Great Powers*, Random House, New York, 1989.

6   GUARDIANS OF THE PLANET

1. This and subsequent quotations from Lynn White Jr, 'The Historical Roots of Our Ecological Crisis', *Science* 155: 1203–7 (1967).

2. This and subsequent quotations from Beatrice Willard, 'Ethics of Biospheral Survival', in N. Polunin (ed.), *Growth or Ecodisaster?*, Macmillan, London, 1980.

3. The Gaia hypothesis first appeared in James Lovelock and Sidney Epton, 'The Quest for Gaia', *New Scientist* 65: 304–6 (1975).

4. Ali Shariati, *On the Sociology of Islam*, trans. Hamid Algar, Mizan Press, Berkeley, CA, 1979, p. 87.
5. This and subsequent quotations from Parvez Manzoor are from his paper, 'Environment and Values: The Islamic Perspective', in Z. Sardar (ed.), *The Touch of Midas: Science, Values and the Environment in Islam and the West*, University of Manchester Press, Manchester, 1984.
6. Othman B. Llewellyn, 'The Objectives of Islamic Law and Administrative Planning', *Ekistics* 47: 11–14 (1980).
7. Othman B. Llewellyn, 'Desert Reclamation and Islamic Law', *The Muslim Scientist* 11: 9–30 (1982).
8. *Ibid.*
9. Alison Ravetz, *Remaking Cities*, Croom Helm, London, 1980.
10. This and subsequent quotations from Gulzar Haider, 'Islam and Habitat: A Conceptual Formulation of an Islamic City', in Z. Sardar (ed.), *The Touch of Midas: Science, Values and the Environment in Islam and the West*, University of Manchester Press, Manchester, 1984.

7   MUSLIMS AND PHILOSOPHY OF SCIENCE

1. Majid Fakhry, *A History of Islamic Philosophy*, Longman, London, 1983.
2. Donald Hill, *Islamic Science and Engineering*, Edinburgh University Press, Edinburgh, 1993.
3. George Hourani, *Reason and Tradition in Islamic Ethics*, Cambridge University Press, Cambridge, 1985.
4. Oliver Leaman, *An Introduction to Medieval Islamic Philosophy*, Cambridge University Press, Cambridge 1985.

9   ARGUMENTS FOR AN ISLAMIC SCIENCE

1. A. N. Whitehead, *Adventures of Ideas*, Cambridge University Press, Cambridge, 1938, pp. 13–14.
2. Chu Cahi and Winberg Chai (eds & trans.), *The Essential Works of Confucianism*, Bantam Books, New York, 1965, p. 13.
3. *Ibid.*, p. 15.
4. From Aristotle's *Nicomachean Ethics*, W. D. Ross (trans.), R. Mckeon (ed.), Basic Books, New York, 1941.
5. Quoted in Colin A. Ronan's abridgement of Joseph Needham, *The Shorter Science and Civilisation in China*, vol. 1., Cambridge University Press, Cambridge, 1978, p. 144.
6. *Ibid.*, p. 158.
7. Farrington, *Greek Science*, pp. 50–2.
8. *Ibid.*, p. 97.
9. For a detailed description of various Muslim classification schemes, see Rosenthal, *Knowledge Triumphant*.
10. Chejne, *Ibn Hazm*, p. 64.
11. *Ibid.*, pp. 64–5.
12. *Kash al-Mahjub*, R. A. Nicholson (trans.), Brill, Leiden, p. 11.

13. Particularly G. E. Von Grunebaum has been very hostile to Muslim interpretation of knowledge. See his *Islam: Essay in the Nature of Growth of a Cultural Tradition*, Barnes and Noble, New York, 1961.

14. This example is taken from Seyyed Hossein Nasr, 'Reflections on Methodology in the Islamic Science', *Hamdard islamicus* 3(3), 00. 3–13 (1980).

15. Al-Biruni, *The Determination of the Co-ordinates*, p. 175.

16. *Ibid.*, p. 2.

17. For a detailed analysis of how al-Biruni came up with this figure and the theory behind his calculations, see Willy Hartner and Matthia Schramm, 'Al-Biruni and the Theory of Solar Apogee: An Example of Originality in Arabic Science', in A. C. Crombie (ed.), *Scientific Change*, Heinemann, London, 1962.

18. Quoted by Roger Arnaldez, 'The Theory and Practice of Science According to Ibn Sina and al-Biruni', in Said, *Al-Biruni Commemorative Volume*, p. 431.

19. See S. Pines, 'La conception de la conscience de soi chez Avicenne chez Abul Barakat al-Baghdad', *Archives d'histoire doctrinale et litteraire du Moyen Age XXI*, 1995, p. 97.

20. Ibn Sina, *Tis Rasail*, Cairo, 1908, p. 120.

21. S. Pines, 'Ibn al-Haytham's Critique of Ptolemy', in *Actes du Xe congres internatinale d'histoire des sciences*, Paris 1, 1964, p. 574.

22. In particular, see Anton Heinen, 'Al-Biruni and al-Haytham: A Comparative Study of Scientific Method', in Said, *Al-Biruni Commemorative Volume*, pp. 501–13.

23. Quoted by Naseer Ahmad Nasir from al-Haytham's *Tabaqat-ul-Attiba*, in his paper, 'Ibn al-Haytham and His Philosophy', in Said, *Ibn al-Haytham*, pp. 80–93.

24. *Ibid.*, p. 80.

25. *Ibid.*, p. 84.

26. Young, 'Polymathy in Islam.'

27. Mitroff, *The Subjective Side of Science*, p. 79. Mitroff's table compares the norms of science with 'counternorms' which are considered by more radical scientists to form the basis of more enlightened paradigm of scientific research.

28. Cambridge Univesity Press, Cambridge, 1969, p. 554. For a really arrogant defence of untamed reasons, see Gerald Feinberg, *The Prometheus Project*, Doubleday, New York, 1969.

29. See the classic paper by Lynn White Jr., 'Historical Roots of Our Ecological Crisis'; see also Willaim Leiss, *The Domination of Nature*, George Braziller, New York, 1972.

30. Anees, 'Islamic Science: An Antidote to Reductionism.'

31. For a detailed account of how science is being used to justify oppression and inequality, see the brilliant work of Philip Green, *The Pursuit of Inequality*.

32. Ashis Nandy, 'Science Severed from Source'.

33. J. R. Ravetz, 'The Social Function of Science: A Commemoration of J. D. Bernal's Vision', *Science and Public Policy*, October 1982. I owe the

diagrams to Ravetz. See also his classic, *Scientific Knowledge and its Social Problems*, Oxford University Press, Oxford, 1982.

34. Ford, 'Liberating Science with Islamic Values'.

35. See Ziauddin Sardar, *Science, Technology and Development in the Muslim World* and *Science and Technology in the Middle East.*

10　ISLAMIC SCIENCE: THE WAY AHEAD

1. From an article in the *Bulletin* of The American Association of University Professors, quoted by Margaret C. Jacob, 'Science and Politics in the Late Twentieth Century', in Margaret C. Jacob (ed.), *The Politics of Western Science*, Humanities Press, New York, 1994.

2. Lewis Wolpert, *The Unnatural Nature of Science*, Faber and Faber, London, 1992.

3. The quotes are from the preface to the reprinted edition of J. D. Bernal's, *The Social Functions of Science*, MIT Press, Cambridge, MA, 1967.

4. 'They Shoot Pigs Don't They?', *Independent*, Section 2, 26 January 1995.

5. *Time*, January 1994. For a detailed analysis see Chip Brown, 'The Science Club Serves its Country', *Esquire*, December 1994.

6. Ron Rosenbaum, 'Even the Wife of the President of the United States Sometime Had to Stand Naked', *Independent*, 21 January 1995 – a reprint of the *New York Times* story.

7. *Independent*, 15 February 1995.

8. The classic study by Thomas S. Kuhn, *The Structure of Scientific Revolutions*, University of Chicago Press, 1962; second edition, 1972.

9. See Paul Feyerabend's *Against Method*, NLB, London, 1975; and *Science in a Free Society*, Verso, London, 1978.

10. See J. R. Ravetz's classic work, *Scientific Knowledge and Its Social Problems*, Oxford University Press, Oxford, 1971; and *The Merger of Knowledge and Power*, Mansell, London, 1990.

11. See D. Bloor, *Knowledge and Social Imagery*, Routledge, London, 1976; and 'The Strength of the Strong Programme', in J. R. Brown (ed.), *Scientific Rationalist: The Sociological Turn*, Reidel, Dordrecht, 1984.

12. Robert Young, 'Science *Is* Social Relations', *Radical Science Journal* 5: 65–131 (1977).

13. Harry Collins and Trevor Pinch, *The Golem: What Everyone Should Know About Science*, Cambridge University Press, Cambridge, 1993, pp. 1–2.

14. Sandra Harding, *The Science Question in Feminism*, Open University Press, Milton Keynes, 1986; and Sandra Harding and Merrill Hintikka (eds), *Discovering Reality: Feminist Perspectives on Epistemology, Metaphysics, Methodology and Philosophy of Science*, Reidel, Dordrecht, 1983.

15. Ashis Nandy, *Science, Hegemony and Violence*, Oxford University Press, New Delhi, 1988.

16. Claude Alvares, 'Science', in Wolfgang Sachs (ed.), *The Development Dictionary*, Zed, London, 1992, p. 219; and *Science, Development and Violence*, Oxford University Press, Delhi, 1992.

17. See Depak Kumar, *Science and Empire*, Anamika, Delhi, 1991; Satpal Sangwan, *Science, Technology and Colonialism*, Anamika, Delhi, 1991;

Susantha Goonatilake, *Aborted Discovery: Science and Creativity in the Third World*, Zed, London, 1984; R. K. Kochar, 'Science in British India', *Current Science* 63 (11): 689–94 (December 1992) and 64 (1): 55–62 (January 1993); and George Sheverghese Joseph, 'Cognitive Encounters in India During the Age of Imperialism', *Race and Class* 36 (3): 39–56 (1995).

18. Karin Knorr-Cetina, *The Manufacture of Knowledge*, Pergamon, Oxford, 1981.
19. B. Latour and S. Woolgar, *Laboratory Life*, Sage, Beverly Hills, 1979.
20. See Richard Dawkins' *The Selfish Gene*, Oxford University Press, 1976 and 1989 and *The Blind Watchmaker*, Penguin, London, 1986. For the social import of Dawkins' theories of genes as totally aggressive mafiosos see Andrew Ross, *The Chicago Gangster Theory of Life*, Verso, London, 1994.
21. See Muhammad Abdus Salam, 'Islam and Science', *MAAS Journal of Islamic Science* 2 (1): 21–6 (1986); and 'Notes on Science, High Technology and Development for Arab and Islamic Countries', *MAAS Journal of Islamic Science* 7 (2): 83–100 (1991).
22. For a critique of postmodern science see Ziauddin Sardar, 'Conquests, Chaos, Complexity: The Other in Modern and Postmodern Science', *Futures* 26 (6): 665–682 (July/August 1994).
23. Margaret C. Jacob, 'Science and Politics in the Late Twentieth Century', in Margaret C. Jacob (ed.), *The Politics of Western Science*, Humanities Press, New York, 1994, p. 6. For a discussion of the global knowledge system, its structure and what role the non-west plays in it, see Philip G. Altbach, *The Knowledge Context: Comparative Perspectives on the Distribution of Knowledge*, Sunny Press, Albany, 1987.
24. Alan Beyerchen, *Scientists Under Hitler: Politics and the Physics Community in the Third Reich*, Yale University Press, New Haven, 1977.
25. David C. Cassidy, 'Hisenberg, German Science and the Third Reich', in Jacob (ed.), *Politics of Western Science*.
26. Stuart W. Leslie, 'Science and Politics in Cold War America', in Jacob (ed.), *Politics of Western Science*, pp. 209–10.
27. *Ibid.*, pp. 212–13.
28. *Ibid.*, p. 216.
29. *Ibid.*, p. 217.
30. In the introduction to his *Science, Hegemony and Violence*.
31. William W. Lowrance, *Modern Science and Human Values*, Oxford University Press, Oxford, 1985, p. 8.
32. Nancy Cartwright, *How the Laws of Physics Lie*, Oxford University Press, Oxford, 1983, p. 15.
33. On the whole question of risk, confidence-limits and the question of values in statistical inference see Silvio Funtowicz and J. R. Ravetz, *Uncertainty and Quality in Science for Policy*, Kluwer, Dordrecht, 1990.
34. C. V. Seshadri, *Equity is Good Science*, Murugappa Chettier Research Centre, Madras, 1993.
35. Sandra Harding (ed.), *The Racial Economy of Science*, Indiana University Press, Bloomington, 1993.
36. See, for example, Maureen Mcneil (ed.), *Gender and Expertise*, Free Association Books, London, 1987.

37. This daft theory is presented by Paul R. Gross and Norman Levitt, *Higher Superstition: The Academic Left and Its Quarrels with Science*, Johns Hopkins University Press, Baltimore, 1994.

38. Ziauddin Sardar, 'A Revival for Islam, A Boost for Science?', *Nature* 282: 354–7 (22 November 1979).

39. Ziauddin Sardar, *Science, Technology and Development in the Muslim World*, Croom Helm, London; Humanities Press, New Jersey, 1977.

40. Ziauddin Sardar, 'Can Science Come Back to Islam?', *New Scientist* 88: 212–16 (23 October 1980); 'Science for the People of Islam', *New Scientist* 93: 244–5 (28 January 1982) and 'Why Islam Needs Islamic Science', *New Scientist* 94: 25–8: (1 April 1982).

41. The study sponsored by the International Federation of Institutes of Advance Studies was published as Ziauddin Sardar (ed.), *The Touch of Midas: Science, Values and the Environment in Islam and the West*, Manchester University Press, Manchester, 1982.

42. The proceedings appeared as *Islamic Scientific Thought and Muslim Achievements in Science* (2 vols) and *Science and Technology Potential and Its Development in the Muslim World* (2 vols), Ministry of Science and Technology, National Hijra Centenary Committee and Organization of the Islamic Conference, Islamabad, 1983.

43. The proceedings of the Aligarh Seminar appeared as Raid Ahmad and S. Naseem Ahmad (eds), *Quest for a New Science*, Centre for Studies on Science, Aligarh, 1984.

44. J. R. Ravetz, 'Prospects for an Islamic Science', *Futures* 23 (3): 262–72 (1991).

45. Pervez Hoodbhoy, *Islam and Science*, Zed Books, London, 1991.

46. For a more recent, and perhaps a more complete, appreciation of his view on science see Seyyed Hossein Nasr, *The Need for a Sacred Science*, Curzon Press, Richmond, Surrey, 1993. For a derivative perspective see Osman Bakr, *Tawheed and Science*, Secretariat for Islamic Philosophy and Science, Kuala Lumpur, 1991.

47. As developed in his *Islamic Science: An Illustrated Study*, World of Islam Festival Trust, London, 1976. For a deconstruction of Nasr's view of history of Islamic science see Ziauddin Sardar, *Explorations in Islamic Science*, Mansell, London, 1989, chapter 5.

48. Maurice Bucaille, *The Bible, the Qur'an and Science*, Seghers, Paris, 1976. On the truly banal nature of Bucaillism see *Abstracts of Paper Presented at the First International Conference on Scientific Miracles of the Qur'an and Sunnah*, Islamabad, 18–21 October 1987, International Islamic University, Islamabad and World Muslim League, Jeddah.

49. Munawar Ahmad Anees, 'What Islamic Science is Not', *MAAS Journal of Islamic Science* 2 (1): 9–19 (1984).

50. See 'Statement on scientific knowledge seen from Islamic perspective' and 'Islamabad declaration on science and technology' in the brochure of the 'International Conference on Science in Islamic Polity in the Twenty-first Century', 26–30 March 1995, COMSTECH, Islamabad.

51. Nasim Butt, *Science and Muslim Societies*, Grey Seal, London, 1991, provides a good overview of the Islamic science debate and attempts an explanation of how the ideas of Islamic science can be integrated in

modern textbooks. See also Munawar Ahmad Anees and Merryl Wyn Davies, 'Islamic Science: Current Thinking and Future Directions', in Ziauddin Sardar (ed.), *The Revenge of Athena: Science, Exploitation and the Third World*, Mansell, London, 1988, pp. 249–60.

52. For the outcome of this seminar see Sardar, *Touch of Midas*.

53. For a more detailed analysis of the Ijmali position see Sardar, *Explorations in Islamic Science*.

54. For the work of the Aligarh school see M. Zaki Kirmani, 'A Critique of Criticism on Science', *MAAS Journal of Islamic Science* 1 (2): 39–52 (1985); Riaz Kirmani, 'Structure of Islamic science', *MAAS Journal of Islamic Science* 1 (2): 31–8 (1985), 'Some More Thoughts on the Structure of Islamic Science', *MAAS Journal of Islamic Science* 5 (1): 41–68 (1989) and 'Iman, Ilm and the Qur'an', *MAAS Journal of Islamic Science* 7 (2): 7–18 (1991); M. Kaleemur Rahman, 'Preface to Islamic Science', 3 (1): 45–56 (1987); Hamid Ahmad Khan, 'How to Identify Islamic Science', *MAAS Journal of Islamic Science* 6 (2): 7–18 (1990); Rais Ahmad, 'Islamic Science: Its Scope and Purpose', *MAAS Journal of Islamic Science* 6 (2): 19–31 (1990) and Zaki Kirmani, 'Islamic Science: Moving Towards a New Paradigm', in Ziauddin Sardar (ed.), *An Early Crescent: The Future of Knowledge and the Environment in Islam*, Mansell, London, 1989, pp. 140–62.

55. Andrew Jamison, 'Western Science in Perspective and the Search for Alternatives', in Jean-Jacque Salomon et al. (eds), *The Uncertain Quest: Science, Technology and Development*, United Nations Press, Tokyo, 1994, pp. 131–67.

56. S. Parvez Manzoor, 'The Unthought of Islamic Science', *MAAS Journal of Islamic Science* 5 (2): 49–64 (1989).

57. Sandra Harding, 'After the Neutrality Ideal: Science, Politics and "Strong Objectivity"', in Jacob (ed.), *Politics of Western Science*, p. 100.

58. *Ibid.*, p. 100.

59. Lowrance, *Modern Science and Human Values*, p. 6.

60. See David Hillel, *Rivers of Eden*, Oxford University Press, Oxford, 1994.

61. Michael Warren, Guus W. von Liebenstein and L. Jan Slikkerveer, 'Networking for Indigenous Knowledge', *Indigenous Knowledge and Development Monitor* 1 (1): 2–5 (1993).

11   SCIENCE WARS: A POSTCOLONIAL READING

1. For a concise survey of Islamic science, see Donald R. Hill, *Islamic Science and Engineering*, Edinburgh University Press, Edinburgh, 1993.

2. Ziauddin Sardar, *Orientalism*, Open University Press, Philadelphia, 1999, p. 5.

3. G. Galileo, *Dialogue on the Great World Systems* (1633), ed. G. de Santillana, University of Chicago Press, 1953, p. 63.

4. A. G. Chejne, *Ibn Hazm*, Kazi Publications, Chicago, 1982, p. 64.

5. R. Descartes, *Discourse on Method* (1638), trans. A. Wollaston, Penguin Books, 1960; part II, p. 41.

6. Edinburgh University Press, Edinburgh, 1990. See also George Makdisi's *The Rise of Colleges: Institutions of Learning in Islam and the West*, Edinburgh

University Press, Edinburgh, 1981, which shows how Europe appropriated the idea of the university, complete with 'professorial chairs', from the Muslim civilisation.

7. Bishop George Berkeley, 'A Defence of Freethinking in Mathematics', in *The Works of George Berkeley, Bishop of Cloyne*, A. A. Luce and T. E. Jessop (eds), Nelson, Edinburgh and London, 1951, vol. 4, 64–138; p. 117.

8. Hessen's paper can be found in N. Bukharin et al., *Science at the Crossroads*, Frank Cass, London, 1971.

9. For a discussion of the concept of 'development', see Ziauddin Sardar, 'Development and the Location of Eurocentrism', in Ronaldo Munck and Denis O'Hearn (eds), *Critical Development Theory*, Zed Press, London, 1999, pp. 44–62.

10. J. D. Bernal. *Science in History*, Pelican, London, 1954, vol. 1, p. 1.

11. See Karl R. Popper, *Conjectures and Refutations: The Growth of Scientific Knowledge*, Routledge and Kegan Paul, London, 1963; see also, Karl R. Popper, *The Logic of Scientific Discovery*, Hutchinson, London, 1959.

12. Thomas S. Kuhn, *The Structure of Scientific Revolution*, University of Chicago Press, Chicago, 1962, p. 10.

13. *Ibid.*, pp. 5–6.

14. Represented by Paul Feyerabend, *Against Method: Outline of an Anarchistic Theory of Knowledge*, New Left Books, London, 1975 and Imre Lakatos, *Proofs and Refutations* (1976); see also Imre Lakatos and Alan Musgrave (eds), *Criticism and the Growth of Knowledge*, Cambridge University Press, Cambridge, 1970.

15. Published in *Social Text* 46–47: 217–52 (1996) as 'Transgressing the Boundaries: Towards a Transformative Hermeneutics of Quantum Gravity'. In the interest of constructivist objectivity, I should mention that Sokal cites this humble author in his bibliography!

16. For a detailed discussion of non-Western ideas on nature, time, and logic see Susantha Goonatilake, *Towards Global Science: Mining Civilisational Knowledge*, Indiana University Press, Bloomington, 1998.

17. William A. Henry III, *In Defense of Elitism*, New York, Doubleday, 1994, pp. 29–31.

18. Floyd E. Bloom, 'The Endless Pathways of Discovery', *Science* 287: 229–31 (14 January 2000).

19. Don Ihde, 'Timeline Travails', *Science* 287: 803 (4 February 2000).

20. Brill, Leiden, 1967–.

21. Summarised in Roshdi Rashed (ed.), *Encyclopaedia of the History of Arabic Science*, Routledge, London, 1996 (3 vols).

22. Ekmeleddin Ihsanoglu (ed.), *History of Mathematical Literature During the Ottoman Period*, Organization of the Islamic Conference's Research Centre for Islamic History, Art and Culture, Istanbul, 1999 (2 vols); there are also sister volumes on astronomy, chemistry, geography and other disciplines.

23. D. M. Bose et al. (eds), *A Concise History of Science in India*, National Commission for the Compilation of History of Sciences in India, New Delhi, 1971; P. V. Sharma, *History of Medicine in India*, Indian National Science Academy, New Delhi, 1992; and Debiprasad Chattopadhyaya

(ed.), *Studies in the History of Science in India*, Asha Jyoti, New Delhi, 1992.

24. The strongest proponent of this position, and a good stereotype of the colonial view of history of science, is Toby Huff. See his *The Rise of Early Modern Science: Islam, China and the West*, Cambridge University Press, Cambridge, 1993. See also my review of this book in *Nature* 368: 376–8 (24 March 1994).

25. See Deepak Kumar, *Science and the Raj*, Oxford University Press, New Delhi, 1995; and Deepak Kumar (ed.), *Science and Empire*, Anamika Prakashan, New Delhi, 1991. See also Satpal Sangwan, *Science, Technology and Colonisation: The Indian Experience 1757–1857*, Anamika Prakashan, New Delhi, 1991; Susantha Goonatilake, *Aborted Discovery: Science and Creativity in the Third World*, Zed, London, 1984; R. K. Kochar, 'Science in British India', *Current Science* 63 (11): 689–94 (December 1992) and 64 (1): 55–62 (January 1993); and George Sheverghese Joseph, 'Cognitive Encounters in India During the Age of Imperialism', *Race and Class* 36 (3): 39–56 (1995).

26. Ashis Nandy (ed.), *Science, Hegemony and Violence*, Oxford University Press, New Delhi, 1988; and Ashis Nandy, *Alternative Sciences: Creativity and Authenticity in Two Indian Scientists*, Oxford University Press, New Delhi, 1980.

27. Claude Alvares, *Decolonising History: Technology and Culture in India, China and the West, 1492 to the Present Day*, Other India Press, Goa, 1991; and *Science, Development and Violence*, Oxford University Press, New Delhi, 1992.

28. Ziauddin Sardar (ed.), *The Touch of Midas: Science, Values and the Environment in Islam and the West*, Manchester University Press, Manchester, 1982; and *The Revenge of Athena: Science, Exploitation and the Third World*, Mansell, London, 1988.

29. On the Islamic science debate see Ziauddin Sardar, *Explorations in Islamic Science*, Mansell, London, 1989; the special issue on 'Islamic Science', edited by Ahmad Bouzid, of *Social Epistemology* 10 (3–4) July–December 1996; and numerous articles in the *Journal of Islamic Science* (Aligarh, India).

30. On contemporary rediscovery of Indian science, see the proceedings of 'Indian Congress on Traditional Sciences and Technologies of India', 28 November–3 December 1993, Indian Institute of Technology, Bombay, Conference Programme, pp. 101–2.

31. Oxford University Press, Oxford, 1971; second edition, Transaction Publishers, New Brunswick, 1996.

32. Sardar's *Revenge of Athena* is based on the conference and contains 'The Penang Declaration on Science and Technology'.

33. Steve Fuller, *The Governance of Science*, Open University Press, Buckingham, 2000, p. 110.

34. 'Science for the Post-Normal Age', *Futures* 25 (7): 735–55 (September 1993) (text slightly modified – private communication).

35. S. O. Funtowicz and J. R. Ravetz, 'Three Types of Risk Assessment and the Emergence of Post-Normal Science', in S. Krimsky and D. Golding (eds), *Social Theories of Risk*, Praeger Westport, CN, , pp. 251–73 at p. 254. For

further discussion on post-normal science see Jerome Ravetz (ed.) 'Post-Normal Science', *Futures* 31 (7): September 1999 (Special Issue).

12   COMING HOME: SEX, LIES AND ALL THE 'I'S IN INDIA

1. Leslie A. Felmming, *The Life of and Works of Saadat Hassan Manto*, Vanguard, Lahore, 1985, p. 63.
2. Saadat Hassan Manto, 'The Dog of Tay Wal', translated by Tahira Naqvi in Felmming, *Life of and Works of Saadat Hassan Manto*, p. 166.
3. Saadat Hassan Manto, 'The Progressive' in *Khanyan* (*Stories*), Sang-e-Meel Publications, Lahore, 1995, (in Urdu), p. 268.
4. *Ibid.*, p. 268.
5. *Ibid.*, p. 278.
6. Purushottam Agarwal, '"Kan Kan Mein Vyape Hein Ram": The Slogan as a Metaphor of Cultural Interrogation', *The Oxford Literary Review* 16 (1–2): 245–64 (1994), p. 249.
7. Dilip Simeon, 'Tremors of Intent: Perceptions of the Nation and Community in Contemporary India', *The Oxford Literary Review* 16 (1–2): 225–44 (1994), p. 228.
8. *Ibid.*, p. 231.
9. Saadat Hassan Manto, 'Hindi and Urdu', in *Manto Nama*, Sang-e-Meel Publications, Lahore, 1991, (in Urdu), p. 560.
10. Quoted by Felmming, *Life of and Works of Saadat Hassan Manto*, p. 32.
11. Saadat Hassan Manto, 'The New Law', translated by Tahira Naqvi in Felmming, *Life of and Works of Saadat Hassan Manto*, p. 290.
12. Ayesha Jalal, *The Sole Spokesman: Jinnah, the Muslim League and the Demand for Pakistan*, Cambridge University Press, Cambridge, 1985.
13. Charu Gupta and Mukul Sharma, 'Communal Constructions: Media Reality vs Real Reality', *Race & Class* 38 (1): 1–20 (July–September 1996), p. 1.
14. On the process of Othering see Ziauddin Sardar, 'When Dracula Meets the "Other": Europe, Columbus and the Columbian Legacy', *Alternatives* 17: 493–517 (1992); 'Terminator 2: Modernity, Postmodernity and Judgement Day', *Futures* 25 (5): 493–506 (June 1992); 'Do Not Adjust Your Mind: Post-modernism, Reality and the Other', *Futures* 25 (8): 877–93 (October 1993); and Ziauddin Sardar, Ashis Nandy and Merryl Wyn Davies, *Barbaric Others: A Manifesto on Western Racism*, Pluto Press, London, 1993.
15. See Marshall Hodgson, *The Venture of Islam*, Chicago University Press, Chicago, 1974 (3 volumes).
16. For the opposite view, the ideals of tolerance in Hinduism, see Arvind Sharma, *Hinduism for Our Times*, Oxford University Press, Delhi, 1996.
17. Agarwal, '"Kan Kan Mein Vyape Hein Ram"', p. 250.
18. *Ibid.*, p. 251.
19. For the orientalised language used in the Rushdie affair see Ziauddin Sardar and Merryl Wyn Davies, *Distorted Imagination: Lessons from the Rushdie Affair*, Grey Seal, London, 1990; for the language that became common during the Gulf War see Hamid Mawlana, George Gerbner and Herbert Schiller, *The Triumph of the Image: The Media's War in the Persian Gulf – A Global Perspective*, Westview Press, Boulder, 1992.

20. Gupta and Sharma, 'Communal Constructions', p. 6.
21. *Ibid.*, p. 5.
22. Simeon, 'Tremors of Intent', p. 232.
23. See the series of articles by Girilal Jain in *The Times of India*: 10 September, 8 October, 29 October, 12 November 1986.
24. See Naipaul's interview with Dilip Padganokar, *The Times of India*, 11 July 1993.
25. Gupta and Sharma, 'Communal Constructions', p. 8.
26. Simeon, 'Tremors of Intent', p. 235.
27. For a brilliant analysis of the Babri Masjid destruction see Ashis Nandy et al., *Creating a Nationality: The Ramjanmabhumi Movement and the Fear of the Self*, Oxford University Press, Delhi, 1995.
28. The emergence of Sikh militancy is well chronicled in Dipankar Gupta, *The Context of Ethnicity: Sikh Identity in Comparative Perspective*, Oxford University Press, Delhi, 1996.
29. M. S. Golwalkar, *We or Our Nationhood Defined*, 1938; cited by Semeon, 'Tremors of Intent', p. 241.
30. Dipankar Gupta, *The Context of Ethnicity*, p. 3.
31. *Ibid.*, p. 6.
32. Saadat Hassan Manto, 'Toba Tek Singh', translated by Tahira Naqvi in *The Life of and Works of Saadat Hassan Manto*, Felmming, p. 288.

13 THE A B C D (AND E) OF ASHIS NANDY

1. Ashis Nandy, *The Savage Freud, and other essays on possible and retrievable selves*, Oxford University Press, Delhi, 1995. See the dedication.
2. Ashis Nandy, *Alternative Sciences: Creativity and Authenticity in Two Indian Scientists*, Oxford University Press, Delhi, 1995. See the dedication.
3. *Ibid.*, p. 15.
4. Ashis Nandy, *The Intimate Enemy: Loss and Recovery of Self Under Colonialism*, Oxford University Press, Delhi, 1983, p. x.
5. *Ibid.*, p. x.
6. *Ibid.*, p. xi.
7. *Ibid.*, p. xiii.
8. *Ibid.*, p. xvi.
9. *Ibid.*, p. xvi.
10. *Ibid.*, p. xiv.
11. *Ibid.*, p. 74.
12. *Ibid.*, p. 74.
13. *Ibid.*, p. xvii.
14. Nandy, *Alternative Sciences*, p. 100.
15. Ashis Nandy, *Science, Hegemony and Violence: A Requiem for Modernity*, Oxford University Press, Delhi, 1990; The United Nations University, Tokyo, 1988. See the dedication.
16. A. K. Saran is a thoroughgoing anti-positivist who is totally disdainful of all social science discourse. He is heavily influenced by Coomaraswamy as well as by marginalised western traditions, represented by such people as Marco Pollis, Simone Weil, Wittgentstein, and others. He writes in a

peculiar scholastic style where footnotes often tend to be longer than the text itself.

17. See Dharampal's classic studies *Indian Science and Technology in the 18th Century*, Delhi, 1971, and *The Beautiful Tree*, Delhi, 1983.

18. Mohammad Idris founded and led the Consumer Association of Penang (CAP) which is perhaps one of the most influential environmental pressure groups in the Third World. He also established the Third World Network, an information and media service on Third World issues based in Penang; and the Kuala Lumpur based Just Trust which campaigns for social justice and champions the cause of the marginalised and the oppressed.

19. Nandy, *The Intimate Enemy*, p. 107.

20. Ashis Nandy, *Traditions, Tyranny, and Utopias: Essays in the Politics of Awareness*, Oxford University Press, Delhi, 1987, p. 46.

21. *Ibid.*, p. 11.

22. Richard Rorty, *Philosophy, the Mirror of Nature*, Princeton University Press, Princeton, NJ, 1979.

23. Fred Inglis, *Cultural Studies*, Blackwell Publishers, Cambridge, MA, 1993, p. 204.

24. *Ibid.*, p. 229.

25. Richard Rorty, *Contingency, Irony and Solidarity*, Cambridge University Press, Cambridge, 1989.

26. Inglis, *Cultural Studies*, p. 231.

27. *Ibid.*, p. 215. On neo-orientalism in general, and Naipaul in particular, see Ziauddin Sardar and Merryl Wyn Davies, *Distorted Imagination: Lessons from the Rushdie Affair*, Grey Seal, London, 1989.

28. Inglis, *Cultural Studies*, p. 218.

29. *Ibid.*, p. 220.

30. Quoted by Nandy, *The Illegitimacy of Nationalism*, Oxford University Press, Delhi, 1994, p. 16.

31. *Ibid.*, p. 85.

32. *Ibid.*, p. 7.

33. Ashis Nandy, *The Tao of Cricket: On Games of Destiny and the Destiny of Games*, Penguin Books, Delhi, 1989. See the dedication.

34. Nandy, *The Intimate Enemy*, p. xx.

35 *Ibid.*, p. 30.

36. *Ibid.*, p. 40.

37. *Ibid.*, p. 73. For a more detailed discussion of the relationship between the coloniser and the colonised see Ziauddin Sardar, Ashis Nandy and Merryl Wyn Davies, *Barbaric Others: A Manifesto on Western Racism*, Pluto Press, London, 1993.

38. Nandy, *Traditions, Tyranny, and Utopias*, p. 22.

39. *Ibid.*, p. 22.

40. *Ibid.*, the dedication.

41. *Ibid.*, p. 13.

42. Ashis Nandy, 'Bearing Witness to the Future', *Futures* 28 (6/7), Aug/Sept 1996, p. 638.

43. Nandy, *The Savage Freud*, p. ix.

44. Nandy, *The Intimate Enemy*, p. 111.

45. Nandy, *Traditions, Tyranny, and Utopias*, p. 34.
46. *Ibid.*, p. 30.
47. *Ibid.*, p. 31.
48. Nandy, *The Savage Freud*, p. 59
49. Thomas Szasz, *The Second Sin*, Routledge and Kegan Paul, London, 1979, p. 20.
50. Nandy, 'Bearing Witness to the Future', p. 638.
51. *Ibid.*, p. 637.
52. Nandy, *The Intimate Enemy*, p. xiii.
53. Nandy, *The Illegitimacy of Nationalism*, p. 82.

15   MANAGING DIVERSITY:
IDENTITY AND RIGHTS IN MULTICULTURAL EUROPE

1. Amartya Sen, 'The Predicament of Identity', *Biblio*, March–April 2001: 48–50, at p. 49.
2. *Ibid.*, p. 49.
3. The Parekh Report, *The Future of Multi-Ethnic Britain*, Profile Books, London, 2000, p. xvii.
4. For a detailed discussion of American self-perception see Ziauddin Sardar and Merryl Wyn Davies, *Why Do People Hate America?* Icon Books, London, 2002.
5. Parekh Report, p. ix.
6. John Stuart Mill, *Essay on Liberty*, 1859.
7. John Rawls, A *Theory of Justice*, Harvard University Press, Cambridge, MA, 1971.
8. Will Kymlicka (ed.), *The Rights of Minority Cultures*, Oxford University Press, Oxford, 1995.
9. Darlene M. Johnston, 'Native Rights and Collective Rights: A Question of Group Self-Preservation', in Kymlicka (ed.), *Rights of Minority Cultures*.
10. Jonathan Sacks, *The Dignity of Difference*, Continuum, London, 2002.

16   BEYOND DIFFERENCE:
CULTURAL RELATIONS IN THE NEW CENTURY

1. For critiques of modernity see J. Herbermas, *The Philosophy Discourse of Modernity*, Polity, Cambridge, 1981; and A. Giddens, *The Consequences of Modernity*, Polity, Cambridge, 1990.
2. Ashis Nandy and Giri Deshingkar, 'The Futures of Cultures: An Asian Perspective', in Eleonora Masini and Yogesh Atal (eds), *The Futures of Asian Cultures*, Unesco, Bangkok, 1993.
3. Martin Rose and Nick Wadham-Smith, *Mutuality, Trust and Cultural Relations*, Counterpoint, British Council, London, 2004, p. 9.
4. *Ibid.*, p. 10
5. The ruling on *Brown v. Board of Education* can be found at <www.nps. gov/brvb>.
6. Unesco, *The Futures of Cultures*, Paris, 1994.

7. Ziauddin Sardar, *Postmodernism and the Other: The New Imperialism of Western Culture*, Pluto Press, London, 1998.
8. The classical text is D. Lerner, *The Passing of the Traditional Society*, The Free Press, New York, 1958.
9. Ziauddin Sardar, *Introducing Chaos*, Icon Books, Cambridge, 1998.
10. John Vidal, 'Noble Peace Prize for Woman of 30m trees', *Guardian*, 9 October 2004.
11. Arthur Schlesinger Jr, *The Disuniting of America: Reflections on a Multicultural Society*, Whittle Books, New York, 1998, p. 134.
12. For the Canadian Multiculturalism Act, see the Canadian government's multiculturalism website: <www.pch.gc.ca/progs/multi>.
13. Quoted in 'Canadian Diversity: Respecting Our Difference' at <www.pch.gc.ca/progs/multi/respect_e.cfm>.

Ziauddin Sardar Bibliography

Compiled by Gail Boxwell

This bibliography comprises Sardar's books and papers as well as longer essays from the 'Ideas' section of *Afkar: Inquiry* magazine from 1984 to 1987. Also included are a selection of key articles on Islamic science, from *Nature* and *New Scientist*; as well as major review articles from *The Muslim World Book Review*. Books that have appeared in different editions, as well as translations (although it has not been possible to trace all of the translations of Sardar's work into other languages) and papers and articles published in more than one journal, are grouped together under the year of the original publication.

FOR SARDAR'S EARLY WRITING, SEE:

Sixth Form Opinion, Fountain Press, London, 1969–71
Zenith, Muslim Educational Trust, London, 1969–72
The Muslim, FOSIS – Federation of Students Islamic Societies in the UK and Eire, London, 1972–73
Impact International Fortnightly, News and Media, London, 1972–75

FOR HIS JOURNALISM, ESSAYS AND REVIEWS, SEE:

Nature, London, 1978–80
New Scientist, London, 1980–82
Independent, London, 1991–94; 2001–
Herald and *Sunday Herald*, Glasgow, 1998–2000
New Statesman, London, 1997–

1976

(ed. with A. A. Ashraf) *A Time to Speak: Anecdotes from Sadi Shirazi*, Islamic Foundation, Leicester
'The Quest for a New Science', *The Muslim Institute Papers – 1*, The Open Press, Slough

1977

Science, Technology and Development in the Muslim World, Croom Helm, London; Humanities Press, New Jersey; Arabic translation: Al Bait Foundation, Amman, 1982; Malaysian translation: Yayasan Dakwah Islamiah, Malaysia, Kuala Lumpur, 1981; Urdu translation: All India Urdu Board, New Delhi, 1982

'Science Policy and Developing Countries', in I. Spiegel-Rosing and D. de Solla Price (eds), *Science, Technology and Society: A Cross-Disciplinary Perspective*, Sage Publications, London and Beverly Hills; *Science Policy and Developing Countries*, Royal Book Company, Karachi, 1978

1978

Muhammad: Aspects of a Biography, Islamic Foundation, Leicester
'The Information Unit of the Hajj Research Centre', *Aslib Proceedings* 30 (5): 158–64
'Separate Development for Science', *Nature* 273: 176
'On Calculating an Appropriate Sense of Confidence', *Nature* 280: 530–1

1979

The Future of Muslim Civilisation, Croom Helm, London; 2nd edition: Mansell, London, 1987. Indonesian translation: Penerbit Mizan, Bandung, 1986; Turkish translation: Insan Yayinlari, Istanbul, 1986; Malaysian edition: Pelanduk Publications, Kuala Lumpur, 1988
Islam: Outline of a Classification Scheme, Clive Bingley, London; K. G. Saur, Munich and New York
(ed.) *Hajj Studies*, Croom Helm, London
'The Middle East', in D. S. Greenburg (ed.), *Science and Government Report Almanac 1978–1979*, Washington, D.C.
'Where will we be in the Year 2000?' (in Arabic) *al-Muslim al-Ma'asir* 5 (19): 29–49
'Cultural Dimensions of Strategy', *Islamic Defence Review* 3: 46–8
'Science Policy in the Developing World', *Nature* 281: 85
'A Revival for Islam, A Boost for Science', *Nature* 282: 354–7
'Scientific Thinking Behind Khomeini', *Nature* 282: 439–41
'Science in Turkey: Choosing the Wrong Priorities', *Nature* 282: 668–70

1980

'The Fight to Save Malaysia', *New Scientist* 87: 700–3 (4 September)
'Can Science Come Back to Islam?' (cover story) *New Scientist* 88: 212–16 (23 October) (translated into Arabic, Turkish, Chinese and Japanese)
'Islamic Awakening', *Resurgence* 23: 26–7
'The Real Face of Islam', *Vole* 3 (4): 31–3 (January)
'Ayatollah's Dilemma', *New Scientist* 87: 51–2 (2 July)
'Meaningful Gestures', *New Scientist* 87: 724–5 (4 September)
'The State of Arab Science', *Nature* 283: 30–1
'Nostalgia for Empire', *Washington Post* (Book World) 11 (14 September)

1981

Hadith, Umran Publications, London; second edition: East-West University/ Umran Publications, 1986

'What Does the Third World Really Want? Expectations and Reality in the North–South Dialogue at UNCSTD', in *World Interdependence and Economic Cooperation among Developing Countries*, Centre for Applied Studies on International Negotiations, Geneva

'Between Gin and Twin: Meeting the Information Needs of the Third World', *Aslib Proceedings* 33 (2): 53–61 (February)

'Islamic Science', *British Journal for the History of Science* 14 (48): 285–6

'Integrated Knowledge Transfer', *Technology and Culture* 22 (3): 683–6

'Why the Third World Needs Nuclear Power', *New Scientist* 89: 402–4 (12 February)

'The Day the Saudis Discovered Technology', *New Scientist* 90: 481–4 (21 May)

'Masterplan for a Tropical Paradise', *New Scientist* 91: 230–5 (23 July)

'Last Chance for World Unity', *New Scientist* 91: 334–41 (6 August)

'Hadith and Sira Literature in Western Languages', *Muslim World Book Review* 1 (4): 6–8

'Dispossessed: The Ordeal of the Palestinians', *Muslim World Book Review* 1 (3): 38–9

1982

(ed.) *The Touch of Midas: Science, Values and the Environment in Islam and the West*, Manchester University Press, Manchester; Pelanduk Publications, Kuala Lumpur, 1988; The Other India Press, Goa, 1997

Science and Technology in the Middle East: A Guide to Issues, Organisations and Institutions, Longman, Harlow

'The Hajj: A Select Bibliography', *Muslim World Book Review* 3 (1): 57–67

'Technology for the South', *Geographical Magazine* 56 (10): 591–2

'Development: Interdependence and Terrorism', *Geographical Magazine* 54 (1): 608

'Development: Who Benefits?', *Geographical Magazine* 54 (5): 246–7

'Development: Is It So Desirable?', *Geographical Magazine* 54 (7): 367–8

'Digging Deep in Development Studies', *Geographical Magazine* 54 (8): 430–3

'Science for the People of Islam', *New Scientist* 93: 244–5 (28 January)

'Sheesha Cancer', *New Scientist* 459–560 (18 February)

'Why Islam Needs Islamic Science', *New Scientist* 94: 25–8 (1 April) (translated into Arabic and Turkish)

'The Astronomy of Ramadan', *New Scientist* 854–6 (24 June)

'Art and Literature', *Muslim World Book Review* 3 (2): 53–6

'Science and Technology', *Muslim World Book Review* 2 (3): 49–53

1983

'The Future of Islamic Studies', *Islamic Culture* 57 (3): 193–205; *al-Muslim al-Ma'asir* 39: 25–39

(with R. T. Bottles et al.) 'Changes in the Communication of Chemical Information 1: Some Effects of Growth', *Journal of Information Science* 6: 103–8
'When Islam Prevailed in Europe', *Geographical Magazine* 55 (2): 104

1984

'Arguments for Islamic Science,' Centre for Studies on Science, Aligarh, 1985; Urdu translation: Centre for Studies on Science, Aligarh, 1985; also in Rais Ahmad and S. Naseem Ahmad (eds), *Quest for New Science*, Centre for Studies on Science, Aligarh, 1984; Malaysian translation: *Hujjah Sains Islam*, translated by Abdul Latif Samian, Dewan Bahasa dan Pustaka, Kuala Lumpur, 1992
'Islamic Science or Science in Islamic Polity?', *Pakistan Studies* 2 (3): 3–16; *Journal of Islamic Science* 1 (1): 31–44 (1985)
'Is There an Islamic Resurgence?', *Afkar: Inquiry* 1 (1): 35–9
'The Need for Islamic Science', *Afkar: Inquiry* 1 (2): 47–8
'Timbuktu and the History of Ideas', *Afkar: Inquiry* 1 (2): 68–9
'Muslim Marxists: Victims of Methodology', *Afkar: Inquiry* 1 (3): 44–8
'Prepare for a Brave New World', *Afkar: Inquiry* 1 (4): 20–1
'Hajj: The Greatest Gathering of Mankind', *Afkar: Inquiry* 1 (4): 25–32
'The Elegance of Mud', *Afkar: Inquiry* 1 (4): 70–1
'Al-Nadim: Books Smile as Pens Shed Tears', *Afkar: Inquiry* 1 (5): 62–4
'The Crown of Islamic Civilisation', *Afkar: Inquiry* 1 (5): 68–9
'Laying the Foundation of Intellectual Revival', *Afkar: Inquiry* 1 (5): 75–6
'Reconstructing the Muslim Civilisation', *Afkar: Inquiry* 1 (6): 39–44
'Islamization of Knowledge, Or Westernisation of Islam?', *Afkar: Inquiry* 1 (7): 39–45
'Alternatives to Hightech' *Afkar: Inquiry* 2 (5): 66–7
'Development: Who's Afraid of Population?', *Geographical Magazine* 56: 506
'Appropriate Technology', *Geographical Magazine* 56: 495
'Physics and Faith', *Nature* 312: 216–17
'The Future of Hajj: Some Basic Considerations', *Islamic Culture* 58 (4): 307–26
'Islamic Cities and Conservation', *Muslim World Book Review* 4 (4): 34–6
'Intellectual Space and Western Domination: Abstracts, Bibliographies and Current Awareness', *Muslim World Book Review* 4 (2): 3–8
'Science and Technology in the Muslim World: A Select Bibliography', *Muslim World Book Review* 4 (3): 58–65
'The Other Side of History: The Future in Contemporary Muslim Literature', *Muslim World Book Review* 5 (1): 26–31

1985

Islamic Futures: The Shape of Ideas to Come, Mansell, London; Indonesian translation: Penerbit Pustaka, Bandung, 1987; Malaysian translation, Divan Bahsa dan Purtika, Kuala Lumpur, 1988; Turkish translation: Insan Yaninlari, Istanbul, 1988; Malaysian edition (English): Pelanduk Publications, Kuala Lumpur, 1988

'Science Policy: India', in Jon Turney (ed.), *Sci-Tech Report: Current Issues in Science and Technology*, Pluto Press, London
'Towards an Islamic Theory of Environment', *Arts and the Islamic World* 3 (1): 12–23
'Making History', *Afkar: Inquiry* 2 (1): 7
'Pakistan: A State of Borrowed Ideas', *Afkar: Inquiry* 2 (3): 39–45
'Islamic Economics: Breaking Free From the Dominant Paradigm', *Afkar: Inquiry* 2 (4): 40–7
'Technology: From Sweet Virtuosity to Domestic Self-Reliance', *Afkar: Inquiry* 2 (5): 39–45
'Between Two Masters: The Qur'an or Science?', *Afkar: Inquiry* 2 (8): 37–41
'Lies, Damn Lies: And a Way of Getting Out', *Afkar: Inquiry* 2 (8): 66–7
'Utopia and Love', *Afkar: Inquiry* 2 (9): 53–4
'Future Worlds, Present Realities', *Afkar: Inquiry* 2 (9): 66–7
'The Other Jihad: Muslim Intellectuals and Their Responsibilities', *Afkar: Inquiry* 2 (10): 40–7

1986

'Redirecting Science Towards Islam: An Examination of Islamic and Western Approaches to Knowledge and Values', *Hamdard Islamicus* 8 (1): 23–34
'Civilisational Dialogue, Captured Minds and the Technology of the Intellect', *Muslim World Book Review* 7 (1): 3–10
'On Being a Writer: Painful Seats', *Afkar: Inquiry* 3 (1): 35
'Turkey: Refloating The Intellectual Enterprise of Islam', *Afkar: Inquiry* 3 (2): 32–7
'Inside a Miniature', *Afkar: Inquiry* 3 (2): 59–62
'What Makes a University Islamic?', *Afkar: Inquiry* 3 (4): 39–44
'Pedantic Vacuum', *Afkar: Inquiry* 3 (7): 68
'Let the Children Be', *Afkar: Inquiry* 3 (8): 39–44
'Separating the Wood From the Trees', *Afkar: Inquiry* 3 (9): 68
'Medicine and Metaphysics: The Search for Healthy Lifestyles', *Afkar: Inquiry* 3 (10): 42–7
'South African Lives', *Afkar: Inquiry* 3 (11): 72–3
'Tail Leading the Dog', *Afkar: Inquiry* 3 (12): 68–9
'Is There a Third World?', *Geographical Magazine* 58 (1): 3
'Islamic Thought', *Revision* 9 (1): 41–3 (1986), Special Issue: 'Critical Questions About New Paradigm Thinking', numerous contributions 14–89

1987

'Reformulating the Shari'ah', *Afkar: Inquiry* 4 (1): 40–5
'Intellectual Paths', *Afkar: Inquiry* 4 (1): 51–42
'Enchanting Journey', *Afkar: Inquiry* 4 (8): 25–33
'Civilisation of the Book', *Afkar: Inquiry* 4 (5): 33–9
'Old Cities, New Cities', *Afkar: Inquiry* 4 (3): 66–7
'What Human Rights?', *Afkar: Inquiry* 4 (7): 67
'Fact and Fiction', *Afkar: Inquiry* 4 (8): 65–6

'The Holy Qur'an and Sciences of Nature', *Muslim World Book Review* 7 (4): 21–3

'Contemporary Librarianship and Information Science in the Muslim World: A Select Bibliography 1970–1987', *Muslim World Book Review* 7 (3): 58–65

1988

Information and the Muslim World, Mansell, London, 1988; Indonesian translation: Penerbit Mizan, Bandung; Malaysian edition: Pelanduk Publications, Kuala Lumpur; Bhasa Malaysian translation: Divan Bahsa dan Purtika, Kuala Lumpur, 1994

(ed.) *Shaping Information Systems of the Islamic World*, Mansell, London; Malaysian edition: Pelanduk Publications, Kuala Lumpur

(ed.) *The Revenge of Athena: Science, Exploitation and the Third World*, Mansell, London; Third World Network, Penang; The Other India Press, Goa, 1997

The Manifesto, International Islamic Conference, 'Dawa and Development in the Muslim World: The Future Perspective', Muslim World League, Makkah al-Mukarramah

'Reformist Ideas and Muslim Intellectuals: The Demands of the Real World', in Abdullah Omar Naseef (ed.), *Today's Problems, Tomorrow's Solutions: Future Thoughts on the Structure of Muslim Society*, Mansell, London

'Islamic Technology', *Middle East Journal* 42 (2): 325–6

'Ideas, Ideologies and Intellectuals: What's Left, Right and Islamic in Pakistan?', *Muslim World Book Review* 8 (3): 3–10

'The Political Theory of Islam: A Select Bibliography', *Muslim World Book Review* 9 (1): 67–78

'Where's Where? Mapping Out the Future of Islamic Science', *Journal of Islamic Science* Part I: 4 (2): 35–64; Part II: 5 (1): 69–110 (1989)

'Against the Common Man: Authoritarianism and the Greek Intellectual Heritage', *Muslim World Book Review* 9 (2): 3–17

1989

Explorations in Islamic Science, Mansell, London; Centre for the Studies on Science, Aligarh, 1996

(ed.) *An Early Crescent: The Future of Knowledge and Environment in Islam*, Mansell, London

Unfinished Journeys: Adventures in Familiar Places, Barita Books, Kuala Lumpur

(ed. with Merryl Wyn Davies) *Faces of Islam: Conversations on Contemporary Issues*, Barita Books, Kuala Lumpur

'Freedom to Develop', *Futures* 27 (2): 666–8 (December)

1990

(with Merryl Wyn Davies) *Distorted Imagination: Lessons from the Rushdie Affair*, Grey Seal, London; Barita, Kuala Lumpur, 1991

'Surviving the Terminator: The Postmodern Mental Condition', *Futures* 22 (2): 203–10 (March)
'Deep Ecology to the Rescue', *Futures* 22 (9): 976–7 (November)
'Secularism's Grand Project', *Impact* 20 (4): 12–14 (23 February–8 March)
'Islam and Intellect', *Listener* 123: 12–15 (25 January)
'Philosophy and Science in the Islamic World', *Middle East Journal* 1: 159 (Winter)
'A Postmodern War of the Wor(l)ds: Putting Rushdie and His Defenders Through Their Paces', *Muslim World Book Review* 10 (3): 3–17
'The Rushdie Malaise: The Orthodoxy of Doubt in the "Little Room" of Postmodernist Fiction', *Muslim World Book Review* 11 (1): 3–19

1991

(ed.) *How We Know: Ilm and the Revival of Knowledge*, Grey Seal, London
(with M. A. Anees and S. Z. Abedin) *Christian–Muslim Relations: Past, Present and Future*, Grey Seal, London
(ed.) 'Special Issue: Islam and the Future', *Futures* 23 (3), April
'Editor's Introduction: Islam and the Future', *Future* 23 (3): 223–30 (April)
'Total Recall: Aliens, Others and Amnesia in Postmodern Thought', *Futures* 23 (2): 189–203 (March)
'The Ethical Connection: Christian–Muslim Relations in the Postmodern Age', *Islam and Christian Muslim Relations* 2 (1): 56–76 (June)
'Arabic Science and Philosophy', *Nature* 353: 459 (3 October)
'Darwin', *Journal of Islamic Science* 7 (2): 115–22
'The Alger Manifesto About the Future of Islam: A Response', *WFSF Newsletter* 17 (2–3): 40–2 (August)

1992

'When the Pendulum Comes to Rest', in Sheila M. Moorcroft (ed.), *Visions for the 21st Century*, Adamantine Press, London.
(with Merryl Wyn Davies) 'The Future of Eastern Europe: Lessons from the Third World', *Futures* 24 (2): 150–7 (March)
'Cultural Diversity: Learning to Live as One', *Leaders* 15 (1): 70
'The Paradise I Seek', *Arts and the Islamic World* 21: 65–7 (Spring)
'Paper, Printing and Compact Discs: The Making and Unmaking of Islamic Culture', *Media, Culture, Society* 15: 43–59
'When Dracula Meets the "Other": Europe, Columbus and the Columbian Legacy', *Alternatives* 17: 493–517
'Lies, Damn Lies and Columbus: The Dynamics of Constructed Ignorance', *Third Text* 21: 47–56 (Winter)
'Islam in the Modern World: A Christian Perspective', *Journal of Islamic Studies* 3 (2): 255–7 (July)
'Conventional Wisdoms', *Nature* 360: 713–14 (24/31 November)
'What Utopia?', *Futures* 24 (1): 97–9 (January–February)
'On Serpents, Inevitability and the South Asian Imagination', *Futures* 24 (9): 942–9 (November)
'Terminator 2: Modernity, Postmodernity and Judgement Day', *Futures* 25 (5): 493–506 (June)

1993

(with Merryl Wyn Davies and Ashis Nandy) *Barbaric Others: A Manifesto on Western Racism*, Pluto Press, London; Westview Press, Boulder, CO.

'Colonising the Future: The "Other" Dimension of Futures Studies', *Futures* 25 (3): 179–87

'Do Not Adjust Your Mind: Post-Modernism, Reality and the Other', *Futures* 25 (8): 877–93 (October)

'The Door Beyond the Door', *Focus on Pakistan* 2–7 (Winter)

1994

Muhammad for Beginners, Icon Books, Cambridge; American edition: Totem Books, New York; Australian edition: Allen & Unwin, St Leanards, NSW; Norwegian edition: Bracan Forlag, Oslo, 1995; Italian edition: Feltrinelli, Rome, 1995; also issued as *Introducing Muhammad*, 1999; *Introducing Islam*, 2001

(ed., with Jerry Ravetz) 'Complexity: Fad or Fashion?', Special Issue, *Futures* 26 (6), August

(with Jerry Ravetz) 'Introduction: Complexity – Fad or Future?', *Futures* 26 (6): 563–7 (July–August)

'Conquests, Chaos, Complexity: The Other in Modern and Postmodern Science', *Futures* 26 (6): 665–82 (July–August)

'Asian Cultures: Between Programmed and Desired Futures', in Eleonora Masini and Yogesh Atal (eds), *The Futures of Asian Cultures*, Unesco, Bangkok, 1993; also in Unesco, *The Futures of Cultures*, Unesco, Paris

'What Chaos? What Coherence? Across the River I Called', in Mika Mannermaa, Sohail Inayatullah and Rick Slaughter (eds), *Coherence and Chaos in Our Uncommon Futures: Visions, Means, Actions*, Finland Future Studies Centre, Turku

'Can Small Countries Survive the Future?', in *Problems and Futures of Small Countries*, Institute of Forecasting, Slovak Academy of Science, Bratislava

'Logic and Laws', *Nature* 368: 376–8 (24 March)

1995

(ed. with S. Z. Abedin) *Muslim Minorities in The West*, Grey Seal, London

(with Richard Appignnesi et al.) *Postmodernism for Beginners*, Icon Books, Cambridge; American edition: Totem Books, New York; Australian edition: Allen & Unwin, St Leanards, NSW; numerous translations

(ed. with Jerry Ravetz) 'Cyberspace: To Boldly Go…', Special Issue, *Futures* 27 (7), September

'Introduction: Cyberspace – To Boldly Go…', *Futures* 27 (7): 695–8 (September)

'Islam and Nationalism', *Concilium: International Review of Theology* 262: 103–10

'Understanding Postmodernism', *Pemikir* 1 (2): 131–58 (October–December)

'alt.civilisation.faq: Cyberspace as the Darker Side of the West', *Futures* 27 (7): 777–94 (September); also in Ziauddin Sardar and Jerome R. Ravetz (eds), *Cyberfutures: Culture and Politics on the Information Superhighway*, Pluto Press, London, 1996; and in David Bell and Barbara M. Kennedy (eds), *The Cyberspace Reader*, London, 2000

'Cruising for Peace', *Nature* 373: 483–4 (9 February)

'Bosnia and the Postmodern Embrace of Evil', *Bulletin of the World Futures Studies Federation* 21 (3): (10–12 October)

'The Shape of Things to Come', *Nature* 378: 110 (2 November)

'The A B C D (and E) of Ashis Nandy', *Emergence* 7/8: 126–45 (1995–96); also *Futures* 29 (7): 649–60 (September 1997); and 'Introduction' to Ashis Nandy, *Return from Exile*, Oxford University Press, Delhi, 1998

1996

(ed. with J. R. Ravetz) *Cyberfutures: Culture and Politics on the Information Superhighway*, Pluto Press, London; New York University Press, New York; Korean edition: Shi YuShi, Seoul, 1997

'Other Futures: Non-Western Cultures in Futures Studies', in Richard A. Slaughter (ed.), *The Knowledge Base of Future Studies: Directions and Outlook* (vol. 3), DDM Media Group/Futures Study Centre, Hawthorn, Victoria

'The Future of Islam', in George T. Kurian and Graham T. Molitor (eds), *Encyclopedia of the Future*, Macmillan, New York

'Some Thoughts on an Alternative to the Imperium of Human Rights', in *Human Wrongs: Reflections on Western Global Dominance and its Impact Upon Human Rights*, Just World Trust, Penang

'Future Challenges of Human Rights and Democracy', *Futuresco* (Unesco) 5: 17–24 (June)

'Beyond Development: An Islamic Perspective', *European Journal of Development Research* 8 (2)

'Walt Disney and the Double Victimisation of Pocahontas', *Third Text* 37: 17–27

'Islamic Science: The Task Ahead', *Journal of Islamic Science* 12 (2): 57–88

'Cycling Through Arabic History', *Nature* 383: 492–3 (10 October)

'Natural Born Futurist', *Futures* 28 (6–7): 665–8

1997

Cultural Studies for Beginners, Icon Books, Cambridge; American edition: Totem Books, New York; Australian edition: Allen & Unwin, St Leanards, NSW

'Islamic Philosophy of Science', in Edward Craig (ed.), *Routledge Encyclopedia of Philosophy*, Routledge, London

'Islamic Science: The Contemporary Debate', in Helaine Selin (ed.), *Encyclopedia of the History of Science, Technology and Medicine in Non-Western Cultures*, Kluwer, Dordrecht

'Science and Values', in Helaine Selin (ed.), *Encyclopedia of the History of Science, Technology and Medicine in Non-Western Cultures*, Kluwer, Dordrecht

'British, Muslim, Writer', in Juliet Steyn (ed.), *Other Than Identity: The Subject, Politics and Art*, Manchester University Press, Manchester

'Beyond Development: An Islamic Perspective', in Vincent Tucker (ed.), *Cultural Perspectives on Development*, Frank Cass, London
'Development Ladder', *Nature* 389: 145–6 (11 September)
'Return of the Repressed', Nature 389: 451–2 (2 October)
(ed. with Jerry Ravetz) 'Rethinking Science', Special Issue, *Futures* 29 (6), August
(with Jerry Ravetz) 'Introduction: Rethinking Science', Special Issue, *Futures* 29 (6), August
(ed.) 'South Asia: Fifty Years On', Special Issue, *Futures* 29 (10), December
'Coming Home: Sex, Lies and All the "I"s in India', The Sadat Hasan Manto Lecture, *Futures* 29 (10): 891–908 (December)
'Introduction: South Asia – Fifty Years On', *Futures* 29 (10): 883–90 (December)
'The Problem', Special Issue on 'Futures', *Seminar* 460: 12–18 (December)

1998

Postmodernism and the Other, Pluto Press, London; Turkish edition: Soylem Yayinluri, Istanbul, 2001
Chaos for Beginners, Icon Books, Cambridge; American edition: Totem Books, New York; Australian edition: Allen & Unwin, St Leanards, NSW
(ed.) *Rescuing All Our Futures: The Future of Futures Studies*, Adamantine Press, London; Praeger Publishers, Westport, CT
'Dilip Kumar Made Me Do It', in Ashis Nandy (ed.), *A Secret History of our Desires*, Oxford University Press, Delhi; Zed Press, London, 1998
'Development and the Location of Eurocentism', in Ronaldo Munck and Denis O'Hearn (eds), *Critical Holism: (Re)Thinking Development*, London, Zed Books
'Postmodernism and the Other', *Worldview* 2 (4): 32–5
'Machines R Us?', *Motif* 5: 3–17
(ed. with Sean Cubitt), 'Fictions and Futures', Special Issue, *Futures* 30 (10), December

1999

Orientalism, Open University Press, Buckingham; German translation: Verlag Klaus Wegenbach, Berlin, 2002; Turkish edition: Yonelis Yayinlari, Istanbul, 2002
(with Jerry Ravetz) *Introducing Mathematics*, Icon Books, London
(ed. with Richard A. Slaughter) 'Dissenting Futures', Special Issue, *Futures* 31 (2), March
'European Muslims and European Identity', in John Coleman (ed.), *The Conscience of Europe*, Council of Europe, Strasbourg
'The Changing Face of Futures', *Futures* 31 (1): 1–6 (February)

2000

The Consumption of Kuala Lumpur, Reaktion Books, London

Introducing Media Studies, Icon Books, Cambridge, 2000
Thomas Khun and the Science Wars, Icon Books, 2000; also in Richard Appignanesi (ed.), *Postmodernism and Big Science*, Icon Books, London
(ed.) 'The Morning After', Special Issue, *Futures* 32 (1), February
'Introduction: Waking Up to a New Century', *Futures* 32 (1): 1–6 (February)

2001

'Above, Beyond, and at the Centre of Science Wars: A Postcolonial Reading', in Keith M. Ashman and Philip S. Bringer (eds), *After the Science Wars*, Routledge, London
'Other Cities, Other Futures', in Iwona Blazwick (ed.), *Century City: Art and Culture in the Modern Moteropolis*, Tate Publishing, London
'Waiting for Rain', *New Scientist* 2321 (15 December)
'Critical Muslims', *Harvard Asia Quarterly* 5 (4): 24–6 (Autumn)
'El Nou (Des)Ordre Comunicatiu', *TD: Debats Tecnologics* 17: 8–15 (November) (in Spanish)
'Het muticulturalism deugt neit', *Eutopia* 1: 57–62 (January)
'Terrorists, Islam and the American Attack', *Futures Research Quarterly* (Winter)
'The Jihad for Peace', in Anna Kiernan, *Voice for Peace*, Scribner, London

2002

The A to Z of Postmodern Life, Vision, London
(ed. with Sean Cubitt) *Aliens R Us: The Other in Science Fiction Cinema*, Pluto Press, London
Introducing Science, Icon Books, London
(ed. with Rasheed Araeen and Sean Cubitt) *The Third Text Reader on Art, Culture and Theory*, Continuum, London
(with Richard Appignanesi and Ralph Edney) *Introducing Learning and Memory*, Icon Books, London
(with Merryl Wyn Davies) *Why Do People Hate America?* Icon Books, London, and translations
(ed. with Annabelle Sreberny and Daya Thussu) 'Marginalisation as Violence', Special Issue, *Inter-Sections* 2 (1), Summer
'Rethinking Islam', *Seminar* 48–52 (January)
'Healing the Multiple Wounds: Medicine in a Multicultural Society', in Bill New and Julia Neuberger (eds), *Hidden Assets: Values and Decision-Making in the NHS*, Kings Fund, London
'The Ambassador from India', in Peter Wallen and Joe Kerr (eds), *Autopia: Cars and Culture*, Reaktion Books, London
'The Excluded Minority: British Muslim Identity After 11 September', in Phoebe Griffity and Mark Leonard (eds), *Reclaiming Britishness: Living Together After 11 September and the Rise of the Right*, The Foreign Policy Centre, London
(ed.) 'Islam: Resistance and Reform', *New Internationalist* 345 (May)
'Mecca', *Granta* 77: 223–54 (Spring); German translation: *Lettre International* 57 (24–31 June)

'Medicine and Multiculturalism', *New Renaissance*, 6–8 (Summer)
'Der König des Qawalli', *Lettre International*, 58: 63–5

2003

Islam, Postmodernism and Other Futures: A Ziauddin Sardar Reader, edited by Sohail Inayatullah and Gail Boxwell, Pluto Press, London
'The Dambuster', in David Cotterrell, *The Impossible Project*, Black Dog, London,
'God Save America', *Resurgence*, 19–21 (May/June)
'Europe: The Legacy of Islam', Action Centre for Europe Ltd, London
'Why People Hate US', *European Business Review* 15 (5): 347–451

2004

Desperately Seeking Paradise: Journeys of a Sceptical Muslim, Granta Books, London, and translations
(with Merryl Wyn Davies) *The No Nonsense Guide to Islam*, Verso, London
(with Merryl Wyn Davies) *American Dream, Global Nightmare*, Icon Books, Cambridge and Nexus Audiobook, London, 2005
'What Does it Mean to be a "British Muslim"', in *What is British?*, British Council, London
'Healing the Multiple Wounds: Medicine in a Multicultural Society', in Sohail Inayatullah (ed.), *The Casual Layered Analysis Reader*, Tamkang University, Taipei
'Mecca', *Lettre Internationale* 51: 22–31 (Summer)
'Terrorists "R" Us', *Adbusters* 13 (1), January/February
'De Islam En Europa', *Eutopia* 7: 43–54 (May)
'Drowning in a Universal River', *New Humanist*, 28–9 (September/October)

2005

'Same Again…', in Linda Carroli (ed.), *The Ideas Book*, University of Queensland Press, Brisbane
Islam Tanpa Syariat, edited by Abdul Muti and Ahmad Najib Burjani, British Council, Jakarta
'The beginning of knowledge' in *Belief* edited by Joan Blackwell, BBC/ Duckworth, London, p155–68

2006

What Do Muslims Believe? Granta Books, London
'What do we mean by Islamic futures' in *Blackwell Companion to Contemporary Islamic Thought* edited by Ibrahim Abu Rabi, Blackwell, Oxford
'Transmodernity: Art Beyond Modernity and Multiculturalism' in *Navigating Difference: Cultural Diversity and Audience Development*, Arts Council England, London

Index

Compiled by Sue Carlton